Moments with God

Refreshing Daily Meditations

Edward Grube

CONCORDIA PUBLISHING HOUSE • SAINT LOUIS

For Renee...
wonderful wife,
magnificent mom,
excellent educator.

Concordia
Publishing House

Published 2006 Concordia Publishing House
3558 S. Jefferson Avenue
St. Louis, MO 63118-3968
1-800-325-3040 • www.cph.org

Unless otherwise marked, scripture quotations are from THE HOLY BIBLE, ENGLISH STANDARD VERSION, copyright © 2001 by Crossway Bibles, a division of Good News Publishers. Used by permission. All rights reserved.

Scripture quotations marked NIV are from the HOLY BIBLE, NEW INTERNATIONAL VERSION®. Copyright © 1973, 1978, 1984 by International Bible Society. Used by permission of Zondervan Publishing House. All rights reserved.

This publication may be available in braille, in large print, or on cassette tape for the visually impaired. Please allow 8 to 12 weeks for delivery. Write to the Library for the Blind, 7550 Watson Rd., St. Louis, MO 63119-4409; call 1-866-215-6852; or e-mail to blind.mission@blindmission.org.

Manufactured in the United States of America

1 2 3 4 5 6 7 8 9 10   15 14 13 12 11 10 09 08 07 06

CONTENTS

As You Begin . . .

Moments with God: Refreshing Daily Devotions contains 365 brief devotions—ideal for a year's worth of mediations for any person in any work setting. Whether you work outside your home or in it, whether you get paid or work out of love, whether your chores are difficult or easy—take a break and do a little reading. Schedule about five minutes of any part of your day to read the meditations in this book. Perhaps you will find them a welcome break from your daily routine as you refresh yourself with reminders of God's love and Jesus' work in your life.

In this book you'll find a little light humor and lots of Gospel integrated into things you observe or experience in everyday life. Nearly anything can remind us of Jesus and of what God has done for us. Look around you. What you see has potential to give you a spiritual boost—by the power of the Holy Spirit, of course. I pray this book will help you too.

Speaking of the Spirit's power, these devotions mean nothing without it. Take a few moments after each reading to thank God for His mercy and grace. Ask Him to strengthen your faith. Ask Him to help you narrow the gap between spiritual matters and the "rest of the world." In reality, God is truly in the world, though He isn't of this world. The same is true of Christians; however, we might need an occasional nudge and a timely Bible passage to remind us of that. You'll find both in these pages. Each daily devotion includes a Scripture passage but it doesn't include a prayer. Your own will be far better than any I could provide. Reflect on your personal needs and those of others. Take those needs, either on your lips or in your heart, to God. He promises to hear you.

May God the Father, Son, and Holy Spirit bless your meditation.

Edward Grube

They'll Wonder Why You're Smiling

Bless those who persecute you; bless and do not curse them.
Romans 12:14

Do you feel their eyes on you? Don't be surprised—especially if you're reading this in a public place or in the presence of your family. Especially if they know you're reading something "religious." Look up, flash a smile, and return to your reading. Even if you're a bit timid about your co-worker's or family's curiosity, you can witness your faith. Let their eyes see it on your lips. Smiles are so powerful. They can even break the ice!

You have much to smile about. Smile as you remember that cooing baby nestled in the hay. Smile as you think about the man mistaken for a landscaper that misty Sunday morning in a cemetery near dark Gethsemane. Then imagine yourself with the disciples, hunkered down in a stuffy room, and suddenly Jesus enters—through a locked door! Go ahead, smile. Perhaps they will wonder what you're smiling about.

Maybe they will ask. Then what will you do? You could tell them you're reading a funny book. After all, our Savior acted "funny." Many who witnessed His ministry laughed at Him. A few laughed with Him. He probably laughed too. (But never at anyone's expense.) He did many funny things—like forgiving His enemies, associating with potentially dangerous strangers, getting within infectious range of contagious people, obeying His Father perfectly, and blessing His enemies.

Reading this book may be risky. Each meditation should make you smile. Sometimes you might even chuckle. At the very least, your heart should be lighter. So be ready. Be ready for inquisitive looks, rolling eyes, even mockery for your devotion. But smile anyway. Who knows? You might ruin the day for a grouch!

Note: This book may not be suitable for people on diets. The first thing dieters usually lose is their good mood!

Fine Print I

But God, being rich in mercy, because of the great love with which He loved us, even when we were dead in our trespasses, made us alive together with Christ—by grace you have been saved. Ephesians 2:4–5

How do you answer when people ask you, "What must I do to be saved?"

If you tell them to find the answer in the Bible, they might page through the Old Testament and get bogged down in all the rules and regulations—the fine print—in Deuteronomy and Leviticus. Like most legal writ, it doesn't make for happy reading. In fact, some of it is downright demanding and frightening. Left by itself, this legalistic fine print can only condemn and destroy any hope of living forever.

Skeptics also look for the fine print in the New Testament. Jesus often said that He is the only thing necessary for salvation. Just believe, and live forever! And how does one believe? Why, it's a free gift of the Holy Spirit! Free! Gift! Still, people look for loopholes—something like successfully observing at least 7.5 of the Ten Commandments to earn eternal life. Or maybe paying God a 10 percent tax to avoid the angelic auditors.

There is indeed fine print involved in answering "What must I do to be saved?" Reread today's Bible passage.

Nothing could be finer! Saved by grace—God's gift of unconditional love. He saves us while we are still sinners. Such love is unheard of these days. Such love was unheard of in Jesus' day too. But true love it is. After all, doesn't the fine print always spell out the truth?

Oh yes, there is more fine print. It's true that believers contribute nothing toward their salvation. Christians don't need a perfect 10 on the Commandment scale, nor are they required to tithe. They don't have to associate with the oppressed or other needy people. If the fine print requires none of this for salvation, why do it? Read the next meditation to find out. The print is fine, but it won't be small.

Fine Print II—It Will Make You Dizzy

For the grace of God has appeared, bringing salvation for all people, train-
ing us to renounce ungodliness and worldly passions, and to live self-con-
trolled, upright, and godly lives in the present age, waiting for our blessed
hope, the appearing of the glory of our great God and Savior Jesus Christ,
who gave Himself for us to redeem us from all lawlessness and to purify
for Himself a people for His own possession who are zealous for good
works. Titus 2:11–14

Someone said that people rarely get dizzy from doing good turns!
While God doesn't require goodness as a prerequisite for faith, faithful people do good because they have faith. Now you could sit down and create a list of good deeds for the day or spend the morning pondering potential
situations to which you might contribute your good deeds. *Warning:* Such
activities can consume so much time that you won't have any left to actually
activate the list.

The best way to do good is to be good. Titus offers reliable advice about
the ingredients of a good life. Self-control is the key. The key to self-control is
to turn all your sins over to Jesus. He took them away and made you
righteous, thereby supplying a means to resist temptation. While Jesus' death
and resurrection made us righteous, we still sin as we await that time when
He comes again and brings us to complete perfection. The fine words from
Titus address that situation too.

We have the blessed hope that Jesus will come again. Living with that
hope comforts us in times of pain, sorrow, failure, and sin. We know that
despite our own troubles, Jesus knows our needs and He will treat those problems. While we wait for that blessed day, we can be good. We can share His
comfort with those in need; forgive as we have been forgiven; care for those
who can't care for themselves; support missionaries and charities; help out
around church, etc. (The etc. is limited only by your imagination and effort.)

One more thing. If anyone calls you a dizzy Christian because of your
good works, take it as a compliment.

A Perfect Ten

Then Jesus answered, "Were not ten cleansed? Where are the nine? Was
no one found to return and give praise to God except this foreigner?"
Luke 17:17–18

The moral of the passage above is that we should thank God for His blessings. Unfortunately, often our response is to click our tongues at the nine who didn't bother to say thank You.

These verses are relived every day in the modern world. So much good happens to so many people—without regard to their religious background. Have you noticed that God doesn't care whom He blesses? Pagans and unbelievers get their crops watered by the same God who nourishes farmland worked by Christians. Profane, reckless, and rude drivers on the interstate arrive as safely at their destinations as those who practice patience and brotherly love. The seriously ill patient who never uttered a prayer enjoys a miraculous recovery; the Christian in the next bed dies even as a host of believers pray diligently. It's enough to make our tongues click until they're all clicked out!

Why does God love and bless those who don't love Him? Someday we'll understand the depths of His love, but for now this paradox baffles us. For now, God expects us to love as He loves. Listen to Jesus as He says, "But I say to you, Love your enemies and pray for those who persecute you, so that you may be sons of your Father who is in heaven. For He makes His sun rise on the evil and on the good, and sends rain on the just and on the unjust" (Matthew 5:44–45).

God bestows His love on all regardless of race, creed, ethnic origin, height, weight, eye color, church attendance, income, language, or breed of dog they own. We don't know how many people recognize His grace and thank Him for His goodness. Perhaps it's only 10 percent. Hopefully, it's higher. Our only task is to remain among the 10 percent and use our tongues to pray rather than click. Pray that more and more people recognize God's grace and come to Him for His final blessing when Jesus comes again.

Your Sleep Will Be Sweet

If you lie down, you will not be afraid; when you lie down, your sleep will be sweet. Proverbs 3:24

Have you ever noticed that your soundest sleep is the sleep you're in when the alarm clock rings? Or do you find it difficult to sleep—tossing, turning, snoring—working so hard at sleeping that you're too tired to get up? As you have noticed, Proverbs talks about sweet sleep—an unusual topic for a Biblical book. Let's examine the context of this piece of proverbial wisdom. (If you have a Bible handy, read Proverbs 3:21–26.)

Solomon begins this section of Proverbs talking about judgment and discernment—two gifts from the Holy Spirit. Solomon says that good judgment and spiritual insight decorate the lives of believers like an ornament. But even more important, wisdom provides safety. And this wonderful security makes it easy to enjoy sweet dreams and refreshing sleep. By now, you may wonder if you have access to this wisdom. If you know the kind of wisdom to which Solomon is referring, you can stop reading and catch a little nap instead. But if you're not sure, read on.

Godly wisdom is believing that God loves you, that He has an angel watching over you right now. And while that angel might not protect you from distressing engagements with sin and Satan, it will keep the devil from taking you away from God. Godly wisdom is knowledge that nothing can separate us from God's love, not even death itself. Godly wisdom is an awareness that we belong to the Savior and not even sudden disaster can tear His hand from ours. God's gift of wisdom lets us see the Savior through blind eyes, talk to Him with mute lips, and turn to Him with paralyzed bodies. When we can't come to Him, He comes to us. After all, that's how we became believers, isn't it?

Changeless Variety

The heavens declare the glory of God, and the sky above proclaims His handiwork. Psalm 19:1

Sit near a window today so you can "see" the topic of this meditation. Look out once in awhile even if you're in a place that doesn't seem to "declare the glory of God." What does the sky look like today? What did it look like 12 hours ago? What will it look like 12 hours from now?

Weather conditions change, and the sky differs greatly between noon and midnight. In some locales, the sky smiles or storms on beautiful surroundings, while in others it falls on environments defaced by human folly. Yet, as the psalmist says, "the heavens declare the glory of God." God's glory shines and glistens on His creation and creatures every day regardless of weather conditions. Day after day, night after night, God displays His creative power in a paradoxical mixture of variety and changelessness. Only one thing never changes: Our expectation of change! In a world of change, it's good to know we have a permanent God.

God brings the same glory into our daily lives. His dependable presence soothes our anxieties with knowledge that He is just a prayer away. Better yet, He watches us and knows our changing needs even before we know them. And should illness or accident strike, God doesn't abandon us. He heals, if not physically, then spiritually by bringing us closer to Him—perhaps even making us totally dependent on His love and care.

Some people greet each morning with "This is the day that the LORD has made. It must be good for something." No, wait. How about "Let us rejoice and be glad in it" (Psalm 118:24). How true! The Lord makes each day for us to find joy in serving Him—from the kitchen table, the office desk, the factory workbench, the road or rail, the furrows or curbs. So rejoice again. Be glad again. And get back to work again!

Wave Your Shoe if You Agree

*Now this was the custom in former times in Israel concerning redeeming
and exchanging: to confirm a transaction, the one drew off his sandal
and gave it to the other, and this was the manner of attesting in Israel.
So when the redeemer said to Boaz, "Buy it for yourself,"
he drew off his sandal. Ruth 4:7–8*

Picture this. A strategic business deal worth millions of dollars approaches closure. Company lawyers have dotted every *t* and crossed every *i*. (Then they turned it around and did it the right way.) Hours of negotiation finally reach a climax when one businessman takes off his shoe and hands it to his counterpart, thus sealing the deal. *Warning:* Do not actually try this. You may get the boot in exchange!

That's exactly what happened when Boaz bargained to marry and care for Ruth. (Read Ruth in your spare time. It's only four heart-warming chapters long.) Instead of signing legal documents or conducting a church ceremony, they passed a sandal to legalize the marriage. With that act, Boaz and Ruth became husband and wife.

Don't wave your shoe right now (unless you're alone), but at least wiggle your foot if you agree with the following:

1. *God loves me, and I love Him.*

2. *I will invite God to show me His will as I pray for His wisdom.*

3. *I will hate evil but pray for my enemies.*

4. *I will ask God's forgiveness daily.*

5. *I will forgive myself and others as God has forgiven me.*

6. *I will spend a few moments each day meditating on God's Word, and I will accept the blessings that come from it.*

7. *I will bring all my needs to Jesus and gratefully accept His answers to my prayers.*

By now your ankle probably aches, and if anyone is watching they probably think you need a clear path to the bathroom. But don't let that bother you. Be like Boaz and Ruth after he waved the sandal. Go off and live happily ever after—in God's grace, of course.

A Way Out

"When you see these things taking place, you know that the kingdom of God is near. . . . But watch yourselves lest your hearts be weighed down with dissipation and drunkenness and cares of this life, and that day come upon you suddenly like a trap. For it will come upon all who dwell on the face of the whole earth. But stay awake at all times, praying that you may have strength to escape all these things that are going to take place, and to stand before the Son of Man." Luke 21:31–36

The fire was especially smoky and hot. The hotel's guests crawled through the hallway until they saw the faint glow of an exit sign—the door to a stairway and escape! Those who made it to the fresh air gratefully recalled the room instructions that normally are so easy to ignore. "Locate the nearest exit before occupying the room." Such a simple task. Look down the hallway for the familiar exit sign, and mark it in your memory. Sadly, not all the guests heeded the advice. When the heat was on, their cool was off.

How good for us that Jesus gave safety instructions! In Luke 21:36, He says, "But stay awake at all times, praying that you may have strength to escape all these things that are going to take place, and to stand before the Son of Man."

This valuable counsel may sound a bit ominous. But if we're not offended or frozen in fright over common safety warnings, then this Word from God need not lurk on the dark side either. Just as we need to prepare ourselves for fire, we also need to be ready to "escape all that is about to happen."

What is "about to happen"? Nothing short of the end of the world. (Just what you needed to lighten up your day!) "Now wait," you may say. "Nobody escapes the end of the world. Everyone will see God face to face—believers and unbelievers alike."

Yes, it's true that Judgment Day will fully involve all creation. But if you're reading this book, be confident that you will escape God's wrath. No, this book doesn't contain an asbestos shield; you're probably reading it because you're a Christian. Maybe a very strong one. Maybe a very feeble one. One thing is certain, however; you're equipped for escape. The Holy Spirit has brought the Gospel into your heart. If you know Jesus Christ died for your sins and rose for your victory, then you're prepared to escape.

When the final trumpets sound and all around you quakes and burns, look for the exit sign. It will look just like Jesus. It will glow gloriously through the flames and smoke. You're sure to make a safe exit in the arms of Christ.

What the Devil Looks Like

*Again, the devil took Him to a very high mountain and showed Him all
the kingdoms of the world and their glory. And he said to Him, "All these
I will give you, if you will fall down and worship me." Matthew 4:8–9*

A preacher claimed that the Bible identified more than 500 different sins. After the service, several parishioners asked for a list. Apparently, they didn't want to miss anything.

We often blame sin on the devil. If only we could see him coming, we could arouse our defenses. But the devil is hard to see. If only the devil were really that ugly, crimson-skinned, sharp-horned, pointy-tailed character, we could easily avoid him.

When the devil tempted Jesus, he exposed his real character. Jesus had spent over a month alone, seriously contemplating His ministry and what it would require of Him. No doubt He hungered for a break from His routine of fasting and meditation. The devil saw an opportunity to approach Jesus as a "friend" and perhaps trap Him into ruining God's plan. Far from a hideous beast bearing a red-hot pitch fork, the devil approached Jesus with something that would make Him feel better. (Doesn't sin usually start out as fun?) Jesus detected the trap and told the devil where to go.

The devil approaches us the same way. He offers what looks like gifts to make us feel better. Unhappy with a spouse? Maybe you should ditch him/her . . . Too tired to pray at night? Don't—a day without God can't hurt a strong Christian like you . . . Doesn't it hurt when they mock you? Be like them. Curse and swear more often. Vile language releases your pent-up hostilities.

Yes, the devil may be hard to identify, but the results of his treachery aren't. Sin always brings us down. So thank God for Jesus Christ. We always know Him. He's the one who says, "Come to Me. I'll forgive you. Go in peace, and cling to what is good."

Now go back to work. In peace.

Watch Your Language

But the evil spirit answered them, "Jesus I know, and Paul I recognize, but who are you?" And the man in whom was the evil spirit leaped on them, mastered all of them and overpowered them, so that they fled out of that house naked and wounded. Acts 19:15–16

As we read above, violence erupted when several unbelievers attempted to profit by driving out evil spirits in Christ's name. Unexpectedly, the devils turned on the frauds and knocked them silly. I think it's safe to presume that the frauds watched their language from that point on. They weren't punished so much *for* their sins as *by* their sins.

We hear God's name used most every day. It's used on the loading dock, at the hair stylist, in the factory, and on the farm field. We hear it on radio and TV and in the classroom. God's name even pervades our pastimes—on the golf course, in the fishing boat, at the card party. Would that God was really so popular!

Of course, we realize that God's name is used in two ways. As demonstrated by the unbelieving frauds (who probably articulated more "choice" words after their experience), there is the profane way of calling on Him. Sadly, this seems the most common use of His name. Worse, misusing God's name is acceptable and even expected in some circles.

When misuse of God's name is so common, isn't it frustrating that proper use invites derision? To utter "Jesus Christ" when something goes wrong seems more acceptable than proclaiming the same name in public prayer or words of forgiveness.

I guess God is used to hearing His name mentioned so often. He always sticks around to listen. Those who call Him in the name of Jesus Christ receive power to overcome evil and live peacefully, knowing that God is good, and that He is in charge of every minute of our lives.

You're entitled to use God's name freely. Watch your language. Let others watch it too, for it is the language of love.

What Do Christians Look Like?

But the Lord said to Samuel, "Do not look on his appearance or on the height of his stature, because I have rejected him. For the Lord sees not as man sees: man looks on the outward appearance, but the Lord looks on the heart." 1 Samuel 16:7

Stop reading. (I know. You just started.) Find a mirror, and look at yourself. Take the book with you, and answer the following questions:

1. *How would you describe your complexion?*
   Light   Dark   Ruddy   Cosmetically challenged

2. *What color are your eyes?*
   Brown   Blue   Gray   Hazel   Red striped

3. *How would you describe your overall appearance?*
   Attractive   Plain   In-between
   I don't use that kind of language

4. *If you were a motor vehicle, which would you be?*
   Subcompact   Family sedan   Sport/utility   Beater

5. *What expression appears on your face?*
   Frown   Smile   Non-committal

Okay, get your face out of the mirror before someone thinks you're vain.

You just caught a glimpse of what Christians look like. Were you happy about it? If not, don't worry. The prophet Samuel had doubts about one of God's chosen people too.

Samuel was to anoint David as king. In Samuel's time, kings were normally tall, strong, and—well—kingly looking. Samuel went through all of Jesse's sons, several of whom possessed appropriate physical qualifications. But then David stepped forward. He was rather young, and he lacked the general size and demeanor common to kings at the time. But God chose David to lead His people. And God made David the right person for the job.

God worked the same way with us. He chose us to be His people regardless of how we look. Our physical looks are far less important than the beauty that resides in our soul—for Jesus is there. With Jesus in our soul, His beauty radiates through our body, just waiting to escape into the eyes of others.

Almost Persuaded

Agrippa said to Paul, "In a short time would you persuade me to be a
Christian?" And Paul said, "Whether short or long, I would to God that
not only you but also all who hear me this day might become such as I
am—except for these chains." Acts 26:28–29

Some people buy newspapers only for the ads. It's hard to understand, but then the ads are probably as believable as the news! At least they have something good to say, and they usually say it in large letters. Just look at the car ads in any major newspaper. They advertise shockingly low prices for the car of your dreams. But instead of decimal points, the ads usually have * ** *** **** ***** behind them. Each asterisk leads you to microscopic print secluded somewhere on the page. Each stands for limitations on the deal. Those ads can nearly persuade normal but suspicious buyers, while those less skeptical make the cost of the ads justifiable.

Ancient King Agrippa was the target of some classy advertising by Paul. He listened to eloquent, honest testimony, yet Agrippa was more likely to buy a dream car direct from the Saturday morning ads than he was to believe the truth. "Agrippa said to Paul, 'In a short time would you persuade me to be a Christian?' And Paul said, 'Whether short or long, I would to God that not only you but also all who hear me this day might become such as I am—except for these chains.'" (Acts 26:28–29).

How persuasive are you? Do you place Jesus on a pedestal wherever you go? Would you succeed in the advertising world as a walking billboard? Hard questions, aren't they? Yet we can tap the same source of confidence that Paul had 2,000 years ago. The Holy Spirit is the highest-powered ad agency in the universe, and He wants us to work for Him.

What a product we have to sell! Who wouldn't want it? Do you feel your enthusiasm growing? You want to throw down this book and get right out there and . . . Wait a minute. We need to get real. If Paul couldn't persuade Agrippa, how can we expect success?

We can't expect success—at least not a success that we can always see. As you talk and act as a Christian, people will take notice. Some will want to know more, and there's your big chance. Some people will ignore you. Others will think your news is too good to be true. Don't let that discourage you. Proclaim Jesus' love for the world in BIG LETTERS. And you don't need a single asterisk!

When You Feel Like Shouting

Clap your hands, all peoples! Shout to God with loud songs of joy!
Psalm 47:1

You probably know someone who thinks his horsepower is judged by the amount of his exhaust!

The Bible has many examples of shouting. In one New Testament incident, some unbelievers (who thought they were real believers) shouted at Paul, angry because he told them they couldn't obey God's law well enough to save themselves. And Paul shouted back something about their resemblance to poisonous snakes. From Paul's point of view, it was a loud but righteous argument.

Not all the biblical shouting was done in anger. Remember the inspired crowd on Palm Sunday welcoming Jesus with whoops of praise? Psalms and other Old Testament books speak of cheerful shouting.

As modern Christians our shouts can be more delightful. We can attempt to say, "I forgive you," as loudly as others accuse. We can say, "I'm sorry," with the same intensity as we argue our defense. Let God hear your shouts of thanksgiving at the same volume as grumbles of discontent.

If you're too shy or self-conscious to shout out loud, do it in a whisper. You know how a whisper shouts—like when Mom wanted you to stop popping your bubble gum during the movie. Blare out a boldly whispered "Praise the Lord," "Amen," or "Thank You, Jesus" whenever the occasion suggests.

You can also shout without saying a word. A hefty smile on your face, even when you're troubled about something, nearly screams that you have hope—hope in Jesus. A warm handshake or hug for a downhearted person speaks louder than hollow words of comfort.

If you dare, be like David, who often shouted his psalms. Once he even danced so uninhibitedly that he embarrassed his wife. But he just couldn't contain His joy in God. If David could write poems and offer a footloose frolic, we also have freedom to express our joy in Jesus. Shout. Whisper. Or at least offer some polite applause.

Don't Miss the Boat

*Therefore, my beloved, as you have always obeyed, so now, not only as in
my presence but much more in my absence, work out your own salvation
with fear and trembling, for it is God who works in you, both to will and
to work for His good pleasure. Philippians 2:12–13*

Mackinac Island is one of the Midwest's premier locales for beauty
and relaxation. No cars. Every conceivable flavor of fudge. Ample
souvenir shops—even for the most devoted shopper. Scenic beauty in rocky
cliffs and pristine lake water. Carriage rides and a historic fort. Something for
everyone—except for those who tend to wander and lose track of time.

The only way from Michigan's mainland to the island is by ferry. The fer-
ries do not operate on a 24-hour schedule. Oh, there are many opportunities
to board and return to the mainland, but eventually the opportunities end.
Those who wander aimlessly, fail to watch their watches, or defy the deadlines, get stranded up the Straits of Mackinac without a paddle.

Jesus has already claimed us, but we have many opportunities to wander
away from Him. It's easy to become sidetracked and miss the boat. We trade
one opportunity for another. And when we hear a knock at the door, it's hard
to know whether it's opportunity or temptation that's doing the knocking.

How can we recognize opportunity? The passage from Philippians has a
suggestion phrased in somewhat curious words. The idea here is to grow in
Christ. Jesus died once to save us. But we can miss the boat and lose that salvation if we become disoriented by sin or if we decide to work for salvation
without Christ.

Growing in Christ comes from reading and meditating on His Word—
like you're doing now. A steady diet of His Word in regular worship and Bible
study makes our faith stronger so we can live "according to His good pleasure."

Next time you hear opportunity knocking, don't grumble because the
noise woke you up. Get up and answer the door. Then again, it might just be
one of your relatives.

What's It Doing in the Bible?

Warning: The following Bible passage contains violence, sex,
and adult themes.

"Bring out the man who came into your house, that we may know him."
And the man, the master of the house, went out to them and said to
them, "No, my brothers, do not act so wickedly; since this man has come
into my house, do not do this vile thing. Behold, here are my virgin
daughter and his concubine. Let me bring them out now. Violate them
and do with them what seems good to you, but against this man do not
do this outrageous thing." Judges 19:22–24

It could be a story from the *New York Times*. Worse, it could be a made-for-TV movie. But this true story line comes from the Old Testament. The report ends predictably tragic. The concubine was tossed to the perverts and died from their abuse. The concubine's master wasn't too pleased, either. Revenge was exacted.

The Bible chronicles the history of salvation—and how much people need it. Wickedness is nothing new. Violence and sexual abuse have been around since Adam and Eve vacated the Garden of Eden. The first reported sin was selfish idolatry. The second was murder. Why do these stories appear in the Bible—the *Holy* Bible?

God didn't plant this malice and corruption into the hearts and minds of people. They easily absorbed it through their own flesh and through ardent tutoring from the devil. But God also prevented this depravity from getting in the way of His plans. Many vicious events described in the Bible told of ways the devil tried to prevent God from keeping His promises. And regardless of how ugly and repulsive the sinfulness was, God overcame. Nothing can stand in the way of God's promises.

There was nothing to smile about in today's meditation. Humor has no place in brutality or savagery. But you can leave your chair smiling because nothing can stand in the way of God's promises either. The Savior will come again and gather us where the News is always Good.

Change

And Balaam took up his discourse and said, "Rise, Balak, and hear; give ear to me, O son of Zippor: God is not man, that He should lie, or a son of man, that He should change His mind. Has He said, and will He not do it? Or has He spoken, and will He not fulfill it? Behold, I received a command to bless: He has blessed, and I cannot revoke it. He has not beheld misfortune in Jacob, nor has He seen trouble in Israel. The LORD their God is with them, and the shout of a king is among them. Numbers 23:18–21

How would you define change? Change is . . . Change is . . . Having trouble? The best definition of change is found in your pocket or purse. You know, two dimes and a nickel?

Sometimes change is bad. Newspapers report changes that adversely affect people—crimes, accidents, obituaries, and the scores of your favorite losing team, to name a few. You easily could add to the list with more personal accounts of unwanted changes—jobs lost, marriages broken, health failing, relatives rebelling, etc.

Sometimes change is only what you make of it. The Internet is widely assailed as a tool of those who wish to poison hearts and minds. Yet that same Internet carries many Christian sites that unite believers and evangelize. The same could be said of books, magazines, television, nuclear energy, and the supermarket.

The Scriptures speak often of change—and changelessness. Consider this from Numbers 23:19–20: "God is not man, that He should lie, or a son of man, that He should change His mind. Has He said, and will He not do it? Or has He spoken, and will He not fulfill it?"

God is no "small change." In fact, He isn't change at all. God is never bad nor is He neutral. While some may foster evil in His name, He doesn't support them. God keeps His promises. He's proved that many times—through Noah, Abraham, Jesus, and (insert your name).

You have the blessing of God. The devil and his agents would love to hear God curse sinners and give up on them. God knows we deserve it! Despite sinfulness, God refuses to give up sinners if they cling to Him with even the smallest fleck of faith. And no one can change that.

What Good News we have because we know that God's love doesn't change! But because God doesn't change, we should. God's love through Jesus Christ changes us, drives us to hate sin and live the way He wants us to live.

Next time some coins cross your palm, think about the change Jesus brought to you. Thank Him for it. Now that really makes some sense.

Equal-Opportunity Employer

And there is salvation in no one else, for there is no other name under heaven given among men by which we must be saved. Acts 4:12

If you want a humbling experience, open your local newspaper to the job guide section, and mark all the jobs you're not qualified to do. Feeling humble yet? Don't go too far. Humility is like underwear. We should wear it but not show it off. Of course, humility isn't always as popular as it should be. Consider the Pharisees in Jesus' time, for example.

Pharisees prided themselves on independence—not needing a Savior to take away their sins. They imagined they obeyed God's Law and lived according to His will. When Jesus pointed out their error, they became angry. They felt quite capable of living perfectly, and they didn't need anyone doing a job they could do themselves.

People of the Old Testament hadn't set a good example, either. God wanted them to call on Him for deliverance from their enemies. Occasionally, God's people forgot the source of their strength and went to battle without His help. Their inventory of spears, arrows, and warriors were no match for the enemy on such occasions. Without God they lost and remained lost.

"Equal-Opportunity Employer" is an important phrase today. But it doesn't apply to God's choice of a Savior. Only one qualified for the job. And what a job He did! From birth, to career, to death, to resurrection, to ascension into heaven, Jesus did all the right things to keep us in God's graces.

God is an equal-opportunity employer in one way, though. Regardless of the attributes we possess or lack, we are qualified to share the Gospel with others. Jesus qualified us, and the Holy Spirit authorizes us to tell others what He has done.

See whom you can recruit for His task force. Tell others the many benefits you have as one of His workers. The retirement plan is especially good too!

Telling the Story

For we cannot but speak of what we have seen and heard. Acts 4:20

When a terrorist's bomb shattered a federal building in Oklahoma City (1995), more than 10,000 people called the witness hotline with information. People felt compelled to report anything that could help authorities. Eventually, several reports yielded useful information.

That same bomb shook the air waves with bold Christian witness. People shed their shyness trying to make sense of the tragedy. They knew there was no sense, so they relied on God to work it out—and they shared their trust over national TV and radio networks. In such adverse times, it was refreshing to hear their sincere testimony.

The Apostle Peter also felt obliged to tell what he had seen and heard. His story must have warmed many hearts, and it made more than a few angry, or at least uncomfortable. (That's how it is with truth. Some people keep a respectable distance from it!) Peter's passion burned for the Gospel, and he couldn't help but tell the authorities what they needed to know. But it wasn't what they wanted to know, so they told him to be quiet.

Picture this. It's a quiet Sunday morning when a passer-by notices a squad of soldiers flat on their backs, out cold. A huge stone stands beside an open tomb behind the soldiers. The witness peers in and sees nothing. How do you report nothing? Yet that is what Peter did. He reported that nothing inhabited the tomb where Jesus was buried. He told those who would listen, as well as those who wouldn't listen, that nothing could stand in the way of salvation now that Jesus rose from the dead. He was their Savior.

Despite Peter's impassioned testimony, some chose not to believe. But others, like us, rejoiced in the news. Our joy remains even though the event is long past.

Don't wait for a bomb blast to shake your testimony loose. Give it freely. Give it bravely. Tell the story.

Act of God

*Give thanks to Him; bless His name! For the Lord is good; His steadfast
love endures forever, and His faithfulness to all generations.*
Psalm 100:4–5

The Arkansas legislature didn't like the terminology, so they struck it
from common use in legal documents. An "act of God," they said,
gives God a bad name for something He didn't do.

They replaced the term with "act of nature," though they might have
shown more candor and termed such random destruction "acts of Satan."
Perhaps they thought it risky to offend him too.

"Why, God?" is a common question after disasters, natural or human-
made. The emotions of a tragic moment tempt people either to blame or to
question God. We know that terror and destruction afflict the world. Evil
events are the result of sin, and we can expect calamity and adversity to affect
believers and nonbelievers alike. (Keep in mind that God showers both with
blessings too.)

The psalmist says, "For the Lord is good; His steadfast love endures forever, and His faithfulness to all generations" (Psalm 100:5). Our good God
has not shielded us from the consequences of sin. Rather, He uses those occasions to draw us closer to Himself.

The Old Testament contains many examples of how God faithfully cared
for His people though they were beset with grief and distress. He demonstrated His power by strengthening the Israelites throughout their four centuries of slavery. (Talk about getting physically and mentally prepared for an
arduous trip in the wilderness!) When the Israelites were threatened with
annihilation from myriad enemies, God always saved a few of the faithful to
carry His Word and promise to future generations. How precious that Word
became when endangered with extinction! People clung desperately to it
because it was the only possession they had.

Later, we marvel at God's promise come true in the birth of baby Jesus.
We hear how He lived a perfect life—for our sake. Then, tragedy. He was
wrongfully executed, but it was for our sake. The sky turned black on that
Friday. The earth quaked, and the temple suffered major damage to its finest
curtain. Then all was quiet. God's Son was dead.

But not for long. Some distraught women discovered the truth in the
quiet hours a couple days after the horrific spiritual storm. An empty tomb. A
living Jesus. A promise of eternal life. Now there's an act of God!

If the Clothing Fits, Wear It

I put on righteousness, and it clothed me. Job 29:14

A joy to some and a bane to others—that describes shopping for clothes. Finding fashionable clothing in the right size, made of comfortable material, and priced reasonably is always a challenge. The Bible has some excellent counsel for style-conscious clothing shoppers. It's almost like the departments in a clothing store. Care for a tour?

The first stop is Psalm 45:3, which advises "Gird your sword on your thigh, O mighty one, in your splendor and majesty!" Considering the date of this advice, the psalmist probably isn't talking about evening gowns and tuxedos. But what style could be more magnificent than the look and feel of salvation? What splendor there is in going in style!

The second stop is Isaiah 52:1—the durable clothes department. "Put on your strength." Nothing lasts as long as life in Christ, does it? It literally lasts forever. You need only one of these garments. Move on.

The next department is Colossians 3:12: "Put on then, as God's chosen ones, holy and beloved, compassion, kindness, humility, meekness, and patience." Christians find compassion always in style, though sometimes hard to find. We can get so caught up in our own spiritual "looks" that we forget what Christians are all about. Take several of these outfits so you can give them to those in need.

The fourth stop is 1 Peter 5:5—perhaps the most confusing department: "Clothe yourselves, all of you, with humility toward one another." Most designers create alluring clothing that attracts attention. Nevertheless, it is good to don this outfit often enough to remind us that the best-dressed people remain sinful and dirty unless they bathe themselves in much-needed forgiveness.

As with any shopping spree, the time comes to pay for the "prizes." If we think the clothes are stunning, they are nothing compared to the bill. It would take a lifetime to pay it. And that's what Jesus did. He gave His life to clothe us in the garments of righteousness. Feel free to fill your closet.

Trust Fund

But I have trusted in Your steadfast love; my heart shall rejoice in Your salvation. Psalm 13:5

Trust can be as elusive as a treasure chest filled with priceless jewels. But trust can be quite common too. We trust many things because they are dependable. When you sit down, you expect the chair to be there. Turn the handle on a water faucet, and you expect water. Trust is common when we believe that ordinary (though quite remarkable) things will do what they're supposed to do and be where they're supposed to be. Experience teaches who and what we can trust.

Cynical sages advise us to trust no one. Distrust comes from experience too. Just let the car not start once, and you won't easily trust it again—at least not soon.

We may find God hard to trust at times too. Ardent prayers seem to go unanswered—at least on our terms and timeline. Disease and disaster afflict the believer as well as the heathen. Sometimes we may doubt that anyone could love us as much as Jesus did. Trust can indeed be frail. Perhaps what we need is a good role model to show us what trust is all about.

King David had one of the richest trust funds ever. He often took his task to God for guidance and help. He simply trusted God to support him.

God is a trustworthy fixture in our life too. When we need rest and comfort, we can trust Him to hold us up. If we need refreshment for heart and soul, we can turn our thirst over to Him.

Look around you. Choose an object that is always near where you read this book. Every time you see it, trust that God is always just as common, just as near. Your trust fund is as well supplied as David's.

By the way, someone probably trusts that you'll get back to work now.

You Are What You Eat

"Blessed are those who hunger and thirst for righteousness, for they shall be satisfied. . . . Blessed are the pure in heart, for they shall see God."
Matthew 5:6, 8

Have you heard the expression "You are what you eat?" Let's hope you don't make a steady diet of nuts! Perhaps you prefer food that sticks to your ribs. But you know, of course, that's not really where the food sticks. Our tastes might better be served by hash. When it comes to hash, at least we know the cook put everything he had into the dish.

Jesus created some heavenly hash when He mixed ample portions of righteousness and purity. We can't cook up righteousness and purity ourselves. Nor can we buy it. The Master Chef put everything He had into it, even His life. Jesus Christ followed God's recipe for righteousness and purity. The ingredients included a one-of-a-kind perfection commonly known as sinlessness. Jesus' life fulfilled all the daily requirements for spiritual nourishment. His death and resurrection make this a miracle food that sustains those who indulge through eternal life. It's a true miracle food—the miracle is that it's free. All we need for an ample supply is a hunger for it.

The portions of this heavenly hash available to us on earth are only a ration of what we'll receive in heaven. Even though we dine regularly on God's righteousness and purity, we're not completely filled yet. What we are left with is a genuine, insatiable hunger. We want to be exactly like Jesus. We want to be sinless in God's sight. We hate sin and love good. Those are the degrees of righteousness and purity we possess as sanctified Christians. And it's enough for now.

Dietary experts recommend that we stop eating while we are still hungry. That's good advice for ordinary foods, but our spiritual life is sustained by stuffing ourselves with the righteousness and purity served by Jesus.

Are you ready for another helping?

Grow Down

At that time the disciples came to Jesus, saying, "Who is the greatest in the kingdom of heaven?" And calling to Him a child, He put him in the midst of them and said, "Truly, I say to you, unless you turn and become like children, you will never enter the kingdom of heaven. Whoever humbles himself like this child is the greatest in the kingdom of heaven."
Matthew 18:1–4

Have you discovered the secret of staying young? Lie about your age! Of course, there are those who look forward to growing old(er) and finally reaching their eternal rest. The Bible is an excellent source of information about living forever. The mystery isn't in finding ways to grow older but in ways to grow younger.

It wasn't in the context of living forever or finding a fountain of youth that Jesus spoke the words of Matthew 18:3, unless, of course, we realize that the disciples were acting like children. Instead of telling them to grow up, however, Jesus said they should grow down.

The message is clear. Disciples need to adopt the genuine humility of children. Children have much about which to be humble. The beauty of that humility is that they're naively modest about it. They are not consciously aware of their humility, so they live naturally with the condition. You don't hear them saying things such as "It's with great humility that I accept this racy, red bicycle on my birthday." They simply ride off with a smile stretching from training wheel to training wheel.

That's how we are called to live with the faith God gives us. Grow down and act like a kid who just got the gift she has always wanted. Free of thoughts about being deserving or undeserving, worthy or unworthy, we can romp and carouse in the generosity of God's love and blessings. We joyously accept our role in life because nothing could be better than living with the special gift that never grows old—the gift of salvation and eternal life.

True humility probably involves a little selfishness. Oh, not the bad kind, rather a selfishness that approaches a gift-giver with bold confidence, assured that a gift is forthcoming. That's exactly how we can approach God. Despite how bad we've been, we can approach the lap of our heavenly Father, knowing that He won't reject us—that He wants us to come to Him in faith.

Grow down. You won't have to lie about your age to keep from growing old. In truth, you're getting younger every day. You're growing down until that time when you'll be born again, never to grow old.

Christian Chameleons

To the weak I became weak, that I might win the weak. I have become all things to all people, that by all means I might save some. 1 Corinthians 9:22

Hopefully, you're not one of those people whose weaknesses are the strongest thing about them. Do you know people like that?

Now, if you were to follow Paul's example, how would you reach those who need to know that Jesus isn't some stuffed toga who cares only about people who go to church and read religious books? Does Paul suggest that you adopt sinful ways to attract sinful people to Christ?

Paul's Jewish colleagues thought he was guilty of breaking God's law because he ate with Gentiles—non-Jewish people. He not only ate with them, he ate what they ate. Therein was the problem. Devout Jews restricted their diets to certain types of food; all others were forbidden. But Paul considered none of these old laws as important as winning new believers. All believers were freed from such ceremonial laws by Jesus.

Which religious practices may we ignore and which must we practice? God guided Paul to know where to draw the lines. He led Paul to know when to act like a chameleon and when to hold firm to his beliefs and practices. Study Paul and you'll find that He wouldn't compromise when it came to faith in Jesus or acceptance of God's authority over all of life. But he did step away from common traditions and religious practices when it was incidental to real faith.

We don't have to curse with the verbally deprived nor need we dabble with other religions to win others to Christ. We simply need to act like Christ when in the presence of these people. He didn't threaten and He didn't give in. He simply lived what He spoke and taught.

Your break is over. See how weak you can become to win someone for Christ.

Window Decorations

*The men said to her, "We will be guiltless with respect to this oath of
yours that you have made us swear. Behold, when we come into the land,
you shall tie this scarlet cord in the window through which you let us
down." Joshua 2:17–18a*

They come in many sizes and designs depicting everything from hummingbirds to flying fish to the skyline of beautiful, downtown
Holyrood, Kansas (a general store dwarfed by colossal waves of grain). Sun
catchers make a statement. Occasionally, they evoke statements too—such as
when the little suction cups malfunction in the middle of the night and you
think an invader is crawling through your window!

What sun catcher would you design to tell the world you believe in Jesus?
What would you want Jesus to see when He returns on Judgment Day?

The Old Testament relates the story of a prostitute named Rahab whose
fame involved protecting some spies. She hung something in her window—
something that would save her life when Israel invaded and destroyed Jericho.
It's found in Joshua 2:17–18a: "The men said to her, 'We will be guiltless with
respect to this oath of yours that you have made us swear. Behold, when we
come into the land, you shall tie this scarlet cord in the window through
which you let us down.'"

Rahab's red rope identified her as someone to be saved. It made a statement both to the invading army and to herself. Every time she looked out her
window, she saw that scarlet ribbon shimmering in the sun or standing in joyful contrast to cloudy gloom. She believed the army would come and victoriously destroy the evil that surrounded her.

While we might wish to announce our Christianity to passersby via sun
catchers, we might consider the way we live as the best window dressing. Our
lifestyle provides a window to our soul. When others hear how we talk, see
how we act, notice how we forgive, and accept how we love, they can't help
but see the Son shining on these symbols of His influence in our lives.

Like Rahab, we expect something of an invasion. Jesus will come back,
and at His Word, every wicked and evil thing will be utterly destroyed—except
us. Jesus will see our scarlet cord and recognize us as numbered among those
cleansed by His blood. He will recall how He brought us to faith and how we
harbored Him in our heart, waiting for the day when He would return to
make life better.

Hang something in the window of your soul. A big, bright thankful heart
would be a good way to begin.

Heart Condition

Keep your heart with all vigilance, for from it flow the springs of life.
Proverbs 4:23

We must subscribe to the same school of wisdom as Solomon. The heart remains the seat of desire. Doctors know the heart beats the rhythm of life. Poets and lovers see the heart as the place where affection and emotions dwell. The Bible cautions against hard hearts like the stony one inside Pharaoh when he wouldn't free captive Israel. (It's said that the only thing worse than hard-heartedness is soft-headedness.) And so, as Proverbs indicates, the heart, in whatever context, is a wellspring of life.

Place your hand over your heart. You're not a doctor, but you know you're alive. *Thump thump. Thump thump. Thump thump.* That little thumper is pushing blood through thousands of miles of veins and arteries inside your body. You depend on its operation to keep you alive, yet it works on its own, without your planning or management!

Paul said, "For with the heart one believes and is justified, and with the mouth one confesses and is saved" (Romans 10:10). Paul's view of the heart was less clinical, but he recognized its life-supporting significance just the same. He would probably promote activities that maintain healthy hearts too.

First, exercise is vital. Doctors often recommend vigorous walks. Paul might recommend the same—with Jesus for a companion. Although Jesus isn't here to match us step for step, we walk with Him in our meditation and prayers. He's close by, and He promises to guide us.

Second, diet is important. Debates toss about pros and cons of every conceivable food and nutrient, and it's hard to be sure that we're eating the right foods. But Paul's spiritual diet consists of only one item—God's Word. How pleasant to know that we can never consume too much of His nutrition!

Coffee breaks are great times for exercise and snacks, aren't they?

Memories

But the Helper, the Holy Spirit, whom the Father will send in My name,
He will teach you all things and bring to your remembrance all that I
have said to you. John 14:26

You know your memory is failing if you . . .

forget the words to "Happy Birthday."

can't recall your last mistake.

don't remember how long your break lasts.

thought the TV rerun was new.

Oh, to be that proverbial elephant that never forgets! Then again, what do they have to remember?

Memories play a prominent role in life. It seems the older we get, the more we live with memories. When you think about it, that's not very profound. Naturally, the older we are the more memories we have. Memory is important from a spiritual vantage point too.

As you read in today's passage, Jesus told His disciples that the Holy Spirit would teach them new things and also remind them of all that He had said. The memories of Jesus preaching, teaching, healing, forgiving, laughing, crying, dying, and rising would come to the disciples when they needed to proclaim Christ. The Holy Spirit would also refresh their memories when they needed to recall all that Christ had done for them. The key to their memories was the Holy Spirit—not their own untrustworthy memory banks. How comforting for us who have poor or deteriorating memory!

An old friend once worried, "I'm afraid I might get Alzheimer's—then I might forget about Jesus my Savior." As tragic as Alzheimer's is, and as unsettling as normal memory loss may be, we can be certain that we'll never forget our faith. The Holy Spirit just won't let us forget. Besides, He placed faith in our souls, not our minds.

Jars

*For God, who said, "Let light shine out of darkness," has shone in our hearts
to give the light of the knowledge of the glory of God in the face of Jesus
Christ. But we have this treasure in jars of clay, to show that the surpassing
power belongs to God and not to us. We are afflicted in every way, but not
crushed; perplexed, but not driven to despair; persecuted, but not forsaken;
struck down, but not destroyed; always carrying in the body the death of
Jesus, so that the life of Jesus may also be manifested in our bodies. For we
who live are always being given over to death for Jesus' sake, so that the life
of Jesus also may be manifested in our mortal flesh. 2 Corinthians 4:6–11*

Have you noticed how some people collect jars? You'll find them (the jars and the collectors) in antique shops, skillfully buying and selling these precious collectibles. And why not? The ancestors of modern jars—urns and other vessels—festoon the shelves of many museums.

Jars of clay weren't worth any more in Paul's time than jars of glass are today. They were simple containers. What was on the inside was far more valuable and important than the jar itself. That's good news for us Christian "jars."

Our bodies are worth little, subject as they are to chipping, cracking, and gradual deterioration. Someday they'll be so worthless that they will end up buried in landfills we politely call cemeteries. Yet the faith and power that lives and breathes inside us will live forever. We contain, as Paul calls it, a treasure within ourselves. That fabulous fortune is nothing less than Jesus Christ.

Like all jars, we get jostled, dropped, or simply develop loose covers. Sickness, family problems, accidents, and other tragedies dribble and spill us out of our bodies and senses. Even this can be a blessing! As our treasure spills, we have opportunity to witness our faith despite our frailties. In fact, it's during those troubled times that our testimony about God's love can have the greatest impact. Besides, our treasure will never leave us empty.

Undoubtedly, we want to retain this treasure forever. But we know our bodies will not last that long. Isn't it just like our loving God to recycle the old into something new? Although our old jars are crushed into dust by sin, God will make that dust into a better jar—one whose quality we can't begin to imagine. That makes us part of a priceless collection too.

It Doesn't Count

Blessed is the one whose transgression is forgiven, whose sin is covered.
Blessed is the man against whom the Lord counts no iniquity, and in
whose spirit there is no deceit. Psalm 32:1–2

I magine this newspaper article:

SIN IS DEAD

WASHINGTON, D.C.—Today the courts unanimously and unequivocally declared sin dead and gone. In a cleverly worded decision, the courts have made all sins legal.

David had something else in mind when he declared the words of Psalm 32. He had recently confessed his worst atrocity. In an attempt to cover his lust and illicit affair with Bathsheba, he had her husband killed so he could legally marry her. But God knew exactly what happened. He let guilt play some useful havoc on David's conscience.

David says, "When I kept silent, my bones wasted away. . . . Day and night Your hand was heavy upon me" (Psalm 32:3–4). Perhaps you've had similar experiences?

We commonly experience guilt for wrongdoing. How many family arguments have kept you awake nights? What have you tried to cover up so others won't know? These are the aching bones and heavy hands David talked about. Good thing David shared with us what he did next. He repented.

Repentance is the gracious loophole through which God lets us escape eternal damnation for Jesus' sake. Repentance begins with sorrow over sins. Sorrow invites confession. David confessed before the prophet Nathan and God Himself. Praise God for accepting the apologies of sinners! He accepted David's, and He will always accept ours too.

Repentance also involves a change of behavior—a desire to do good rather than evil. (This is the hard part. The devil is rather fond of sin, and he'll do everything possible to prevent its extinction!) The desire, like the forgiveness, springs from the Holy Spirit, who empowers us to hate sin and fight it.

The bottom line is that God completely forgives and forgets. Why cover up sins ourself when Jesus does such a complete job of it?

Together with Thomas

Then He said to Thomas, "Put your finger here, and see My hands; and put out your hand, and place it in My side. Do not disbelieve, but believe." Thomas answered Him, "My Lord and my God!" John 20:27–28

Thomas believed his doubts and doubted his beliefs. He put a question mark where God put a period. We, like Thomas, also need to touch the scars of Jesus once in awhile.

The best way to combat doubt is to fortify our faith. Prayer—talking things over with God—is one good way of reinforcing faith. You already know how "talking things out" works with others. For example, one day your daughter comes home and remarks, "I don't think you love me anymore." You would want to know why she felt that way, and reassure her of your love. A heart-to-heart talk, along with further evidence of your love, would likely resolve the situation.

Like Thomas, we need to talk over our doubts with God:

> "Good morning, God. I'm on break now, so I have only a
> few moments to talk to You. I'm sorry, but sometimes
> You're just unbelievable. So little on earth confirms Your
> existence. How can You be three Persons, yet only one God?
> And I don't understand how You could send Yourself to
> earth so You could actually die, then raise Yourself from the
> dead! Sometimes I think You've given up on me because I
> don't feel very holy. That's what You're supposed to do,
> isn't it—make me holier every day?"

This conversation could continue through many breaks—as long as we have time to think up more doubts. We sometimes doubt because nothing in our present existence equals God's goodness. Instead of relying on experience, we must trust His Word. Through the Bible, God assures us of His love and drives away our doubts. When we pray to God, we need to read rather than hear or see His answers, promises, and comfort. Then we can exclaim together with Thomas, "My Lord and my God!"

Cater Walls

*Oh come, let us sing to the Lord; let us make a joyful noise to the rock of
our salvation! Let us come into His presence with thanksgiving; let us
make a joyful noise to Him with songs of praise! For the Lord is a great
God, and a great King above all gods. Psalm 95:1–3*

The director said it was a special group created for singers like me who
had, uh, similar vocal qualities—qualities that deserved to be distinct
from the group known as A Capella Chorus. I overheard the director explaining this new group to the principal. He said it would be called the Cater
Walls—probably a Latin word for something melodious.

One safe axiom is that singers like to sing, notes on the harmonic scale
notwithstanding. Some singers hold membership in singing groups such as
the Crows or the Grackles—certainly never attaining the height of a Cater
Wall—and thus believe that because others think they are lousy singers, they
are, indeed, lousy singers. But what they lack in quality, they compensate for
in volume.

How do you sing? Whether lyrically or raucously, you have a right, maybe
a responsibility, to sing. Perhaps Psalm 30:12 was written for the vocally challenged: "That my glory may sing Your praise and not be silent. O Lord my
God, I will give thanks to You forever!" Singing hearts cause less aesthetic
damage than twanging vocal chords, but as singers of every kind know, sincere singing rises from the heart.

Throughout the history of God's people, songs played an important role
in praising Him. Some songs were so good that they were recorded—in the
Bible, that is. The most popular songwriter was David, who rose from the rank
of shepherd to fearless warrior and eventually to king. His songs reflected
what was in his heart—sometimes anguish, sometimes fear, but mostly trust
and praise. A little-known fact is that David probably created the first rock
concert. After all, we hear in the words of Psalm 95:1: "Oh come, let us sing
to the Lord; let us make a joyful noise to the rock of our salvation!"

Sing a song today. Or at least whistle an original composition dedicated
to Jesus. Our Lord isn't a music critic. He doesn't care how well or how loudly we sing as long as the notes and lyrics spring from our heart. Despite circumstances, we have much for which to sing. Even if few on earth love us,
One faithfully loves us from above. Even if employment, health, weather, or
wealth abandon us, the treasure of salvation is always ours. So even if you're
shy about singing, have a Rock concert in your heart. God will happily take
note, even an off-key one.

February 1

Who Needs It?

And when the Pharisees saw this, they said to His disciples, "Why does your teacher eat with tax collectors and sinners?" But when He heard it, He said, "Those who are well have no need of a physician, but those who are sick." Matthew 9:11–12

The easiest way to make friends is with a warm heart (as opposed to a hot head). The biggest barrier to making friends is holding your nose higher than your head.

Jesus really knew how to make friends, not that He needed them, but because they needed Him. Though He was God in the flesh, He was neither pompous nor conceited. And He wasn't shy, either. He gently but persistently befriended people.

Some Christians seek to shelter their life with only the company of other Christians. Fellowship with other believers is important and desirable, but who benefits from associating only with others of similar beliefs?

It's possible these days to associate exclusively with "announced Christians." Christian business directories lead us to faithful plumbers, contractors, printers, florists, and even used car dealers. (Sorry.) Presumably, this helps Christians share their faith and fees with each other, and that's okay. But carried to an extreme, it can lead to the kind of religious aristocracy Jesus dealt with in today's text.

Dear Christian, you are free to associate with anyone who might be influenced by your faith. So if you employ a pagan plumber, maybe your language, kindness, and the cross on your wall will give him something to stick in his pipe. And you may impress the used car salesperson with your integrity, fairness, and gentle tire kicking.

Don't abandon your Christian companions, and above all, don't let others lead you astray. But don't be afraid to eat lunch or share coffee or do business with sinners. You may even discover that they are just like you—also saints. And even if they are unbelievers, the Holy Spirit can work through your words and actions to bring Jesus into their lives.

Other Reasons

"For God so loved the world, that He gave His only Son, that whoever believes in Him should not perish but have eternal life. For God did not send His Son into the world to condemn the world, but in order that the world might be saved through Him." John 3:16–17

It's not an enjoyable way to begin a devotion, but recall some of the bad times in your life. Maybe you don't have to tax your memory, but perhaps you'll think back to a death, a serious illness or accident, a failed marriage, a rebellious child, or an economic calamity. Worse yet, perhaps you faced several of these difficulties at once. It's enough to make you wonder if God is mad at you, right?

The Old Testament reveals numerous occasions of God's anger. It was always just—just horrible! He destroyed whole cities or infested fields with grasshoppers or turned rivers into bloody baths. In every case, God was punishing the wickedness of unrepented sin. If God got mad back then, is it a sign of divine indignation when we suffer?

The answer is in the Bible. One of many places we can find an answer is John 3:17, which says, "For God did not send His Son into the world to condemn the world, but in order that the world might be saved through Him." And the verse immediately before this is the famous one that tells how much God loves us. So when we suffer, it must not be God's fury that afflicts us. There must be other reasons.

Affliction and adversity are the result of sin, but not necessarily a one-to-one correspondence with personal sins. Risky behaviors certainly invite direct consequences, but anguish and hardship do not discriminate on the basis of personal saintliness. Worldly dilemmas might be traced to the first man and woman, whose foray into sin was so earthshaking that God called it original. Since then, humankind has introduced many new and improved, giant-sized varieties. The world is wracked—and wrecked—by the general nature of sin. Everyone becomes victims of it, from the most prurient pagan to the most chaste Christian.

Sin and its ugly, painful, and constrictive results were not introduced by God. Spiritual mutation results from the devil's deeds to alienate us from God. Sin is separation from God.

Thank God we suffer only a temporary taste of that separation. Isn't it true that we seek a closer relationship with God in times of trouble?

God is not mad at you. He spent His anger on Jesus. Now all is well, though we did nothing to deserve this treatment. There must be other reasons.

Happy Campers

And he said to them, "Look at me, and do likewise. When I come to the
outskirts of the camp, do as I do." Judges 7:17

Camping is the happy pastime of millions of people, but it's certainly not new. Just ask Gideon.

Gideon sounds like a helpful campground director in the brief verse above. But he was about to embark on dangerous business for God in Jericho. The inhabitants of Jericho were God's enemies, and Gideon's job was to defeat them. But Gideon had a unique problem—too many soldiers! God wanted an army of 300 rather than the 32,000 at Gideon's disposal. God didn't want these soldiers to carry conventional weapons either. Trumpets, jars, and the Secret Weapon would do the job. When the day of the battle came, God's enemies crumbled in defeat.

Lest we get sidetracked, the moral of the story is not to look for uncrowded campgrounds. What we learn from Camp Commander Gideon is to trust God, especially when we face powerful, frightening, spiteful enemies. God is our Secret Weapon. The devil and our own human nature are the enemies.

Sin builds a dense wall around itself, but it doesn't stay inside its fortress. It makes well-planned raids against God's people. If all the Christians in the world formed an army to crush sin, it couldn't win. Too many soldiers. God needed only one soldier, and He won the war even though He appeared to lose it.

The war is over, but sin continues its terrorist attacks. To remain happy campers, we need to know who fights our battles because we can't do it alone. Today, we rely on the Holy Spirit as our Secret Weapon. When the Spirit directs us to Christ, we can survive sin's onslaught, even when we become our own worst enemy. The Spirit speaks to our hearts and minds by revealing God's will to us in the Holy Scriptures.

Trust God with all that threatens or attacks you. And don't forget your trumpet and jar.

Christ-Confidence

*Therefore let anyone who thinks that he stands take heed lest he fall. No
temptation has overtaken you that is not common to man. God is faithful,
and He will not let you be tempted beyond your ability, but with the
temptation He will also provide the way of escape, that you may be able to
endure it. 1 Corinthians 10:12–13*

Some define confidence as what a person feels before he knows what's
really going on! For the average person, confidence is something we
have until it's shaken from us. And then we remain shaken—and shaky.

Temptations challenge our confidence. Conversion, Baptism, Communion, Bible study, and Christian fellowship all work to assemble and
strengthen our faith. We become confident Christians, poised to live devout-
ly in a sin filled world. We fend off confrontations with the worst of sins—
murder, adultery, witchcraft, rape, and robbery. Confident that we can withstand anything Satan and the world flings at us, we confidently ignore our
"little sins"—until they devour our confidence.

Shaken and frightened sinners were part of Paul's world too. That's why
God directed Paul to write the words in today's passage. How good for
Christian confidence! We can (and must) ask God to help us abandon *all* our
sins. (Little sins are inclined to grow like cancerous tumors!) But what about
the "bigger" temptations that lead to bigger sins?

Indeed, some temptations are too big for us to face. But when they attack
and we retreat, we can be confident that God won't let us be assaulted by anything we can't handle. He keeps those temptations from claiming us.

Confident Christians walk a thin line. We err when we become self-con-
fident, counting on our own noble nature to resist temptation. We walk in
complete confidence only when we have Christ-confidence.

Did You Turn Off the Coffee?

Rejoice in the Lord always; again I will say, Rejoice. Let your reasonableness be known to everyone. The Lord is at hand; do not be anxious about anything, but in everything by prayer and supplication with thanksgiving let your requests be made known to God. And the peace of God, which surpasses all understanding, will guard your hearts and your minds in Christ Jesus. Philippians 4:4–7

Getting away from the front door was always a bittersweet accomplishment when my family left for vacation (or even a Sunday drive). Dad would slide behind the wheel. Mom would slip into the passenger seat and slip right out again. Fumbling for the house key, she would say, "I don't know if I turned off the coffee." Dad would grunt, and I would groan. But it wasn't long before Mom was in the front seat again. And if Dad didn't screech away from the curb, Mom was back out again. "I don't remember locking the door after checking the coffee," she would say.

Stress and tension are nothing new. The disciples had plenty of it, which gave Jesus a chance to address the problem. He told His disciples (and that includes us) stories about birds and lilies and how they didn't need to worry about food or how they looked. Later, Paul told the Philippians, "Do not be anxious about anything, but in everything by prayer and supplication with thanksgiving let your requests be made known to God" (Philippians 4:6).

Paul wasn't talking about practical anxieties such as locked doors or brewing pots. Those are things we can and should do something about. His advice concerned worries about future events—the "what ifs" that keep us awake nights, as well as the realities of present stresses. "Take it to the Lord in prayer," was Paul's counsel.

But did you notice something else in Paul's words? Thanksgiving. How hard it is to feel thankful in bad times! How can you be thankful when you're worrying about your teenager, or about Uncle Harry's abusive alcoholism, or about tomorrow's edition of pink slips?

Paul knew that worries subside when you trust your life to God. God cares more for you than the birds and flowers that mindlessly exist with His blessings. Thank God for His care. He loves you in good times and bad and in sickness and health. Even death won't part you from Him. Little worries or big, give thanks that you can give them all to God. With Paul, we exclaim, "And the peace of God, which surpasses all understanding, will guard your hearts and your minds in Christ Jesus" (Philippians 4:7).

The Do-It-Yourself Syndrome

Peter said to Him, "You shall never wash my feet." Jesus answered him,
"If I do not wash you, you have no share with Me." John 13:8

Peter was developing a reputation for denials. But this one was dire. At face value, his refusal to let Jesus wash his feet seems admirable. Why would any devout person permit the King of kings and Lord of lords (Hallelujah!) to perform a task so menial that servants even avoided it? Would you or I tolerate such servitude, say, from the President of the United States? He's too important for lint-picking. How about from someone we love and respect more than anyone else? We love them too much to allow them to stoop so low. We can do it ourselves.

Peter had to be stunned when Jesus responded, "Unless I wash you, you have no part with Me." With that said, a chastised and wiser Peter asked for a whole bath! His story teaches us not to toy with the Do-It-Yourself Syndrome.

Oddly enough, many of us fail to fully appreciate the magnitude of Jesus' humility. We think of Him as gentle, kind, meek, caring, and—humble. But we sometimes miss how humiliating humility was for Him. Washing a pair of filthy feet was one thing. But worse was His bout with the sins of the world. He could have turned this cesspool of sin into pure water with a single command. Instead, He followed the laws that He Himself established for people. He suffered and died in place of sinners because of their self-imposed broken relationship with Him—but only after obeying all the laws for them. Did the gods of any other people ever so humiliate themselves? Of course not. The devil never humiliates himself, either. He only humiliates his victims.

Peter was momentarily the devil's victim. At first he wanted to clean himself. But then he learned that Jesus was the only one who could make him clean enough for God.

Next time you're washing your feet, remember Jesus. Invite Him to give you a whole bath. You'll never be cleaner.

Enough Is Enough

*For now we see in a mirror dimly, but then face to face. Now I know in
part; then I shall know fully, even as I have been fully known.*
1 Corinthians 13:12

"What do you know?" was once a common greeting. Usually the
response was brief, and no one gave it serious thought.

Wise people seem unsatisfied with what they know, and they constantly
strive to learn more. Ignorance is not bliss. (We can be happy about that.) Is
the same true for Christians?

Close your eyes for a moment (but not if you're tired). Think of three
things you would like to know about God that you don't know now.

Perhaps you can find the answers to your questions by using a topical
Bible or asking a pastor. But the most difficult questions may not have
answers readily available. Some examples? How about a practical explanation
of the Trinity? How could Jesus rise from the dead? How can anything have
no beginning or end? How did God really create giraffes? Did Pontius Pilate
repent and go to heaven? What did Jesus really look like? If you're involved in
a lively Bible class, you're likely to hear even more questions and speculation
as to the answers. To use a religious term, the questions could go on for eternity.

Did you notice anything all the questions had in common? Not one
asked anything truly important. None inquired as to how we are saved or
what we must do to receive forgiveness. Is it because we don't care about those
answers? Hardly. It is because we already know the answers! A truly wonderful thing about the Bible is that it makes us question many things. But even
better, the Bible makes the most important information so simple that even
children understand it. What could be less complicated than Jesus' love for
you? He took your sins away. You will live with Him in heaven. Those aren't
answers. Those are promises.

Study your Bible. But know when enough is enough.

Locked in or Locked Out?

On the evening of that day, the first day of the week, the doors being
locked where the disciples were for fear of the Jews, Jesus came and stood
among them and said to them, "Peace be with you." When He had said
this, He showed them His hands and His side. Then the disciples were
glad when they saw the Lord. Jesus said to them again, "Peace be with
you. As the Father has sent Me, even so I am sending you." And when
He had said this, He breathed on them and said to them, "Receive the
Holy Spirit." John 20:19–22

Have you heard of the satellite system that unlocks your car from outer space if your keys are trapped in inner space? It used to take a coat hanger and a little ingenuity to do the same thing.

Locks are flexible mechanisms. They can lock people in, and they can lock people out. Consider the disciples in this incident recorded in the Bible passage above.

The disciples feared their enemies. Even the lightest knock on the door or the faintest sound of approaching footsteps alarmed them. They felt much safer behind the sturdy door and the lock that separated them from their enemies. While the lock worked to protect them, it didn't keep out their best Friend, who greeted them with calming words. So shook up was that crowd that Jesus repeatedly said, "Peace be with you."

How often are we like those disciples—secure in our insecurity? We spend most of our lives locking out our fears. We want to keep the bad out, and at the very least, keep the status quo inside. So we lock the doors of our hearts, the windows of our minds, and the portals of our souls. Some good results. We may succeed in reducing the perils of evil and sin that lurk in the world's darkness. But wickedness is so powerful that it seeps in through cracks and crevices. It attacks our bodies with illness and injuries, infects our minds with doubts and despair, and seduces our souls with temptations. Our own defenses prove inadequate.

Just when we realize the weakness of our locks, Jesus breezes in to bring us peace. Through His forgiveness earned on the cross, Jesus broke Satan's bonds that so firmly locked us to sin. Jesus gave us power to resist sin and finally to escape its power to destroy us. We are locked inside His grace, and the devil is locked out in an eternity of darkness.

Each day when you lock your doors, remember that Jesus is with you to provide total security. Even if you misplace your keys, Jesus has a way to get inside.

Star Struck

And those who are wise shall shine like the brightness of the sky above;
and those who turn many to righteousness, like the stars forever and ever.
Daniel 12:3

Today's passage sounds like a poetic goal of someone seeking success. In reality, it's more like the motto of someone who spent a lifetime becoming an overnight success.

These words from Daniel provide a picture of the end times—when earth ends and we join all other believers in the indescribable delights of heaven. Therefore, they don't speak of the present as much as the future. If the words have struck your soul, however, you're headed for stardom yourself.

Most present stars, movie or otherwise, didn't achieve success by sitting around and waiting for it. They discovered that the secret of success is hard work, or as someone put it, they started from scratch and kept on scratching! But we Christians have an advantage—we are successful right now! Christ gave us all the success we need. Now He wants us to use our success to successfully lead others to Him. And He will even help us do it.

If our goal is to become a star, we've missed the point of being Christ's chosen ones. Besides, the sky has so many stars that only astronomers can tell them apart. Christ's chosen stars must shine on those who live in the darkness of ignorance—on those who don't recognize the true star, Jesus Christ. How, then, can we burn brightly?

As God's stars, we burn with energy created by Jesus Christ. We warm those in our presence with love, compassion, and understanding. We light the way through black holes of sin. We share God's warmth and light through our actions and our words. And as we grow in faith—through Bible study, prayer, and the Lord's Supper—we shine even brighter.

Look up at the sky tonight. Think of each star as one of your fellow Christians working to lead others to their Savior.

Twinkle, twinkle little star.

Looking Up

As they were looking on, He was lifted up, and a cloud took Him out of their sight. And while they were gazing into heaven as He went, behold, two men stood by them in white robes, and said, "Men of Galilee, why do you stand looking into heaven? This Jesus, who was taken up from you into heaven, will come in the same way as you saw Him go into heaven."
Acts 1:9–11

Warning: Practical jokes are sometimes dangerous, especially around humorless people. You might want to try this one when you're on a busy street corner or at the mall. Look up. That's right. Crane your neck and aim your eyes at the ceiling or the sky. Every once in a while, cast a shifty glance at the people around you (watch out for the ones sporting a badge). What are they doing? Probably the same thing you are—at least before they storm off in a huff or flee in terror.

The Bible tells about some men of Galilee who were staring at the sky. One minute Jesus was talking with them, and the next He was ascending into heaven. The disciples lost their good Friend once, and now it was happening again. As they gazed into the void, two angels addressed the group. "'Men of Galilee, why do you stand looking into heaven? This Jesus, who was taken up from you into heaven, will come in the same way as you saw Him go into heaven'" (Acts 1:11). It was just another way of saying that things were looking up—even if it didn't seem that way to Jesus' closest followers.

Like those early believers who witnessed the first Ascension Day, we might find ourselves looking up to heaven and feeling very much alone here on earth. Wouldn't it be good to see Jesus face to face, to hear His voice, to thrill to His blessed touch? Jesus would seem so much more real if only . . . If only we avoided these thoughts. Like the disciples, we're not alone.

Just 10 days after the disciples lost sight of Jesus, God filled them with another Friend—the Holy Spirit. We have the Holy Spirit too. We no longer need to selfishly guard our friendship with God. Instead, God enables us to share His love and companionship with everyone we meet. Others won't always accept the way we look up to God. But as our words and deeds point up to our Savior, others might want to know more. Then you can tell them about how God loves you—and them too. You can borrow the words of the angels and let people know that Jesus will come again.

Things are looking up, all right. No joking!

Party Time

*I tell you, there will be more joy in heaven over one sinner who repents
than over ninety-nine righteous persons who need no repentance.*
Luke 15:7

Earthly parties could never match the heavenly celebration over repentant sinners. Can you see the banner stretching from cloud to cloud? It says "Welcome Back" in a rainbow of colors.

Do you note any cynicism in today's passage? When Jesus spoke these words, He wasn't conceding that sinners comprise a 1 percent minority of the population. He was referring to people who *think* they are righteous. They are lost until they lose their sense of self-righteousness.

"Repentant sinner" might be an embarrassing name tag to wear in public. Imagine the stares and the snickers. Neighbors might whisper, "I wonder what he did?" Scoffers might comment, "There goes another victim of the church!" Others would dismiss us as unstable fanatics. The repentant sinner label was equally regarded in Jesus' time. Otherwise He wouldn't have spoken these words.

The minority of us who appreciate our title know the importance of repentance. Through repentance Christians take hold of Jesus' invitation to salvation. Much to our chagrin, the angels conduct "welcome back" parties a little too often. Daily, in fact. But God certainly is gracious. Make a fool of yourself at someone's backyard party, and you probably won't get invited again. But God is different—for Jesus' sake. Instead of saying, "Not you again," He says, "Welcome back." And He will say it over and over until that time when you join the angels in heaven.

It's true that repentance includes more than sorrow. We need to abandon our sins. With our human frailty, when we abandon one sin, another usually takes its place. Sometimes the best we can do is just abhor sin, and return to God's profuse forgiveness.

Next time you're outside, aim a wave and a smile into the sky. The angels are holding a party to celebrate *you.*

Separation Anxiety

*For I am sure that neither death nor life, nor angels nor rulers, nor things
present nor things to come, nor powers, nor height nor depth, nor anything else in all creation, will be able to separate us from the love of God
in Christ Jesus our Lord. Romans 8:38–39*

The little boy peered over the service counter in the department store. An announcement had summoned his mother several minutes ago. As Mom came into view, her little boy raced up and stood squarely, hands on hips, before her. Before she could speak, he asked, "How come you wandered away from me?"

We can get it backwards too. Take the Romans passage, for example. For many, it may seem to guarantee that believers would never fall away from God—you know, once saved always saved. How could this be true when all believers experience lapses in faith?

Christians may regress into a self-centered focus on Bible passages. We do that when we concentrate exclusively on what *we* can do rather than what *God* has done and continues to do. This book, like many others, encourages readers to act on their faith. But I pray that you will always know why you obey God's will. All the good we do is a response to God's love through Jesus Christ. Pray that the Holy Spirit enables us to strike the proper balance between recognizing God's love and applying it.

The affirmation in Romans 8 refers to God's faithfulness. God remains available to us. We must never ask, "Where were You?" Nor may we accuse Him of wandering away. Like the young child in the opening anecdote, we must realize that God is here even when we are there.

Nothing can destroy God's love for us. Our sins may sadden or anger Him, but He still loves us. We may exercise too much spiritual freedom, but He still loves us. Our faith may weaken, but He won't—He still loves us.

P.S. Next time you're out with your Father, try not to wander. But in case you do, He'll find you again.

Dream Come True

How precious to me are Your thoughts, O God! How vast is the sum of them! If I would count them, they are more than the sand. I awake, and I am still with You. Psalm 139:17–18

Do you dream of a castle in the sky? Before you leap into a commitment to live there, it's good to list pluses and minuses. Pluses: Great view, good neighbors, and no flooding. Minuses: Watch the first step, unstable foundation, a bit drafty, and long-distance phone bills.

The trouble with most dreams is that eventually you have to wake up. However, one dream will come true. The psalmist identified it this way: "How precious to me are Your thoughts, O God! How vast is the sum of them! If I would count them, they are more than the sand. I awake, and I am still with You" (Psalm 139:17–18).

"I awake, and I am still with You." What loving words! Take a moment to think about someone—maybe someone who lives far away or seems to live far away; maybe it's a new love in your life or an old one; perhaps you haven't seen each other in years or it's been only minutes. What are you thinking? Are they fond memories or bitter disappointments, future hopes or past history, dreams or realities?

Enough dreaming for now! Has it changed anything? Some dreams come true; others don't. That's only half true with God. When He thinks of us, He isn't sleeping. Although we sleep and dream, when we awake, God is also in our company.

If God sent a "thinking of you" card, what do you suppose He would write? Realizing that He knows everything about us, we might hesitate to open the envelope. Don't fear, though. God thinks of us as redeemed, saved people—thanks to Jesus Christ. Here is what God might write:

Thinking of you? I always think of you! I know how hurt you are when others let you down. I knew you were in danger on your last trip to Wal-Mart, so I sent an angel to protect you. (Didn't know about that one, did you?) Oh yes, and I thought about what makes you laugh, so I'm planning to send more joy your way. Watch for it and think of Me next time you chuckle. There is so much more I'd like to tell you, but notes are just too short. I'll always remember you, and someday I want you to move in with Me. I've got a real castle in the sky.

You're Not Getting Older, You're Getting . . .

Even to your old age and gray hairs I am He, I am He who will sustain
you; I have made you and I will carry you; I will sustain you
and I will rescue you. Isaiah 46:4 NIV

D on't be discouraged by gray hair. You're not getting older, you're getting better.

We are all headed toward our next birthday. And our next birthday brings us closer to our final birthday. Some may not want to think about that prospect, but we need not fear it. Before we get there, God has promised to care for us. He uses words like *sustain, carry,* and *rescue.*

Sustain means that God will keep us going. Regardless of our age, our Father is always older—and wiser and stronger and everything else that makes a good father. He promises to bolster our faith even though our bodies sag and bend. A newspaper once interviewed a woman who had passed her 100th birthday. When asked how she got that old, she responded, "I think maybe God forgot about me." Isaiah assures us that God does not forget about us. He promises to keep our most important function—faith—in good health.

Carry was another of God's promises to the aging. Many older people fear loss of mobility. Legs weaken, hips break, and strokes paralyze. But God promises to carry us, not to the grocery store or bingo game, but through disappointments, pain, and even death.

Lastly, God promises to *rescue* us wherever we are: living alone, in a retirement villa, from a hospital bed. He also promises to rescue those who've aged only a little bit—from the crib, the classroom, the busy office, or the endless interstates. And, of course, He takes care of all the time in-between.

We're not getting older, we're actually getting younger. We are counting down to the time when we'll open our eyes like a newborn. And we'll never close them again.

Workers Unite!

Slaves, obey in everything those who are your earthly masters, not by way of eye-service, as people-pleasers, but with sincerity of heart, fearing the Lord. Whatever you do, work heartily, as for the Lord and not for men.
Colossians 3:22–23

How many people work where you do? (Ask the same question of your boss and the answer may be, "About half of them!")

Today's meditation doesn't address organized labor as the title might suggest. Instead, it deals with the work ethic. Paul makes laboriously clear what God expects from Christian workers. (Paul does not encourage slavery, nor does he treat it as a social issue. He simply addresses those who find themselves in that position. We could substitute the word *workers* in the same way.)

Christian employees should take God's Word seriously. They strive to be honest, fair, and hard-working even when nobody is watching. (Paul also addresses "masters" or employers in Colossians 3. If you are one—a boss or employer, that is—be sure to read it.)

Christian workers advertise the Gospel through their work ethic. They show that their hearts and minds have changed from a what-do-I-get-out-of-it attitude to a what-can-I-do-to-help attitude. Their perspective comes from what they know about Jesus Christ. Never one to stretch His coffee break (Are you watching the clock?), Jesus used every waking moment on the job. He didn't fret about how many days He was away from home. He didn't even have one! He traveled constantly as He preached and taught, healed and forgave, listened and loved. As Paul implies in Colossians, work doesn't always result in fair rewards. But the Christian worker's reward is in heaven even if it doesn't happen on earth.

Why don't you surprise everyone today? Quit your coffee break early, and get back to work. And if nobody is watching, feel doubly blessed. Jesus has awarded you a wonderful bonus—a true Christian work ethic. Workers unite! Unite with Christ!

Three's a Crowd

In the beginning was the Word, and the Word was with God, and the Word was God. He was in the beginning with God. All things were made through Him, and without Him was not any thing made that was made.
John 1:1–3

Our God is triune—three in one in a way too divine for human comprehension. Human efforts have tried in vain to define or describe the Trinity, but one of the best illustrations comes from John Wesley. He said that the Holy Trinity is like three lighted candles in a dark room. Though each candle is a candle, they provide one light.

Scripture never uses the word *trinity*. It only implies this description of the true God, who introduced His three-fold-ness in Genesis 1:26 when He spoke in the plural, saying, "Let Us make man in Our image."

Perhaps you took time to read the opening passages of John 1—that familiar and mysterious "In the beginning was the Word. . ." One of the clearest references to the Trinity appears in Matthew 3:16–17: "And when Jesus was baptized, immediately He went up from the water, and behold, the heavens were opened to Him, and He saw the Spirit of God descending like a dove and coming to rest on Him; and behold, a voice from heaven said, 'This is My beloved Son, with whom I am well pleased.'" Do you see it there? Jesus . . . Spirit . . . Father.

It's unwise to dissect this doctrine because it remains central in the foundation of Christianity. We can, however, appreciate God's comprehensive nature. Three's a crowd—a powerful crowd that spreads unique love and abundant blessings to all creation. Think about it. God the Father not only created "the heavens and the earth," He continues to care for it. Everyone has air to breathe, water to drink, food to eat, and shelters to protect. And, of course, there's Jesus, whose single, unselfish, courageous act on the cross changed the course of eternal history. The Holy Spirit works for our benefit too. The Spirit carries God's merciful love to us now that Jesus finished the job of forgiveness. It's the Spirit who tapped you on the soul and brought you to meet your Savior. It's the Spirit who continually fans the flames of faith in you. What a God! What a God! What a God!

Have you heard the old adage, "What you don't know can't hurt you"? Sometimes it's true. We don't have a logical clue as to the concept of the Trinity, but we do have faith. You're here, aren't you? And you know where you're going, right? Someday, you'll join millions of other believers in praising a Triune God that you fully understand. You'll follow the crowd forever!

Durable Finish

He has told you, O man, what is good; and what does the Lord require of you but to do justice, and to love kindness, and to walk humbly with your God? Micah 6:8

For years, one of the most durable countertop finishes was called Formica. (Warning! Pun ahead.) For Micah, and for God, believers must wear a durable finish composed of justice, mercy, and humility. These traits come not so much from conscious effort as they do from methodical reaction to God's love.

Anyone can be just, merciful, and humble without a personal relationship with God. Some of the world's most generous philanthropists would certainly qualify, even without a declaration of faith. But their mercy and their behavior may be motivated by gratitude for good luck or a belief in the goodness of humanity in general. Micah would probably agree that positive attributes without faith in no way spiritually benefit the giver.

But is it fair for Micah to even ask what the Lord requires of us? After all, didn't Jesus do everything necessary? And isn't faith the only thing required of us? The answer to both questions is yes. However, as we might expect, a loud *but* intervenes. But what?

Jesus did it all, *but* now He expects (yes, *expects!*) us to act like Him. While grace is free and no prerequisites hinder its distribution, grace actually costs us our sinful lives. But, that may not be as radical as it sounds.

Christian workers perform their duties out of love for Jesus. The service may be the same without Christ, but the motivation makes a meaningful difference. Without that motivation, a person would stop serving as soon as that service is unappreciated, unnoticed, ridiculed, or scorned. The motivation of Christ puts a durable finish on relationships—relationships built on love, commitment, and obedience to Christ.

How about you? For Micah, it was justice, humility, and mercy. Micah knew about those things because he received all of them from God. You have too. Be a durable Christian—and don't worry about the scratches or mars.

Who's Who

Then King David went in and sat before the Lord and said, "Who am I,
O Lord God, and what is my house, that You have brought me thus far?
. . . Because of Your promise, and according to Your own heart, You have
brought about all this greatness, to make Your servant know it.
2 Samuel 7:18, 21

"The family that prays together stays together" is a popular expression. After a recent hedge-trimming episode in consort with my wife, she quipped, "The family that prays together stays together, but the family that trims bushes together grows apart!"

God richly blessed David's family. That doesn't mean that his family avoided serious strife. David himself didn't always act like God's gift to His children. So it was entirely appropriate that David, knowing what was behind and suspecting what was ahead, recognized God's Gospel influence in his life. (Even before the word *Gospel* was invented!) Who was he to receive so many blessings? Certainly a miserable sinner with no merit of his own. Yet God loved David and had a purpose for him.

How blessed is your family? (Should that be a question mark or exclamation point?!) Why should God bother with you? If you're busy thinking of reasons for God's attention, take a deep breath and go back to David's prayer. While you may have no murderers, adulterers, or rebellious children, your family is not without sin. Yet He comes to you and has a purpose for your life too.

God wants to accomplish His will through us. For David, it meant victoriously leading a nation through endless wars. As a result, David made the Who's Who of Kings. But God's will went beyond battle victories. God promised that the Savior would be from David's clan. God's will for us is to bring His Word into the world, and He preserves us to carry out His wishes. Isn't that wonderful news? Even though we're sometimes weak and often sinful, He wants us to bring His Good News to others just like us. And when we do a good job of that, people will really know Who's Who!

Parts of Speech

Know this, my beloved brothers: let every person be quick to hear, slow to speak, slow to anger; for the anger of man does not produce the righteousness that God requires. Therefore put away all filthiness and rampant wickedness and receive with meekness the implanted word, which is able to save your souls. James 1:19–21

Color drained from the teacher's face as he corrected my English test. Unfortunately, it drained all over my paper. Red ink nearly obliterated my response to the question "What are the parts of speech?" I still think I deserved partial credit for my answer: The parts of speech are nouns, verbs, adverbs, and expletives. Ha!

One part of speech that needs more teaching is the part called listening. The apostle James valued listening. He said, "Know this, my beloved brothers: let every person be quick to hear, slow to speak, slow to anger" (James 1:19).

Listening—genuine listening—is such a lost art that students often practice specific exercises to build the skill. They learn active and reflective listening strategies designed to help them understand what others say. However, James probably was not talking about active listening. So how do you listen to God?

First, you tell God what you need and what you want. He already knows this information, but He invites you to make your requests known. God hears so many requests for personal, sometimes selfish, attention that He probably enjoys hearing what others need. (Words of thanks and praise are certainly in order too.) You can talk to God about anything.

The second step in listening to God is to quit talking. Do some reading instead. God told us everything we need to hear in the words of the Bible. Regular readers have discovered that God speaks to their needs, often before they even know their needs. In addition, a good topical or indexed Bible helps to pinpoint what God says about specific topics.

The third phase of listening is to sit still and let God talk to your soul. Quiet reflection on God's Word gives the Holy Spirit wonderful opportunities to help you. Try it now. Ask yourself these questions:

1. *What do I need help with now?*

2. *What does the Bible say? (Take time to look.)*

3. _____ *(That's you listening.)*

Mind Your Own Business

Aspire to live quietly, and to mind your own affairs, and to work with your hands, as we instructed you, so that you may live properly before outsiders and be dependent on no one. 1 Thessalonians 4:11–12

Some people just can't mind their own business. Perhaps it's because they have small minds and even less business.

Paul's counsel to those who are tempted to gossip and meddle in other people's business was to keep quiet and keep busy. It was godly guidance too, because we find Jesus observing that practice even as He minded His Father's business. Jesus exercised good timing when He talked. We don't find Him interrupting His friends and followers. He wasn't rude to His enemies, either. And when it came to keeping busy, He was (and is!) the champion. Jesus even knew when someone in a crowd touched His clothing because she believed He could heal her. As He taught on a hillside, He observed that His audience was hungry, so He literally made a meal for all of them. Jesus was even busy under the torture of the cross. He saved a thief, made provisions for His mother, and forgave His murderers. He was too busy to say, "I knew we shouldn't trust Judas," or "You should have seen what I saw in Pilate's house." Jesus' business was God the Father's business.

God's business is our business too. We mind it by doing it. When we see something that others drool to know about, we need to "tell it all"—to God. Oh, He already knows all the dirt about everybody (including us), but it's good to express our concerns and ask Him to intervene or carry out His will.

Minding your own business has fringe benefits too. As Paul said, those who do, often win the respect of others. It's a good thing for people to respect Christians—to say things like "He never has a bad thing to say about anybody." Now that's a good piece of gossip!

The Same Old Story

Finally, my brothers, rejoice in the Lord. To write the same things to you is no trouble to me and is safe for you. Philippians 3:1

Some people are bored at those Sunday school Christmas programs. They complain, "It's the same old story over and over and over again." You've probably noticed that this book also is redundant. You read repeatedly about what God has done for us. And you're constantly summoned to respond to God's love. That's how it is with life in Christ. The same old thing—over and over again.

We could become defiant or despondent if the "same old story" wasn't such Good News. How horrific if we had nagging replays of Jeremiah's doomsday prophecies or if Lent were not followed by Easter! Such news would tempt us to hate God, or at least fear Him beyond approach. Thank God for His annual reruns of Christmas and Easter!

Regardless of how often we hear it, God still loves the world so much that He sent His only Son to save it. Jesus' story always includes His unconditional love for sinners. And though few stories survive retelling without losing meaning, the narrative of Jesus' life, death, and resurrection always means that we who live in Christ, will die in Christ and rise to live with Him forever.

If we ever get bored with the Good News, we can always look at the disgusting repetition of bad news. Newspapers assault our values with graphic accounts of violence, murder, cheating, and stealing. When we review our own life, we recognize our feeble attempts to live according to God's will as well as our outright refusal to obey Him. And yet the Good News persists. For each sin and every crime, Jesus offers forgiveness. Redundantly! And as often as we repeat the phrase "I'm sorry," we hear Jesus say, "I forgive you." The same old story remains the same old story. It's God's way of safeguarding us. So "Rejoice in the Lord always; again I will say, Rejoice" (Philippians 4:4).

Get Your Kicks

But for you who fear My name, the sun of righteousness shall rise with healing in its wings. You shall go out leaping like calves from the stall.
Malachi 4:2

In the good old days, dancing tested a person's agility in moving feet nimbly and accurately—mostly to avoid your partner's prancing. For some of us, the best way to describe our dancing is to watch a calf finding its first legs! They don't do very well. But they surely are happy doing it.

It is good for Christians to kick up our heels once in awhile. For those who can't or won't dance with their feet, there are alternative forms of dancing.

Alternative 1: Dance with your eyes. As you consider all God has done, let the joy travel up your optic nerve. Let it shine on those whose glance (or glare) meets your gaze. Eyes can twinkle as well as toes! I suppose it's no coincidence that you see similar looks in the eyes of lovers as they discover the exhilaration of unconditional, unexpected, and unmerited love. That's like our relationship with Jesus. (Solomon thought so too. Read Song of Solomon sometime.)

Alternative 2: Dance with your lips. Lips dance in several ways. Obviously, singing gets the lips moving. God likes many different kinds of singing—the praise can be soft, loud, beautiful, or discordant. The Bible says the angels dance with their lips, and they're probably good singers. But our lips need only move to the rhythm of our heart to stay in step.

Lips also dance when they pucker out humor. Good humor. The kind that laughs at self or human foibles but never destroys with cruel snickers. Too bad the Bible doesn't record Jesus' laughter as it does His tears. Surely He laughed when He healed the sick, welcomed little children, and rose from the dead. Our lips too can dance with jovial verbs and jubilant nouns. If life gets dull, just picture yourself leaping like a calf!

Something to Crow About

*And the word of the Lord came to [Elijah], "Depart from here and turn
eastward and hide yourself by the brook Cherith, which is east of the
Jordan. You shall drink from the brook, and I have commanded the ravens
to feed you there." So he went and did according to the word of the Lord.
He went and lived by the brook Cherith that is east of the Jordan. And
the ravens brought him bread and meat in the morning, and bread and
meat in the evening, and he drank from the brook. 1 Kings 17:2–6*

The similarities between crows and ravens are such that only bird
experts and the birds themselves know the differences. The only difference I can see is that crows live in my neighborhood and ravens don't.
Human experience with crows is often unpleasant. The birds are brassy, noisy,
and they eat disgusting things. On the positive side, though, crows remind us
of ravens, and ravens remind us of God's love, which is something to crow
about.

As reported in the Bible, God's perpetual care rode the wings of ravens
several times. The first occurrence was when the floodwaters receded and
Noah needed information about the risks of disembarking from the ark. We
hear about ravens again in the story of a hungry Elijah. Listen to how God
took care of His prophet: "And the ravens brought him bread and meat in the
morning, and bread and meat in the evening, and he drank from the brook"
(1 Kings 17:6). (Perhaps this is the thought behind the phrase "on a wing and
a prayer.")

God has both expected and unusual ways of caring for people. Often, He
mixes both the spectacular and the unremarkable. Consider how He feeds us.
Seeds are deceptively simple. You can regain a sense of wonder and apprecia-
tion if you imagine yourself in the tiny shoes of a kindergarten child who
wonders aloud how a plump radish can pop out of such a small seed. The
only satisfactory explanation is God. Yes, God continues to provide for us
with or without ravens, and that's something else to crow about.

The most important way God ever cared is through His Son—a curious
mix of true God and true Man. God could have solved everyone's problems
simply by uttering a creative word. Instead, He chose to use things to which
we can relate—such as birds and people. Jesus, as true man, talked with people as He healed them, forgave them, and died for them. He was God in
human flesh—quite demeaning for God when you think about it. Yet God
sent Jesus to feed us with His Word, a diet that nourishes forever. That's even
more to crow about. In fact, it's something you could go on ravin' about for
a long time!

Rising to the Bottom

"It shall not be so among you. But whoever would be great among you must be your servant, and whoever would be first among you must be your slave, even as the Son of Man came not to be served but to serve, and to give His life as a ransom for many." Matthew 20:26–28

D o you have any secret goals in life? Some people aim at their goals, but they're lousy shots. Take Jesus' disciples, for example. The mother of two of them aimed high. She wanted her sons to have the highest ranking among His followers. Jesus warned that such high status was no picnic. It would cost them their lives. Then Jesus told them the real secret of success in the company of Christians. Aim low.

Modern corporate executives might reject Jesus' protocol for rising through the ranks. But Christians are in the business of serving others. Jesus was able to start out at the bottom and stay there. He was the perfect servant, obeying God and serving people. He was the only one who could reach low enough to save us, and His job was successfully completed on the first Easter. Now, as any good leader does, He inspires us to ever lower levels of service.

As we labor and grow in the company of Christians, we do well to imitate those who founded the company. The Apostles weren't just a bunch of junior executives making decisions for others. They went into the field and cultivated new Christians. They sometimes ended up with dirtied hands and bloodied bodies. Several of the most prominent execs were killed on the job.

Thousands of Christians have retired, and we're here to replace them. What service can we offer? Will it be driving Mr. Thomas to church every Sunday? Will it be reading a preschooler the story of Josiah—743 times? Will it be cleaning the seats in church? Will it be suffering scorn and mockery as we try to outdo one another in kindness? One thing is certain. To reach the top, you have to strive for the bottom.

Horn Tooters

And the king of Israel answered, "Tell him, 'Let not him who straps on his armor boast himself like he who takes it off.'" 1 Kings 20:11

Flattery gets you nowhere; especially when you give it to yourself. Some people even brag about their humility! We all know a few horn tooters, and perhaps we even see one each time we pass a mirror. Boastful people might be compared to monsters with heads full of *I*'s. The king's advice in the passage above applies equally well to us. Don't toot your horn unless you play in the band.

Braggarts usually feel insecure about who they are. They fear nobody will notice or value them unless they point out their worthiness. Often this leads to a vicious circle in which acquaintances avoid the boaster so the boaster feels an even stronger need to gain attention. Braggarts, even occasional ones like ourselves, need prayer.

We can be confident that Jesus notices us. He chose to befriend us—and even more! He knew that we were born sinful, that we would remain sinful, and that we would lose our life as a result. And there was nothing we could do about our condition except, perhaps, talk about it. But no amount of talk could make us worthy or righteous. We could brag that we were sinless or that we could do enough good deeds to make up for our sinfulness, but that would just be empty talk. So Jesus said, "I love you, *(insert your own name)*. You don't need to toot your own horn in front of Me. I'm the whole band! I'll play the tune for you, and I won't flub a note or miss a beat. Yes, _____, you are Mine."

We don't need to flaunt our goodness before God. When the world ends and we appear before God, we won't need to invent stories about how good we are. Instead, we will tell God how good Jesus is—for us. In fact, maybe some bragging is good. Paul advocated boasting to the Corinthians. He said, "Let the one who boasts, boast in the Lord" (2 Corinthians 10:17).

Mint Condition

And if you call on Him as Father who judges impartially according to each one's deeds, conduct yourselves with fear throughout the time of your exile, knowing that you were ransomed from the futile ways inherited from your forefathers, not with perishable things such as silver or gold, but with the precious blood of Christ, like that of a lamb without blemish or spot. He was foreknown before the foundation of the world but was made manifest in the last times for your sake, who through Him are believers in God, who raised Him from the dead and gave Him glory, so that your faith and hope are in God. 1 Peter 1:17–21

The salesperson claimed the car was in mint condition. She was right. It would have taken the entire Denver mint to pay for it. The term "mint condition" probably refers more to what the seller can receive than what the buyer can expect.

Speaking of mint condition, what are you worth? Please don't run off for your calculator and investment portfolio (or your wallet and piggy bank!) Look in your Bible instead. A good place to start is 1 Peter 1:18–19: "Knowing that you were ransomed from the futile ways inherited from your forefathers, not with perishable things such as silver or gold, but with the precious blood of Christ, like that of a lamb without blemish or spot."

There are two ways to think about that passage. First, we were worth so much to God that He spent His Son, Jesus, to buy us back from Satan. Second, it cost Jesus' life to fix us and make us presentable to our original Owner. Which thinking is correct? Both are. Let's examine them in reverse order. It's not pleasant to think of ourselves as worthless, yet our sins make us that way—at least in the eyes of Satan, who may be the universe's most renowned junk collector. He loves what he hates, namely, worthless, sinful, despairing humans—especially because they were created originally in God's image.

We are worthless. Worse, we might even be called a deathtrap for God's Son. Sadly, it took Jesus' life to remake us in God's image. Jesus' life was the only thing worth enough to make us worthy to be called the children of God.

Why did God expend the effort and sacrifice to save us? Certainly it was nothing He saw in us. He wasn't partial to blue eyes, dark skin, straight hair, or pointed noses. He didn't need us. We treated Him badly. He saved us because He loved us. That's it, and that's all.

Now go out and show everyone your shiny, restored self. Tell others about the God who is powerful enough to save you, and be sure to stay close to your owner. He'll keep you in mint condition forever.

All the Same

By this you know the Spirit of God: every spirit that confesses that Jesus Christ has come in the flesh is from God, and every spirit that does not confess Jesus is not from God. This is the spirit of the antichrist, which you heard was coming and now is in the world already. 1 John 4:2–3

"It doesn't matter what you believe, as long as you're sincere." "I can worship in any church. All religions are the same anyway." Tolerant attitudes, for sure, but dangerous ones. Such statements come from those who claim no religious prejudice, but the dismal truth is that no prejudice often equals no religion.

What Christians need to do, according to John, is to be intolerant (as opposed to intolerable). This doesn't mean that Christians should desecrate Jewish synagogues, Muslim mosques, or Buddhist temples. But they shouldn't credit those places as dwellings of God either. As John says, unless Christ is confessed, the religion is phony and evil. Note that John didn't use the word *harmless*. He calls the priests of false religions antichrists—against Christ! Pray that the Holy Spirit reaches these lost people before it's too late!

Christians must be alert to even more subtle and subversive religions, though. Some religions look like Christianity but fail to qualify with the only thing that counts: Christ as the only Savior from sin. Watch out for churches devoid of crosses. (Sometimes they just don't want to scare visitors away with religious symbolism, but who except the devil fears the cross?) Stay away from those who concentrate exclusively on you at the expense of Jesus and what He has done for you. Be cautious about churches that focus on success rather than humility and service in the name of Jesus. If it doesn't proclaim Jesus, it serves the devil.

Doomed to Success

Then [David] put garrisons in Edom, and all the Edomites became
David's servants. And the Lord gave victory to David wherever he went.
1 Chronicles 18:13

Sometimes success is measured in dollars. If you make them faster than the government can take them away, you're successful. On the other hand, if you don't feel successful, there's probably lots of people who will gladly offer advice. Some of these individuals even do it in the name of religion. Perhaps you've read some success books: *How to Grow Perfect Bananas the Adam and Eve Way* or *37 Ways to Raise Children Who Honor Their Father and Mother* or perhaps *The Abraham Principle: How to Succeed in Business Even with a Large Family*. Well, maybe you won't find those exact titles, but you get the idea.

Some people consider success elusive. Is it? There seems to be a lot of it going around—even if it's going around you. As much as we seek success, we also must identify its origin. King David, successful by most standards, knew the truth about success. He identified the source in 1 Chronicles 18:13: "Then [David] put garrisons in Edom, and all the Edomites became David's servants. And the Lord gave victory to David wherever he went." David's response? Many psalms proclaim his revelry.

Success comes from God. That means others' successes as well as our own. Sometimes the success of others may come at the expense of our own. Like rain and sunshine, God bestows success to many people. He doesn't discriminate on the basis of race, sex, or even religion.

Behind every successful person stands God. Believers know this, though sometimes success is accompanied by serious bouts of forgetfulness. At such times, successful people might become like the children of Israel. In their heady successes, they forgot their source of victory. As a result, God often caused other nations to succeed against Israel to bring His beloved people back to their senses.

Successful people need not be doomed to success, though. Not if they're as conscious of the Power behind the success as David was. Not if they refuse to use God and His people as stepping stones to ungodly success. Not if they remember Jesus, who succeeded in history's most important venture.

True success does not lie in accomplishments, wealth, or status. True success lies in knowing who succeeded beyond a sinner's wildest dreams and who is willing to share that success with His friends. But you already know that, don't you? Ah! The sweet taste of success. His success.

Chip off the Block

Blessed be the God and Father of our Lord Jesus Christ, the Father of mercies and God of all comfort, who comforts us in all our affliction, so that we may be able to comfort those who are in any affliction, with the comfort with which we ourselves are comforted by God. 2 Corinthians 1:3–4

Have you ever felt like knocking the chip off somebody's shoulder? Is there someone at work or in your neighborhood who needs a good kick in the pants? What they really need to displace that chip is a little comfort. There's nothing like a pat on the back to knock a chip off the shoulder. And while a pat on the back is only 18 inches higher than a kick in the pants, it works better.

God is the greatest source of encouragement and comfort. When God's Old Testament people fell (or leaped) into bad times, they retreated to God for counsel and aid. God's admonishment was always the same: Return to the Lord, give up your evil ways, and He will help you. Another way of putting it was "Return to Me, and I'll return to you." When Christ came to earth, the command was similar as Jesus invited people to follow Him and evade sin.

How can we help others to find this comfort? A curt "Go to God with your troubles" is likely to place a whole log on that person's shoulder. When someone is distressed or angry, we can help by getting that person to talk to us—especially if he or she is not accustomed to talking to God. Once the problem has been "confessed," it's time to relate with compassion. Tell the person that you know how it feels to be bitter, depressed, or frightened (without going into details), and that you find relief in prayer. Share your trust in God—your absolute confidence that He will work things out. Offer to pray with the troubled and afflicted. And if the person wants to talk more after praying, make time to do so. Maybe you're God's answer to his or her prayer—and a chip off the divine Block.

Oh yes, when you're all done, give Him a big pat on the back.

Too Many Pots Spoil the Cook

*Then everyone who survives of all the nations that have come against
Jerusalem shall go up year after year to worship the King, the LORD of
hosts, and to keep the Feast of Booths. . . . And [on that day] the pots in
the house of the LORD shall be as the bowls before the altar.*
Zechariah 14:16–20

Some cooks find it easy. Most amateurs, however, would struggle to
manage four pots on a cook top, especially if all of them needed constant attention to prevent the contents from congealing, boiling over, or sticking to the bottom of the pot.

Pots, however, can remind us of an interesting Bible passage and at least
one lesson to learn from it. The prophet Zechariah continued, "And every pot
in Jerusalem and Judah shall be holy to the Lord of hosts, so that all who sacrifice may come and take of them and boil the meat of the sacrifice in them.
And there shall no longer be a trader in the house of the Lord of hosts on that
day" (Zechariah 14:21).

About the closest thing to "holy pots" today is when the contents resemble a burnt sacrifice. Not surprisingly, sacrifices were exactly what Zechariah
was talking about. In his day, many people couldn't make it to Jerusalem, the
location of the temple, to offer sacrifices. Zechariah, speaking for God,
assured them they could make a sacrifice anyplace they found themselves.
They didn't have to use the special pots for sacrifices located exclusively in the
temple. They could use the ones in their kitchens. This was good news for
everyone who wanted to observe this holy day. But what does this mean for
us?

Next time you see a pot, think of how you honor God—the modern
equivalent of the Old Testament sacrifice. Do you contribute generously to
the Lord's work? Do you tell God how thankful you are and how much you
love Him? Have you applied your skills by serving others to His glory? Your
pot of sacrifices may be brimming over or the contents may barely cover the
bottom, but you surely honor God in some ways.

One danger, however, is keeping other "pots" cooking in addition to the
one dedicated to God. Those other "pots" are anything that distracts us from
love of and obedience to God. So much of life needs attention to keep it from
boiling over, blazing up, or becoming a mess. At those times, we're tempted
to forget our Lord—to try to manage without Him. That's a mistake. Our Lord
invites us to worship Him not only with thanksgiving, but with trust. Honor
God by trusting Him with everything you've got cooking.

Call Me in the Morning

*And Elisha sent a messenger to him, saying, "Go and wash in the Jordan
seven times, and your flesh shall be restored, and you shall be clean." But
Naaman was angry and went away, saying, "Behold, I thought that he
would surely come out to me and stand and call upon the name of the
Lord his God, and wave his hand over the place and cure the leper." . . .
But his servants came near and said to him, "My father, it is a great word
the prophet has spoken to you; will you not do it? Has he actually said to
you, 'Wash, and be clean'?" 2 Kings 5:10–11, 13*

Have you visited a doctor's office lately? It seems they found a cure for
what to do with old magazines!

Today's Bible selection finds Naaman indignant when Elisha (a prophet,
not a physician) refused to see him personally regarding a disease. Naaman
heard that Elisha worked many miracles, and he hoped that Elisha would
work one on him. But Elisha simply pronounced God's prescription of washing in the Jordan River. Elisha's prescription must have seemed like an imper-
sonal "Take two and call me in the morning." Naaman was so angry that he
stormed off without filling the prescription. Later, Naaman reconsidered
Elisha's presumably preposterous proposal, and he was cured.

We are sick too—sick with sin. The symptoms include everything that
makes us miserable. It's a terminal disease for which there is only one cure,
and only one Physician can work the miracle. Yes, miracle.

Many of us might think miracles happen only to others or exclusively in
Bible history. But each of us has received the healing miracle of forgiveness
from Jesus Christ, the Great Physician. None of us has yet seen Him face to
face, so we—like Naaman—rely on His Word. If He says we're forgiven, we're
forgiven! Jesus does comprehensive surgery on our souls. He removes the sin,
and we are healed.

Thank God for sending Jesus on house calls. And thank Him for footing
the bill too.

Hard Heads

*Because I know that you are obstinate, and your neck is an iron sinew
and your forehead brass. Isaiah 48:4*

Car makers would make history if the government forced them to recall defective drivers! While that seems improbable, government agencies do seem determined to protect people from themselves. You probably have your own opinions about seat belts, cycling helmets, four-way railroad crossing gates, and other such devices. But have you stopped to think about why we don't exercise common sense in protecting ourselves—without government intervention?

God and Isaiah saw the same flaws in people. (Didn't Isaiah have a unique expression for hardheadedness?) The people in Isaiah's time also refused to practice common sense and self-preservation. God promised His people that He would be their God and they would be His people. God would protect them and make them flourish. That was an excellent deal and certainly more than fair. But like drivers buzzing along at 85 sans seat belts, they refused to protect themselves. They took chances.

Seat belts confine and restrict movement. Obeying God limits our normal activities and keeps us in line with all that God has provided to keep us happy and safe. And when we collide with major temptations, God's will keeps us in place. Why would He bother to protect us that way?

God loves us. He saw our helplessness and took our safety into His own hands. He placed Jesus at our disposal. God continues to send the Word accompanied by the Holy Spirit. Many heed His direction and submit to the safety of His law and love. Yet others rebel. The rebels and the careless need our prayers even more than those who refuse protection from earthly harm. As for ourselves, may God always keep us from sin and the devil, and may the Holy Spirit ever give us the faith to take advantage of God's love.

Remember, each time you awaken to a new day, buckle up with Jesus.

Hop to It

*And he said, "Take the arrows," and he took them. And he said to the
king of Israel, "Strike the ground with them." And he struck three times
and stopped. Then the man of God was angry with him and said, "You
should have struck five or six times; then you would have struck down
Syria until you had made an end of it, but now you will strike down Syria
only three times." 2 Kings 13:18–19*

The setting of today's reading was a somber room in which God's
prophet Elisha was about to die. Israel's king had come to pay his
respects and also get some of God's power through Elisha. Now Elisha seemed
a man of few but potent words, so his conversation with the king was brief—
as you can see in the passage. The king half-heartedly struck the ground with
the arrows. He probably thought this was a silly exercise ordered by a feeble
man. His lack of enthusiasm, however, was really reluctance to trust God.
Elisha predicted the outcome of the king's indifference and then died.

As we might guess, there's a lesson here. When the Lord empowers us, we
need to hop to it. And keep on hopping! One benefit of faith is forgiveness.
God commissioned us to forgive as we have been forgiven. Translated loosely, that means a lot. How angry God must get when He sees us half-heartedly
attempt to carry out His will, or when He sees us forgive only a few times.
How many more battles we could win with forgiveness than with anger and
bitterness! Isn't that the way He won us? We didn't come to Jesus because we
feared what He would do to us. Instead, the Holy Spirit delivered His words
of invitation and forgiveness. It was love that drew us to Him, and it's His love
that we can use to draw others.

Hopefully, you're fired up and ready to strike a few arrows. Get the point?

No Minors

For You are not a God who delights in wickedness; evil may not dwell
with You. The boastful shall not stand before Your eyes; You hate all evil-
doers. . . . But I, through the abundance of Your steadfast love, will enter
Your house. I will bow down toward Your holy temple in the fear of You.
Lead me, O Lord, in Your righteousness because of my enemies; make
Your way straight before me. Psalm 5:4–8

You don't always see the sign, but the rule exists anyway. No minors. The rule applies in bars and cigarette shops and that steamy corner of the video store. Then there's all the hoopla surrounding the Internet and television and ways to prevent sensitive young eyes from scenes and words that threaten indelible damage on fragile values. The judicial system sometimes singles out minors too. What do you think of laws that carry more severe penalties for minors when the same acts bring only a slap on the hand to adults? It seems unfair, but would God agree?

"For you are not a God who delights in wickedness; evil may not dwell with You. The boastful shall not stand before Your eyes; You hate all evildoers" (Psalm 5:4–5). Note the phrase "hate all evildoers." Not those under 21 or 18, but ALL. If you are squirming like an adolescent caught with an "adult" magazine, you're not alone. If you're not taunted by some degree of discomfort, you're probably not—excuse me—honest with yourself or with God.

We are all sinners. We tend to group sins into categories such as "not too bad," "everybody does it," "I would never get caught doing such a thing," or "Why would anyone want to do that?" Sins in the last two categories are those from which we most want to shield children—though those "of age" don't mind dabbling in them at the movies, in the tavern, or on the mattress.

When it comes to spiritual life, all humans are minors—spiritually immature, feeble, and all too susceptible to temptation. We shouldn't be exposed to "certain things," but there they are. The devil dangles them in front of us. Good thing Someone is out there to help us minors.

Confess and pray this: "But I, through the abundance of Your steadfast love, will enter Your house. I will bow down toward Your holy temple in the fear of You. Lead me, O Lord, in Your righteousness because of my enemies; make Your way straight before me" (Psalm 5:7–8).

Because Jesus took away our sins on that best of days, God welcomes us into His presence. When temptation wins over us, the victory is only temporary. God's forgiveness is permanent. And that's no minor accomplishment.

Litterbugs

When iniquities prevail against me, You atone for our transgressions.
Psalm 65:3

The window descends, an arm extends, and from a hand some trash offends. (Littering isn't very poetic, is it?) Litterbugs! They leave trash everywhere but the garbage can. I suppose they become overwhelmed by trash. When your dashboard litterbag bulges, what can you do but pitch it from the car?

Some of us accumulate quite a cache of sins too. When our conscience becomes bloated, we are overwhelmed. Where can we dump our trashy sins? One technique works like the litterbag. We store our sins until we can store no more. Then what? We probably get another litterbag. Another technique avoids the inconvenience of storage and appropriate disposal. We simply toss off our sins like gum wrappers out the car window. Out of sight, out of soul. But this simple "redistribution" method doesn't clear up the problem either.

The Bible tells us where to place our trash. Give it to Jesus. Now it might sound disrespectful to talk about loading Jesus down with the garbage of our lives, but that's the only way to properly dispose of it. In fact, Jesus gave His life for our sins at a place adjacent to the city dump.

Unlike litterbags or even huge Dumpsters, Jesus has unlimited capacity to remove our sins. His death and resurrection have incinerated our transgressions beyond a trace. Then He recycles our sinful self into an entirely new creation, designed to serve Him and others.

We don't need to stockpile our sins because we don't know what else to do with them. Jesus takes out the trash every time we call, not just when we're weighed down. So place your sins at His disposal. And open your heart to the Holy Spirit that you may help others take out their trash.

Three Crosses

*He went out, bearing His own cross, to the place called the place of a
skull, which in Aramaic is called Golgotha. There they crucified Him, and
with Him two others, one on either side, and Jesus between them.*
John 19:17–18

This is the first of three meditations on crosses. Not the three crosses
on Golgotha, but three crosses we readily see today. Our first cross is
the crucifix—the cross with Jesus nailed to it.

I don't like crucifixes much. They're too real and not real enough at the
same time. How they remind us of our sins! There we see Jesus, arms stretched
and ribs protruding. We see the holes dotted with blood on His hands and
feet. And what you don't see hurts too. There, on His bare and scrawny shoul-
ders, lie the sins of the world. All that weight pulling on His arms, crushing
His lungs, pushing down on His feet. It's almost too repulsive. Yet we must
gaze on this cross, the crucifix. Although they realistically depict the Savior's
suffering, somehow crucifixes can't fully symbolize the pain and agony. We
can close our eyes and we won't hear the labored breathing or gasps of
anguish. We can touch the crucifix and it's cold and hard, not clammy flesh
on splintered wood. Good thing it's not. We couldn't bear to know just how
much He agonized on that cross. Yet the fact remains, we must take a distressing look at the crucifix now and then. But not to make us feel guilty.

Jesus removed our guilt on the cross. All of it. He doesn't want us in
throes of extended mourning either. He has prepared a place for us where
tears will be extinct. But the crucifix does serve one excellent purpose. It makes
us thankful. It could be us up there, for hell holds equal terrors for unbelievers. Jesus did in six hours what would have taken us an eternity.

Now get back to work, and have a good mourning.

Clean Cross

After these things Joseph of Arimathea, who was a disciple of Jesus, but secretly for fear of the Jews, asked Pilate that he might take away the body of Jesus, and Pilate gave him permission. So he came and took away His body. John 19:38

As decorations go, crosses are often the pride of Christian churches. Some are cut from rare and expensive imported wood. Others are cast in gleaming steel or aluminum. Often, their towering presence becomes the focal point of our attention. And well they should. This instrument of execution is a symbol for Christ Himself.

The empty cross reminds us that Christ's story—and ours—doesn't leave us hanging. And the bare beams of wood or steal imply much more than we read in John's report above. True, some of Jesus' admirers didn't want to leave Him suspended there like some common criminal. Finally, one of the wealthy believers risked the contempt of his peers to bury Jesus in his own plot. But that was one body that would not decay into dust. Jesus would simply not go away.

The clean lines of modern crosses remind us of what Christ did for us. His death on the cross made us clean. When God looks at us, He sees squeaky-clean Christians, polished by Jesus' love and sacrifice.

The vacant cross would mean nothing if the tomb had remained occupied two days later. Neither brutal cross nor damp, dark tomb can defeat God. So unoccupied crosses also remind us of Jesus' resurrection. We can almost hear the words of God's angels: "Why do you seek the living among the dead? He is not here" (Luke 24:5–6). The same might be said of us someday. The empty cross and the risen Savior mean that we won't remain dead either. Perhaps we'll rest in the grave beyond the third day, but we will rise, never to fall again.

Look around. Find any object that resembles a cross. Look at it several times each day. Christ isn't on it, is He? He's in heaven. He's someplace else too.

Cross my heart.

Take It with You

Then Jesus told His disciples, "If anyone would come after Me, let him
deny himself and take up his cross and follow Me." Matthew 16:24

I'm certain that Jesus wasn't talking about lapel pins or necklaces in the
verse above. But at least those are crosses we can easily wear—on our
lapel, around our neck, on our finger, or pinned to our ears. Crosses are not
just banal jewelry. People notice the difference when we wear the cross on our
heart.

To wear His cross worthily, we must meet the requirement that Jesus
established for His disciples. We must deny ourselves as we take up the cross.
That's what Christ did. He denied His divine power to serve us and to die for
us. Would we not have cheered if Jesus struck the taunting high priest dead?
Would it not have served the crowd right if Jesus pronounced a plague of
muteness as they chanted, "Crucify Him! Crucify Him!"? And certainly we
would have rejoiced had Jesus sprung from the cross and tossed His antagonists straight into hell. That would have served them right. Jesus would have
done Himself a favor too. But the Savior wasn't self-serving. He served His
Father and us instead.

When Jesus tells us to deny ourselves, He means that we can't be the cen-
ter of our own life. The Savior doesn't want us to deny ourselves through
seclusion or solitude. He doesn't want us to devote our time exclusively to
singing hymns and chanting prayers. Who would ever see our crosses that
way? Serving Jesus means serving others. Sometimes the service involves simple acts of kindness or assistance. At other times, it may entail private or public prayers for someone in need. Service may consist of giving some of our
treasures to the needy. And yes, we must also serve by telling others what we
believe. Maybe if you wear a cross, someone will ask.

Don't Look Down

Brothers, I do not consider that I have made it my own. But one thing I do: forgetting what lies behind and straining forward to what lies ahead, I press on toward the goal for the prize of the upward call of God in Christ Jesus. Philippians 3:13–14

For many people, the future comes too soon! If the future frightens you, think of it as climbing a rope to the top of the gym. You'll be okay if you just don't look down.

Looking down or looking back shows where we've been rather than where we are going. The sight may not be pretty. As we age, we store many memories. Some of those memories are things we might want to forget or that make us dread the future. But, to paraphrase what St. Paul told the Philippians, don't look down. Look up. Press on. After all, the future is looking up.

Try this sometime when you're frightened or feeling low. Whistle a happy tune. No, wait. That's from a movie. Look up, for that is the direction of heaven. As you look up, imagine Jesus looking down at you. Picture Him saying the words He put into Paul's mouth. He calls you heavenward to receive your reward.

Don't be misled. Your reward isn't something you earned or won on your own. Jesus earned your right to live with Him here on earth and later in heaven. But by faith you believe that Jesus is your Savior. Faith too is a gift of the Holy Spirit. God wants us to use our faith to face the future. He wants us to grow in faith so we can continue our climb into the future. The reward for faithfulness is everlasting life, and it's a life that begins right now. So keep climbing, and if you're afraid, don't look down. Jesus is at the top, urging us on. Things certainly are looking up, aren't they?

You're Elected

Even as He chose us in Him before the foundation of the world, that we should be holy and blameless before Him. Ephesians 1:4

Want an inexpensive way to trace your family history? Run for office. Reporters and opponents will expose every skeleton in your closet! And then, if you win the election, people will criticize every decision you make. Don't let all this influence your reaction to the biggest (and perhaps only) election that lists you in the winner's circle.

God elected you. As Paul said in Ephesians, He chose you even before He created squash or Saturn or sea cucumbers. God didn't research our relatives to determine our worthiness either. He is at the very root of our family tree.

We didn't deserve to win the election. An examination of our past would uncover pits filled with sin. What we deserve is an eternal term in hell. But Jesus cleaned up our record and placed us on His winning ticket. He won the election for us even if the election was unfair—unfair to Him.

It's one thing to begin with a clean slate, but quite another to maintain it. Did you notice why God elected us? Like politicians who make promises they can't keep, we're in trouble. So it's Jesus to the rescue again—erasing our slate of sins and forgiving us far more than voters forgive those whom they elect. Each time the Lord forgives, He renews our will to lead blameless and holy lives.

There is only one way to be blameless and holy. Locking yourself away with the Bible, isolating yourself from all that might tempt you is not it. Instead, we are blameless and holy when our sins are washed away from us by Jesus Christ.

Go out there now and shake a few hands and kiss a few babies. Take out your neighbor's trash and give shut-ins a ride to church. Help anyone in need. Do favors—especially for your family. After all, you've been elected!

How Do We Do It?

See what kind of love the Father has given to us, that we should be called
children of God; and so we are. The reason why the world does not know
us is that it did not know Him. 1 John 3:1

A certain man was praying in public. A passer-by noticed the folded hands, closed eyes, and moving lips, but he didn't hear anything. He said, "Speak up. I can't hear you." The man opened his eyes and replied, "That's okay. I wasn't talking to you."

The disciples were, at first, equally confused about prayer. They wanted to know to whom they should pray and what they should say. Jesus taught them words that have been on the lips of millions of people throughout history. If you're like most Christians, the Lord's Prayer is a staple in your spiritual diet. This and the next six devotions focus on what we say each time we use the most perfect prayer.

"Our Father in heaven, hallowed be Your name" (Matthew 6:9). Jesus wants us to call God "our Father." How that must have stunned His early followers! For centuries, people didn't believe they could directly address God. God was so mighty that sinners calling on Him would perish if they spoke of anything but the somewhat distant "Name of the Lord." Jesus changed all that. He made it possible not only to call God God, but also to call Him Father. It takes only a small assumption to realize how we're related to the Savior if Jesus was God's Son. As if that relationship isn't good enough, the Bible even tells us that we're friends with Jesus! (See John 15:13–15.) When Jesus took away the sins of His friends, He brought us into His Father's family. And what a name that family has! Not just any name—but a holy (hallowed) one.

Call your Father every day—for praise, help, or thanksgiving. You know how to do it. After all, you had a good Teacher.

Dual Citizenship

He who testifies to these things says, "Surely I am coming soon." Amen.
Come, Lord Jesus! Revelation 22:20

Even liberty has limits beyond which we may not take liberties. Historically, most kingdoms were led by kings who gave their subjects the liberty to pay outrageous taxes and swear absolute allegiance or else spend lots of free time in a cold dungeon. Is this the kind of kingdom for which we ask in the Lord's Prayer?

Let's realize at the outset that we hold a dual citizenship. Jesus considered our earthly citizenship important. He told people to pay taxes and obey laws. Jesus wants us to understand that God empowers governments to keep order. Some governments keep order in oppressive ways. Others outlaw God's Word. And some want to make God's Word available but keep it out of the government.

"Your kingdom come." Our other citizenship is in God's kingdom, where we live now. (Our move to the mansion comes later.) God made us His subjects when He sent the Holy Spirit into our heart. We might call His kingdom the Church. (Notice the capital *C*.) His Church is believers in all time and all places. We are subject to His will and commands, but He is most merciful. He even forgives our acts of weak loyalty and occasional consorts with the enemy.

Good citizenship in God's kingdom means much the same as good citizenship in earthly kingdoms. We strive to lead a godly life by regularly honoring our King in everyday language as well as in worship. Since He is a good listener, we talk to Him and tell Him our needs. We can be sure that He has our best interests in mind as He meets those needs. We also want to tell everyone the good He does for us so they too will recognize Him as our good God.

God's kingdom is a great place to live. And we don't even have to pay taxes!

Will Power

I do not understand my own actions. For I do not do what I want, but I do the very thing I hate. Now if I do what I do not want, I agree with the law, that it is good. So now it is no longer I who do it, but sin that dwells within me. For I know that nothing good dwells in me, that is, in my flesh. For I have the desire to do what is right, but not the ability to carry it out. For I do not do the good I want, but the evil I do not want is what I keep on doing. Now if I do what I do not want, it is no longer I who do it, but sin that dwells within me. Romans 7:15–20

Do you, like Paul, also argue with yourself when it comes to problems of will power? Martin Luther said that will power is the most powerful power we have. The dynamics of will power presents some stubborn problems. Will power inevitably results in clashes. Take a moment to consider your own involvement in each of the following conflicts.

Sometimes the contest is between my will and the will of someone else. (Maybe you already had one of these today.) At other times, the conflict is between God and me. Still other occasions find me experiencing the "Paul syndrome." The peace treaty in any war of wills demands an application of a short phrase in the Lord's Prayer—"Your will be done."

We pray it all the time. We ask God to do His will. When His will overpowers our will, then we're bound for spiritual serenity. Right?

Not exactly. The sin within us won't die easily. And that's exactly why we pray "Your will be done." God's will is to keep sin out of our life. He also wants to save us. He wants to keep our faith strong so we can praise Him and live with Him forever.

Now go out there and practice some will power. Try some "won't power" too—the power God gives to battle and hate sin.

Enough Daily Bread

Remove far from me falsehood and lying; give me neither poverty nor riches; feed me with the food that is needful for me, lest I be full and deny you and say, "Who is the Lord?" or lest I be poor and steal and profane the name of my God. Proverbs 30:8–9

The words flow so smoothly. "Give us today our daily bread." Of course, we would like it buttered on both sides, and some cake would be nice too. And make sure we have enough to last us the whole week, Lord.

With or without prayers, God supplies food to the world—even to unbelievers. That's just the way God is. He cares for everybody. The difference is that believers know who to thank and praise for all good things.

Bread is sometimes called the stuff of life. When we pray for daily bread, we acknowledge that God provides everything our bodies need. In addition to food (even cauliflower!), God provides the roof that shelters us, family and friends to provide affection, jobs, good weather, and even coffee breaks. God grants it all!

When you think of the amount of edible food trashed from American tables and the acres of farmland that purposely remain unproductive, it's a miracle of mercy that God gives us anything. It's also a shameful sin that hunger reigns in the bellies of so many. Good thing God doesn't say, "Enough is enough!" and strike us all with famine.

Christians need to know when enough is enough. Have you noticed how we pray, "Give us *today* our daily bread"? Our prayer takes us beyond greed or stockpiling. It expresses confidence that God will provide what we need each day. History suggests that when God's people have more than they need, they tend to forget where they got it. When enough is enough, we are more likely to keep our focus on God.

Isn't it good to know who butters our bread?

Perilous Prayer

Be kind to one another, tenderhearted, forgiving one another, as God in Christ forgave you. Ephesians 4:32

Some people find forgiving much easier after they've gotten even! Others forgive because they know it really annoys the trespasser. Of course, the only proper motivation for forgiving is that we ourselves have been forgiven.

If we really concentrate when we say, "Forgive us our sins as we forgive those who sin against us," we recognize the serious deal we make with God. We give up our eternal life if we reject God's forgiveness by refusing to forgive others. Rather than dig through archives of sins committed against us, fearing that we forgot to forgive some, let's complete our "deal" with God right now.

> Dear heavenly Father, sometimes I'm a real flop at forgiving. I still store some bitterness in my heart from things past. Warm my heart with kindness for those who have done wrong to me. And fill me with compassion for those who will sin against me today, tomorrow, and next year. I don't deserve Your mercy or grace any more than those who do wrong to me. Yet, as You forgive me, strengthen me to forgive others. Fill me with the peace that comes from forgiving, even when it's not appreciated or acknowledged. Make me more like You. Amen.

Forgiveness feels good. It lightens our heart both when we get it and when we give it. God's forgiveness enables us to pray with a clear conscience. Forgiveness is also evidence that we believe God's forgiveness is real. To know that reality, we must recognize and confess the huge inventory of sins we garner each day. Only then do we also grasp the magnitude of God's grace and realize our obligation (yes, obligation!) to forgive others.

Is the Lord's Prayer truly perilous? It can be. But God's forgiveness gives us power to forgive too. Do some forgiving today. Then forget it.

Let's Have Some Fun

Count it all joy, my brothers, when you meet trials of various kinds,
for you know that the testing of your faith produces steadfastness.
James 1:2–3

Temptation is patient. It always gives a second chance. How wise Jesus was to instruct us to pray, "Lead us not into temptation."

God is the last one we would suspect of enticing us with temptations. Would He really do that? Of course not. Between the unholy trinity of the devil, the world, and our own flesh, temptation abounds in all shapes and sizes. Jesus knew all about those temptations because He encountered them Himself—with very personal attention from the devil. Jesus wanted His disciples—us included—to pray for strength to resist temptations.

Take a moment—an agonizing moment—to recall your most persistent temptations. Now take another moment to recall what happened the last time you foiled your tempter. Check out the Bible passage at the beginning of this meditation. The best thing about temptations is what happens when you repel them.

Temptations test our faith. Now God was and is prone to testing faith even if He refuses to tempt us to evil. He did it to Abraham in the incident when Isaac, Abraham's long anticipated son, was to be the family sacrifice. What faith it took for father Abraham to wield the knife, trusting that God knew what He was doing. The story ends with God providing a substitute sacrifice for Isaac. "Lead us not into temptation." Will God answer this prayer? Listen to what Paul says:

> No temptation has overtaken you that is not common to man. God is faithful, and He will not let you be tempted beyond your ability, but with the temptation He will also provide the way of escape, that you may be able to endure it. (1 Corinthians 10:13)

March 18 ~~

Shipping and Handling

But He said to me, "My grace is sufficient for you, for My power is made perfect in weakness." Therefore I will boast all the more gladly of my weaknesses, so that the power of Christ may rest upon me. 2 Corinthians 12:9

When we have problems, we often either try to bury them or blame them on someone else. Paul didn't appreciate his problems either, so when he prayed "Deliver us from evil," he expected an answer. He shares God's answer in the passage above. God delivered Paul from much evil, but he also endured much more than most of us would want to face—beatings, jail, shipwreck, and eventually death. Paul had another mysterious problem. He simply called it a "thorn" and asked God to take it away. God let him live with it instead.

We know that God doesn't lead us into temptation and that He fortifies our faith through tests tailor-made for us. And although we ask him to deliver us from evil, He sometimes says, "Live with it." (Of course, we never know just how much evil He delivers us from!) It's all part of God's shipping and handling plan to take us from birth to eternity.

Make no mistake. God has already delivered us from the worst evil through the sacrifice and victory of His Son, Jesus Christ. Now He commands His angels to protect us as we move toward our final destination in His mansion. They handle us well, but they allow us to experience bumps, bruises, and detours along the way. Those problems are good if we respond as Paul did. He recognized that Jesus keeps us close to Himself through our weaknesses. We don't ever want to forget that we need Him. And we also don't want to neglect our praise for Him.

Thank God for your weaknesses. Boast if you must—especially if someone questions how a sinner like you can be a Christian. Then run to the Savior who has paid all the shipping and handling charges for your delivery.

Think of Yourself

For by the grace given to me I say to everyone among you not to think of himself more highly than he ought to think, but to think with sober judgment, each according to the measure of faith that God has assigned.
Romans 12:3

It's time to think of yourself. You say we already do more of that than we should? You're probably right. If you browse the self-help section of most bookstores, you'll see title after title of self-help, self-evaluation, self-promotion, and self-esteem books. Self-esteem is a popular subject, so we must be careful not to confuse self-esteem with selfishness. (We all know people who are all wrapped up in themselves. They're grossly overdressed.)

Psychologists tell us that we need to love ourselves before we can love others. Does that also imply that we must serve ourselves before we can serve others?

Let's think of ourselves for a moment. Do we count our assets before we identify a few token liabilities? Do we find more faults than "goods" about ourselves? Chances are good that we hope someone will come along and give us a little esteem. And that's what we can expect from others—little! But God comes along and gives us lots of esteem. He loves us though we don't deserve it. He loves us even when we don't love ourselves.

Why should we possess self-esteem? God loved us so much that He sent Jesus to live and die and live again to save us. If God loved us, we can love ourselves. He gave us faith to accept and use our strengths to love and serve others. He gave us faith to forgive ourselves our shortcomings too. After all, why shouldn't we forgive what He forgave?

Think of yourself for a while. Not too highly, though. But love yourself as Jesus loves you.

What a Friend!

No longer do I call you servants, for the servant does not know what his master is doing; but I have called you friends, for all that I have heard from My Father I have made known to you. John 15:15

A true friend is one who remains your friend, even after getting to know you!

It's no wonder that "What a Friend We Have in Jesus" is a favorite hymn of many Christians. Believers through all ages have benefited from the presence of their divine friend. Jesus befriends sinners by taking them into His confidence, as friends often do. What does He tell them?

Jesus withholds no important information. While we may wonder about His private life—the years unrecorded in the Bible—He doesn't consider that to be important. We might like to know about our friend's background—the games He enjoyed, the pets He kept, names of His childhood friends (everybody!), the foods He enjoyed most, and how other kids treated Him. But that information would neither build our faith nor save us. Instead, Jesus tells us how to be saved, how to pray, how to serve, and how our friendship will grow.

Jesus tells us some important things about Himself. He says He is God, the Savior inside a body like ours. He taught us how to talk to Him. Jesus also insists that we make friends with others—even our enemies. No secrets here. Jesus tells it all. And much to our delight, He promises to remain friends forever.

Most of us are pleased when some important or popular person claims friendship with us. We're willing to do almost anything to please, and we're proud to be seen in his or her presence. That's how it is with Jesus too. We're happy to be near Him—most of the time. And when we abandon Him in favor of lesser friends, He's always willing to forgive and restore the relationship. He is happy to be with us too.

I guess we might feel the same if we died for someone.

Partly Cloudy

So that the priests could not stand to minister because of the cloud, for the glory of the Lord filled the house of God. 2 Chronicles 5:14

It happened so fast that it took them by surprise. Then, as now, people weren't too surprised by sudden shifts in the weather. But *inside* a building—in the days before sports domes with their mini-environments?

The occasion for the interior cloud was the dedication of God's temple built by Solomon. Years of hard labor yielded a magnificent building—a house for God. The project was financed freely by God's people. When he dedicated the temple, Solomon admitted that even this magnificent building couldn't really confine God, but he asked God to remain with His people anyway. God was so pleased with the righteous intent of Solomon that His spirit filled the temple, appearing as a cloud so thick the priests couldn't see what they were doing.

Solomon's temple vanished long ago, but God still lives with His people. In fact, He lives *in* His people. So what's the weather like in your "temple?" Today's Bible passage hints that good weather conditions include clouds.

Sin beats down on us like a blistering desert sun. Without clouds to shield us, we're inclined to wither and die. Since we can't create friendly clouds, we linger under the control of a force beyond us. No, it's not the meteorologist. Only God can provide a holy cloud to shelter us from the torrid climate of sin. He filters out sin's scorching rays by filling us with Jesus the Christ. And while we enjoy the complete cover He provides, we always push the cloud partly aside, allowing sin to burn us over and over again. Every time we do so, He returns to fill us once again. May God fill our life with the clouds of His Spirit as He did in Solomon's temple!

P.S. Maybe now you can enjoy the next cloudy day.

In over Your Head

O my God, I am ashamed and blush to lift my face to You, my God, for our iniquities have risen higher than our heads, and our guilt has mounted up to the heavens. Ezra 9:6

In some places, garbage landfills are being used for sledding hills. Throngs of young and old dot those hills riding innertubes, toboggans, sleds, snow saucers, and squares of cardboard. What a novel way to cope with our garbage! Otherwise we might be over our heads in junk-food wrappers and Styrofoam artifacts.

The prophet Ezra had some trash predicaments to deal with too. Sins. Heaps of sin and guilt. In a way, those unsightly piles of transgression were a recreation area for Ezra's people. They enjoyed their sinfulness. Only when they were in over their heads did they comprehend that sin's brief satisfactions brought them long-term blight.

Have you ever felt buried beneath the rubbish of your sins? Have you felt like Ezra, who confessed that the sins of his people were more than God should ever have to forgive? Take heart. Remember, while Ezra confessed the magnitude (or should I say altitude?) of their sins, he was indeed talking to God. Although he knew mercy was undeserved, he also knew God was merciful.

Our God is the same God who listened to Ezra centuries ago. As He listened to the confessions of Ezra's followers, He listens to our repentance too. Never do Christians need to feel their sins are too numerous to forgive. Never do Christians need to think they are beyond hope or help. The same God that forgave Ezra's congregation forgives us. After all, God takes His word seriously.

God always promotes repentance and forgiveness. His own Son died near a dump in a sacrifice that ended all sacrifices. If all our sins have been trashed by Jesus, where are the landfills? Jesus might answer, "Oh, I've forgotten them. You should too."

A World without Sin

For the time is coming when people will not endure sound teaching, but having itching ears they will accumulate for themselves teachers to suit their own passions. 2 Timothy 4:3

We can tell when we're dealing with sensible people. They always agree with us. Unfortunately, that's the concept behind the "itching ears principle." Even more unfortunate is that itching ears affect people seeking God too.

A whole new "church" movement, known by critics as "feel good" churches, has gained popularity in our culture. People flock to services to hear what they want to hear, and they worship their favorite people in the process. Preachers and teachers in these popular venues tell their congregation how to be successful and happy—how to tap the vast potential that resides inside them. They're so good at "soft-soaping" that their followers see nothing but the suds. Rarely, if ever, will you hear talk of sin. That would be offensive, humiliating, and otherwise unpopular.

Our entire culture is moving away from the concept of sin. Some mainline churches even prefer to use a synonym like *weakness* to take the repulsive edge off sin. It certainly sounds good to itching ears. Yet, as we shun a word like *sin*, we endanger ourselves. We become callous toward sinfulness even as it abounds around us. We forget that sin is the work of the devil, our surroundings, and even ourselves. Gradually, we may come to believe that we live in a world without sin. But if we believe that, we're as foolish as those who tried to build a tower to heaven.

Let sin be sin in your life. Confess it boldly. If we forget the heinous nature of sin, we also forget the vital need for a Savior. A world without sin doesn't need Jesus. So believe in sin, and believe in your Savior. And if your ears itch too much, scratch them. Even in public.

You Do the Math

Then Peter came up and said to Him, "Lord, how often will my brother sin against me, and I forgive him? As many as seven times?" Jesus said to him, "I do not say to you seven times, but seventy times seven." Matthew 18:21–22

If forgiveness were an animal, it would be an endangered species. (It has, however, been replaced by a wanton mutant identified as "sue.") Have you noticed that to err is human, but to forgive is about as common as a porpoise in Nevada? Of course, when discussing forgiveness, it's easier to receive it enthusiastically, but more difficult to give it. When forced to think about it, our personal archive of forgiveness surfaces from beneath the dust once in a while as we recall how so-and-so did such-and-such to us (approximately 13 years, two months, six days, eight hours, and 27 minutes ago). And now they did it again!

The apostle Peter, being flagrantly human, once questioned Jesus about forgiveness. The scene went like this: "Then Peter came up and said to him, 'Lord, how often will my brother sin against me, and I forgive him? As many as seven times?' Jesus said to him, 'I do not say to you seven times, but seventy times seven'" (Matthew 18:21–22).

You do the math. Perhaps that is 483 times more than reason dictates. Yet even that's not enough. Before we're tempted to hire the accounting firm of Sinbad and Slink to monitor the additional 483 misdeeds, we need to remember that Jesus spoke figuratively. Very figuratively! The Savior meant that forgiveness is never an option. His proclamation of symbolic sevens indicated that forgiveness should be comprehensive and complete. Well He should know. Forgiveness cost Jesus His earthly life.

Our 490 and then-some sins were forgiven completely. Completely. Gone and forgotten. That forgiveness gives us power to forgive others as we have been forgiven—in both quantity and quality. That's not to say that the quality of our forgiveness is the same as the quality of God's forgiveness. If only we could forget what we've forgiven as easily as we forget where we left our car keys! Good thing God forgives both our efficient and deficient memory.

Memory, teamed with guilt, is another plague on forgiven sinners. Have you forgiven yourself as often as God has forgiven you? Next time you remember your own sinfulness, think about Peter's question. And remember Jesus' answer.

Champions

This God—His way is perfect; the word of the Lord proves true; He is a
shield for all those who take refuge in Him. 2 Samuel 22:31

Wouldn't you love to see it? The camera pans the sidelines. Several behemoth linemen and a couple of toothless runningbacks hop in front of the camera. Each holds up four fingers and chants, "We're number 4. We're number 4." Allow the scene an instant replay in your mind. You'll never see it for real. Everyone wants to be the champion.

We Christians know the real Number 1. It's none other than God the Father, Jesus and the Holy Spirit. But through the mystery of divine teamwork, they're all rolled into one Number 1. We are their devoted, victorious fans.

God does everything right. When He battles treacherous rivals on our behalf, it's good to know He always wins. His first victory came in the Garden of Eden, when He had only two fans. The devil briefly won their loyalty, but he couldn't claim their lives.

Later in history, God went to war for those He called the Children of Israel. He fought the Hard-Hearts of Egypt in a series of lopsided plagues that freed His fans from their losers' plight. His greatest victory, though, came in sudden death when everything was at stake. Fans who saw it undoubtedly thought the contest was over when Jesus, sprawled over the cross, closed His eyes, gasped, and stopped breathing. But before His evil opponent could gloat, Jesus sprang back to life and crushed the devil's wicked power.

Warfare with the enemy continues today. But the victory is already ours even when our score lags behind the enemy's. And we cheer the Holy Spirit as He continues to win our contests with the devil.

We are champions—number 1. But not because we won the bout. We're number 1 because the Number 1 won. Isn't that one-derful?

Even If . . .

Though the fig tree should not blossom, nor fruit be on the vines, the pro-
duce of the olive fail and the fields yield no food, the flock be cut off from
the fold and there be no herd in the stalls, yet I will rejoice in the Lord; I
will take joy in the God of my salvation. Habakkuk 3:17–18

B ad news. Newscasters sling it at us every night. Most news is so bad
that we're tempted to watch the soap operas just to cheer up. In fairness, it's not the anchorperson's fault any more than the meteorologist is to
blame for the weather. Sin rages and storms through history, and we're making history right now.

Bad news is nothing new. The prophet Habakkuk witnessed much of it
thousands of years ago. As bad as things were for God's people in those days,
Habakkuk didn't let the news depress him. As you can see by his psalm,
Habakkuk was armed with dozens of "even ifs." Read the verses above again.

You probably don't worry much about barren grape vines, empty olive
trees, or vacant sheep pens unless you make your living by them. But our lives
remain filled with an abundance of other bad news. We might say, "Even if
floods destroy homes and farmland, even if hurricanes shred our coastlines,
even if AIDS decimates our population, even if terrorists unnerve our tranquility, even if domestic violence saturates our floors with blood, even if we
lose our jobs, even then we will be happy with our Lord and God who saves
us."

In fact, God saves the best for last. The last thing we'll ever experience is
eternal life. Why not conclude today's meditation with Habakkuk's prayer?

> O Lord, I have heard the report of You, and Your work, O
> Lord, do I fear. In the midst of the years revive it; in the
> midst of the years make it known; in wrath remember
> mercy. Habakkuk 3:2

Name Dropper

And those who know Your name put their trust in You, for You, O Lord,
have not forsaken those who seek You. Psalm 9:10

Politicians, junior executives, and sales people benefit from knowing names. Drop the right name in the right place and move one rung up the ladder. Of course, name droppers also can become tedious. There are times, however, when dropping the name of Jesus Christ is fundamental. Indeed, we must rely on His holy name instead of our own paltry identity. Consider the following scenarios.

You tell someone that sex is God's gift for enjoyment in marriage. He insists that his relationships hurt no one and that what he does is his business. Who are you to impose your standards on him, anyway? Such a challenge calls for some name dropping. It's God Himself who establishes the rights and wrongs for every situation. God made the rules and offers neither apology nor exception for them.

Scenario two. A co-worker or neighbor asks, "How did you become a Christian?" You might credit years of hearing Bible stories from your mother or how you studied religion in school. But note the emphasis on you. It's time to drop a name again. This time, mention the Holy Spirit who placed faith in your heart. Just think how important you must be if the Holy Spirit would make *you* a believer. You are important to God.

Your last opportunity to drop a name will come on Judgment Day when God will ask, "Why should I admit you to heaven?" Time to drop a name again. You'll want it to be a name you can trust. More important, you'll want it to be the only name that God will trust. Today's psalm reveals the only name that saves us. Just tell God that you and Jesus are friends. Tell Him how much Jesus did for you. You'll get to heaven based on whom you know rather than what you know.

Marriage Vows

When the Lord first spoke through Hosea, the Lord said to Hosea, "Go, take to yourself a wife of whoredom and have children of whoredom, for the land commits great whoredom by forsaking the Lord." Hosea 1:2

One wit (well, maybe he was only a half-wit!) defined marriage as a situation in which two people agree to change each other's habits. This might have been the case with the prophet Hosea and his unusual, albeit God-given, wife, Gomer.

Scripture reports: "When the Lord first spoke through Hosea, the Lord said to Hosea, 'Go, take to yourself a wife of whoredom and have children of whoredom, for the land commits great whoredom by forsaking the Lord'" (Hosea 1:2).

Hosea's marriage to Gomer was ordained as a living parallel to the believers' unfaithfulness to God. (Note: I said "believers.") Can you imagine Hosea's feelings as he embarked on this sea of God-ordained matrimony in a leaky boat? Yet Hosea obeyed, and there was good reason for his obedience.

Believers are God's Gomers. (This includes us, as well as those early believers known as the children of Israel.) Our relationship with God is decidedly one-sided, and the better half is undisputedly God. From the very beginning of humanity, God promised to love and care for His people—in good times and bad, in sickness and health, and in trips to craft shows or auto dealers. We humans, sincerely believing in the powers of spiritual passion, agreed to treat our beloved Creator and Companion in the same way. Both of us knew the predictable results, though we humans tend to be a bit more optimistic (or naive). In reality, believers are constantly unfaithful to God.

The problem is that temptation flirts with us all day and all night. We often succumb to immediate pleasures, temporarily losing memory of our faithful God or brazenly chasing some fleeting joy. We can't help but confess what God already knows. Believers are sinners. Frequent sinners. Sinners who often stray from the One who loves them most. It's an age-old story of unrequited love.

Yet there is hope—hope that doesn't rely on our attempts to improve the relationship. Our only hope for a lasting relationship is grounded in God's commitment to each of us. Ours was a marriage to die for. And He did.

Gone Fishing

While walking by the Sea of Galilee, He saw two brothers, Simon (who is called Peter) and Andrew his brother, casting a net into the sea, for they were fishermen. And He said to them, "Follow Me, and I will make you fishers of men." Matthew 4:18–19

Peter and Andrew probably told lots of fish stories. They were professionals who worked hard at a job they enjoyed. Jesus knew just how to reach them. He had a knack for making ordinary people into disciples. Tax collectors, tent makers, physicians, and homemakers all followed Him when He called.

Jesus called you too. Jesus wants you to do a little fishing, so look at the pond around you and make some plans. If you work or live with other Christians, fishing isn't so challenging. However, Christians need to share their bait!

If unbelievers inhabit your pond, you have some challenges ahead. But if you recall Jesus' words to Peter and Andrew, He said that He would make them fishers of future believers. You're not in the boat alone. Jesus provides energy and vigor for the task. Pray for the angler's chief virtue too—patience. As we share what Christ means to us and invite others into Christ's creel, some will only nibble at the prospect, afraid to commit. Gentle perseverance blessed by the Holy Spirit will eventually win their confidence. Others will take us at our word—hook, line, and sinker. What a joyful catch when the Holy Spirit latches onto those eager to feed on God's Word! Of course, every fisher encounters the ones that refuse to bite.

Go fishing today. Right after coffee break. Whatever you do for a living, you can fish too. Every catch is a keeper regardless of how small. Ask Jesus to guide you. And don't be afraid of getting skunked once in awhile. It happened to the disciples too. Both in the boat and out.

Say Grace

*Let no corrupting talk come out of your mouths, but only such as is good
for building up, as fits the occasion, that it may give grace to those who
hear. Ephesians 4:29*

Even in our violent society, we never need fear getting killed with kindness. No wonder Jesus and His disciples so strongly promoted kindness! And long before Jesus preached on earth, our heavenly Father commanded that we be kind to His children. (Moses had that as item eight on the
tablets.)

It's easy to say "grace" at our tables, so it shouldn't be too difficult to
speak words of grace at other times. Yet gossip, slander, and "trash talk"
remain chronic problems for most of us. It's so much easier to tear people
down than to build them up. We need a good example to follow.

Jesus was a master builder. Not that He didn't know how to aim a well-
placed *whap* upside the conscience when needed, but divine kindness was a
hallmark of His ministry. For example, consider His choice of friends and
eventual followers. Matthew the tax collector was a prime example. If
Matthew was like most others in his business, he skimmed profits at the
expense of taxpayers. This did not make him popular. But Jesus was kind to
Matthew anyway, and invited him to teach God's Word. The tax collector
ended up writing a best-seller—to God's glory.

Zacchaeus must have heard how Jesus even collected a tax collector. He
climbed a tree to see the Savior and ended up having dinner with Him.

Jesus says grace to each of us too. Regardless of our occupation (or pre-
occupation!), Jesus invites us to follow Him. How can He build up such con-
spicuous sinners? He forgives us. Is there any other way? His kindness, mercy,
love, and compassion focuses on poor, pathetic sinners and makes us rich,
cheerful disciples. His kindness commissions us to show the same kindness
to the same kind of people He loved. Namely, everybody!

Be sure to say grace today.

Gate-Crashers

*And when He returned to Capernaum after some days, it was reported that
He was at home. And many were gathered together, so that there was no
more room, not even at the door. And He was preaching the word to them.
And they came, bringing to Him a paralytic carried by four men. And when
they could not get near Him because of the crowd, they removed the roof
above Him, and when they had made an opening, they let down the bed on
which the paralytic lay. And when Jesus saw their faith, He said to the paralytic, "My son, your sins are forgiven." Mark 2:1–5*

There are two things to think about as you look at the neighbor's light
in the window late at night. Either someone is sick or they're giving
a party and you're not invited. If the latter is true, you always could invite
yourself. Gate-crashing isn't uncommon.

The Bible tells about some gate-crashers, or should we say roof-rippers?
Mark recounts the circumstances. "And they came, bringing to [Jesus] a paralytic carried by four men. And when they could not get near Him because of
the crowd, they removed the roof above Him, and when they had made an
opening, they let down the bed on which the paralytic lay" (Mark 2:3–4).

Those who gathered to learn about Jesus witnessed the object lesson of
their lives. The four faithful men who lowered their friend to Jesus' feet heard
the Savior proclaim healing—both of body and soul. And if those who
observed the day's miraculous event were pleasantly astonished, just think
how that man felt when he rose to his feet, free from his horizontal prison!

Of course, there are a few at every party and in every crowd. The scoffers.
The legalists. The troublemakers. Mark tells us they conspired among themselves, criticizing Jesus for forgiving sins! Apparently, they weren't in the
crowd to learn or to enjoy Jesus' message. They wanted to find something
wrong with it. They weren't disappointed.

Today, Jesus holds a huge and happy crowd adoringly spellbound in
heaven. Imagine the angels singing and the souls of saints laughing loudly in
unrestrained glee as they dance in God's dazzling glory. But you're not there.
Yet. Meanwhile, don't be afraid to do some gate-crashing at that heavenly festival. Send your prayers up to God. It gives Jesus another chance to heal
another sinner. Drop in anytime!

Life Savings

"Do not lay up for yourselves treasures on earth, where moth and rust destroy and where thieves break in and steal, but lay up for yourselves treasures in heaven, where neither moth nor rust destroys and where thieves do not break in and steal." Matthew 6:19–20

Aaron was depressed. Asked what he learned in school today, he replied, "I learned that some Americans are so poor that they have only one car and one TV."

On the serious side, the trend in American savings habits indicates that an alarming number of citizens have insignificant or no savings accounts. With easy credit available, it seems that banks are making more deposits in people than people in banks. The words of Jesus recorded in Matthew offer a quick economics course for people of our era.

Jesus says something we may find hard to swallow. He says that true wealth is beyond our reach. It's in heaven. The question is, how do we get it? How can we get rich quick? And the answer is almost too easy. Jesus hands it out to us.

We are spiritually homeless, starved for something to sustain us. Only Jesus has what we need—and lots of it. He doles out the treasures of heaven in His Word. His treasures fill us with awe and love and sometimes fear for His great power, which protects us from the devil. His treasures load us full of forgiveness so sin need never bankrupt us. Then there are the heaps of hope on which we may freely draw when troubled, threatened, or endangered. Yes, the Bible is the biggest bank book in the universe. These meditations only scratch the surface of God's vault of goodies. Make time to look through the investments He has made for you. The New Testament is especially rich. And if you're already in awe of your Savior, read the books after Matthew, Mark, Luke, and John. You have a personal fortune stored there—a treasure of truth and joy on which you can bank.

It Happens So Quickly

And Hezekiah and all the people rejoiced because God had prepared for
the people, for the thing came about suddenly. 2 Chronicles 29:36

The future seemed bleak. God's people forgot Him. They trusted their lives to fate, false gods, and other futile fads. Then Hezekiah became king and, with helpful hints from the Holy Spirit, rediscovered God. He led his people to repentance and worship. They asked God to help them rebuild the long-abused temple. Contributions rolled in to support the project, and the temple was rededicated in a grand festival. Hezekiah and all the people marveled at how quickly it all happened.

Change—especially change perceived as good—remains popular. You probably know people who practice change religiously. They change spouses, friends, cars, homes, and jobs. Of course, they wouldn't think of changing themselves. But that's exactly what Hezekiah and company did. They were amazed at how their change changed their lives.

We can't change God. Sometimes we try with our prayers, but it doesn't work. Then there's the technique that suggests if we just ignore Him maybe He'll go away—but hopefully not too far. When we do those things, we usually fail to recognize just how good He is.

Another change needs to occur every day. We need a personal repentance routine. Put more bluntly, we need to change for the better. We can do it with God's help. The change begins as the Holy Spirit moves us to see how we daily forget God. It happens so quickly. The curse, the meal without prayer, the "one more for the road" drink, the submission to ways of ungodly people. Next, we feel the weight of our godlessness and grieve over our behavior. What a blessing! It leads us to confess our sins. And God forgives us. It happens so quickly!

God will help us make our change more lasting. Just ask Him to keep you in mind when He has some spare change.

Stifled

*For freedom Christ has set us free; stand firm therefore, and do not sub-
mit again to a yoke of slavery. Galatians 5:1*

We may claim to be born free, but hospitals usually charge for the
birth. Besides, from a spiritual standpoint, "born free" is a faulty
concept.

As much as we condemn slavery, we still practice it. All people are born
slaves to sin. Left on our own, not only do we remain slaves, we may actually
think we enjoy our enslavement. We may depend on the devil to satisfy emotional and physical needs. Sometimes we don't need much help from the
devil; we're effective at enslaving ourselves, following our own self-serving
desires rather than God's will.

Jesus is the Emancipator. He set us free when He died and then returned
to life. He sent the Holy Spirit to share freedom with us. It happened the
moment we became believers. We were born sinful slaves to the devil, but
Jesus gave us a new birth, one in which we were truly born free. As Paul told
the Galatians, Christ freed us to enjoy the advantages of freedom. He warned
them—and us—to resist the slavery that once stifled us. Furthermore, freedom is a package deal that implies responsibility.

We are free—free from sin's power to condemn us and free to enjoy a life
of service to God and others. We're even free to make mistakes because God
will forgive us. We're free to praise Jesus by singing hymns from a book or by
making up our own little songs—even if they're off-key. We're free to pray the
Lord's Prayer and proclaim our faith with the Apostles' Creed or we can make
up our own ineloquent prayers or simple declarations of faith. So enjoy your
freedom. And if you ever yearn to return to slavery, call on the Holy Spirit for
some quick help. He will help you stifle it.

The Key to Success

This Book of the Law shall not depart from your mouth, but you shall meditate on it day and night, so that you may be careful to do according to all that is written in it. For then you will make your way prosperous, and then you will have good success. Joshua 1:8

The key to success doesn't always fit our door! If it's any consolation, failure is a far better teacher than success—as long as we actually learn and improve from our mistakes. (Not that we should go out and make better mistakes!)

The success formula recorded in Joshua outlines a difficult road of hard work. In fact, Joshua makes success look impossible. The Book of the Law contains no exceptions, but solid rules for perfect behavior. A person would be prosperous and successful, if only . . .

What is the greatest success anyone could accomplish? Making a billion dollars? Two thousand years from now both the billionaire and his dollar bills will be forgotten molecules of dust. How about discovering a vaccine for cancer? As with the dreaded smallpox, some other fatal disease will replace it. Immortality? God already announced the way to escape death. No, the greatest success is to be perfect. Or at least latch onto someone who can do it for you.

That someone is Jesus Christ, and we're already hanging onto His sandal straps, riding the wave of His Easter success. God does not make us successfully complete a list of requirements for salvation Jesus has already fulfilled those requirements for us. The success of Christ is now attributed to all who believe. We are successful only because Christ was successful for us

Jesus is our key to success. He has opened the door to heaven.

Easy Mark

Then Peter, filled with the Holy Spirit, said to them, ". . . This Jesus is the
stone that was rejected by you, the builders, which has become the corner-
stone. And there is salvation in no one else, for there is no other name
under heaven given among men by which we must be saved."
Acts 4:8–12

Most fisherpersons are easy marks for advertisers. As a boy, I remember responding to an ad for a lure that guaranteed I would catch fish. Forgetting that every lure I ever purchased was similarly destined for success, I bought this marvelous gadget. When it came, I discovered the lure held a battery (not included), a buzzer, and a tiny propeller motor. It was supposed to call fish. It must have called them something offensive because not one fin rippled the water the day I used it.

Advertising is successful because it tells us what we want to hear. It offers answers and hope to all we question or desire. It makes everything sound sooooo good.

The devil would have been a successful advertising tycoon. Can't you see his agency? Satan and Sons, Supreme Sellers of Sin. He could boast a long history of fruitful campaigns, starting with the very first consumers, who eagerly believed his fraudulent claims of glory. Like any effective advertiser, he remains persistent, slinging one angle after another to hook us. One of his largest modern advertising challenges parades itself before our hearts and souls. It might be called "Ways to Get to Heaven."

Admittedly, that doesn't sound like something the devil really wants to sell. Or is it? How often have you tried to do good things because God requires such behavior to enter heaven? Or maybe money is your downfall. Large contributions make God happy, don't they? And a happy God will surely notice your generosity, won't He? Or perhaps someone you know assures you that he has plenty of time to become faithful because God is a sucker for deathbed avowals of faith. We're all suckers for some pitch that the devil broadcasts. Like the worst of advertising, however, his sales pitches are all lies.

Jesus did some advertising of His own. You'll find it in a book on shelves and coffee tables of many homes. Page through it and you'll see this catchy phrase: "And there is salvation in no one else, for there is no other name under heaven given among men by which we must be saved" (Acts 4:12).

You know the name. You know how much it costs. Surely this is the best buy ever.

Overtime

And Hezekiah spoke encouragingly to all the Levites who showed good skill in the service of the LORD. So they ate the food of the festival for seven days, sacrificing peace offerings and giving thanks to the LORD, the God of their fathers. Then the whole assembly agreed together to keep the feast for another seven days. So they kept it for another seven days with gladness. 2 Chronicles 30:22–23

Lots of people would like an occupation that didn't occupy so much of their time. American workers are working more and vacationing less, according to some recent studies. An alarming number of people work overtime just to keep their jobs. And with cellular telephones and other communication technology, overtime can come in the middle of the night, on a fishing trip, during an anniversary dinner, or on weekend outings with family or friends.

Is overtime a good work ethic? We can point to Jesus, who labored overtime serving those He loved (everybody!). Some criticized Him for working on the day of worship. He even died on the job. But Jesus' job was absolutely vital to the welfare of countless people. Regardless of our position, we're not quite so important and neither is our work. If we want to spend some worthwhile overtime, we can take a hint from Hezekiah and his people and take worship into overtime.

When we think how God loves us so much that He sent Jesus to take away our sins, we can't help but adopt a festive mood. Now staying overtime at a festival—that's more up our alley. So you probably won't mind adding a few thank-Yous to your prayers. And while you're at it, add a few more people to your prayer list. Tack an extra 15 minutes to the end of your day to learn more from your Bible or other devotional reading. The pay is great.

Declared Incompetent

Then He went home, and the crowd gathered again, so that they could not even eat. And when His family heard it, they went out to seize Him, for they were saying, "He is out of His mind." And the scribes who came down from Jerusalem were saying, "He is possessed by Beelzebul," and "by the prince of demons he casts out the demons." Mark 3:20–22

You may not know any fanatics personally, but they aren't difficult to identify. They're the people who stick to their guns, whether or not they're loaded.

Two thousand years ago, a well-known figure roamed the regions of Israel. Many thought Him a fanatic. Even His family had doubts, as we hear in Mark 3:20–21: "Then He went home, and the crowd gathered again, so that they could not even eat. And when His family heard it, they went out to seize Him, for they were saying, 'He is out of His mind.'"

Forget the label "fanatic." His family figured Jesus was a lunatic, and they declared Him incompetent. After all, with all His fame, He should have sought His fortune. His entourage should be keeping His name in front of supportive crowds. Instead, He often ordered His followers to keep quiet. Now He was so busy with His job that He couldn't find time to eat!

This section of Mark might be considered hard on families. Later in the reading, we hear Jesus rebuke His family by announcing that His "real" family consisted of those who listened, learned, and believed in Him. Think of how this must have stung Mary and Jesus' brothers—how others must have whispered their opinions about His gruff talk. This was not a rebellious or disobedient son talking. Jesus told the divine truth, and at least some of Jesus' family later believed "their" Jesus was God's Son, the Savior.

As the world, both ancient and modern, views heroes, Jesus certainly was incompetent. His humility and honesty, combined with compelling authority and an unrelenting work ethic, made Him a target for those who view such qualities as characteristics of fanaticism.

Not much has changed. Christians, as you may have experienced, might be accused of incompetency when it comes to dealing with worldly issues and problems. Critics scoff when Christians say they have to pray about something. Then there's the way you spend your time and money. And there's this forgiveness thing. Revenge satisfies more!

Crazy Christians. That's what we are. But we have a great example to follow. So stay with the crowd—the crowd that gathers to learn and listen and believe in Jesus.

Revealing Secrets

And from there He arose and went away to the region of Tyre and Sidon.
And He entered a house and did not want anyone to know, yet He could
not be hidden. Mark 7:24

Can you keep a secret? Probably. It's only the people you tell it to that can't! Why would Jesus want to keep His whereabouts secret in today's text?

Jesus had just fed 5,000 people. That news didn't stay secret for long. People were looking for Him—especially His enemies—who wanted to silence Him and end His miracles. But Jesus wanted time alone with the disciples so He could teach them how to carry on His ministry.

There were other times when Jesus' disciples preferred secrecy. Peter was a notable example. This brash follower claimed to love Jesus more than anyone else. He pledged unflappable loyalty. Yet, when Peter had three successive opportunities to testify about His Savior's innocence and power, he kept it to himself (Mark 14:66–72).

We can't be too hard on Peter. (He was hard enough on himself when he realized what he had done.) Some of us are very good at keeping Jesus' presence a secret. Unlike the episode in today's Bible passage, Jesus doesn't want to be hidden anymore. He wants everyone to know what He did and how they have salvation in Him.

Do we throw a blanket over Jesus in tough times? It's much safer sometimes to keep the shades drawn than to reveal His light in our heart. Like Peter, we're often afraid of what others will think if we say we know Jesus. We tremble to think how others might ridicule us or label us as some sort of religious nut. Just as threatening, they might like what they hear and expect more support, compassion, hand-outs, or better behavior from us!

It's time to tell your secret. Who knows? Maybe others have a few secrets of their own.

Good Luck

And they rose early in the morning and went out into the wilderness of
Tekoa. And when they went out, Jehoshaphat stood and said, "Hear me,
Judah and inhabitants of Jerusalem! Believe in the Lord your God, and
you will be established; believe His prophets, and you will succeed."
2 Chronicles 20:20

Jehoshaphat may be remembered for many thing, but we would do well to note a motto he lived by: "Faith, Not Fate." Some people easily confuse the two.

How often have you (a fine and faithful Christian) wished someone good luck? Frequently, it's a phrase that just slips out—as common a saying as "Have a good day." But some people take luck seriously.

A cross sits atop a well at a Russian village. Those who live around the well think the cross will bring good luck. Of course, baseball fans are familiar with players who cross themselves before each at bat. Perhaps I shouldn't be suspicious, but I wonder if they do it to proclaim their faith, bless their bat, or bring "good luck."

Luck is an impotent substitute for faith. It's another four-letter word we should erase from our vocabulary—even if we don't mean anything idolatrous by it. Consider Jehoshaphat's words for today in the context in which they occurred. He and his army faced oppressive odds. By military standards, they had little hope of winning the battle. Only God's awesome power and Jehoshaphat's genuine trust could win the victory.

That's how it always is. Fate is nothing; faith is everything. We may not know the future, and perhaps we fear the battles that might embroil us. But have faith that God will win for us. He might not always win in the manner we would like, but a single is better than a foul ball any day.

Fragrant Relationship

Your anointing oils are fragrant; your name is oil poured out; therefore
virgins love you. Song of Songs 1:3

My mother wouldn't let me read Song of Songs (or Song of Solomon as it was called then) until I was 21 years old. Even then I had a hard time figuring out why this spicy love poem was in the Bible. It seems so out of place until you make the love connection. What a fragrant parallel the Bible draws comparing the relationship of Christ and the Church (us) with an amorous marriage! It says a lot of what God thinks about marriage and even more of Christ's love for believers.

Our marriage to Jesus began as a gleam in His eye, as He knew He wanted us long before we ever knew His name. He proposed on the eve of our faith, and the marriage was consummated with Baptism. We are now united with Him forever. Unless, of course, we break our vows or go chasing after another lover.

The devil is a shameless flirt, and he enjoys making those married to Jesus unfaithful partners. He plies us with cheap perfume that only masks his foul stench. Jesus, however, purchased a one-of-a-kind fragrance that sweetens our love for Him.

Love, by true description, is sacrificial. Jesus died to keep our love alive. Instead of mourning, however, we celebrate because our love lives on and so does Jesus. We are blessed with perpetual bliss. Like any good marriage, these blessings affect our everyday life.

Hold hands and take long walks with Jesus. And when you begin to stray (or turn your head), you'll feel a gentle tug on your soul-strings as He gently pulls you back to His matchless love.

Every day is an anniversary with Jesus. He never forgets it, even if you do. So when you wake up, thank Jesus for being with you as you slept, and ask Him to stay close during your waking hours too. Just think, this is one honeymoon that never ends.

Lopsided Odds

*Then Elijah said to the people, "I, even I only, am left a prophet of the
Lord, but Baal's prophets are 450 men. Let two bulls be given to us, and
let them choose one bull for themselves and cut it in pieces and lay it on
the wood, but put no fire to it. And I will prepare the other bull and lay it
on the wood and put no fire to it. And you call upon the name of your
god, and I will call upon the name of the Lord, and the God who answers
by fire, He is God." And all the people answered, "It is well spoken."*
1 Kings 18:22–24

The only way to make a small fortune in gambling is to start with a
large one! Most gamblers are out to get something for nothing; in
truth, they get the opposite. Odds always seem stacked against those least able
to lose.

The prophet Elijah understood odds, especially because they were frequently against him. Here's one example: "Then Elijah said to the people, 'I,
even I only, am left a prophet of the Lord, but Baal's prophets are 450 men.
Let two bulls be given to us, and let them choose one bull for themselves and
cut it in pieces and lay it on the wood, but put no fire to it. And I will prepare
the other bull and lay it on the wood and put no fire to it. And you call upon
the name of your god, and I will call upon the name of the Lord, and the God
who answers by fire, He is God.' And all the people answered, 'It is well spoken'" (1 Kings 18:22–24).

The odds were 450 to 1. In fact, they were worse because an additional
400 false prophets threw their support to the prophets of Baal. How could
Elijah face such a disadvantage? What was he thinking to blurt out such a defiant bet in the face of such overwhelming odds? He wasn't thinking, though.
He knew what would happen.

God won the contest; Elijah was just the dealer. In reality, no odds were
involved. God revealed His power that day as He won the battle of sacrifices.
His opponents perished trying to beat Him.

Perhaps you're a gamer of sorts—the kind who plays a friendly game of
canasta, four corners, or even poker. Those games involve odds. Your chances
of winning are just that—a chance. Good thing it's not that way with God.

Winning with God is a certainty. He passed the winnings along to you
when Jesus died for your sins and, against all odds, came to life again, inviting you to share His victory. Next time you play cards, take a moment to savor
your losses. Let them remind you that you're never a loser with your Savior.
Odd, isn't it?

Extra Ordinary

Now when they saw the boldness of Peter and John, and perceived that
they were uneducated, common men, they were astonished. And they rec-
ognized that they had been with Jesus. But seeing the man who was
healed standing beside them, they had nothing to say in opposition.
Acts 4:13–14

How do we describe average Americans? We might say they have an average of three televisions, three cars, three telephones, and three credit card payments. An average American takes more than 19,000 steps each day. The average American has more food to eat than the average citizen anywhere else in the world. Also more diets. Finally, average Americans might have made Jesus' short list of potential disciples.

One striking feature of Jesus' followers was their lack of striking features. They boasted minimal social or employment status. Most of His followers held jobs that didn't require much education. (Don't tell an experienced fisherman that!) Tax collectors, disabled people, and women formed a large contingent of His followers—and those people often were classified as less than ordinary. Critics of Jesus noted this as well. Acts 4:13 says: "Now when they saw the boldness of Peter and John, and perceived that they were uneducated, common men, they were astonished. And they recognized that they had been with Jesus."

The average reader of this book probably considers himself or herself ordinary. Few among us have accomplished things for which we'll be remembered for, say, more than 12 minutes. Yet we're in excellent company considering the likes of Peter and John. How have these ordinary people attained a place in history so lofty that we remember them 2,000 years later?

Behind every successful person is God. God takes common people and empowers us to do uncommon things. You say you don't do anything out of the ordinary? Pig cleanser! (Hogwash.)

You and every other Christian have faith. That's not ordinary. It's miraculous. The Holy Spirit chose you to believe in Jesus as your Savior, and you do. Not enough evidence? You put that faith to work too. You're reading a devotional book. You forgive others too. Right? Ordinary people like us forgive others for only one reason: God forgave us first.

Like the astonished disbelievers in today's Bible reading, there is one thing others may notice about us. It's the "secret" of our uniqueness. We have been with Jesus! Only He can make the extra ordinary extraordinary.

All I Need

But as for me, my feet had almost stumbled, my steps had nearly slipped.
For I was envious of the arrogant when I saw the prosperity of the wicked.
. . . Whom have I in heaven but You? And there is nothing on earth that
I desire besides You. Psalm 73:2–3, 25

A dvertising is the science of making us think we've wanted something our whole life, and now it's finally available. If ads are believable, there is even a way to borrow enough money to get out of debt! If only we owned what ads offered, we would be smarter, happier, sexier, and more successful.

We can't completely blame advertising for leading us to want more than we have. We can't impute blame for the desires and greed that normally infect our all-too-human hearts, either. Nor should we be quick to equate wealth and prosperity with evil, even though we may know of several people with ill-gotten affluence. Money isn't evil—only the exclusive love for it. The psalm for today focuses on the real problem. It's us.

Envy often pushes us until we stumble. Worse yet, we frequently envy what is wicked. We watch others "enjoy" all the sins of life. Does God strike them with lightning bolts? No. Suddenly, we begin to feel like we're missing something in life.

What do we enjoy? The Bible? Humming hymns? Frank, though one-sided, conversations with God? How exhilarating! Exciting? Would you believe satisfying?

Attitude is everything. While earthly delusions of pleasure pull us in one direction, true pleasure beckons quietly from the opposite side.

The psalmist tells us where to find absolute and total satisfaction. We have it in Jesus. As long as we have Him, we need nothing else. Even if we lose our treasures, suffer paralyzing accidents, or lose our senses, we still have all we need. So yearn for whatever good you want, subdue the desire for wicked pleasures, and hold on to all that you need—Jesus.

Minor Keys

I will heal their apostasy; I will love them freely, for my anger has turned
from them. . . . Whoever is wise, let him understand these things; whoev-
er is discerning, let him know them; for the ways of the Lord are right,
and the upright walk in them, but transgressors stumble in them.
Hosea 14:4, 9

We would rather listen to the music than face it. With that, we have something in common with God's rebellious people of long ago. It's to them that the so-called Minor Prophets like Hosea, Amos, and Haggai ministered. Their preaching and prophesying would probably be played in sad and haunting minor keys if set to music.

Have you ever considered it odd that among the Bible's prophetic books, the Minor Prophets are in the majority? Their messages aren't minor either. God considered the themes proclaimed through these men key information for all His people in all times. Therefore, the next 11 days will find us meditating on what the Minor Prophets had to say.

If you haven't read the Minor Prophets, take some brief excursions to these tiny islands of prophecy in God's Word. But not on an empty stomach. These prophets portray God at His angriest since the great flood. God talked through these prophets, but His stubborn people refused to listen and obey. But even as God pronounced grisly judgment on the traitors, He graciously offered them an "if only." If only they would repent and return to Him, they could be His people again.

Do the Minor Prophets have anything major to say? Look at the verses from Hosea again. We hear that God indeed is liberal with forgiveness. But Hosea also has a word to the wise. God's ways are still right even though they receive heavy criticism from those who believe that only we ourselves know what's right for us.

Our God hasn't changed since the time of the prophets and neither have people. They still rebel. He still loves and offers forgiveness. Now that's something we can profit by!

Holey Hearts

Rend your hearts and not your garments. Return to the Lord, your God,
for He is gracious and merciful, slow to anger, and abounding in steadfast
love; and He relents over disaster. Joel 2:13

You can't always judge people by what they wear. Sometimes there just isn't enough evidence!

People living in Old Testament days lamented their sinfulness by ripping their clothes. Left with little to wear after such episodes, they changed into fresh sackcloth to further demonstrate their repentant hearts. While the prophet Joel was no fashion critic, he was savvy enough to know that torn clothing might still hide hardened hearts. That's when he suggested that people should rip their heart rather than their raiments.

Echoing the key theme of other Minor Prophets, Joel demanded that people change their mutinous hearts and defiant behavior. God isn't fooled. To be truly repentant, says Joel, we need to bare our hearts and soften the hard parts.

God's people are frequently guilty of the fatal flaw of hard-heartedness. Each time we choose to act in ways that God wouldn't approve, we harden our hearts. Perhaps the greatest contributors to stoney hearts are our "pet" sins—the ones we commit so often that they don't seem serious anymore. Joel might say, "Poke a few holes in your hard heart. Soften up and come back to God!"

We can trust Joel's teachings. God told him what to say—not only to ancient believers but also to modern Christians. He describes God's reaction to our repentance with words like *compassion, grace,* and *love.* We receive those blessings not through some outward expression of sorrow or desperation, but through contrite hearts that seek to do God's will. And when He forgives, our hearts no longer weep and cower before Him. We can celebrate, adorned in His grace.

Who Did It?

*For behold, He who forms the mountains and creates the wind, and
declares to man what is His thought, who makes the morning darkness,
and treads on the heights of the earth—the Lord, the God of hosts, is His
name! Amos 4:13*

It's a marvel that He did all the above without benefit of a diversified
holding company or manufacturing empire. And He didn't quit there.
He assumed human form and became one of us. He offered immortality by
dying and coming back to life long before Ponce de Leon searched for a fountain of youth. He sent Paul on business trips that changed the lives of millions
of people without using a scheduled airline or rental car. And now He keeps
the earth tilted at just the right angle without the help of cranes or scaffolds.
He knits cells together into the cutest bundles even though He lacks a degree
in molecular biology, and He gathers thousands into His kingdom without
immigration or equal opportunity quotas. Who is He? You know Him
already. He is God, of course. His name is one to both fear and revere.

Fearing God suggests we recognize His ultimate authority for what it is—
authority! How modern society rebels against authority! We want the right to
make decisions that directly affect us—even if we haven't a clue about long-
term consequences. We often want God's love, but not His rule in our lives.

God doesn't flaunt His authority, though. Nor is He secretive. Instead, as
Amos points out, God tells us His thoughts. His thoughts carry more weight
than human opinions. His thoughts were the very power that created the
heavens and earth and preserves them yet today. He reveals His thoughts
about us too. He loves us so much that He's willing to forgive and forget our
faults. He wants us to love Him and be happy—and He tells us how: Believe
in Him who died on the cross for our sins.

Who is "Him"? Why Jesus, of course.

Minority Report

For the day of the Lord is near upon all the nations. Obadiah 1:15

Each tick of the clock brings us closer to judgment, or as we read in Obadiah, the Day of the Lord. Some people deny the reality of Judgment Day. Perhaps that's an easy way to live, never admitting that we'll need to account for our actions someday. That viewpoint is as foolish as killing some time because the boss isn't around—at the time. Very risky.

Others joke about judgment. Perhaps you've heard some Judgment Day jokes, complete with verbal imagery of pearly gates, St. Peter monitoring the entrance, and devilish creatures rubbing their hands in ghastly anticipation of heaven's castoffs.

Sadly, some people dread the coming judgment. They fear they won't have a good enough lawyer to protect their reputation. Or maybe they fear that God really knows their reputation is true! But saddest of all are those who know their unworthiness in all its expansive dimensions, and either hate God or despair because of it.

Christians can welcome Judgment Day because we know what will happen. The Bible says that Jesus will return suddenly, with the sound of trumpets blasting the air. All people shall rise from the dead. All. Not just believers, but all the rebellious unbelievers as well. They, together with all those still alive, will appear before God for His judgment. Not that He doesn't already know where we belong. The Bible says God will thumb through the Book of Life to find our name. If we're registered, we proceed to everlasting bliss. If not, we spend eternity suffering in hell. We're also told we need to account for our behavior. (No excuses accepted.) And we better have some answers.

Are you ready to answer? Remind God (respectfully, of course) that although you're a weak sinner, you're also a firm believer that Jesus took those sins away. Just ask God to check the book under F—for *forgiven*.

Shucks

And he prayed to the Lord and said, "O Lord, is not this what I said
when I was yet in my country? That is why I made haste to flee to
Tarshish; for I knew that You are a gracious God and merciful, slow to
anger and abounding in steadfast love, and relenting from disaster."
Jonah 4:2

Have you ever prayed for something and then complained when God delivered what you wanted? Look at Jonah's prayer above. As you might remember, Jonah never wanted to take God's business trip to Nineveh—even if God would have sent him first class.

Nineveh was a horrid city filled with fierce opponents of God. Jonah wasn't about to go overboard telling them to repent—or so he thought. When, after a soggy detour, he ended up telling the citizens they were miserable sinners, Jonah was disappointed that they actually repented. Jonah's prayer came at that point. It's as if he was saying, "Why did I go through all this trouble to tell these sinners that You would destroy them when we both knew that You would extend Your mercy and grace to spare them?"

For those who repented in Nineveh, and millions of other sinners, what better news could we have? God is merciful. He spares us from calamity. God's grace even goes further back than Jonah and Nineveh. He had every right to wipe out Adam and Eve for infecting the world with sin, but instead He gave them some new clothes and promised them a Savior. (This greatly disappointed the devil!) And well after Nineveh, sinners continued their old tricks. All creation should have trembled the day God's Son hung on the cross. But that was just another act of grace and love. Once again, the devil was heaving out puffs of smoke and yelling, "Shucks!" (It's possible the devil used some other words.)

The moral of this story? Pray for unbelievers, even if you would rather see them get what they deserve. If you think about it, we don't get what we deserve either. Nineveh isn't too far from our own neighborhood.

Stamp Out Sin

Who is a God like You, pardoning iniquity and passing over transgression for the remnant of His inheritance? He does not retain His anger forever, because He delights in steadfast love. He will again have compassion on us; He will tread our iniquities under foot. You will cast all our sins into the depths of the sea. Micah 7:18–19

Picture this: A large crowd marches around the county building. You squeeze your way in to read the demands scrawled on their placards: "Stamp Out Sin!"

Unlikely, you say? Sadly, you're right. Today, anyone demonstrating to stamp out sin would face ridicule. Besides, there isn't much we can do about sin, can we?

Sin is a fact of life. A fact—not a figment of radically religious imagination. For centuries, people have tried to stamp out sin with laws. (Even people who weren't religious.) The result? Millions of people apply rules and regulations to daily life—especially the daily life of other people. But the only law that everyone obeys is the law of gravity!

If we really want to stamp out sin, we must lobby with the only one who can do anything about it. In fact, He already has done something about it. God sent Jesus to abolish sin. In so doing, He abolished our sins forever. Jesus obeyed all the laws for us and summarized them with only two. Love God and love others. Love springs from a godly heart and soul, with a willing desire to serve and show mercy.

Because God has trampled our sins underfoot, He has prevented sin from claiming our lives. God stamped out sin, not in some violent confrontation with the forces of evil, but through self-sacrifice on the cross. When the world ends, there will indeed be a final, fatal confrontation with the devil. Until that time, we live with the comforting words of Micah. God is delighted to show mercy. And most of us sinners surely bring Him much delight!

Ho Hum

The Lord is good, a stronghold in the day of trouble; He knows those who take refuge in Him. Nahum 1:7

Would you believe that Nahum had a younger brother named Ho? (Think about it . . .) There was nothing ho hum about Nahum. From the sound of his words, he didn't take God's care and protection for granted. Are we sometimes guilty of spiritual complacency?

Consider this scenario. The alarm clock summons us from our beds. We wipe the sand from our eyes and process our bodies for another day of work. We begin our chores with various degrees of enthusiasm, and we usually sense relief and relaxation at the end of our workday. In a few hours, our heads burrow into the pillow as the alarm clock once again waits to perform its once-a-day ritual. Ho hum.

Such ho-hum existence lulls our senses and numbs our awareness of God's presence. We may forget that He and His angels accompany us in the routine times, the good times, and the times we're unaware of how much we really need Him. Then something happens to take the hum out of the ho. Perhaps it's serious illness or just a nagging toothache. Maybe it's financial problems or a brutal argument with someone we love. Whatever intrudes on our ho-hum routines usually sends us straight to our Savior's side, where we can expect comfort, security, and hope.

In some ways though, perhaps it's okay to have a ho-hum trust in God. Our trust in Him can be as routine as the alarm clock waking us every morning. What else, who else is more trustworthy? Horoscopes and rabbits feet can't compare. They differ little from the impotent idols that people trusted in Old Testament days. And saving for the proverbial rainy day is futile in a full-fledged flood. Our only hope is the constant, routine, habitual, even ho-hum hope in the Lord.

Isn't it great to have a God who cares? Aren't we contented knowing we can always count on God? What else is new?

April 21

Speak Up!

*You who are of purer eyes than to see evil and cannot look at wrong, why
do you idly look at traitors and are silent when the wicked swallows up
the man more righteous than he? Habakkuk 1:13*

In some large cities, you can walk a mile and never leave the scene of a
crime! Headlines mourn the loss of children killed by an abusive mother. Our cries of injustice usually prompt a flurry of activity by legislators hopeful of averting more violence. But such "solutions" are only temporary. And
how rightfully indignant do we get when a guilty party escapes the justice system on a technicality? Surely, it would help if God would only speak up.

Things were indeed bad in Habakkuk's time: rampant crime; random violence; deadly marauders; masses of wicked sinners refusing to worship and
obey the true God. Habakkuk would feel right at home in our society. But he
probably wouldn't get much press if he brought up the issue of people
unfaithful to God. And if he asked God to speak up, people would dismiss
him as a religious fanatic. Yet the root of our problems is our refusal to con-
form to God's way of life—and our resistance to acknowledging that God is
God. But before we complain to God about His silence, we better think of a
response in case He turns the question back to us.

God gave us His Word. We know what it says. As in Habakkuk's time,
God's words often fall on deaf or mocking ears. Yet we must carry on the tradition of believers. Being motivated by the power of Christ we can speak up
and let God's Word be heard—heard in the ears of our neighbors, co-workers,
civic leaders, and everyone else. Let those ears hear words of hope, words that
extend the forgiveness that we know so intimately. Remember, God speaks to
us too.

A Refreshing Thought

The Lord your God is in your midst, a mighty one who will save; He will rejoice over you with gladness; He will quiet you by His love; He will exult over you with loud singing. Zephaniah 3:17

We all like people who come right out and say what they think—especially if they admire us. Then there are those less high on our list who probably know us better. Regardless of what happens to us, they knew we had it coming. How refreshing, then, it is to read what Zephaniah said about us! Go ahead, read it again.

God breaks into song because He's so delighted in us! God's love quiets us—calms and soothes our troubled soul and body. Yet once in a while, isn't it normal to feel disquieted—to hear loud clanking coming from the vicinity of our soul?

An honest appraisal of ourselves can't help but suggest one thing—God has little to rejoice and sing about. We have trouble imitating Jesus' attitude toward other sinners. Even if forgiveness comes easily, forgetting doesn't. Not much for God to croon about there. We have those temporary but persistent lapses in our language and thoughts—the kind that integrate disobedience of the Second, Fifth, and Sixth Commandments into one fiery ball of sin. God is anything but delighted.

Time to turn to Zephaniah again. As much as we like to hear God's joy about us, it makes no lasting sense unless we remember the real reason God is happy. Jesus Christ the Savior is our Lord God. He wiped out sin's power to control us. True, we're not completely empowered in this matter yet, but we're on our way to perfection. In the meantime, our Savior dabs our guilty brows with forgiveness in equal measure to our sins.

God is indeed happy with us for Jesus' sake. How else could a Father feel about His children?

Get Back to Work

Yet now be strong, O Zerubbabel, declares the Lord. Be strong, O Joshua,
son of Jehozadak, the high priest. Be strong, all you people of the land,
declares the Lord. Work, for I am with you, declares the Lord of hosts.
Haggai 2:4

I hope you didn't attach any immediacy to the title. After all, you deserve a break, don't you? Just don't stretch your break too long. (You wouldn't want to miss quitting time.)

We may find it hard relating to Zerubbabel or Jehozadak's son, but God's Word to them is also good for us. That's why God kept this message in the Bible. Perhaps we can relate to these two men if we consider a little background information.

Zerubbabel and Joshua were land developers of sorts. They were to manage the building of a temple to replace the one destroyed earlier by the Babylonians. That task might not seem overwhelming except for one thing: Solomon built the original temple. It was a huge, ornate, and splendid edifice.

The new builders worked with a drastically smaller budget. After they completed the foundation, some people complained about how it was shaping up. Naturally, their reaction discouraged Zerubbabel and Joshua. That's when God stepped in and said, "Be strong. I'll be with you. Now get back to work."

Do you find your work satisfying? Granted, not everyone has a job they enjoy. Is there anything else that you would rather be doing?

However you feel about your job, God's Word comes to you through Haggai. Your work is important, and you need to get busy again. God promises to be with you, and that implies much about the attitude and effort that you'll put into your work. So get back to work now. It's okay to smile. The best Helper is with you. Together you'll do a great job.

Singed, Soiled, and Saved

Then he showed me Joshua the high priest standing before the angel of the Lord, and Satan standing at his right hand to accuse him. And the Lord said to Satan, "The Lord rebuke you, O Satan! The Lord who has chosen Jerusalem rebuke you! Is not this a brand plucked from the fire?"
Zechariah 3:1–2

It's probably no surprise that whatever their working role, everyone is the same in God's sight. What we might not be so eager to confess, however, is that everyone is the same in the devil's sight too! Take Joshua, for example. Even a high priest couldn't escape the devil's indictments! How Satan must have contemplated his dramatic affect! He was really living up to his name, which, not surprisingly, means "accuser."

If there was one time when we would welcome Satan's lies, it would be when he prosecutes us before God. But the devil doesn't have to lie about us. The truth is enough to damn us to a death sentence. Like Joshua, we're nothing but a burning stick and one without a legitimate defense, at that.

Accusations are always unpleasant and even frightening. More so if they're true. Thank God we share something else with Joshua. Though singed by Satan's fire and soiled by our own dirty life, we're also saved. Jesus always has a ready ear for our self-accusations. We can confess all that we've done wrong—not that He doesn't already know. But as we tell Him how sorry we are and how much we hate our sins, we can also be confident that He forgives and energizes us to go on living in freedom. So next time the devil points his fiery finger at you, tell him to stick it in his ear. He'll be able to hear the Judge better.

Little Change

For I the Lord do not change; therefore you, O children of Jacob,
are not consumed. Malachi 3:6

Do you know anyone operating under the delusion that if they wait long enough, God will change? Kids are experts at applying this principle to parents and teachers. They know that the longer they ignore a request or command, the greater the likelihood that adults will abandon their efforts.

This, the last meditation in the series based on the Minor Prophets, features Malachi. Actually, like all other prophetic books, it features God speaking through a prophet. God is telling us what He has done for us and what He expects from us. God still expects people to love one another as He has loved them.

God really doesn't need our dollars and cents. However, He blesses us with money and expects us to support ourselves and share with others from what He gives. He knows that true giving doesn't come from the wallet, but from the heart. That was Malachi's message to God's selfish people too. A few verses after the ones above, we hear God accusing His people of robbery! Not only did they allow greed to govern their giving, but they gave half-heartedly.

God tells people of all generations what He has done. He tells us in plain English that He loves us and that He sent Jesus to take away our sins. That story will never change! But another story never changes either. It's the one where God's Word tells us to send missionaries throughout the world. And He doesn't want us to forget the physical needs of poverty-stricken people either. And while the tithe, or 10 percent, rule is an Old Testament law, giving from the heart is a changeless rule for all ages.

At your very next opportunity, give generously to God's work. And don't ask for any change—except a change of heart.

We Just Don't Know

Have you not known? Have you not heard? The Lord is the everlasting
God, the Creator of the ends of the earth. He does not faint or grow
weary; His understanding is unsearchable. Isaiah 40:28

By the time you read this, you're probably a bit fatigued. That's why
you're taking a break. Can you imagine what would happen if you
worked seven days a week, 24 hours each day? That's exactly how God operates.

We can't understand it—how God works, that is. Consider these questions: **Q:** Where did God come from? **A:** We just don't know. **Q:** How is the
Trinity possible? **A:** We don't even understand the question, much less the
answer. **Q:** How can anyone put in the time God does creating and maintaining the world? **A:** His ways aren't our ways. (Now you know.) **Q:** If Jesus
is God, and Jesus died on the cross, how is it possible that God could die?
A: Huh?

God left many things unknown. For our purposes, those things either
aren't important or they are left to faith as opposed to proof. What God wants
us to know is in the Bible. And it's all the important things. Consider these
questions: **Q:** Does God really love *me?* **A:** Yes. **Q:** Why? **A:** Now we're back to
unfathomable things again. **Q:** What did Jesus do for me? **A:** He took away
your sins through His life, death, and resurrection. **Q:** Why? **A:** Because He
loves you. **Q:** Me? **A:** Yes, and don't ask why. **Q:** Am I now His disciple? **A:** Yes.
Q: What should I do? **A:** Tell others that Jesus died to save them too. **Q:** What
happens next? **A:** Jesus will come again and take us to heaven. **Q:** How long
will we be gone? **A:** Forever. **Q:** You're not making this up, are you? **A:** No. It's
all in the Bible.

Q: Should I read it now? **A:** Not unless you want to stretch your coffee
break all the way to the unemployment office.

New Punctuation

*How long, O Lord? Will You forget me forever? How long will You hide
Your face from me? How long must I take counsel in my soul and have
sorrow in my heart all the day? Psalm 13:1–2a*

Have you ever wondered who invented punctuation marks? I haven't
either, and it's probably good that we don't know. Can you imagine
what it would cost if the inventor of the comma had patented the device and
we had to pay to use it? Then again, many modern students wouldn't spend
much according to current assessments.

After ages of commas, question marks, periods, and exclamation marks,
the time might be right to invent a new mark. The mark would represent a
question to which no current or complete answer exists. The new mark would
be useful for spiritual people like us. The psalmist David might have appreciated it too. He could have used it in passages such as: "How long, O Lord?
Will You forget me forever? How long will You hide Your face from me? How
long must I take counsel in my soul and have sorrow in my heart all the day?"
(Psalm 13:1–2a).

Let's examine each of David's questions. "Will You forget me forever?"
Those separated from loved ones might relate to David's anguish. Perhaps
you've even felt the ultimate loneliness—separation from God. Although people may be gone, they're often not forgotten. And we don't want them to forget us, either, though it sometimes seems that way. Perhaps it's a time when
our fervent prayers seem to go unnoticed. Has God forgotten us?

"How long will You hide Your face from me?" We might reason that our
perfect God cannot forget, so if He doesn't appear to hear our prayers, maybe
He is hiding from us. Have we done something unforgivable? Have we
exceeded our sin quota? Why don't You look at me when I'm talking, God?

"How long must I take counsel in my soul?" I read the Bible, but it does-
n't have the answers I want. Why don't You tell me more, Lord? I want to
know.

These questions shouldn't end with question marks. I'd like to suggest a
new mark that is actually an old symbol. It's a †. How do you like it? When
prayers don't get answered according to our schedule and when our curiosity
isn't satisfied by the Bible, we can look to the cross and end our questions
there. The one-and-only most-important answer was given at the cross. Wait
patiently. Someday we'll have all the answers. When God is ready.

April 28 〜

You Are Here

For if you keep silent at this time, relief and deliverance will rise for the
Jews from another place, but you and your father's house will perish.
And who knows whether you have not come to the kingdom for such
a time as this? Esther 4:14

Don't you love those signs in public places that proclaim "You Are Here?" If you get lost easily, the signs may offer token comfort. At least you know you are here even if you don't know where "here" is!

Have you sometimes wondered why you are here? Perhaps God has you in the right place at the right time just as He had Queen Esther.

Esther was one of many women "collected" into King Xerxes' harem. The king's crown must have twirled when he saw Esther because she immediately became his favorite. Xerxes made her his queen, but they probably never discussed family on their dates because the king didn't know Esther was Jewish. (This might have doomed their marriage from the start!) Some wicked officials plotted to exterminate the Jews, but Esther's uncle uncovered the conspiracy. He reported the evil to Esther, who probably said something like, "What can I do?" Her wise uncle answered her in the words of today's Bible reading.

Surely, you are here for some vital reasons too. Your mission is to work for the Holy Spirit, saving or sustaining the lives of your co-workers, family, and neighbors. You see, there is a devilish plot to exterminate them, and you're in the right place at the right time. You are here to declare and live the Gospel. You know that Jesus died to take away the sins of the world. You know that His sacrifice guarantees everlasting life to all believers. And now that you are here, you can share it all. Tell your friends, family, and coworkers about your Savior—even if they already know. Life is even better when everyone knows where they are.

A Little Culture

*Your boasting is not good. Do you not know that a little leaven leavens
the whole lump? Cleanse out the old leaven that you may be a new lump,
as you really are unleavened. For Christ, our Passover lamb, has been sacrificed. Let us therefore celebrate the festival, not with the old leaven,
the leaven of malice and evil, but with the unleavened bread of
sincerity and truth. 1 Corinthians 5:6–8*

Some social scientists predict that our culture will last another 200
years. Maybe they can tell us when it will start too! American culture
may suggest that we shouldn't get too much of a good thing; therefore, we
have a convenient excuse for not having much—culture, that is.

Before we hop on the culture bandwagon, we need to define the term.
Culture can refer to the finer things of civilization and society—music, literature, arts, technology, and yes, even religion. Culture also may be defined less
nobly—as in yogurt or yeast. Then there's the bottom stratus of culture—
mold and other oddities that frolic in petri dishes. In human form, sinners
match the last definition! Clearly, then, the word culture is used in different
ways. Perhaps we can use it several ways at once.

Paul warns Christians about "culture" in 1 Corinthians 5:6–8: "Your
boasting is not good. Do you not know that a little leaven leavens the whole
lump? Cleanse out the old leaven that you may be a new lump, as you really
are unleavened. For Christ, our Passover lamb, has been sacrificed. Let us
therefore celebrate the festival, not with the old leaven, the leaven of malice
and evil, but with the unleavened bread of sincerity and truth."

Jesus used a similar example of yeast's power to permeate when He
described how the worst features of society—even religious society—can
spread and negatively influence spiritual life. In less "politically correct"
terms, sinful society has the same effect on spiritual nourishment that yeast
would have if you swallowed it raw. Lots of gas. Bad gas.

Much sinfulness has seeped into religious life in the form of faulty doctrine, pride, self-sufficiency, and an emphasis on success rather than Scripture.

There's the other side of yeast too. It produces great bread when it's
allowed to work with good ingredients. Christian spiritual culture doesn't
have to be victimized by society. Christians can turn the tables and influence
society and its culture. We can share the Gospel along with the Law. The sincerity and truth to which Paul refers is the truth about Jesus. He came to save
all sinners, whether or not they have culture.

Revelation from Research

"Be faithful unto death, and I will give you the crown of life. He who has an ear, let him hear what the Spirit says to the churches. The one who conquers will not be hurt by the second death." Revelation 2:10–11

Church attendance prolongs life. A respected journal of public health studied longevity in two groups of people—those who regularly attended worship and those who didn't. The annual death rate was 36 percent higher in the group that didn't attend church regularly.

This study spanned 28 years and included more than 5,000 subjects. Actually, they could have discovered the same thing in a few minutes had they listened in Sunday school. (One side note: The government reacted favorably to this research because it can collect several more years of taxes from at least one segment of society.)

God revealed this: "Be faithful unto death, and I will give you the crown of life" (Revelation 2:10b). Remaining faithful to death usually includes a lifestyle of regular worship. Simply going to church, of course, doesn't guarantee salvation. Faithfulness includes trusting God, living according to His will, talking to Him regularly, loving and serving others and, because we aren't consistently good at any of the above, asking and accepting forgiveness.

The research study didn't differentiate between Christians and non-Christians. The results were solely attributed to healthier lifestyles and supportive social and emotional interaction. It only makes sense that happy and healthy people would live longer. But to be genuinely happy and healthy, we depend on faith. Oh, not our own. It's often weak and sickly. But God's faithfulness is what makes us live longer.

How old are you? Perhaps God has been faithful to you for many years. In fact, He was faithful even before you were! He sent the Holy Spirit to deliver faith to your soul. That faith soon circulated to your intellect and emotions, but it requires constant maintenance. God faithfully does that—by the day, even by the minute if necessary. He loves you even when you neglect or avoid Him. He also takes advantage of those times when you're weak or sick or depressed or disgusted to bring you closer to Himself.

God is faithful until death. Not His death, of course, but ours. Because of His faithfulness, we'll be another statistic that indicates longevity runs in God's faithful family. Those researchers were right. Faithful people do live a long time.

Nomads

*My brothers, if anyone among you wanders from the truth and someone
brings him back, let him know that whoever brings back a sinner from
his wandering will save his soul from death and will cover a multitude
of sins. James 5:19–20*

Sometimes you need to let your conscience be someone else's guide.
Every Christian spends some time as a spiritual nomad in need of a
guide.

James doesn't mince words. (Just read his short book if you don't believe
me.) He says that calling mutual believers to repentance will cover a multitude of sins. In other words, we are responsible for helping others see how
they've wandered. Most of them already know their way back and can probably return without our preaching, nagging, or any other -ing except praying.
The flip side, of course, is that we tend to wander too. (Have you noticed that
enormously attractive person over by the water cooler? Did that extra glass of
wine make you happier? Did you break the speed limit today? What did you
say under your breath when you made that last mistake? Repent, you sinner!)

While neither God nor James wants us to assist the devil in prosecuting
other sinners, our role is to watch out for others *for their own good.* Pointing
out every sin isn't the way to help others, but if we notice a trend away from
faithfulness and obedience, it's time to act. Spiritual wandering usually begins
in such small ways that wanderers don't even realize how nomadic they've
become. Being moved by the love of Christ we can pray and point the way. We
can remind the wanderers how much Jesus loves them, and ask them if they
really want to stray. We can always invite them back to the forgiveness that
Jesus so freely offers. And we can always share stories about the times we wandered away and what we found when we returned.

The Other Side of the Ditch

But a Samaritan, as he journeyed, came to where he was, and when he saw him, he had compassion. He went to him and bound up his wounds, pouring on oil and wine. Then he set him on his own animal and brought him to an inn and took care of him. Luke 10:33–34

Ancient Jews despised Samaritans; Samaritans weren't especially fond of Jews either. So when Jesus told about a wounded, pain-racked Jew who lay dying in a ditch, the last person you might expect to help was a Samaritan.

I wonder if anyone listening to Jesus that day dared to ask, "Why help?" Why risk helping others in such a dangerous and prejudiced society? Perhaps we can understand why if we get on the other side of the ditch. Lie down in the cold, stagnant water. See your blood mix with water and mud into a color God didn't include in the rainbow. Feel the mosquitoes and flies stick to your wounds. Try to crawl up where someone might help you. But how it hurts to breathe, much less move! What's that in the distance? Someone is coming! Perhaps . . . Well, I guess he was late for an appointment or something. Someone else is coming, perhaps . . .

Sin has beat us bloody. Satan has left us wallowing in filth with no hope for help. Modern society and science have many remedies and cures, but all are powerless to treat sin. The only One who can and will help is really foreign to us. He's perfect. A resident of heaven. Will He really stoop low enough to pick us up?

We already know the answer. God stooped all the way from heaven to give us Jesus. And Jesus stretched across some rough timbers to heal us. Now He leaves us in the care of the Holy Spirit, who delivers healing doses of the Gospel every day. Our Lord raised us from the ditch to love Him and serve others. Are there any better reasons for being a "Good Samaritan?"

May 3

Grave Dangers

A good name is better than precious ointment, and the day of death than the day of birth. It is better to go to the house of mourning than to go to the house of feasting, for this is the end of all mankind, and the living will lay it to heart. Sorrow is better than laughter, for by sadness of face the heart is made glad. The heart of the wise is in the house of mourning, but the heart of fools is in the house of mirth. Ecclesiastes 7:1–4

Okay, so it's not a good way to start a devotion, but today's title begs the question. For what kind of death do you hope? Most people hope to die of natural causes—you know, that's when you die naturally. There are some things worse than death, however. For some, it's life.

The wise writer of Ecclesiastes had an intriguing outlook on death. He talks about funerals in this passage: "It is better to go to the house of mourning than to go to the house of feasting, for this is the end of all mankind, and the living will lay it to heart" (Ecclesiastes 7:2).

That might seem morbid, especially coming from someone like Solomon, who had every reason to live festively. But Solomon understood that all people die. It's a natural consequence of living—with or without doctors. He advises us to anticipate our own passing—in a healthy way, of course.

Why think about death? One good reason is life. For example, how do you feel today? Have you been sick recently? What do you fear most in life—storms, loneliness, family crises, neighborhood violence, demonic drivers, cancer, your next dental visit? The list probably could go on, but suffice it to say that life isn't always what we would like it to be. Suffering is common. What do we say when someone dies after a particularly agonizing illness? "Well, at least she's at peace now."

Solomon warns of grave danger in loving life too much, probably because it can be so disappointing. But we also can experience peace alongside reality. We know death is temporary. But that suggests another grave danger—belief in reincarnation

Christ's reality, which He so graciously shares, is that death is just another stage of life. Moreover, it's the last unpleasant stage! We know that because Jesus returned to life, we also will live again. Which brings us to one last misconception about death—that we'll return as angels.

Not so. The Bible tells us that we'll have brand-new bodies and that we'll be ourselves. So don't worry about how you'll keep your halo straight or your wings strong. Don't avoid funerals because they're surrounded by sadness. In death's grief, we find the reality of the resurrection. Don't be so grave!

May 4

Lifetime Guarantee

*And I am sure of this, that He who began a good work in you will bring
it to completion at the day of Jesus Christ. Philippians 1:6*

Is your automobile covered by an extended warranty? Three miles or 30
minutes (whichever comes first) after the warranty expires, so will
your car!

God guarantees His workmanship. We can read the terms of the warranty
in Philippians. Note the period of coverage—until Christ returns. (Most of us
probably don't think the warranty expires any time soon, but Christ may
return before our next coffee break!) Like any guarantee, we should read this
one closely.

Christ began a good work in us—the work of setting us free from sin. He
placed faith in our hearts and gave us the Bible, Baptism, and the Lord's
Supper to carry on that good work. All this makes us confident that we will
continue to work as Christians until He returns and retires us from earthly
service. But while the warranty has its short form in Philippians, we find a
complete edition of it in the rest of the Bible. We find that this warranty, like
most, is limited.

The only unlimited part of the guarantee is that Christ died to take away
our sins. And it's true that the Holy Spirit brought us to faith and helps us
grow. But we can violate the guarantee by abusing God's workmanship. The
Bible chronicles many sad events when God's people decided they didn't
need the good work started in them. They followed other gods, refused to
obey the real God, and, in one very tragic instance, even betrayed the Savior.
Since history tends to repeat itself, we must guard against breaching our own
warranty too.

Put your confidence into action. Continue to study God's Word and worship Him. Confess your sins and accept His forgiveness. Thank God for giving you a lifetime guarantee.

Scum of the Earth

And we labor, working with our own hands. When reviled, we bless;
when persecuted, we endure; when slandered, we entreat. We have
become, and are still, like the scum of the world, the refuse of all things.
1 Corinthians 4:12–13

Picture this. You rise early in the morning, read your Bible, say your prayers, brush your teeth, and dress for the day. Doesn't it feel good to start your day with God? You go about your daily routine wearing the bright smile and airy attitude that Jesus' love placed in your heart. You treat those around you with dignity, respect, and friendliness. With Christ in your heart, your day is bound to blossom into fragrant, beautiful fruit of the Spirit—until someone poisons the atmosphere with ridicule or slander. "Wait," you say. "Something is wrong here. I'm a Christian. I'm nice to you and you appreciate it so much that you're nice to me. At least it's supposed to be that way, isn't it?"

St. Paul would understand. This letter to the Corinthians expressed the same experience, so we're in good company if some consider us the scum of the earth. Jesus understood too. While some welcomed and worshiped Him, others spit, slapped, mocked, and conspired. Persecution is a way of life for Christians. If you display and proclaim your Christ-centered focus on life, some will love you, some will tolerate you, some will avoid you, and others will persecute you.

Don't be afraid. Jesus stands with you. Remember how He answered jeers and reacted to the violence? He endured, blessed, and forgave. Christians like you have been doing this for centuries. Go ahead. Keep the Gospel evident in everything you do. You're in good company even when you're in bad company.

Don't Tell a Soul

They brought to Him a man who was deaf and had a speech impediment,
and they begged Him to lay His hand on him. And taking him aside from
the crowd privately, He put his fingers into his ears, and after spitting
touched his tongue. And looking up to heaven, He sighed and said to him,
"Ephphatha," that is, "Be opened." And his ears were opened, his tongue
was released, and he spoke plainly. And Jesus charged them to tell no one.
But the more He charged them, the more zealously they proclaimed it. And
they were astonished beyond measure, saying, "He has done all things well.
He even makes the deaf hear and the mute speak." Mark 7:32–37

Don't you love secrets? A secret makes you feel so important when you tell it to friends! Keeping secrets is difficult because you must forget the secret.

Several times during Jesus' ministry, He gave what seems a strange command. He wanted His work kept secret. Mark reports one such incident in the passage above.

Sometime after seeking to surround His ministry with secrecy, Jesus told His disciples to do just the opposite. He wanted them to tell the world about Him. So why the initial secrecy?

Perhaps Jesus didn't want to focus exclusive attention on His miracles. Crowds followed Him, hounded Him for healing from all types of sickness—physical and demonic. His great compassion never failed, but He probably worried that the crowds would miss His message about faith, forgiveness, and forever. That happens today, too, as people look for miracles to solve their problems. Faith healers and other miracle workers still ply the crowds, but how often is the message of salvation by grace alone hidden behind the mystery and marvel of miracles?

Jesus was more than just a miracle worker. Well, maybe not. What miracle was greater than God loving sinners so much that He sent His Son to take the form of a human and suffer and die for them? What a magnificent miracle was Christ's coming back to life, defeating death and the devil for us! Yet another miracle, one we personally have experienced—the miracle of faith! We have it not by our learning or goodness. (Thank God!) The Holy Spirit gave it to us. Not only that, but He nourishes us each day and keeps us close to Jesus.

Maybe the Holy Spirit wants you to share some "secrets" today. Go ahead, but just share your faith. Leave the miracles to Him.

The Good Old Days

We remember the fish we ate in Egypt that cost nothing, the cucumbers,
the melons, the leeks, the onions, and the garlic. Numbers 11:5

Remember the good old days? For the most part, a poor memory greatly enhances the good old days. However, some people have such perfect memories of the good old days that they even remember things that never happened! Let's review the good old days to see if we can find something truly good about them.

The best place to start is the beginning. Now those really were good old days. Husband and wife living in perfect harmony with each other and with God—in complete freedom. They were even free to disobey God. And that's where the trouble began. The first couple wasn't satisfied with their blessings. Eve was curious about the snake's invitation. Adam was curious about Eve's invitation. One bite into the forbidden fruit forever destroyed the good old days. But God remained good. He protected Adam and Eve, promised them a Savior, and gave them children.

The children of Israel longed for some good old days as they slaved in Egypt for Pharaoh. After 400 years God sent Moses to rescue them. But they soon forgot how precious their freedom was. As today's Bible text tells, they yearned for the bad old days. Later, God sent prophets to remind them of His good old promises. But the Israelites tried to relive the old days, to their own destruction.

The good old days aren't all bad, though. Among the best are Christmas, Good Friday, Easter and Pentecost—good old days we fondly celebrate yet today. As you remember the good old days, be sure to remember just how good they were. And confidently face the future knowing that the best days are yet to come.

Cobwebs

Ah, you who hide deep from the Lord your counsel, whose deeds are in the dark, and who say, "Who sees us? Who knows us?" Isaiah 29:15

It started as a few specks of dust. Soon it had grown into a gossamer cobweb. No time to take care of it now; you'll get it later. A week later you see it again and remember your pledge. But it can wait. Nearly anything is more important than cobwebs. Months pass and the cobweb remains. In fact, it has grown, perhaps so much that it's also strung between your ears! Ah. Ignorance is bliss and it's so good to be happy.

Let cobwebs remind us of sin. Sins may begin small, like specks of dust. It's hard to notice them, and they're nearly impossible to combat until they accumulate and knit together like a cobweb. At first, they may seem an illusion, just a shadow of unavoidable human nature. Then the illusion becomes a delusion. "What harm will a few sins do? Let them build up, and when I have enough, I'll take them to Jesus for disposal." But then, like cobwebs, our sins pile up, ignored and looming larger every day. We procrastinate, forget, or risk total disregard.

When it comes to sinfulness, we can't let "forget" come before "forgive." Jesus invites us to clean up our sin-filled corners daily. He knows all our corners, and there is no hiding. And even though He soils His holy hands with our dirt, He forgives our filthiness. Then He hands us a mop. With forgiveness accomplished, He gives us power to eliminate sin's sticky webs from our life. But once again, we must remain vigilant for sin, like dust, is stubborn, and it has a tendency to regroup.

Thank God that no cleaning job is beyond Jesus' power to cleanse. Brush away those sins as soon as you see them. Ask Jesus to help you shake the cobwebs loose.

Spiritual Economics

Now to the one who works, his wages are not counted as a gift but as his due. And to the one who does not work but trusts Him who justifies the ungodly, his faith is counted as righteousness. Romans 4:4–5

These days, we seem to need higher pay to pay the higher prices caused by higher pay (Economics 101). And take-home pay doesn't stay home long.

The Apostle Paul imparted a critical economics lesson to the believers in Rome. Wages aren't gifts. Employers agree to pay those who work for them. They rightfully expect diligence and effort. Workers rightfully expect pay that fairly compensates them for their thoughts and actions.

Spiritual economics operates in quite the opposite manner. Let's examine the implications of this supernatural economy.

By all appearances, those who work for their eternal living should be worthy of high reward. We might expect God to commend those who toil to earn His favor and a room in His executive suite. God, however, sees things differently. He notices flaws in what others perceive as goodness and quality. He knows when we resentfully attempt to do His will rather than eagerly work to serve Him. His annual evaluation (as if He needed to wait a year!) indicates the less-than-perfect and completely unsatisfactory exertion of our thoughts and deeds. That's why we need to quit the chores of earning salvation.

Our inability to do God's will dooms us. We cannot possibly work hard enough, contribute enough money, or say sufficient prayers to earn eternal living. God saves through faith, not work. We simply trust God, who sent Jesus Christ to work for us. God credits Jesus' work to us. Talk about unearned income! Jesus made us truly wealthy, and now we have ample free time to use that wealth. Perhaps it's time to stop reading and go on a spending spree!

Misery Loves Company

He had to be made like His brothers in every respect, so that He might
become a merciful and faithful high priest in the service of God, to make
propitiation for the sins of the people. For because He Himself has suffered
when tempted, He is able to help those who are being tempted.
Hebrews 2:17–18

D on't say you haven't been told! Flee from temptation. Run from it!
Needless to say, speed records aren't endangered by people racing
from temptation. In fact, most who run from temptation leave an obvious
trail for new temptations to follow. Then there are those who are ever vigilant
for temptation. The more they see, the better it looks!

Temptation is an ever-present fact of life. While sinful enticements change
specifications with each passing stage of life, their basic allure and potential
destructiveness remain the same. For example, children seem beset by temptations to challenge authority. Not coincidentally, their decisions often conflict with what their parents would decide.

Next, we have young adult temptations so frequently associated with sexual matters and justified by claims of personal freedom. Middle-age temptations continue with much of the same and add financial discontent, career
pressures to succeed at any cost, and anxieties associated with both. Then
comes old age. It seems that in old age, hope sags along with everything else.

Those outside Christian circles, as well as those within, sometimes think
that Christians should somehow be devoid of temptation. But listen to what
the book of Hebrews has to say: "For because He Himself has suffered when
tempted, He is able to help those who are being tempted" (2:18).

The "He Himself" is Jesus. He suffered human temptations during childhood, adolescence, and young adulthood. In fact, He probably suffered more.
The Bible relates how the devil gave Jesus personal attention! If misery loves
company, Jesus is right there with us. But don't despair.

One resource Jesus provides to fight temptation is communication. He
willingly listens when we share what tempts us most. Perhaps He'll remove
that temptation from the devil's repertoire; perhaps He'll strengthen us by letting us struggle more with it.

Another "temptation tool" is what Jesus used in His personal battle with
Satan—God's Word. When we know what the Scriptures say, we're able to
fling those words at the devil just as Jesus did. The catch, of course, is that we
need to know what the Bible says. You're working on that now as you meditate, but get involved in Bible classes and daily Bible reading too. Misery does-
n't really love company, but Jesus does.

Take That!

Do not repay evil for evil or reviling for reviling, but on the contrary, bless, for to this you were called, that you may obtain a blessing. 1 Peter 3:9

You only need to drive through a metropolitan area to discover a significant urban maxim: It's easier to forgive once you've gotten even. What is it that motivates us to get revenge? Before we impulsively agree with the passage from first Peter, we need to assess our own R.Q.—revenge quotient. (Anyone who drives, works, or breathes should get high marks here.)

Unless you have already absorbed 1 Peter 3:9 into your temper cells, you may have already qualified for the revenge award. For example, you're exercising safe driving habits (including using your turn signal before you cut someone off, driving only five miles over the speed limit, etc.) when a impatient fool roars alongside, glares in your direction, holds the steering wheel with one hand, and delivers an emphatic hand gesture with the other hand. What is your immediate reaction?

The workplace affords ample opportunity for reprisals too. And if that's not enough, home can be the scene of the most meaningful, permanent, and satisfying retaliation. But if revenge is so sweet, why does it make life so sour?

We Christians have power to retaliate in a God-pleasing way when people mistreat us. We can repay insults with blessings; hand gestures with an apologetic wave; scowls with smiles; slights with compliments; mistreatment with kindness; unfairness with grace; meanness with mercy; bitterness with forgiveness.

At first, our reactions will surprise—and possibly anger—our antagonists. But it's a great way sharing Christ's love with others.

May 12

Lawless

For Christ is the end of the law for righteousness to everyone who believes.
Romans 10:4

Although our legislature backs laws, it is powerless to bring about obedience. Crowded courts and jammed jails provide ample testimony to the efficacy of law.

Even if laws govern our actions, they never completely govern our hearts. And that's what Paul was getting at when He wrote to the Romans. Paul told them that the law is great for exposing our sinfulness and condemning us to hell, but it doesn't have power to bring the kind of obedience that God expects.

Paul knew much about the law. If ever there was a devoted law-abider, it was Paul. He was an honor student in the synagogue. He obeyed all the Jewish laws perfectly to the letter. And he vehemently prosecuted (or was that persecuted?) those who didn't. Paul thought he was perfect. But Paul's heart was bad. He didn't believe in Jesus—until God knocked him off his high horse. When Paul emerged from the blindness that accompanied his fall, he saw God's law in a brand-new light. Scrutiny under God's Law showed Paul he was fooling himself, he wasn't perfect, and that the law didn't help him one bit.

Like Paul, we need to throw ourselves on God's mercy. Any attempt to conduct a loving relationship with God is futile without Jesus. Jesus ended the law in that He saved us from the eternal consequence of our failure to keep it. He obeyed it perfectly and shared that obedience with us. Now we are judged as He is—righteous. Now we have a loving relationship with God, not because we've been so good, but because we've been so blessed. And God still empowers us to obey Him. We want to obey Him too. But salvation is already ours.

Branch Office

Hear now, O Joshua the high priest, you and your friends who sit before
you, for they are men who are a sign: behold, I will bring my servant the
Branch. For behold, on the stone that I have set before Joshua, on a single
stone with seven eyes, I will engrave its inscription, declares the Lord of
hosts, and I will remove the iniquity of this land in a single day. In that
day, declares the Lord of hosts, every one of you will invite his neighbor to
come under his vine and under his fig tree." Zechariah 3:8–10

You've heard the one about the forestry company that opened a branch office reserved for small jobs only? Alas, there was so little business that most employees packed their trunks and took leave. (It's knot polite to groan!)

Now might be a good time to introduce the first of today's Bible passages. "Hear now, O Joshua the high priest, you and your friends who sit before you, for they are men who are a sign: behold, I will bring my servant the Branch" (Zechariah 3:8). Many years later, Jesus revealed Himself as that branch. From Him would grow and prosper a new way of thinking and living. In Zechariah's years and through the ages (including the present time), people knew much more about sin than about mercy and forgiveness. They especially knew about sins committed by others, and they freely unveiled these for all to see. The Branch tried to change all this and ended up nailed to a tree. This didn't stop Him from opening global Branch offices.

It began with His closest friends and spread to many more disciples and on to anyone who would listen. Branch offices sprung up anywhere Christians witnessed their faith. It's like Zechariah reported: "In that day, declares the Lord of hosts, every one of you will invite his neighbor to come under his vine and under his fig tree" (Zechariah 3:10).

Reposed in the shade of God's love through Jesus Christ, Christians can spread the Good News of eternal life wherever they are. That's how faith spreads, with the Holy Spirit's help. Each of us is a branch office for Christ. We're part of a vast network of disciples with a long history and a bright future.

You know what sin did to you and what it would still like to do. Everything bad in life is a result of sinfulness. You also know what Jesus did for you when He died and rose to break the bonds of sin. You have the hope—the sure hope—of eternal life in the presence of Jesus, who loves you more than anyone can imagine.

Find a way to branch out and tell how you feel and what you know about the Branch Manager. You may find yourself out on a limb, but He's sure to keep you from falling.

Faceless Names

Vanity of vanities, says the Preacher, vanity of vanities! All is vanity.
Ecclesiastes 1:2

Have you ever walked through a cemetery and wondered about the people resting there? What they looked like? Where they worked? What they accomplished? Now read the Bible passage again.

This isn't starting out well if you anticipated an uplifting meditation today. Persevere. It gets better even though we read the cry of a disenchanted king once known for his wisdom and affluence. Now he believes that all his achievements and possessions are meaningless. Solomon wasn't always that way.

God blessed King Solomon with incredible peace and prosperity for as long as the king acknowledged and worshiped the one true King. As years passed, Solomon abandoned some of His wisdom. And as he approached death, his ears probably rang with a proverb still familiar today—"You can't take it with you."

Think for a moment of all the great inventors you can remember. (Unless you're a historian, it won't take long.) Who created the microwave oven, the nonstick frying pan, and the stethoscope? Who devised our monetary system, forged the first track spike, and mixed the first soft drink? As important as these events are, we've already forgotten the originators and someday society will also forget the invention.

Only a few events are meaningful for all ages. The first seven days of God's earthly creations. Christmas. Easter. And one more—the day each of us came to faith. God chose us before He created camels. He planned to send our Savior even before He hung the first apple. The Holy Spirit knew just where and when to find us well before the first brook babbled. God's love and His work are never meaningless. May God continue to fill our lives with meaning as each day He renews and strengthens our faith.

Broken Hearts

*The sacrifices of God are a broken spirit; a broken and contrite heart, O
God, You will not despise. Psalm 51:17*

How often love results in broken hearts! For Christians, however, broken hearts result in love. Psalm 51 says so. But why would God want a lot of brokenhearted believers around?

The deepest crevice in our heart is the chasm caused by our sins. It's how we feel about our sins that Psalm 51 addresses. God is pleased by heartfelt confession, remorse, and the will to forsake sinfulness.

Confession is the first crack in a broken heart. Some of us prefer to line up in the fast-confession lane—the one for five sins or less. But if we're honest, we probably come to the Lord with a cartload of transgressions every day. How can we ever pay for what we've done? Yet we need not worry because Jesus pays the price in full.

Remorse is confession's first cousin and a second chink in sin-hardened hearts. We all know people who quickly confess wrongdoing in hopes of escaping consequences. Christians, however, experience contrition and remorse as they think about their willful, weak, or even inadvertent lapses into the very things that nailed our Savior to the cross. If our heart condition ended here, though, every Christian would be woefully depressed.

Broken hearts begin to heal when Christ comes into our lives. We abandon sinfulness when we hate the wrong that we do and ask the Holy Spirit to help us resist sins—especially our chronic ones. Of course, Jesus perfected the procedure for healing broken hearts long ago on that ugly hill. He mends our broken hearts with forgiveness and sends us to proclaim healing to others with broken hearts.

Why does God cherish broken hearts? They're the only kind that can be fixed.

Collision Course

Therefore, as you received Christ Jesus the Lord, so walk in Him, rooted and built up in Him and established in the faith, just as you were taught, abounding in thanksgiving. See to it that no one takes you captive by philosophy and empty deceit, according to human tradition, according to the elemental spirits of the world, and not according to Christ.
Colossians 2:6–8

A young girl was reciting the books of the New Testament for her Sunday school teacher. "Matthew, Mark, Luke, . . . Galatians, Ephesians, Philippians, Collisions . . ." A mispronunciation or a profound statement?

Christian faith and the Holy Scriptures are on a collision course with the world. So much of worldly philosophy appeals to our flesh. As the entertainment industry leaves less and less to our imagination, we're tempted to minimize God's will in favor of lust.

Temptations just love to collide with us Christians, getting our attention during weak moments and when we least expect them. Should we fight with words of faith and Scripture, our smiling enemies still wound our feelings with their laughs.

Paul prods us to reach back into our memories. No, he probably wouldn't be impressed by our ability to correctly pronounce Habakkuk—or Colossians for that matter. But he does urge us to remember how the Holy Spirit gave us faith and what God created us to do.

Faith is like an airbag. It doesn't prevent collisions, but it softens the jolt. The Holy Spirit equipped us to withstand clashes with modern immorality and idolatrous philosophies. He taught us to stand up for what we believe, and He gave us an arsenal of love and good deeds to use on those with whom we collide. We may be on a collision course with the world, but now the Holy Spirit empowers us to make a bigger impact!

The Snub

"So everyone who acknowledges Me before men, I also will acknowledge before My Father who is in heaven, but whoever denies Me before men, I also will deny before My Father who is in heaven." Matthew 10:32–33

It leaves emotional bruises that sometimes last for years. Perhaps you've experienced it yourself. Maybe it was the time you were with several acquaintances. They agreed to meet for lunch next Tuesday, but they didn't say, "See you then." Or it could be that child who is just too grown-up to associate with you anymore. He doesn't want you to park too close when you pick him up after school; his friends might see you. Or it might be during that dinner at church when the pastor recognizes several volunteers for their generous service. You've done more but don't get even a smile.

Snubs aren't just emotional dings; they're serious business, especially when applied to our Savior. Jesus said, "So everyone who acknowledges Me before men, I also will acknowledge before My Father who is in heaven, but whoever denies Me before men, I also will deny before My Father who is in heaven" (Matthew 10:32–33).

Snubs may seem to be innocent mistakes, but sometimes they are expressions of conceit. Even conceited people don't like conceited people; of course, they're too conceited to know they're conceited. Right? You may know several conceited individuals, but do you know anyone so conceited she sends her parents a "congratulations" card on her birthday? (I don't either, but we need a little humor to break the tension.) Conceit is when people are all wrapped up in themselves. Not only are such people overdressed, they're often muffled from reality.

So far, today's message has been about other people, right? It's been about the conceited ones who wouldn't give Jesus an invitation to dinner because He dressed oddly, right? We wouldn't be that way . . . or would we?

Most of us could confess that we occasionally snub our Savior. We might do it when we ignore His holy presence during a crude conversation with our friends. Our snub might come when we discuss our problems with everyone but Him. Or perhaps we go out of our way to visit friends and relatives and neglect a short trip to church or the family altar.

Despite our guilt and our shabby treatment of Jesus, He doesn't snub us. He's like that friendly puppy that wags its tail in our direction though we shout and swing newspapers at it. He loves us, and He will to the end. That's nothing to snub our nose at.

Caught in the Middle

But sexual immorality and all impurity or covetousness must not even be
named among you, as is proper among saints. . . . For you may be sure of
this, that everyone who is sexually immoral or impure, or who is covetous
(that is, an idolater), has no inheritance in the kingdom of Christ
and God. Ephesians 5:3, 5

Some people sow enough wild oats to feed every underdeveloped nation on the planet! Thank heavens this meditation isn't about us though. A quick check against today's Bible passage places us in good standing—or at least uttering a sigh of relief.

First, Paul excludes from God's kingdom those who are sexually immoral. ("What is immorality anyway? Doesn't society shape the concept of right and wrong? And who am I to say that certain sexual preferences are immoral? And I can have my fantasies too—just as long as I don't hurt anybody. Besides, I do go to church every Sunday.")

Justifying ourselves on sexual morality, we might proceed to evaluate our greediness. ("Not me. I've fought and scratched for everything I got. It's mine and I intend to keep it. But I'm not greedy.")

Even if we find our heavenly inheritance safe on grounds of good—or at least acceptable—behavior, we can't breathe too easily yet. We're about to get caught in the middle—the verse that comes between 3 and 5. Here it is: "Nor should there be obscenity, foolish talk or coarse joking, which are out of place, but rather thanksgiving."

Now that about does it. There is only one thing to do. Give up.

Give up figuring out how to escape God's anger and rejection. Give up to Jesus, who forgives *every* sin. Finally, give up your sins. Call on the Holy Spirit for help, and hate them out of existence. Take your wild oats to God and pray for a crop failure.

Remember Who Raised You

Now to Him who is able to keep you from stumbling and to present you blameless before the presence of His glory with great joy, to the only God, our Savior, through Jesus Christ our Lord, be glory, majesty, dominion, and authority, before all time and now and forever. Amen. Jude 1:24–25

Who raised you? Your parents? Perhaps you grew up with relatives or adoptive parents. Whoever raised you, you remember the experiences of growing up. Were you one of those children who listened to your parents only when they whispered? Much of the good we experienced came during years when our ability to remember wasn't yet well formed. (That period lasts at least until 40.)

Imagine, then, those early days when you were learning to walk. You crawled on your knees to your launch pad—a couch, easy chair, or coffee table. Flexing your wispy biceps, you pulled yourself up. Standing is half the battle. Mom and dad were so pleased they decided to help (even if you didn't ask). They reached down took your tiny hands, stretched out your arms, and helped you hobble your first steps. How comforting to have those big hands guiding and supporting you in this exciting new phase of life!

Look at today's Bible verse again. Our heavenly Father is the "Him" who keeps us from falling. As we grow in faith, it's good to remember our humble beginnings as well as our fragile progress. Our loving Father reaches down to help us on our walk with Jesus. He provided the support that guided our first steps, and He continues to uphold us as we toddle, walk, run and stumble, limp, and trip through life. Like Jude, we thank Him for keeping us going. And like Christians throughout history, we look forward to the time we can walk completely on our own. Of course, we must wait a while longer—until our Father raises us for good.

How to Get God's Goat

And Aaron shall present the goat on which the lot fell for the Lord and use it as a sin offering, but the goat on which the lot fell for Azazel shall be presented alive before the Lord to make atonement over it, that it may be sent away into the wilderness to Azazel. Leviticus 16:9–10

Yom Kippur is the day when Aaron got God's goat—a holy festival known as the Day of Atonement. The festival begins with two goats. One is sacrificed for the people's sins. The other is set free because of the sacrifice. This symbolic festival celebrated God's plan for His people through the sacrifice of Jesus Christ.

Christians don't celebrate Yom Kippur because Easter replaced it. But it's good to remember the symbolism of Yom Kippur as it suggests how we too, can get God's goat.

We may feel sorry for the poor goat whose lot it was to die for the sins of God's people. This goat was no useless stray, nor had it committed any mischief that contributed to its death. It was a perfect specimen that could have lived a long, productive life. The goat was given to God as an offering so they could receive the forgiveness of the Lord. How easy it is to see Jesus fitting this picture. The only perfect human, both God and man, dying an undeserved death as a sacrifice.

Perhaps we're happier thinking about the goat turned loose, living its remaining days in freedom. We're like that goat. With sins forgiven through Jesus' sacrifice, we gallop off to live as His children forever. Through God's mercy, we escape the burden of our sins. But even in our freedom, we wander through the perils of life in a desert. Like snakes and scorpions, sin either stalks us or just waits until we step on it. But God is with us just as He remained with His Son. We can call on God when sin strikes. So go ahead, get God's holy Goat anytime you need Him.

Tell a Vision

[Zechariah] was chosen by lot to enter the temple of the Lord and burn incense. . . . And there appeared to him an angel of the Lord standing on the right side of the altar of incense. And Zechariah was troubled when he saw him, and fear fell upon him. But the angel said to him, "Do not be afraid, Zechariah, for your prayer has been heard, and your wife Elizabeth will bear you a son, and you shall call his name John." Luke 1:8–13

Early to be bed and early to rise means the TV won't televise!

Most TV programs at the time of this writing (compare it with current shows) involve holdups. Either criminals are holding up victims or doctors are holding up x-rays.

If you're an avid television fan, perhaps you've wondered what people did in the BC (before channels) era. How could anyone be happy without this technology that transforms invisible signals into visions of things such as millionaire sports heroes dribbling tobacco down their chins? You may be happy to know that some of our biblical brothers and sisters had visions without the benefit of cable or satellite. Here is an account from Luke 1:10–13a: "And the whole multitude of the people were praying outside at the hour of incense. And there appeared to him an angel of the Lord standing on the right side of the altar of incense. And Zechariah was troubled when he saw him, and fear fell upon him. But the angel said to him, 'Do not be afraid, Zechariah, for your prayer has been heard.'"

Prayers are almost like a television experience. The TV set loiters in the room. When you turn it on, picture and sound appear. It's almost like a vision is just waiting to be used. In a similar way, God waits around heaven (rather than Hollywood), waiting for you to contact Him.

Zechariah actually saw the messenger who reported God's answer to his prayer. So frightening was it for Zechariah, and so incredible, that he was speechless for nine months afterward! We might not want to see the messenger who reports answers to our prayers, but Zechariah's experience assures us that God is real and that He does respond to prayer.

It's no less miraculous when God answers our prayers, even if it is less dramatic. Like Zechariah, we might hesitate to believe our ears when God says that He's taken action on our behalf. But God loves us for the sake of Jesus, who died and rose to take away our sins. God will give you vision for the future as He answers your prayers. When He does, don't keep the news to yourself. Tell a vision to friends and give the Sponsor all the credit He deserves.

Justin Time

Do not think to yourself that in the king's palace you will escape any more than all the other Jews. For if you keep silent at this time, relief and deliverance will rise for the Jews from another place, but you and your father's house will perish. And who knows whether you have not come to the kingdom for such a time as this? Esther 4:13–14

Who is Justin Time?

A. The inventor of the wristwatch

B. A songwriter

C. A spelling mistake

D. A recent concept of warehousing and inventory

If you answered A or B, you're an incurable victim of puns. If you read the chapter from Esther, you know that she was just in time. Remember what Mordecai said to Esther? "Do not think to yourself that in the king's palace you will escape any more than all the other Jews. For if you keep silent at this time, relief and deliverance will rise for the Jews from another place, but you and your father's house will perish. And who knows whether you have not come to the kingdom for such a time as this?" (Esther 4:13–14). Esther's timeliness saved the whole Jewish population!

The answer to our quiz is also D. Manufacturers have discovered that supplying items "just in time" to meet demand, saves money on storage and inventory.

Just in time. That's part of God's efficiency too. He acts for people exactly when they need Him. The Old Testament reports many "just in times": Abraham about to sacrifice his son; Moses and the Israelites standing before the Red Sea; and David confronted by a king bent on murder. We hear of it in the New Testament, too, especially when "just in time" refers to Jesus, who came at precisely the right time to save us.

The "just-in-time" concept continues with us. As with Esther, God placed us on earth for a reason—a reason that includes sharing the Good News with family, friends, strangers, and even those whom we dislike. Maybe we're here for an even more sensational reason, such as saving someone's life or serving the Savior under difficult circumstances.

When Jesus returns for the world's end, it will be just in time too. No one, not even the angels, know when that time is. Time will tell, and by the time you read this, time may already have told! One thing is certain: Jesus will come just in time. Just in time for the end—of time, that is.

A Good Fight

Fight the good fight of the faith. Take hold of the eternal life to which you were called and about which you made the good confession in the presence of many witnesses. 1 Timothy 6:12

Anger normally surfaces with "fightin' words." But have you noticed that "fightin' words" often produce the best speech you'll ever regret? Most of us would agree that blowing our stack results only in air pollution. But there's nothing like a good fight to protect our faith.

A surefire recipe for a gourmet fray is to combine two young children with one ball. First, one child grabs the ball. This normally results in rapid combustion of the other child's temper. Soon, both lay hold of the ball and engage in a war of tugs, pushes, swipes, and shrill exclamations. How intently both tussle for possession!

While we don't condone battles among children, their example is similar to what Paul suggested to young Timothy. Our faith involved a bloody and deadly battle. The fight occurred on a smelly hill beyond the walls of Jerusalem. To those who witnessed the battle, it seemed the devil had the upper hand. It was all over in six hours. The one on whom generations counted for victory was dead, and the devil danced.

The devil danced with his eyes closed, though, because he didn't see God at work. The death of Jesus was God's way of winning. And to prove it, He raised Jesus from the dead. How Satan's steamy smile must have melted into a fiery frown! Jesus was alive and only sin's power remained in the grave.

The devil isn't dead, and like a vicious animal, he's dangerous when wounded. We will surely fight him before Jesus returns. We can jab with two rights and a left, but that won't be effective. What we really need are "fightin' words." What shall we say? A simple "Jesus Christ" will do.

Epic Proportions

In the beginning, God created the heavens and the earth. Genesis 1:1

It's been a while since the last meditational mini-series, so perhaps you're ready for another one. During the next seven days, we'll relate God's creativity to everyday life. Ready?

We usually think that life began during the six days of creation. Actually, life never began. It always was. That's what we mean when we say that God is eternal. He has neither beginning nor end. That's impossible to understand, so we're left with what Christians have always been left with—faith. Good thing God didn't attempt to explain eternity. Instead, He explained our origins in terms even we could understand. He began with our planet and our universe. "In the beginning"—our beginning—God created the universe.

Do you suppose God enjoyed His work? God's job was so complex that scientists have spent too much time trying to discover the formula for creation. Perhaps God's awesome work should inspire us to ponder our own work.

Most readers of this book have a job at home or in a workplace. (Jobs also provide the only organized way to conduct coffee breaks!) What do you create on the job? Columns of numbers? A clean house? Loaded trucks and railroad cars? Empty trucks and railroad cars? Decisions? More work for someone else? Welded connections? Smarter students? Smooth highways? And how do you approach your daily labor? Those who rely on the quality of your work might hope that you're as conscientious and skilled as the one who created everything.

God made our universe for the same reason that we create goods or services—to glorify Him. That implies something about the quality of our work. As we conclude our coffee break, recall how God so lovingly fashioned a universe for His glory and our existence. He did everything right for us. Now we can return the blessing.

May 25

The Sky Is the Limit

*And God said, "Let there be an expanse in the midst of the waters, and
let it separate the waters from the waters." And God made the expanse
and separated the waters that were under the expanse from the waters
that were above the expanse. And it was so. And God called the expanse
Heaven. And there was evening and there was morning, the second day.*
Genesis 1:6–8

The sky is great for holding things like clouds, sunbeams, and blimps.
It also provides the air we breathe, filters out harmful rays from the
sun, and insulates us from extreme temperatures. The sky is a window
through which we peer into outer space with all its stars, planets, and space
debris. It's clear that the sky (though not always clear) is another of God's
vital, intricate, and comprehensive creations.

God spared nothing when He lavished His love on us. The sky was the
limit. (Not really. Even the sky can't limit God's mercy and grace.)

I wonder how blue the sky was when Adam sucked in his first breath.
Chances are, it seemed even bluer when he woke up next to the woman God
gave Him to love! And after 40 overcast, rainy days, I wonder how Noah felt
when he saw the first patches of dry, blue sky. We even know what the sky was
like some 2,000 years ago on a very particular Friday afternoon near the city
of Jerusalem. Darkness covered the heavens, from 12:00 until 3:00. But blue
skies brightened the bleak cemetery with a curiously empty tomb on the following Sunday.

We relate the sky so easily to our emotions. We Christians should enjoy
perpetually sunny and clear skies, but gloom and gray are far too normal.
Even when little dark clouds hover overhead, we have the reality of Jesus our
Savior shining above it all. Isn't it good to know that He's always there, even
when we can't see Him?

God's Produce Department

And God said, "Let the waters under the heavens be gathered together
into one place, and let the dry land appear." And it was so. God called
the dry land Earth, and the waters that were gathered together He called
Seas. And God saw that it was good. . . . The earth brought forth vegeta-
tion, plants yielding seed according to their own kinds, and trees bearing
fruit in which is their seed, each according to its kind.
And God saw that it was good. Genesis 1:9–10, 12

Imagine yourself back on Tuesday of God's creative week. Like a gardener anxious to plant the first seeds of spring, God wasted no time in garnishing the land with grasses, herbs, flowers, vines, and trees of all kinds. Then He gave plants the ability to reproduce themselves. He planted them, and they carried on with His blessing.

God thought of us on that first Tuesday too. Not just the collective "us" but each individual one of us. Oh yes, He knew all about us then, but that need not frighten us. Like the plants that provided veggies and fruit, He blessed us with the ability to grow and blossom. Now He wants us to carry on.

The Bible says that the gift of faith produces fruit. Confident that the Holy Spirit has planted faith in us, we're ready to bloom with what Paul called the "fruit of the Spirit"—love, joy, peace, patience, kindness, goodness, faithfulness, gentleness, and self-control (Galatians 5:22–23). This is the fruit Jesus produced so perfectly during His earthly ministry. His death and resurrection equipped us to continue His ministry. We can plant new Christians as the Holy Spirit commissions us to share our faith, and we can also strengthen spindly believers through prayer and witness.

Next time you're enjoying a juicy peach or crisp green beans, thank God for the produce He produced. But also remember to imitate what you eat. Be fruitful and feed others with the Gospel that made you grow.

Making Time Count

*And God said, "Let there be lights in the expanse of the heavens to sepa-
rate the day from the night. And let them be for signs and for seasons,
and for days and years." Genesis 1:14*

Time probably ranks second only to money as the most valuable com-
modity in America. Whom can we thank for time? Why God, of
course. He invented it on the fourth day of creation week. Like everything else
God created, time is a blessing.

Instead of counting minutes, we need to make minutes count. God gave
each of us time on earth to accomplish His will—to grow in faith, study His
Word, share the Gospel, and serve other people. In so doing, we glorify Him
and live a useful life. But why should we spend what little time we have doing
God's will when there is so much to see and do?

God has been around a long. (No, I didn't forget to complete the sentence. Remember, time does not exist for God.) Even before time began God
was thinking of us. He knew when and where we would be born. He knew
that the Holy Spirit would give us faith. He also knew we would be sinners,
so He sent Jesus to take away our sins. Jesus spent all His time on earth living
the life we couldn't, and suffering the torment we deserve. Therefore, it
appears we have sufficient motivation to spend our time serving Him who
served us. How do we do that?

Making time count involves setting aside a portion of each day for prayer
and part of our week for worship. More than that, we make time count when
we give it all back to the Lord. But please don't quit your job and set up camp
in church. We really make time count when we're out in the world on our
jobs, shopping, or even traveling on vacation. Wherever we are, the Holy
Spirit empowers us to declare and demonstrate the Good News about Jesus.
The time is coming when our watches will stop but our joy will continue forever.

Believe It or Not

And God said, "Let the waters swarm with swarms of living creatures,
and let birds fly above the earth across the expanse of the heavens."
Genesis 1:20

Every time we see a guppy or listen to a macaw, we can imagine what it was like in the beginning, when God told every kind of sea creature to begin flipping and every fowl to start flapping. It was probably the beginning of noise too, as dolphins squeaked, hummingbirds hummed, robins chirped, crows cawed, and parrots asked for crackers (which hadn't been invented yet.)

You have undoubtedly noticed that the Bible doesn't provide many details about God's creativity. (Can you imagine the media hype if God had created reporters before robins?) For that matter, the Bible also reveals other important information without benefit of illustrations or blueprints. God leaves our acceptance of such biblical reports to something else He created—faith.

Most of us believe that God sent Jesus to rescue us. We believe that Jesus died to take away our sins, that He came to life again, and that He will return some day. That same faith can be applied to other biblical truths of less immediate importance—such as the six day, utterly comprehensive creation. Yet some people pick and choose which parts of the Bible to believe—especially if they think their eternal life doesn't depend on it.

Make no mistake. God expects us to believe the unbelievable—all of it. For if we doubt the creation epic, the parting of the Red Sea, or Jonah in the belly of a fish, we open our minds to doubt other portions of the Bible that deal with our personal salvation more directly. Conclude this meditation with a prayer that the Holy Spirit fill you with enough faith to believe all the wonderful, unbelievable stories in the Bible. Then get back to work. Your employer expects you to be fruitful too.

May 29

Busy, Busy, Busy

And God said, "Let the earth bring forth living creatures according to their kinds—livestock and creeping things and beasts of the earth according to their kinds." And it was so. . . . Then God said, "Let Us make man in Our image, after Our likeness. And let them have dominion over the fish of the sea and over the birds of the heavens and over the livestock and over all the earth and over every creeping thing that creeps on the earth." Genesis 1:24, 26

I wonder if Friday left God as breathless as it leaves us. From the minute aphid to the largest dinosaur, God made all the land animals right before the weekend. If you've ever nursed aching feet after trekking through a zoo, you especially appreciate the abundance of God's living and breathing works of nature. But God also reserved the sixth day to fashion His most prized creation—people!

Did you notice the "Let *Us* make man . . ." God the Father, Son, and Holy Spirit formed a conglomerate to make humans. After all, God wanted to make people in His own image! And God wanted humans to keep busy for the life of the earth. They were to manage God's creation. That should have been enough to keep people out of trouble. But it didn't take long before sin bruised and battered the wonderful creation of God. Yet God retained His original goal for us—to be His children, manage His blessings, and be the prize of His creation. That should be enough to keep us busy!

Busy as we may be with God's business, the devil remains busy trying to disrupt us—usually with much success. Thank God that He's never too busy to continue creating—creating new hearts cleaned by Jesus' blood—creating new energy to serve Him—creating new blessings for us to manage even after we ruin the old ones. When you think about it, we've got quite an image to uphold.

Rest Assured

And on the seventh day God finished His work that He had done, and He rested on the seventh day from all His work that He had done. So God blessed the seventh day and made it holy, because on it God rested from all His work that He had done in creation. Genesis 2:2–3

History isn't what it used to be. The way history is advancing, nearly every day is the anniversary of something terrible! Of course, it doesn't have to be that way—not when history is actually *His story.*

Even for many unbelievers, the Bible is a history book. Most history books record human achievement. It's probably safe to claim that only one history—His story—says anything about the achiever resting. God certainly deserved a rest. After all, He created everything as far as the eye could see and a few things that eyes couldn't see.

God's story is the history of love. His story reveals how He created everything perfect for His people to enjoy. God's story is the history of forgiveness, for soon after creation the apples of His eye turned sour with sin. Even while they were sinners without a clue as to what would happen next, God forgave them. God's story is a history of promises and promise-keeping. He promised a Savior who would bring humanity back into God's image, and He fulfilled that promise on a day historians call Christmas. God's story is one of sacrifice, for He came to earth in a form we humans could understand. He suffered, died, and was buried. But God's story is also one of victory because He rose from the grave, and He rose from the earth into the heavens where He remains our powerful Creator and Savior. God may have rested on the seventh day, but He hasn't rested since. He daily renews and strengthens our faith. The comfort we get from knowing that God is still active helps us rest assured that His story will continue throughout history.

May 31 ⌐

Reform School

Let us test and examine our ways, and return to the Lord!
Lamentations 3:40

O kay, so it's an outdated term—reform school. But we all know some-one who belongs in one. Christ-centered people spend their entire life in reform school. Like many schools, reform school schedules a quiz daily. Here's yours for today.

1. **T F** *The book of Genesis reports the creation of the world.*

2. **T F** *The book of Noah tells about the flood.*

3. **T F** *You can obey the Ten Commandments if you try really hard.*

4. **T F** *Methuselah lived a record 965 years.*

Check your answers. Only the first statement is true. Noah had his own boat but no book, and we cheated Methuselah by four years. Number 3 is why all Christians need reform school. (You have a chance to improve your score with number 5 at the end of this meditation.)

How futile our spiritual education when we realize we can never achieve the perfection God demands. As hard as we might work at reform, we never entirely achieve it. Futile, indeed. But because the Holy Spirit gave us faith, our futility leads not to dropping out or giving up, but into the arms of our Teacher and Savior.

Christ reforms us daily. He removes impediments to our growth and teaches us all we need to know for salvation. Our minds wander, and our con-sciences doze more than a few times every day. But Jesus never gives up on us. He died to give us all we need to "commence" with eternal life. He renews our energy to resist temptation and fight the "classroom bully." He even whispers the answer to the only question that counts:

5. **T F** *I believe that Jesus is my Savior.*

The Case of the Avenging God

The LORD is a jealous and avenging God; the LORD is avenging and
wrathful; the LORD takes vengeance on his adversaries and keeps wrath
for his enemies. The LORD is slow to anger and great in power, and the
LORD will by no means clear the guilty. His way is in whirlwind and
storm, and the clouds are the dust of his feet. Nahum 1:2–3

We Christians probably would agree that the Bible offers comfort as we read the history of salvation—including ours—earned by Jesus Christ on the cross of Calvary. We're pleased to hear how Jesus restored our relationship with God after we both inherited and actively achieved separation from our Father. There's comfort in knowing that God loved us so much, even while we were sinners, that He spared nothing to save us. Then there's Nahum—and perhaps we sense some cold beads of sweat.

The Lord is a jealous and avenging God; the Lord is avenging and
wrathful; the Lord takes vengeance on his adversaries and keeps wrath
for his enemies. The Lord is slow to anger and great in power, and the
Lord will by no means clear the guilty. His way is in whirlwind and
storm, and the clouds are the dust of his feet. Nahum 1:2–3

Nahum offers fearsome meaning to the phrase "We should fear and love God." Is God really like us, with emotions that smolder and explode into an inferno of revenge?

The difference between God and humans is that nothing He does is polluted by sin. He is perfectly just in all He does. That should comfort us, and not because we are sinless or marvelous in His sight. Because we aren't, we're tempted to fear the worst because sinners and God result in a volatile mixture—from God's standpoint. Our comfort comes because we know that God is a jealous lover. He loves us so much that He wants nothing to vie for our attention. He wants us to remain with Him, so He threatens all that seduces us.

While it's wonderful to be popular, the attraction fades when we think of how much the devil wants us and what he's willing to dangle in front of us to win our affection. It's good to know that God will end this someday. He is slow to anger at everyone and everything that jeopardizes our relationship, but those enemies should be forewarned. He will aim His holy vengeance their way and destroy them. Then we'll be out of danger for good.

As you can see, the Case of the Avenging God has a happy ending, depending on whose side you're on.

Getting Directions

May the Lord direct your hearts to the love of God and to the
steadfastness of Christ. 2 Thessalonians 3:5

You've probably participated in a discussion like this:

"Why don't you stop and ask directions?"

"No, I think I'll just turn right at the next corner."

"You said that the last time we turned right. Didn't you look at the map?"

"No, I couldn't get it unfolded."

"If you can't even unfold a map, how do you expect to find the
expressway?"

"Oh, you never trust my judgment. I'll turn right, and we'll be okay.
You'll see."

(Three right turns later.) "Why don't you run into that donut shop and
ask directions?"

We Christians face a similar dilemma. God tells us that we're strangers on earth, far from our home in heaven. As we travel through life, it's easy to get lost. That's why Paul left the Thessalonians—and us—the words of blessing in today's Bible passage.

How we need God's direction in our life! Only God creates faith that leads us to know Jesus as our Savior. Only Jesus paves the way to heaven through His death and resurrection. And only the Holy Spirit delivers directions clearly and accurately.

Certainly, we can read God's Word by ourselves. But it's also good to hear it from others who have studied and meditated. They can tell us about landmarks that make unfamiliar surroundings more familiar—things like the cross and the empty tomb. Things like the bread and wine and river of life. Things like forgiveness and living God's way. All these make our trip to heaven smoother and more enjoyable, though long none-the-less. Don't you feel like reverting to your childhood and asking, "Are we there yet?"

Paul turns to us and says, "Be patient. We'll be home soon."

The Compass

By faith Abraham obeyed when he was called to go out to a place that he was to receive as an inheritance. And he went out, not knowing where he was going. Hebrews 11:8

L ong ago, before cars had satellite navigation systems, people who wanted to know what direction they were headed bought compasses. These devices protruded condescendingly from the dashboard and swiveled merrily every time the car turned a corner. The major advantage of the compass was that at least you knew which direction you were headed when you were lost. Of course, there were always those confident individuals who knew their directions no matter what the compass indicated. ("The compass is wrong. The sun sets over there somewhere, so we must be going north-by-northwest—about 83 degrees I would guess.")

Imagine times much more ancient than the era of auto compasses. Going back to Abraham should be far enough. Listen to his travel dilemma: "By faith Abraham obeyed when he was called to go out to a place that he was to receive as an inheritance. And he went out, not knowing where he was going" (Hebrews 11:8).

Can you imagine the conversation between Abraham and Sarah?

Abraham: God wants to relocate us to a better place. Get packing. We leave right away.

Sarah: Okay, dear. Where are we going?

Abraham: God didn't say, but we'll know when we get there.

Sarah: Oh, I love surprises!

Abraham's compass was faith. He packed his belongings and departed for the destination God intended. The Bible doesn't say if Abraham had any reservations, but that's not important. Concerns or doubts may riddle even strong faith, but strong faith perseveres despite incredulity and misgivings that infiltrate mind and heart.

We may think we know where we're going when we get up each day. But you know how easily plans are interrupted—sometimes pleasantly, but more often in the opposite way. We also face days when we're aware of the many variables that influence us. Plan as we may to provide alternatives, we never can replace Jesus as the supreme leader of life. He points us in the right direction. He takes us around obstacles and keeps us focused during times of uncertainty when we're unsure of the future course of life.

A Long List

First of all, then, I urge that supplications, prayers, intercessions, and
thanksgivings be made for all people, for kings and all who are in high
positions, that we may lead a peaceful and quiet life, godly and dignified
in every way. 1 Timothy 2:1–2

On occasion, we may remember to include the president or the local mayor in our prayers, especially when their administration is particularly stressful. Our prayers may take a different tone when we find our representatives doing things we don't like! The best example of prayer, however, comes from Jesus Himself. Even as He suffered the most unjust judgment a government ever made, He prayed, "Father, forgive them, for they do not know what they are doing." Take a moment now to silently pray for your government. What does it need most right now?

While many Christians have lengthy prayer lists taped to the refrigerator or the cover of their Bible, most every home has an even longer list at its disposal. It's called the telephone book. It's easy to pray for those whom we know or with whom we can identify. But what about the thousands of people we don't know? Don't they too contribute to living what Paul calls peaceful and quiet lives?

The task of praying for all those people may seem impractically large, but it's not so formidable if we break it down to smaller steps. Start with the page on which you find your name. Go to the top and pray for one person each day. (Don't be discouraged. Even Methuselah didn't live long enough to pray for every person in a large city!)

How do you pray for those you don't know? Won't you repeat yourself? Probably. But that hasn't stopped you before, has it? Perhaps the following will help: Lord Jesus, I don't know if _____ knows You, but I know he/she needs You. Come close to _____ and live in his/her heart. Bless _____. I'd like to meet her/him in heaven someday. Amen.

Big Brother Is Watching You

Behold, I am with you and will keep you wherever you go, and will bring you back to this land. For I will not leave you until I have done what I have promised you. Genesis 28:15

How do you react to this: Jesus always knows where you are and what you're doing? Even if you're the most devoted and ambitious worker this side of Father Abraham, there are probably times when you do things you wouldn't want Jesus to see. Big Brother's ever-present watchfulness isn't always welcome. That's the Law side of God's watch over us. When you think about it, even that side of God's care is a blessing.

Have you ever done something wrong and just waited to get caught? Maybe it was that time you skipped school. Or maybe it was that misplaced decimal point that cost your company so much. Just how can these experiences be a blessing?

If God already knows what you've done wrong, what reason is there to hide it deep beneath piles of guilt? Like Adam and Eve after their deliciously sinful snack, God knows all, but He wants us to tell Him about it. Only then are the doors to forgiveness open and the onus of guilt relieved.

On the Gospel side of God's watchfulness, His children also experience great comfort from knowing their Brother's care. When storm winds rattle windows and sweep trees to the ground, it's surely good to know that Jesus sits out the storm with us. When we are so sick we think we're going to die (or afraid that we won't!), it's reassuring to know that Jesus promises to stay close. When we don't know where to turn for help, it's encouraging to realize that Jesus turns even the worst things to good for His brothers and sisters.

Get back to whatever you were doing, unless of course. . . . And smile. Big Brother is watching you.

On-the-Job Training

Then I said, "Ah, Lord God! Behold, I do not know how to speak, for I am only a youth." But the Lord said to me, "Do not say, 'I am only a youth'; for to all to whom I send you, you shall go, and whatever I command you, you shall speak." Jeremiah 1:6–7

Sometimes we feel inadequate to do God's work. Do you feel qualified as a missionary? How about a pastor? Sunday school teacher? Witness? While God didn't intend everyone to be missionaries or pastors, He has equipped each of us for some kind of work. And you're in pretty good company if you feel incapable. Jeremiah, the prophet, felt the same. Did you notice what God said to him?

God provides on-the-job training when we work for Him. It's a good deal too. Where else can you get all the benefits and your entire compensation before you even start the job? You may not become a manager or supervisor, but you will contribute to His glory.

Regardless of the skills and interests God gave you, every Christian has the ability to witness. God commissions us to both live and speak the Gospel. We don't need a theologically impressive vocabulary to witness. We simply need to tell others what we know—in our own words, using terms that others like us understand. But words aren't the real problem. Courage is. Many of us squirm if someone asks why we go to church, why we avoid foul language and dirty jokes, why we pray before eating lunch, or why we're reading this book. Even Jeremiah worried about people's reaction to what God wanted him to say. It's unlikely that anyone will toss you into a mud-filled cistern as they did Jeremiah. But they may sling some dirt at you. How can you witness then? The answer isn't always clear, but God will give you an answer. Just ask Him. He can do what you can't.

Keeping Cool

My eyes are awake before the watches of the night, that I may meditate on Your promise. Hear my voice according to Your steadfast love; O Lord, according to Your justice give me life. They draw near who persecute me with evil purpose; they are far from Your law. But You are near, O Lord, and all Your commandments are true. Psalm 119:148–151

Before there were refrigerators, there were iceboxes. Our ancestors would marvel at how iceboxes now make their own ice! Of course, today's refrigerators have other advantages. Because they are metal, they're great devices for attracting magnets. Thereby they are effectively camouflaged beneath notes, pictures, school papers, calendars, coupons, and the like.

The main purpose of refrigerators is to use cool temperatures to preserve food. Next time you open your refrigerator to see which leftovers will remain leftovers, think of the Gospel. It preserves us from the heat of sin with cool, refreshing waves of God's love. And do we ever need preserving!

David, the psalmist, said, "Plead my cause and redeem me; give me life according to Your promise!" (Psalm 119:154). David had lots of problems with enemies. First, King Saul tried to kill him. Later, even his own son strayed toward murderous intentions. David faithfully laid his problems on God, and God faithfully kept David alive and victorious.

While we ask God to preserve our health and life from physical threats and afflictions, we have a more sinister enemy whose foremost goal is to spoil our relationship with the Lord. For this, we rest in a cool nook of the Gospel. Our only sure hope for preservation lies in the power of God through Jesus Christ.

Sin and its prime perpetrator blast away at us with torrid sheets of hot temptations, blazing walls of guilt, and fiery outbursts of rebellion against God. The Gospel extinguishes these fires because Jesus smothered the flames when He died on the cross and rose from the cool depths of the grave. He adopts and supports us, accepting us even though we still smolder with sin. He encases us in the delightfully frosty confines of forgiveness, reconciliation, and preservation. Sin no longer has power to cover us with fetid mold and bacteria that devour us from the inside out.

As we enjoy the comfort of Jesus' love and mercy, pray that we will end up at the back of His Gospel refrigerator where we can remain leftovers forever. Now that's the best way to remain well-preserved!

What Sacrifice?

I know, my God, that You test the heart and have pleasure in uprightness.
In the uprightness of my heart I have freely offered all these things, and
now I have seen Your people, who are present here, offering freely and
joyously to You. 1 Chronicles 29:17

The word *sacrifice* conjures up many images. We might think of Old Testament days when God's people burned the best of their harvest to honor and worship Him. We may shudder at the Passover celebration when rivers of blood flowed from thousands of lambs slaughtered and cooked for the festival. And yes, we also remember God, who sacrificed His Son, Jesus, to pay for our sins. We rightly associate the word *sacrifice* with loss.

Christ's sacrifice mercifully ended the requirement for all other sacrifices. Yet how else can we thank Jesus for His extraordinary sacrifice on the cross except by making a few sacrifices of our own? We see an example of generous sacrifice in today's Old Testament text, which was part of King David's prayer after he collected special contributions for the temple. The people responded unselfishly to God's love. They gave until it hurt—and they were happy about it!

Giving until it hurts really isn't a true measure of generosity. Some people have a very low tolerance for pain! True giving comes from a happy heart.

Modern Christians still thank God with sacrifices. Sometimes we give our time to manage or maintain our church or to visit the sick and lonely. Sometimes we sacrifice a generous portion of our income for missions or charities. Sometimes we offer our voices to sing praises or tell others what Jesus did for us. Prayer qualifies as a sacrifice too—especially when we talk to God about the needs of others. If someone commented about our sacrifices, we would probably respond, "What sacrifice? I was glad to do it." And that's the whole point of sacrifices.

Drop in Anytime

Beloved, it is a faithful thing you do in all your efforts for these brothers, strangers as they are. 3 John 5

Have you ever looked for a helping hand? We can usually find one at the end of our own arm!

Most of us are in the same position as Gaius, whom John addressed above—able to help and support our Christian brothers and sisters. A good place to start is at God's house. At times, it's easy to snipe (either verbally or within the privacy of our own thoughts) at the choir or the pastor as they display occasional inadequacies. And then there are all those people who aren't paying attention to the sermon. And that noisy kid in the front row! How much did Mr. Hobbs put in the offering basket? Just what would John say if he wrote a fourth epistle to us?

He would probably tell us to drop in on Gaius. Better yet, he might tell us to drop in on Jesus—anytime. Jesus always showed up where He was needed. Once it was among some outcast lepers. He dropped in on them, and they ran off completely cured. Another time, He dropped in on a mob about to stone a promiscuous young lady. And then there were the hours after the resurrection when Jesus strolled alongside two men discussing the recent tragic events. He dropped in at their home for supper too. He not only said "grace" at the table, He *was* grace!

Now it's our turn. Remember the best place to find a helping hand? How might we show kindness and love to others? A phone call and an open ear sometimes meet the need. And the pastor isn't the only one qualified to visit the hospitalized and lonely. How about a little book to keep that noisy kid occupied, and another voice for the choir to savor? Oh yes, one more thing. Sometimes the best helping hand is the one that is folded in prayer.

What a Sight

When I was a child, I spoke like a child, I thought like a child, I reasoned like a child. When I became a man, I gave up childish ways. For now we see in a mirror dimly, but then face to face. Now I know in part; then I shall know fully, even as I have been fully known.
1 Corinthians 13:11–12

If you wear glasses or contacts, you'll identify closely with this meditation. (If you don't, borrow someone's glasses, wear them for a few minutes, then remove them. You'll get a similar effect.) The first time a poor-sighted person brings glasses or contacts to his or her eyes, it's like becoming aware of a new world. What was once a distant blur becomes startlingly clear. Everything becomes lighter and brighter. You probably would exclaim, "What a sight!" if it wouldn't draw curious stares—that you could see!

Experience with corrective lenses is much like our relationship with God. In the dim world of unbelief, sinful ignorance keeps us content with what little we do see. After all, we don't really know what we're missing. Then Someone quietly suggests that we don't know what's out there. That's the Holy Spirit, examining our eyes of faith and concluding that we're all but blind.

We can't see the Savior except through faith. Only the Holy Spirit delivers that faith. Once we have it, we might exclaim, "What a sight!" We see Jesus as true God and true Man. He's off in the distance, hanging on a cross, dying to take away our sins. We see clearly inside an empty tomb—nothing there but some folded burial clothes. Then we look up, farther than we've ever looked before, into heaven and see Jesus waiting for us. What a sight, indeed!

Faith enables us to see what those without faith cannot, but our sight remains a bit imperfect. In 1 Corinthians 13:12, Paul says: "For now we see in a mirror dimly, but then face to face. Now I know in part; then I shall know fully, even as I have been fully known."

We may wish to see better right now, but the view is already good. One heavenly delight we look forward to is perfect faith-sight (as well as 20/20 vision or better!). As wonderful as our Savior seems to us now, He'll be even better when we live together in the presence of God the Father.

Meanwhile, keep your sight as sharp as possible through Bible study, worship, and the Lord's Supper. When the Savior comes again, He'll surely be a sight for sore faiths.

Just What the Doctor Ordered

The light of the eyes rejoices the heart, and good news refreshes the bones.
Proverbs 15:30

One survey indicated that children laugh an average of 500 times daily. Adults, 15 times. If God created humor, I hope it doesn't become extinct. He made us able to smile, grin, chuckle, giggle, laugh, and even howl. He also helps us laugh at our troubles (probably so we never run out of things to laugh at). He enables us to laugh at ourselves too—a wonderful source of amusement. Proverbs tells us that joy is good medicine whether we're sick or not.

Like everything else God created, humor can be misused. We're often eager to laugh at sin. Jokes about sex or race, especially when told in confidential whispers, often prompt fits of laughter when they should really move us to tears. And sometimes cruel laughter escapes our mouths as we enjoy the misfortune or faults of others.

Forgiveness makes humor possible. When life becomes troubled, it's hard to laugh. But as God's forgiveness and comfort begin to soothe and heal, we can look back and laugh at our troubles. It doesn't take much imagination to hear Peter enjoying a shoreline dinner with his friends, recalling the day he almost drowned. "*Ha, ha.* I was *so* brave. I stepped out on those waves, and I was really going to show you guys how much faith I had. Then I thought, 'What am I doing out here?' I thought I'd have to sink to the bottom and run for shore!"

Always be ready to laugh. And when you laugh, make a note of what was so funny. Maybe you can share it with someone who really needs a laugh. Enjoy a good grin a few times each day. A good howl will get your heart pumping too. And you know what they say about he who laughs last. (He didn't get the joke.)

June 12

Prophet Sharing

And the glory of the Lord shall be revealed, and all flesh shall see it together, for the mouth of the Lord has spoken. Isaiah 40:5

A banquet speaker once said, "My job is to speak and yours is to listen. I hope we stop at the same time." In Old Testament days, the prophet's job was to speak. Often, the listeners quit before the message ended. What do you suppose would happen if men like Isaiah, Jeremiah, and Elijah returned to address modern society? We can't meet them in person, but we can rejoice that God recorded and shared their words in His book.

It's easy to see the parallels between Old Testament depravity and today's events. We, like our Old Testament counterparts, tremble to think that God's judgment remains upon us as He punishes sin. It's good that God shared these prophecies with us, for they still show us our sinfulness and need for repentance. They warn us to fear, love, and trust God, as Martin Luther was so apt to say as he explained the commandments.

The old prophets also had Good News. Isaiah shared the Gospel even before anyone knew there was a Gospel! The entire 40th chapter offered welcome relief to his prophecies of doom. For the ancient believers, it pointed toward a Savior who would re-create a right relationship with God. We modern believers know Isaiah's prophecy came true on the first Christmas. But we also share the prophet's words for our future.

Christ will come again. No one will mistake Him for a poor, helpless baby next time. He will come in glory, not humility. He will destroy everything evil, but we need not fear for we are God's people now. He will come to take us home. Isaiah gives us something to hope for as he promises, "they who wait for the Lord . . . shall mount up with wings like eagles" (40:31).

No Crosses to Bear

And stooping to look in, he saw the linen cloths lying there, but he did not go in. Then Simon Peter came, following him, and went into the tomb. He saw the linen cloths lying there, and the face cloth, which had been on Jesus' head, not lying with the linen cloths but folded up in a place by itself. John 20:5–7

What would you think if the government banned all symbols of violence? At first glance, it sounds mighty appealing. Violence pervades our society. Then reality sinks in. The government might prohibit the cross that we cherish as a symbol of salvation. Perhaps we've lost touch with the realities of this gruesome instrument of torture and execution.

What would you have in your house to symbolize Christ even if religious symbols were forbidden? What would you keep as a visual reminder of Jesus? Today's Bible reading hints at a replacement: "And stooping to look in, he saw the linen cloths lying there, but he did not go in. Then Simon Peter came, following him, and went into the tomb. He saw the linen cloths lying there, and the face cloth, which had been on Jesus' head, not lying with the linen cloths but folded up in a place by itself" (John 20:5–7).

Bed sheets! You can think of Jesus every time you see bed sheets. (Just think how blessed those housekeepers in large hotels would be!) Come to think of it, crosses don't need to be banned for us to use other things to remind us of Jesus. (That's the point of this book. Anything and everything can help us keep Jesus in our thoughts.)

When the disciples saw those strips of linen and the burial cloth, they were stunned—with surprise and joy. Their Friend wasn't dead after all. What He had said was true, unbelievably true! How foolish they were to doubt the Messiah's claims that He would come return to life after dying. Sin certainly plays havoc with faith, even the faith of those who lived and ate with the Savior for three years. It can do the same to us. That's a good reason to surround ourselves with symbols of our Savior.

Do you find it difficult to believe that you will experience what Jesus did? It's natural for doubts to tarnish our faith, especially if the news seems too good to be true. Does heaven seem far from reality? Oh, those qualms make us queasy. But look at the bed sheets. As sure as they are real, the linen strips and burial cloth, neatly folded after only brief use, were real. So is the risen Savior.

Even if someone takes away your cross, cling to your bed sheets. You're sure to have a restful sleep—and a great awakening.

June 14

Once Upon a Time

You should remember the predictions of the holy prophets and the commandment of the Lord and Savior through your apostles. 2 Peter 3:2

Call it want you want—recall, recollection, reminiscence, or memory. It's one of those fleeting things in life. Memory is that function of the mind that suggests you've probably forgotten something.

Some things are unforgettable. They constitute a treasury of "once upon a times" for us. Perhaps it was a special birthday surprise, a wedding, or the birth of a child. Maybe it was a once-in-a-lifetime trip or first car or family reunion. Like fine wine, recalled events get better as they age—even if a few sour grapes contaminated the original version.

The Apostle Peter knew the value of memory too. Far from just an ingredient of sentimentality, he considered memory a vital link between God's Word in the past and life in the present and future. The Bible provides indispensable "once upon a time" stories still valuable today.

Once upon a time—actually before there was a time—God created a splendid place to live.

Once upon a time, God was so angry with the evil world that He flooded it, destroying all but a few lives. In His incredible mercy, He rescued a few faithful people and a boatload of animals. Then He placed a rainbow in the sky to remind people that He still loved them.

Once upon a time, God took the form of a common Man so He could live a holy life for hopeless sinners. He obeyed all the laws perfectly. He loved people unselfishly and unconditionally. Then He carried our sins to the cross, suffered, died, and was buried. He showed Himself victorious over the devil when He rose back to life.

Once upon a time, He will also return and take us to heaven where we'll live happily ever after. And that's no fairy tale.

Willpower

May you be strengthened with all power, according to His glorious might,
for all endurance and patience with joy, giving thanks to the Father, who
has qualified you to share in the inheritance of the saints in light. He has
delivered us from the domain of darkness and transferred us to the
kingdom of His beloved Son, in whom we have redemption, the
forgiveness of sins. Colossians 1:11–14

God works in and through us when we do His will. Of course, some people are so contrary that His will becomes their won't! Yet to those whose faith makes them open to God's intentions and desires, He gives willpower.

Colossians 1:9 says: "And so, from the day we heard, we have not ceased to pray for you, asking that you may be filled with the knowledge of His will in all spiritual wisdom and understanding." This was Paul's prayer for the Colossians, a prayer that God is happy to answer according to His will.

One important phrase in that passage contains the words "spiritual wisdom and understanding." What is the source of this component of faith? Can we equate it with human or secular wisdom and understanding? If so, we might be tempted to think that our own wealth of experience and dedication to study makes us wise and knowledgeable. But we can't obtain or attain spiritual wisdom and understanding through our own will or efforts. God reveals His will in the Bible. Anyone can read it. But it's the faith we received from the Holy Spirit that makes God's revelation meaningful. It's the Holy Spirit who gives us power to actually do God's revealed will.

We truly do God's will when we apply to daily life what He has revealed. That gives us experience that contributes to wisdom and understanding. Translated into practical terms, applying God's will to daily life means that we persist in doing good. Christian do-gooders have the advantage of knowing and experiencing God's goodness to them. In fact, God made us good through Jesus; therefore, good people like us do good things for others.

As we do God's will, we find ourselves extending forgiveness (even when it's not asked for), showing compassion (What can I do for that homeless guy on the corner?), generously supporting God's work in mission fields and in the local congregation (What can I sacrifice this week?), and smiling through it all (It's not like we were asked to sacrifice our son or anything!). As we continue to practice God's will, we realize that it isn't some parenthetical expression appended to our lives. It's the main idea.

Hypocrites and Other Sinners

In the meantime, when so many thousands of the people had gathered
together that they were trampling one another, He began to say to His dis-
ciples first, "Beware of the leaven of the Pharisees, which is hypocrisy."
Luke 12:1

A re you a hypocrite? Consider the following questions:

1. *You smile contentedly as you write a large check to the IRS.*

2. *You must always think before putting the best of your two faces forward.*

3. *You stay away from church because there are too many hypocrites there.*

4. *You know 27 people other than you who should read this meditation.*

5. *You agree with everybody.*

A real hypocrite is one who simply pretends to be a Christian. A real hypocrite may attend church and recite the creed but deep down inside does not
believe Christ is the Savior. A real hypocrite is a nonbeliever. We also act like
nonbelievers whenever we do that which is inconsistent with our faith—sin.
So in other words there are times when nonbelievers act like Christians, and
there are times when Christians act like nonbelievers. No wonder things get
so complicated.

The difference between Christian sinners and the nonchristian hypocrite
is that Christians recognize two faces of their faith—the perfect face that is a
gift of the Holy Spirit and the beaten face scarred by wars with the devil and
our own natural desires. Those around us may see only the beat up face of a
sinner. They make us feel guilty—like hypocrites—if they point out inconsis-
tencies between what we believe and how we act. Should Christians guzzle
one-too-many? Should Christians curse when cut off by a motor moron?
Should Christians laugh hysterically at filthy jokes?

Jesus is the cure for hypocrisy. And while scars remain, we're also cleansed
of our sins as well. And even though we stumble and fall repeatedly, our
clumsiness as saints is only a stage from which we'll pass someday. God forgives when repentant sinners run to Him for healing, even when we're repeat
offenders.

June 17

A Tender Kiss

Whoever gives an honest answer kisses the lips. Proverbs 24:26

You'll probably agree that the verse above is better than the old adage about honesty being the best policy. As of this writing, kissing remains one of the more pleasant ways of spreading germs. And honesty still pays more than it costs. Or does it?

Here are some times when you may be tempted to be less than truthful: Completing a resume; filling out any form with the number 1040 on it; answering questions about sex; reporting last Saturday's golf score; telling children how well you did in school; selling your car with 212,000 miles on it; describing your athletic heroism before you injured your knee (falling off the bench); how many oysters you can eat; and how fast you thought you were going in that 25 mph zone. You could probably create additional paragraphs about honesty, but then kissing might take on a bad flavor. Or become extinct.

One reason people resort to dishonesty is to protect their image. Or their income. Or their freedom. Or their eternal life? Wouldn't you know it? The only time the devil is truly honest is when he's telling God about us. Before the divine throne the devil accuses us. (And he's proud of it!) He's not very discreet either. The devil tells all. But God made it possible to beat the devil at his game. God makes it possible for us to be honest with Him. There is nothing He can't or won't forgive (except not believing in Him). He forgives even the most appalling sins.

God's response to our repentance is indeed like a kiss—especially as one psychologist defines a kiss: It's when you're so close that you don't see anything wrong.

Tabloid Targets

Be sober-minded; be watchful. Your adversary the devil prowls around like
a roaring lion, seeking someone to devour. Resist him, firm in your faith,
knowing that the same kinds of suffering are being experienced by your
brotherhood throughout the world. And after you have suffered a little
while, the God of all grace, who has called you to His eternal glory in
Christ, will Himself restore, confirm, strengthen, and establish you.
1 Peter 5:8–10

It's time to pretend again. You're probably familiar with supermarket tabloids that beckon to you at the checkout counter. They usually have outrageous headlines such as "Pet Canary Swallows a Cat" or "Hero Brings Down Purse Snatcher with False Teeth."

Now back to your imagination. Imagine that a reporter from the Globe Enquiring Star is assigned to watch you. He has access to all your financial, tax, and legal records. You can't escape his observation. He follows you everywhere, noting everything you do and don't do.

He heard you swear when you read today's weather report and curse when you saw what the puppy did on the floor. He read your lips when you mocked your best friend. He saw the lusty look in your eyes when the neighbor pranced around in a skimpy bathing suit. The reporter's stopwatch tattled on how much time you took for breaks and lunches. What was that you shouted when the rude driver slipped into the last parking space? Then there were those three martinis to calm your nerves and the movie you rented with the scenes your kids couldn't watch. Next, . . .

If you made the headlines, you probably wouldn't want to read farther. Perhaps you would feel like the psalmist, who said, "I am an object of scorn to my accusers; when they see me, they wag their heads" (Psalm 109:25).

Our accusers have good reason to shake their heads, don't they? We're lion food. Peter writes: "Be sober-minded; be watchful. Your adversary the devil prowls around like a roaring lion, seeking someone to devour" (1 Peter 5:8). The reporter has all the evidence he needs to make us lion food, except for one thing.

Jesus edits our life. He takes out all the bad stuff, which leaves the devil with exactly nothing to report. As we stand before God our judge, the accusing (and accurate!) reporter is dumbfounded. Pages of the tabloid are blank, except for a short article. It describes how Jesus took away the sins of the world—including yours and mine. Oh yes, the devil knows that story. He just doesn't devote much space to it.

No God

Oh, the depth of the riches and wisdom and knowledge of God!
How unsearchable are His judgments and how inscrutable His ways!
Romans 11:33

An 18-year-old girl once said she couldn't believe in God. Her friend's mother suffered an excruciating death from cancer. A friend had AIDS. Another friend was killed on his way to school. All this seemed sufficient evidence that no God existed. You probably hear similar stories from other skeptics.

God doesn't always make sense. The truth is that *we* often have no sense—not His kind anyway. That's what Paul told the Romans. Comparing God's thoughts and actions with those of humans is like comparing apples and orangutans! How sad it is when people bring God down to their level of understanding. It's even worse when they blame God for something He hasn't done.

God didn't bring sin into the world. Adam and Eve's first sin so defiled the world that sin has been epidemic ever since. Sin is a random terrorist and killer. Sin's greatest promoter loves to have us believe that there is no God because there is so much sin! Isn't that just like shrewd old Satan?

God never promised to keep sin from hurting us. But He does promise that should sin even take our life, He won't let it defeat us. We have the hope of eternal life even when earthly life seems like a living hell. There is only one way to be sure that God's promise is stronger than sin's grasp. Faith is the answer. Faith is trusting God to make the best of every situation. Faith drives us to read the Bible where we find many stories of God's love in the lives of His suffering and dying people. And the only way we can respond to declarations like "No God" is to say, "Know God."

Upward Mobility

"In My Father's house are many rooms. If it were not so, would I have told you that I go to prepare a place for you?" John 14:2

This is the first in a series of seven meditations on Jesus' promises as recorded in John 14. The first promise involves moving—moving to a better location. In fact, the move is into a mansion.

If you're like most Americans, you've moved several times during your life. People move often and for various reasons, mostly work-related. But did you hear about the man who read that most accidents happen within 25 miles of home? He moved 50 miles away just to be safe! Some people move so often they don't even feel at home at home. And anyone who has ever packed and unpacked their own moving boxes probably yearns for the day they can stay put. The day is coming.

Jesus knew His followers didn't want Him to leave. Even after His Easter return, the disciples wanted Him to stay longer. This time He would withdraw His physical presence until the world ended.

Jesus went ahead of all His friends to get a new place ready. It's spacious enough for all His friends to live together. No ordinary house, our new home will be a mansion with many rooms. And our life there will add new depth to the phrase "happy home."

We often think of our future heavenly happiness in terms of what makes us happy now. Perhaps that's a good way of visualizing the joy that still awaits us, but nothing we enjoy now will come close to what we will enjoy at our new home. The greatest earthly pleasure is likely to be the simplest heavenly pleasure—if it even ranks! Our most exalted ecstasy will involve living in the presence of our Savior—actually seeing Him and worshiping Him. And as we settle in for an eternity of bliss, we'll praise God that we never need move again.

Get Moving

"And if I go and prepare a place for you, I will come again and will take you to myself, that where I am you may be also. And you know the way to where I am going." John 14:3–4

Has this ever happened to you? You approach the stop sign and dutifully obey. You wait. And wait. And wait. Suddenly you realize the sign will never turn green.

We sometimes act the same as we travel the road to our heavenly home. As Jesus promised in the text above, He's returning to take us to heaven. We may want to sit back and patiently wait for that moment when the sign turns green—when the sound of trumpets announces His second arrival. Christians, however, can't sit around and wait.

We can become so preoccupied by our blissful future that we fail to move toward that goal. Furthermore, we sometimes fail to realize that our eternal life already began when we were baptized. Like most roads, the one to heaven isn't always smooth. But at least we know the way.

God cleared the way for us when He sent Jesus to take away our sins. Then the Holy Spirit delivered faith in Jesus as the only way to heaven. Now He's honking at us to get moving. Sitting still and waiting around makes us prime targets for getting rear-ended by the devil.

The pages of our Bibles provide a road map that makes clear the way home. And when the road is suddenly filled with forks, dangerous intersections, and steep grades, we need to slow down and go over God's map again. Going the wrong way has tragic consequences; there is only one way to go.

One more thing—as we travel to the place Jesus prepared for us, we need to be alert for others who need a lift. Sometimes, the Holy Spirit makes us the vehicle for a spiritual hitchhiker's trip to heaven. Maybe it's the driver who should hold up his thumb!

Promise of Success

"Truly, truly, I say to you, whoever believes in Me will also do the works that I do; and greater works than these will he do, because I am going to the Father." John 14:12

The secret of success remains a secret to many people. Not that there's any lack of formulas, especially those that follow the familiar injunction "If at first you don't succeed . . ." Here are some you might enjoy.

If at first you don't succeed . . .

read the directions.

retrieve the directions from the wastebasket.

do it the way the boss told you.

give up. Why make a fool of yourself?

Promises of success are usually misleading. God's promises, however, are reliable and true.

At first glance, Jesus' promise recorded in today's Bible passage seems astounding—or at least too good to be true. But His promise is also built on a premise. Faithful Christians do what Jesus did. Like many premises, this one is slightly flawed, but it's not God's fault. We do as Jesus did, but we don't do it nearly as well. Sin often messes up our work, but God's forgiveness patches up the problem and enables us to copy the Savior's behavior. And rather than focus on our shortcomings, Jesus promised that we will do "greater things." How can sinners—even forgiven sinners—possibly do that?

It's not easy. But Jesus meant that we're here on earth, surrounded by needy sinners, while He's up in heaven getting things ready for us. We continue the work He started. Oh, we're not alone. Not when we pray. And just wait till you see tomorrow's promise.

Tomorrow's Promise Today

"Whatever you ask in My name, this I will do, that the Father may be glorified in the Son. If you ask Me anything in My name, I will do it."
John 14:13–14

You've heard it before. It's not *what* you know, but *who* you know. And how would you like to know someone who could and would give you whatever you asked? Dream a moment. Just what *would* you ask?

Back to reality now before your garage is overcrowded with Rolls Royces or your job begins to interfere with exotic vacations or . . . Jesus' promise, as it appears above, is in context of the preceding meditation. Remember? Jesus told believers they will not only continue His work on earth, but they will also do great things when they pray in His name.

Praying in Jesus' name means more than simply adding a few words at the end of our prayers. When our prayers harmonize with everything that Jesus was, did, and is, then we are praying in His name. So forget about luxury cars and a multimillion-dollar income. They aren't important—nor are they covered under the terms of this promise. In fact, this promise promises more than most of us can dream.

Now that we have the promise in focus, what would you ask for? Want to be another Billy Graham? Would you like to feed 5,000—no, make it 15,000—with only the contents of your lunch? Just ask. Right? Great things lurk within the sound of your prayers!

Once again, we need perspective. The greatest thing we can do for God may be far less great in our minds than it is in God's will. That's why we pray not only in Jesus' name but according to God's will.

Great things don't always mean startling statistics, dramatic deeds, or fabulous fame. Yet God challenges us, and we can ask His help to succeed. Why not ask Him right now? Then watch for the opportunities.

Faithful Friend

"And I will ask the Father, and He will give you another Helper, to be with you forever." John 14:16

How many friends do you have? You'll never really know until you buy that new home with a guesthouse, swimming pool, and tennis court. Of course, we're talking about good friends—faithful friends—here. We all could use a good friend. (And we often do!) The fifth promise in John 14 is about just that—a friend whom Jesus called "Counselor."

A good friend is someone who listens to us. And a good friend will counsel us or tell us what we need to know—even if it momentarily offends us.

The Holy Spirit is the Counselor whom Jesus mentions. Notice that the Counselor offers a forever friendship. Jesus spoke these words to the disciples just before He was captured and killed. He knew that even after He rose from the dead and visited with them, He would finally leave them to work without His physical presence. Jesus didn't want to leave them friendless though, so He sent the Holy Spirit. The Counselor's solid friendship rests on Christ's forgiveness and God's power.

Sad to say, we don't always return the Spirit's friendship with much enthusiasm. We're too tired or embarrassed to pray. Worship isn't as important as reading the Sunday paper or sleeping late. We consider Christian witnessing just too risky. And at times, we are downright hostile. "Get thee hence, Spirit! Leave me alone."

In our loneliness, the Spirit is still there—a forgiving friend. The Spirit gently nudges and sometimes powerfully prods us to act out our faith. As much as we allow, the Spirit guides us to know God's will, and we accept His wise counsel. He remains close by, listening to our deepest thoughts and feelings—ready to respond with compassion and love. He's a friend just waiting to be used.

The Best Thing to Leave Behind

*"Peace I leave with you; my peace I give to you. Not as the world gives do
I give to you. Let not your hearts be troubled, neither let them be afraid."*
John 14:27

A move is afoot to eliminate laws about disturbing the peace. Worldwide wars and skirmishes make us wonder if peace is only a period of discontent and perplexity between wars. There isn't much peace left. In fact, about the only sure place to find it is in the dictionary.

Before you slink behind your coffee cup and curl up into a ball, true peace isn't totally out of reach. The sixth promise in John 14 has Jesus telling us that He leaves peace as a legacy for us to share and enjoy.

To take advantage of His peace, we totally surrender to Him. That's both good news and tough news. Good in that the Holy Spirit has already given us the gift of faith, which gives us God's peace. Tough in that we sinners are prone to breaking the peace with God as well as between others and us. Yet the truly peaceful heart remains in Jesus, and Jesus always forgives and maintains the peace. But His peace goes beyond human relationships and into our own personal life as we face our own troubles, failures, sickness, and mortality. Then we begin to understand the nature of peace with God even though our world falls apart around us.

Jesus said, "Do not be afraid." That pretty well sums up His peace. We have nothing to fear because we trust God to bring something good out of everything. We're willing to wait for His mercy and love to show itself too. We're also willing to accept the fact that His peace passes all understanding. And all misunderstanding too.

Glad to See You Go

"You heard Me say to you, 'I am going away, and I will come to you.' If you loved Me, you would have rejoiced, because I am going to the Father, for the Father is greater than I." John 14:28

What would you like engraved on your tombstone? What words would you like to leave behind? Dream big because you probably won't be able to afford much engraving. (Blame it on the cost of living!) I prefer the idea expressed by Jesus in John 14: I'm going, but I'm coming back again. And when we truly understand death, we can also share this comment that might seem strange to some: Be glad to see me go.

You've heard the funeral talk before. "It's such a blessing that Aunt Edna died. Now her suffering is over." And sometimes the conversation isn't so easy. "What a shock about Bobby! He was so young. I guess when your time is up, your time is up."

Did you notice anything missing in those words? It might be considered bad taste to say so, but something is missing if we don't at least think the phrase "Glad to see him go." Why? Not because the suffering is over or because God's love is hard to perceive. We're glad to see Christian people "go" because now they live in heaven where they experience a perfect relationship with God the Father. They've been welcomed by Jesus as if He'd known them all His life. (He did!) And they might even see the Holy Spirit breezing around, delivering faith to that young child, inspiring the words of this preacher, and warming the hearts of believers everywhere. They might even see the Spirit working in us right now as we renew our trust in Jesus and as we confirm our own faith that someday we're "going" too. But not for long—not as God counts time. We'll be back as good as new—even better—in heaven. Meet you there. And that's a promise too.

Hot Heads

If your enemy is hungry, give him bread to eat, and if he is thirsty, give him water to drink, for you will heap burning coals on his head, and the Lord will reward you. Proverbs 25:21–22

It's been said that conscience keeps more people awake than coffee. It's also true that we live in an increasingly decaffeinated world—both in coffee and conscience.

Most people would agree that it's good to know your enemies. Fewer people would agree that it's also good to love your enemies, but that's a well-known admonishment straight from God's Word. Regardless of how others feel about enemies, our task is to know our enemies so we can love them. That may leave us asking, "What good will it do?"

First, identify "the enemy." It might be a co-worker, a competitor, a family member, someone at church, or a neighbor. Then ask yourself how you know that person is your enemy.

Second, think about ways to love your enemy. Way down deep, we might want to literally love our enemies to death. But that's not the idea God means in the "heaping coals" image. God's plan for dealing with enemies is to prick their consciences with our own good behavior. We are to make them feel guilty by returning good for evil, kindness for meanness, mercy for cruelty, forgiveness for revenge. We are to make them feel guilty enough to repent! That's God's goal for them and for us.

We bring others to repentance the same way Jesus brought us there. True, our Savior did tell us to repent, but in gentle words and actions. He demonstrated His love not by beating the devil out of us, but by loving us to death— His own. That's exactly the kind of love we need to practice on those who hate us. They may never change, but they'll wonder about us. And someday, maybe they will figure it out.

Reason to Live

To this end we always pray for you, that our God may make you worthy of
His calling and may fulfill every resolve for good and every work of faith
by His power, so that the name of our Lord Jesus may be glorified in you,
and you in Him, according to the grace of our God and the Lord Jesus
Christ. 2 Thessalonians 1:11–12

God put us on earth for a reason. He wants to accomplish something through us while we're here. Some of us are already so far behind that we might live through the 21st century.

Social science suggests that people are only genuinely fulfilled when they have purpose in life. For some people, that purpose is a life spent teaching or in public service; for others, purpose is achieving some significant scientific breakthrough such as Teflon or the polio vaccine. Some create majestic works of art to be admired through the ages. Others take piles of notes and arrange them into unforgettable melodies. Of course, there are those whose purpose seems dedicated to useless and sometimes malignant endeavors in those same fields.

Through Paul, God revealed our purpose: "To this end we always pray for you, that our God may make you worthy of His calling and may fulfill every resolve for good and every work of faith by His power, so that the name of our Lord Jesus may be glorified in you, and you in Him, according to the grace of our God and the Lord Jesus Christ" (2 Thessalonians 1:11–12).

God created people for many different purposes. Note that He didn't want all of us to be preachers or construction workers or librarians or computer programmers or even Sunday school teachers. He gives purpose to our lives whatever we do, putting numerous blessings at our disposal. He gives purpose to our lives not because of what we are or what we have, but for the sake of Jesus and by the power of the Holy Spirit.

What tremendous reason we have to live! From the time we're old enough to realize that we're not here only for horseback rides and talking cereal, we have opportunity to respond to God's love

Stop and consider the ways in which you might respond. Oh, there's the usual "go to church and pray before meals" answer. But what about integrating your response to God's love into your normal activities? Bring closure to this devotional on your own. Decide right now what you'll ask the Holy Spirit to help you do because of all that God has done for you. Don't put if off. Living to 1,000 probably isn't all that it's cracked up to be.

Shots That Miss

*And do not fear those who kill the body but cannot kill the soul. Rather
fear him who can destroy both soul and body in hell. Matthew 10:28*

D rive-by shootings are no longer confined to squalid streets in sprawl-
ing metropolises, and victims aren't restricted to gang members.
Terrorism no longer happens only in other countries. It may strike just across
the street. Horrific diseases like AIDS no longer afflict only those with risky
life styles, but it stalks the innocent as well. All these things scare us, and make
us fear for the future of those we love.

Even as dread and apprehension drip from daily headlines, we're tempted to miss even greater dangers. As Jesus said in today's text, life-threatening
danger goes beyond bullets, dynamite, viruses, and steering wheels. Certainly,
those physical things can put us in an early grave. More perilous are those less-
visible perils that can put us in an eternal grave.

How does Satan stock his arsenal for spiritual terrorism? It's no real
secret. We might even help him. The devil's goal is to lure us away from God.
It's not hard to accomplish that satanic intent when intended victims get lazy
about regular prayer and worship.

The devil also plots our demise by enticing us away from the way God
wants us to live in relation to others. He merrily envisions warehouses full of
body parts as we get eyes for eyes, teeth for teeth, toes for toes, elbows for
elbows—well, you get the idea. And we all too often comply with his ambitions. Soon our desire to forgive and be forgiven has been erased. Then we
drown in a lake of trespasses and sins.

It doesn't have to be that way if we're on our guard. We can't whip the
devil with karate chops or 9mm semi-automatic handguns. But we can slash
away with the pages of our Bibles and the pleas of our prayers. God will protect us and keep us safe. Even death won't defeat us.

Apple Polisher

He found him in a desert land, and in the howling waste of the wilderness; He encircled him, He cared for him, He kept him as the apple of His eye. Deuteronomy 32:10

A literal rendering of the phrase "apple of His eye" would be "little man of His eye." I guess I prefer apple. A little man—even if he's a pupil—trying to keep his balance on my slippery eyeball sounds painful. Besides, this meditation is more about apples than eyes.

Apples—especially large, crispy, shiny red ones—capture our imagination as well as our taste buds. Many of us probably retain the appetite for applesauce that we first developed as a child. And in our mind's eye we can feel our teeth stick to the nutty caramel on our first taffy apple. (Now our teeth might stick better to the taffy apple than to our mouth!) Of course, we can't forget steamy vapors rising from the flaky crust of apple pie with ice cream on it either. Apples are, indeed, something special and a true delight to our eyes.

Apples, however, don't always retain their positive image. You probably know someone who is rotten to the core or the one bad apple that spoiled the bunch. And even great apples, when you get down really deep, are seedy, and they have those little shavings of core that taste like cellophane. Makes one wonder if "apple of His eye" is a good metaphor for our special relationship with God.

Good thing God loves even rotten apples. How often aren't the "apples of His eye" soft, bruised, and moldy? Like apples fallen from the tree and attacked by bees and worms, we apples sometimes feed what seeks to consume us. Yet we remain the apple of His eye. He doesn't concentrate on the soft spots or decay. Jesus polished us through His victory over sin, which He earned hanging on the tree from which we fell. Jesus, the apple of His Father's eye, waxed us with forgiveness and created a whole new saying: One Good Apple saved the whole bunch!

That Bugs Me

What then shall we say? That the law is sin? By no means! Yet if it had not been for the law, I would not have known sin. I would not have known what it is to covet if the law had not said, "You shall not covet."
Romans 7:7

Arthropodiatrists (scientists who specialize in bugs with lots of feet) recognize about 425,000 species of beetles. (Whoops, make that 424,999. I think my wife squished the last one of a kind in the kitchen sink!) That's more than half the species of insects, spiders, and crustaceans put together. A famous bug biologist was once asked what theological ramifications this might have. He theorized that God just had a special fondness for beetles!

So how do we turn beetles into something that reminds us of our own spirituality? My theological theory is that a beetle is like guilt. It's meant to bug us. (If you're fond of beetles, bugs in general, or Volkswagens, you probably won't like this meditation.)

God put beetles and other arthropods on earth so we could call common things by names that defy pronunciation. No, that's not right. Even beetles have a God-given role in our complex ecosystem (or is it eek-o-system?). They annoy some and benefit others. It's the same with guilt.

Hear what Paul says in Romans 7:7: "What then shall we say? That the law is sin? By no means! Yet if it had not been for the law, I would not have known sin. I would not have known what it is to covet if the law had not said, 'You shall not covet.'"

Guilt may bug us, but its God-given purpose is to reveal our sins. We need not worry about divulging our sins to others. (They probably are well aware of them already!) But we need to personally know about and admit our sins, otherwise we would continue living in ways that angered God and fractured our relationship with His creations—human and otherwise. We wouldn't know what we've done to earn eternal destruction. Without that knowledge, we would go about our normal routines completely ignorant of God's willingness to forgive for Christ's sake. We'd be unaware of the majesty of God's mercy and the generosity of His grace. And to make matters worse, guilt would still bug us!

Like prolific beetles, just as one episode of guilt gets extinguished, another appears. Thank God for guilt anyway! Thank God for His opulent opportunities to repent and receive forgiveness. Thank Him for His lavish love. And thank Him that we can bug Him about our guilt and His forgiveness anytime.

Don't Ask

*Then He said to them, "But who do you say that I am?" And Peter
answered, "The Christ of God." Luke 9:20*

When is the last time you expressed an opinion? We probably share
opinions more frequently than we realize. Most liberal thinkers
believe that opinions must be pliable, and that only fanatics maintain their
views without compromise. My opinion is that opinions are sometimes foolish. Millions of opinions shared by millions of fools are still foolish opinions.
So there.

Whoops. We can really get caught up in our opinions, can't we?
Sometimes we confuse them with facts. Sometimes we mistakenly label facts
as opinions too. Take the matter of Jesus and Peter recorded in the passage
from Luke above. Did Jesus seek fact or opinion from Peter?

Today, as always, facts must be based on proof. Opinion, on the other
hand, is often what we think about facts. When Jesus asked Peter that famous
question printed above, Peter answered with a fact. In those days, as well as
today, people expressed diverse opinions about Jesus. Some thought He was
a great prophet. Others, no doubt, thought Him a silly fool. His enemies
thought He was a heretic. Only Peter correctly identified Him. Jesus was the
Savior sent by God. Fact.

We can claim that the Bible clearly identifies Jesus as our Savior, the Son
of the only true God, who is still active today in the Holy Spirit. But others
also convincingly claim other gods. So what makes Christians right and everyone else wrong?

Faith is the answer. Believing an opinion doesn't make it right unless the
Holy Spirit has planted that belief in our hearts and minds. He did. Thank
God for faith to believe what otherwise would be an incredible opinion!

July 3

The One and Only First of Many

"For God so loved the world, that He gave His only Son, that whoever believes in Him should not perish but have eternal life." John 3:16

You're probably not alone if today's title leaves you puzzled, so perhaps I owe a quick explanation. You're embarking on a series of meditations built on significant Bible passages known as the 3:16s. During the next several days we'll consider the third chapter, 16th verse of several books, but today's 3:16 is a universal favorite.

God so loved the world that He didn't form a committee to plan it, hire a consulting firm to improve it, or look the other way and pretend not to notice its problems. God so loved the world that He didn't send someone else to save it. He did it Himself.

Now God appointed Himself to deal with sin from the very beginning. He made promises, and He also made threats. Quite often people forgot His promises and ignored His threats. It seems that people had difficulty putting their trust solely in one God. So God put some flesh on His promises by taking the form of a human so the world He loved could actually see Him.

As you know, much of the world didn't like what it saw. (It still doesn't.) Jesus was humble, gentle, forgiving, and law abiding. He had power to overpower, but He didn't use it except in cases where someone needed healing or help. As might be expected, He was arrested on trumped-up charges and executed. God died. Think of that. The second person of the Trinity was actually dead. But not for long. He came back to life and promised that we would do the same. Now He's waiting for us.

God so loves the world that His Holy Spirit is still with us. God so loves the world that He will keep us with Him until the end of time. And even longer.

Wisdom 316

Long life is in her right hand; in her left hand are riches and honor.
Proverbs 3:16

Wouldn't it be great if you could enroll in a college course numbered Wisdom 316? Some claim that age brings wisdom, but age sometimes travels alone. And when it does come with old age, it's too late to do us much good! A course to teach wisdom? Hardly possible. You can buy an education, but wisdom is a gift from God.

Some define wisdom as knowledge at work. Others claim wisdom is learning from our foolishness. The writer of Proverbs had his own definition of wisdom. He said that trust in God was wisdom (3:5). In that verse, he also advised the "wanna be" wise not to "lean on their own understanding." That seems to warn that our own life experiences can be misleading or useless.

Life may teach us to keep quiet, save our money, and otherwise look out for Number 1. Keeping quiet is fine when we have nothing good to say, but wise Christians just can't be mute when it comes to sharing the Gospel. It's not always the popular thing to do, and some will think it unwise, but we can trust God's wisdom in His command to proclaim His Word.

Saving or investing money is a wise way to approach retirement, but spending some of that money on God's work is an even wiser practice. After all, there is no mandatory retirement age for Him, and His work needs to proceed. Spending money on God's work requires the trust Solomon wrote about too. Did it ever strike you that he was exceedingly rich even though he spent fortunes for God's work?

Looking out for Number 1 is a wise thought too. As long as we remember who Number 1 is! True wisdom comes with recognizing God as Number 1 in our life and trusting Him more than we trust ourselves. He provides plenty of guidance in His Word and through His Spirit. We're wise when we trust Him. If we don't, we're otherwise.

Accounting 316

Then those who feared the Lord spoke with one another. The Lord paid attention and heard them, and a book of remembrance was written before Him of those who feared the Lord and esteemed His name. Malachi 3:16

Business students must take several accounting classes before they graduate. Some, like me, took the same accounting course several times before we graduated! My liabilities always exceeded my assets. I guess I just wasn't cut out for Accounting 201.

All Christians qualify for Accounting 316, though. We should probably add verse 17 to really profit from the prophet. He said, "'They will be Mine,' says the LORD Almighty, 'in the day when I make up My treasured possession.'" We should probably remember Revelation too, in which John sees God looking for the names of believers in the Book of Life—the heavenly ledger.

Life is a liability. Filled with sin, we stubbornly cling to the debit side of life's balance sheet. All our numbers seem to be in the left column with no earthly way of paying the debt we accumulate. But God marks the largest number to our credit.

All the credit, of course, goes to Jesus Christ, who paid for our sins with His life. When God looks into that Book of Life on the last day, He'll see one entry that dwarfs the others. Not that we earned that asset ourselves. It was a gift, and it covered all that we owed God for a life of weak faith, unwitting mistakes, and broken commandments.

As we count our daily sins, we need to confess our inability to balance the Book of Life. But this is no time to be timid. God offers free forgiveness. He takes away our sins, and we're able to begin the next day with a clean account. In fact, we really have a credit balance when you think about it. Just count your blessings. They far surpass your troubles.

Quality Control 316

John answered them all, saying, "I baptize you with water, but He who is mightier than I is coming, the strap of whose sandals I am not worthy to untie. He will baptize you with the Holy Spirit and with fire." Luke 3:16

Quality-control departments provide assurance that every product is the best that it can be. But with God, quality control is different. He starts with the best and makes it even better.

Today's Bible passage mentions two baptisms. Now before you run out to get another one, be assured that one Baptism is all it takes to make you a Christian. Our Baptism with water is the only one necessary. When John the Baptist, who did the talking here in Luke, said that his baptism was only with water and that Jesus baptized with the Holy Spirit, he wasn't putting down baptism by water. Baptism is a means of grace—a way of receiving God's love, mercy, and forgiveness. Jesus did everything necessary to bring all the benefits of Baptism our way. He made us holy. The other Baptism of which John spoke referred his listeners to an event yet to come, namely Pentecost. Those already-baptized believers would receive the Holy Spirit, thus enabling them to proclaim the Gospel and baptize even more people.

We start with the best—holiness through the blood of Jesus, which washes away our sins. Then we become better—better people living Christ-centered lives, telling others about Jesus, and applying faith to everyday life.

But there's more to this idea of best and better. John the Baptist indeed was great, but He knew Jesus was greater. In the same way, we Christians have the best right now. We're saved. God is faithful to us. The Holy Spirit keeps the fire in our faith. Yet something better remains in the future. Jesus will come again. Then, together with all the saints, we'll celebrate with an eternal party.

What's Your Doctor's Name?

And His name—by faith in His name—has made this man strong whom
you see and know, and the faith that is through Jesus has given the man
this perfect health in the presence of you all. Acts 3:16

Medical specialization dominates the health-care scene. The names of certain doctors carry status and prestige. If your doctor's name is Salk, Barnard, Menninger, or Mayo (how about Luke?), you probably wonder if he or she is related to THE physician who made that name famous. A doctor's name is also a doctor's reputation. This was always true, even in the days of the early Christians.

Today's Bible verse comes from the story of Peter healing the crippled beggar. People wondered about this medical miracle, and they probably wanted to note the attending physician's name—just in case they needed similar help. Peter bypassed his moment in medical history when he gave all the credit to someone else. Jesus was the specialist, and faith in His power brought true and complete healing.

All of us are disabled and impoverished—in dire need of healing. No covey of specialists has a cure, and even if they did, no insurance company could afford the price. Our sickness is sin. We're hobbled by its power to separate us from God. Thankfully, God isn't paralyzed by it's power. He sent the Great Physician, Jesus Himself, to eliminate sin's power to kill us. Oh, we have our relapses, but the Great Physician has long office hours. He's always ready to hear us describe our despair, and He offers the remedy of His forgiveness. He never sends us a bill either, for He has already paid the price to cure us once and forever. Even more astounding, He writes a perpetual prescription. Just think—no limit on refills and we can even read His writing! So call the Doctor often and be sure to take all His Word too.

Church Bodies

*Do you not know that you are God's temple and that God's Spirit
dwells in you? 1 Corinthians 3:16*

Some people think God lives in church buildings. You can tell by the
reverence they show while in the sanctuary. But our latest 3:16, from
Paul's first letter to the Corinthians, indicates that God's sweetest home is in
the hearts of His people.

Don't you know that you are a place in which to worship God? Don't you
know your body is home to the Holy Spirit? Real churches are places of forgiveness, and so it needs to be in the walking, talking variety.

Just as members of churches serve God, so must the members of church
bodies serve Him. Let's take a look at the body of our church. Starting at the
bottom, we have feet. Isaiah called them beautiful—when they belong to
someone who delivers Good News and peace. Working our way up, we arrive
at the knees—God's great invention for bending. Knees and prayer seem especially good companions. Moving on, we reach the place where we seem to
spend most of our time—our rear end. God gave us some decent padding,
which makes reading our Bibles a comfortable proposition, but He doesn't
expect us spend all our time there.

Heading north again, we migrate past the vital organs. While they might
not play tunes like the one in church, they do keep our service to God moving along. Our church body has an especially warm heart as well as the most
vital organ—one that doesn't show up on x-rays—our soul. Home sweet
home for the Holy Spirit! And off to the sides reside our arms and hands, willing servants for the more physical service to Christ. Finally, we reach the top.
Ears to hear God's Word as it admonishes and blesses. Eyes to see the wonders of His creation. Mouths to house disciplined and kind tongues, and
brains to think of even more ways to serve the Savior.

Who needs stained glass when we have such beautiful churches so close
by?

Dwell on It

Let the word of Christ dwell in you richly, teaching and admonishing one another in all wisdom, singing psalms and hymns and spiritual songs, with thankfulness in your hearts to God. Colossians 3:16

For many years, the Bible was a best seller. It was also the best buy. We may rightfully suspect, however, that if all Bibles were waved in the air at the same time, we would experience the worst dust storm in history!

The only way to let Christ's Word "dwell in you richly" is to dwell on it richly. Yet so many obstacles have us dwelling elsewhere. The biggest impediment is time. If clocks had little pitchforks instead of hands, perhaps we would realize how well the devil uses time. We so cram our calendars that when we have time to rest, that's all we want to do.

God blesses us with several ways to let the Word of Christ dwell in us. In addition to the Bible, there is music. Humming "Jerusalem the Golden" may not be in everyone's repertoire, but nearly everyone enjoys some type of music. Music with Christ-centered lyrics comes in so many varieties that nearly every taste can be satisfied. Have you ever had a tune in your head that just kept coming back? That's the way it is when Christ's Word dwells in us. We live and breathe and speak and hum it without realizing what we're doing.

The indwelling of God's Word enables us to "teach and admonish one another with all wisdom." Note that this is not a one-dimensional activity. "One another" suggests that each Christian is both giver and taker. As we gather with and listen to other Christians, the Holy Spirit opens our souls and minds to new possibilities for living out our faith. When we read our Bibles and sing our spirituals, the Holy Spirit is there too, helping us perceive the awesome majesty of God's power and love—even if a small dust cloud chokes us as we sing off-key.

July 10

Nothing Like a Good Mystery

Great indeed, we confess, is the mystery of godliness: He was manifested in the flesh, vindicated by the Spirit, seen by angels, proclaimed among the nations, believed on in the world, taken up in glory. 1 Timothy 3:16

Mystery stories remain popular both in books and on television. Of course, the mystery is only a mystery until the hero or heroine figures out the puzzle. The same is true for certain mysteries in the Bible.

Paul revealed some important mysteries about God when he wrote to young Timothy. Notice how Paul explains the mystery of Jesus. In doing so, Paul also delivers a brief creed that well capsulizes the life of Jesus. And in explaining the mystery, Paul is careful to avoid any explanation of how God did all these things. That will remain a mystery. Instead, Paul reveals the mystery of who God is.

If you're reading this meditation through the eyes of faith, you may ask, "What mystery?" It doesn't puzzle you because God already revealed the mystery through the Holy Spirit. God chose to give you faith, and now you have received and developed that marvelous—and even mysterious—gift.

But to unbelievers, God's love and the identity of the Savior are a mystery. Without the Holy Spirit's work in uncovering the mystery, the truth remains hidden. To make matters worse, the devil loves mysteries too. Even when the Spirit exposes the truth, the devil tries to hide it, urging us not to believe.

Rejoice that you comprehend the mystery of everlasting life with the Savior. Keep your faith strong in prayer, study, and meditation. Be ready to disclose the mystery to others. You'll have some good opportunities when you find others frustrated, sad, lonely, or sick. They're prime candidates for the Holy Spirit and you. Tell them the truth—even if it hurts. The truth really hurts when you step on the bathroom scale.

Good for Everything

All Scripture is breathed out by God and profitable for teaching, for reproof, for correction, and for training in righteousness. 2 Timothy 3:16

The Bible is good for everything. Sure proof of the Bible's value is the nature of those who dispute it! By the same token, it has survived some of its fanatic and ignorant "friends" as well!

How do you like the phrase "God-breathed?" Older readers may recall that "inspired" was once the word. But perhaps God-breathed is more inspiring. After all, Shakespeare, Louis L'Amour, and Danielle Steel could be considered inspired writers too. But for something to be breathed by God—well, that's another story. Not really a story at all, but divine truth useful for all occasions. Because the Bible's words are God's actual words, we don't have to worry if Paul or Moses or Matthew were having a bad day—perhaps a day when writer's block forced them to leave out some important details or motivated them to fantasize some fiction. We take comfort knowing that God's Word is God's Word!

Writing the Bible, like speaking God's Word, must have been difficult at times, especially when God talked about sinfulness. He told us what we need to know; namely, that we deserve His anger and punishment. But we have Good News in the Bible too. God loved sinners so much that He didn't want them spending eternity in the fiery depths of hell. Jesus brought us close to God through His death on the cross and His victory over sin and Satan. An incredible story but nonetheless believable because God says it's so.

What do we do when someone challenges our belief in the Bible's value and authority? There's no use arguing or trying to prove our point with human logic. Our only ploy is to insist, "God says so." Too simple? Probably. But isn't that what faith is all about? Even children know the answer. Just listen to them sing "Jesus loves me, this I know . . ." They'll tell you why.

July 12

Well Oiled

*The Spirit of the Lord God is upon me, because the Lord has anointed me
to bring good news to the poor; He has sent me to bind up the brokenhearted, to proclaim liberty to the captives, and the opening of the prison
to those who are bound. Isaiah 61:1*

How true it is that the Lord loves cheerful givers! Maybe that's why so
many people enjoy handing out free advice. But Isaiah said that we
should give counsel only to those who really need it. In fact, Isaiah indicates
that God makes Christians well-oiled machines (Isn't that what *anointed*
means?), fully capable of dispensing mercy and grace.

When God anointed people to fulfill a task, it was a sign that He would
be with them, giving them power and wisdom to carry out His holy will for
the people He loved. That's precisely what He has in mind for us too. Let's
take a closer look at two of the tasks He "oils" us to undertake.

First, we're told to "bind up the brokenhearted." What interesting language! God commissions us to mend broken hearts—bind the pieces together again. If you look around, you'll probably find lots of hearts that need
repair.

Quoting a Bible passage may seem to be the right bandage for a broken
heart. But as much as people need God's Word, they also need good listeners.
They need someone willing to hear gut-wrenching emotions spend themselves in words. Then they need someone willing to say, "Jesus loves you in
good times and bad. Trust Him to bring you through."

Next we're told to "proclaim freedom for the captives." Some captives are
imprisoned by drugs, sex, or alcohol. Others are prisoners of greed, gossip, or
hate. We can share what it's like to be a forgiven child of God, freed from guilt
and condemnation by our loving Savior. Only words? Yes, but we need not
feel guilty or inadequate. Just as we might not understand how glue bonds
objects, we don't need to know how Christ's love binds broken hearts and
frees captives. What we do know is that it works.

Back from the Dead

"If they do not hear Moses and the Prophets, neither will they be convinced if someone should rise from the dead." Luke 16:31

The funeral industry enjoys downward trends in business. Okay, the humor is morbid, but it's here to suggest something that certainly isn't a new idea to believers. For faithful people, death is the only currently available portal to that immortal, glorious life in God's presence—a place where all jokes are actually funny. Death does bring grief to loved ones, but bereavement is easier to bear knowing it's not permanent. Our comfort—and even joy—is absent in the lives of some, though.

Did you read today's Bible passage? It's the sad and frightening story of a man who had opportunity to be saved but didn't take it. He pleaded for help to Abraham from hell—someone to warn his family to accept the faith offered them. But here is the tragic finale: "He said to him, 'If they do not hear Moses and the Prophets, neither will they be convinced if someone should rise from the dead'" (Luke 16:31).

Father Abraham's words ring true today. Unbelievers often are skeptical, seeking proof of God's almighty existence. Believers may wish for the same in hopes of convincing unbelieving loved ones before it's too late. Sadly, father Abraham was and remains right. No proof is solid enough to those bent on unbelief, disbelief, or nonbelief. But don't give up trying. We have an advantage. Someone we know came back from the dead.

You probably wouldn't be reading this book if you didn't know and believe that our Savior Jesus Christ defeated sin, death, and the devil. He died. He came back to life because He's more powerful than death and the devil. We've read about it and trust that it is accurate history. As we share that history, we pray the Holy Spirit's power that others may believe. And there ends our responsibility.

Be sure to share what you know about coming back from the dead. Remember that every believer was once dead in sins and has come back to life through the gift of faith. Look forward to that day when the many people you've known and loved will return from the dead to live forever. For now, you are a living link between heaven and earth. You bring truth to people while time remains. You've come back from the dead once. You'll do it again. Things are looking up!

Dead and Buried

For "All flesh is like grass and all its glory like the flower of grass. The grass withers, and the flower falls." 1 Peter 1:24

Does the name Johann August Eberhard ring a bell? He was an author who lived from 1739–1809 and wrote a book entitled *Neue Apologie des Sokrates*. Certainly, Johann was acclaimed in his family and hometown. For most of us, though, his name doesn't even jingle, much less ring a bell. He is dead and buried. Gone and largely forgotten.

We're probably headed for the same degree of renown, and most of us will leave behind only a headstone. One hundred, five hundred, a thousand years from now, will anyone know or care about who we were and what we did? Most of today's population can't remember the name of the first person to walk on the moon, and that was in 1969!

The Apostle Peter's first letter confirms the dismal truth. He compares us with flowers. As beautiful as they are, they all must wither and die. They return to the very ground that nourished them from tiny seed to fruitful adult. Dead and buried. Forgotten. How pathetic for Peter and for us if the end were really the end.

Cemeteries are filled with people who may be anonymous in history and unknown to us personally. But God remembers each of them. He could no more forget than a mother could forget each of her children! God created every one of them and invited them to call Him Father. He sent His only Son Jesus to redeem the world, and to record the names of believers in a special book. The book is called The Book of Life. (Read Revelation if you want to know more.) Your name is in it even though you haven't died yet. Maybe Johann's is in it too. Certainly, we'll find Abraham, Samuel, Ruth, Mary, Lazarus, and Peter there. They're all dead and buried. Gone, but not forgotten. Jesus remembers. And our names will live on forever.

Set Apart

Now may the God of peace Himself sanctify you completely, and may
Your whole spirit and soul and body be kept blameless at the coming of
our Lord Jesus Christ. 1 Thessalonians 5:23

It sure beats "Have a good day." Of course, if we used the farewell that Paul left with the Thessalonians, people might look at us funny. They might think that we are "different" and they might set us apart from themselves in the future. They would be right in one respect. We are set apart.

Paul says the God of peace sanctifies us. To be sanctified means to be set apart. God set us apart to be His own children. He chose us to receive faith from the Holy Spirit so we could believe the extraordinary story of what Jesus did for us. Because God has set us apart, our lives have special meaning.

As much as we might like to bask in the blush of peace and glow of glory that accompanies our status, we don't have time to sit back and admire ourselves. We are set apart to do God's work. So as sanctified Christians, we roll up our sleeves and get busy.

First, it is important to regularly study and reflect on God's Word. Next, we practice His Word in our daily activities and routines. As sanctified Christians we let the Holy Spirit control our lives, and we willingly desire to serve God and our neighbors—both local and global.

Good works are the job of those set apart by God. The possibilities are too numerous to mention, for good works include everything believers do, say, or even think to God's glory or the benefit of others. And the Spirit doesn't let us tackle this work alone. He gives us "tools" to accomplish His will. So what are you waiting for? Quit reading and get back to work. Oh yes—be sure to use some of your new tools.

Show It

*In the same way, let your light shine before others, so that they may see
your good works and give glory to your Father who is in heaven.*
Matthew 5:16

To turn on a light, you must flip a switch. The Holy Spirit has "flipped
our switch" and now our purpose in life is to remain bright beacons
of Jesus Christ. This undoubtedly makes us happy, but perhaps we haven't
told our faces about it.

We let God's light shine when we let our teeth shine. Yes, smiles qualify
as good deeds. Not that we have to be giddy or silly. Some take a smile as an
invitation to generously dump their troubles on you as if you were an old,
close friend. Still others might wonder what you're after—especially if it's the
opposite sex. Lighting up your face with God's love can illuminate a whole lot
more than you expect. But Jesus loves us, and He expects us to show it.

Consider the "dumpers." It's only natural for people to assume that if
you're friendly on your face, you're also friendly in your heart. And your ears.
Your tongue goes along with it too. What better opportunity for witness do
we have than with people who are hurting? Even annoying, whining, selfish
people who are hurting. Maybe you've noticed this on a night ride through a
rural area: the darker the dark, the lighter the light.

Finally, nothing makes a suspicious person more suspicious than a smile.
These people need our sympathy—and our witness—too. Most suspicious
people act that way because they've been misused, abused, or simply used. As
Jesus showed unconditional love even to the worst of His tormentors and the
best of sinners, our light needs to shine even on those who prefer the shadows. *Unconditional* is a key word. Give everything, expect nothing. Not exactly the way of the world, is it? That's what makes it so good. So leave the light
on for someone today.

But I Thought You Said . . .

Beware of practicing your righteousness before other people in order to be seen by them, for then you will have no reward from your Father who is in heaven. Matthew 6:1

The previous meditation dealt with "letting our teeth, er, light shine" as one of many good deeds in our Christian life. Now we read a passage that says we should keep our good deeds hidden!

Good deeds are susceptible to corruption, and the contamination usually comes from within. When it comes to good deeds, it's the motivation that really counts. Rather than contradicting Himself on the "shining lights" verse, Matthew 6:1 is Jesus' comment on those who do good deeds for bad reasons. Only one pure motivation exists for serving God: Loving Him. And even that's not enough.

We love God only when, by faith, we realize how much He loves us. As we meditate daily on His Word, we remember that He sent Jesus to live and die for our sins. We continue to sin, and He continues to forgive. But our vast experience as sinners helps us relate to other sinners who need to know Jesus' love and forgiveness. That's where good deeds—or "acts of righteousness"—come in. And they can't come in from our own hearts and desires. They are totally a reaction to God's grace and mercy. Therefore, we have no reason to boast of our own goodness.

So what would you say if someone asked, "Why are you always so helpful (friendly, peaceful, etc.)? No call for false modesty here. Real modesty is best. Confess that you're good (And you are!) because Jesus made you that way. Now He wants us to do good for others—to His credit. He expects us to testify on His behalf, and He gives us the power to make a good name. Not for ourselves, of course. We don't need it. We've already got the best name on earth. Don't we, Christian?

A Short Space

The saying is trustworthy and deserving of full acceptance, that Christ Jesus came into the world to save sinners, of whom I am the foremost.
1 Timothy 1:15

Sometimes there's only a short space between an atheist and a theist. You probably know a few atheists. They're the ones who shake their fists at the God they claim doesn't exist. Atheists can't find God for the same reason that criminals can't find police officers. Atheists have almost as long a history as believers do, which makes one wonder. How could the early inhabitants of our planet not believe in God? They had so much evidence. But then, as now, evidence doesn't make believers. Faith does, and they refused it.

Take the case of Paul, a.k.a. Saul. He was the promoter and supervisor of many persecutions of early Christians. Two thousand years ago, Saul's famous name brought cheer and encouragement to those who hated Jesus. They didn't believe Jesus was God's Son even if they believed in God Himself. They believed in a God they couldn't see, but they couldn't believe in a God they could see! Worse, they wanted to silence forever any lips that confessed Jesus as God and Savior.

Had anyone predicted that Saul's fame as a persecutor would be dwarfed by his fame as a Christian, they would have been laughed all the way to Damascus. But we know what happened (Acts 9). The Holy Spirit performed the miracle of conversion. Paul talked about it in his note to Timothy. If it can happen to Paul, it can happen to anyone.

Pray for all atheists—even successful ones. Pray that they accept the Spirit's invitation to join the worst of sinners who acknowledge the Savior as Lord and King. Pray that the Spirit put some space between them and their unbelief—that they go from atheist to a theist. The Holy Spirit can do it, and Paul is living proof!

Don't be surprised if Christmas displays mysteriously appear on courthouse lawns some day.

Graffiti

Immediately the fingers of a human hand appeared and wrote on the plaster of the wall of the king's palace, opposite the lampstand. And the king saw the hand as it wrote. Daniel 5:5

If you're like many people, you read in the bathroom. If you use public washrooms, chances are good you won't need to provide your own reading material. Just read the stalls. (The term "quit stalling" originated with someone impatiently awaiting available space while experiencing kidney anxiety.) Graffiti poses serious aesthetic problems for building owners, public transportation companies, bridges, garage doors, and anything else that remains immobile for too long.

Graffiti was actually invented as far back as the Old Testament. Daniel 5:5 says: "Immediately the fingers of a human hand appeared and wrote on the plaster of the wall of the king's palace, opposite the lampstand. And the king saw the hand as it wrote."

King Belshazzar of Babylon suffered graffiti on the walls of his banquet room. He even caught the Tagger (to use graffiti language) in the act. Or maybe it was the other way around. God (the Tagger) caught Belshazzar in an act of defiance and disrespect. The slogan on the wall, interpreted by Daniel, foretold the king's death. The graffiti was fulfilled that very night.

Have you seen the handwriting on the wall? If God were to write on our walls, what would He say? He might enumerate the ways we disrespect Him. Would He scrawl something about how we use His name? Might He draw a picture of our wallet or purse to depict how we hoard all His material blessings instead of contributing to His work? Would He record all those evil thoughts we would never reveal to others? Would He redirect our accusations of others to expose our own faults? Would He prophesy our well-deserved death?

No!

God would take His holy finger and probably draw something like a cross. King Belshazzar's graffiti meant death because he refused to acknowledge God. This graffiti on our walls means life because it tells of Jesus who suffered death on our behalf. This graffiti on our walls reminds us that Jesus is our personal Savior who knows and loves us despite our sinfulness.

Next time you see something riddled with graffiti, let it remind you of your sinful life. But look closely—is there a cross somewhere in that tangle of lines?

Unforgivable

*Therefore I tell you, every sin and blasphemy will be forgiven people, but
the blasphemy against the Spirit will not be forgiven. And whoever speaks
a word against the Son of Man will be forgiven, but whoever speaks
against the Holy Spirit will not be forgiven, either in this age or in the
age to come. Matthew 12:31–32*

Do you know the best way to get back at your enemies? Forgive them.
Jesus did that repeatedly. Some of His enemies, however, preferred
not to be forgiven. Those who chose to be condemned, are unforgivable.

Have you ever heard of the deadly Pharaoh Syndrome? Its most conspic-
uous symptom is hardening of the heart. Given numerous opportunities to
repent of his sins and to release God's people whom he enslaved, Pharaoh
refused. Years later, Jesus would tell the disciples to forgive 70 x 7 times. Yet
Pharaoh only had nine chances. Why? The answer, of course, rests (uncom-
fortably) with Pharaoh himself. He refused to believe the true God.

While large numbers of various sins get forgiven each day, the Bible also
cautions that one sin will not be forgiven. Jesus called it the sin against the
Holy Spirit. Before you check back to see if you've inadvertently committed it,
stop and take a sigh of relief. It's unlikely this sin belongs to anyone who takes
time to read this meditation. The sin against the Holy Spirit is refusal to
accept the faith He freely gives. Naturally, those who reject faith reject God
and all that He offers.

We Christians don't need to worry. Our sins were forgiven on a dark hill
2,000 years ago. Each day we come before God and ask Him again to forgive
us for the sake of Him who died on that hill. And each day we can be certain
we are indeed forgiven. As long as you know that and believe it, you can be
sure that you haven't fallen to the unforgivable—and unforgettable—sin.

Sweet Dreams

For since we believe that Jesus died and rose again, even so, through Jesus,
God will bring with Him those who have fallen asleep.
1 Thessalonians 4:14

The call from the hospital came at 3 a.m. The doctor said, "I'm sorry, but your father expired just moments ago." Makes it sound like he was a credit card or a store coupon. Expired?

Many Christians prefer what some consider a euphemism. Death is only sleep. But just as surely as you awoke this morning, you will also awaken after death. Isn't that one of the great comforts we Christians share? Death may extract loved ones from our life, but not forever.

Two things are certain in life—death and taxes. Since we can't escape either, we must live with both. At least death only comes once. And when it comes, it's helpful to use Bible language for death—sleeping. Critics may laugh or think us too soft to face finality. Some people just prefer to think of death as the end of life's story. The truth is that it's only a phase. It'll pass.

If death is sleep, then it's possible to construct some parallels to our limited knowledge about the subject. Some people fear falling asleep because of recurring nightmares. (I had that problem once myself, but it disappeared as soon as I left Latin class.) Cold sweat is a good way of describing such experiences. Christians may experience such discomfort during earthly sleep, but they certainly have nothing to fear as they wait out the death phase of eternal life. In fact, it probably wouldn't be out of order to greet the dying with a sincere "sweet dreams." As John Newton said in his the famous hymn, "How sweet the name of Jesus sounds In a believer's ear!" And as for ourselves, we find comfort in this coming nap too. And this time we'll be eager to wake up when the alarm rings!

Breaking the Habit

*And the Lord said: "Because this people draw near with their mouth
and honor Me with their lips, while their hearts are far from Me, and
their fear of Me is a commandment taught by men, therefore, behold, I
will again do wonderful things with this people, with wonder upon wonder; and the wisdom of their wise men shall perish, and the discernment
of their discerning men shall be hidden." Isaiah 29:13–14*

Do you have any bad habits? If not, ask your neighbor. He probably
has a few to spare. (Or else he'll tell you about the habits you've
been missing!)

Few people would claim that making a habit of regular worship is bad.
But consider these words from Scripture: "And the Lord said: 'Because this
people draw near with their mouth and honor Me with their lips, while their
hearts are far from Me, and their fear of Me is a commandment taught by
men'" (Isaiah 29:13).

Has it occurred to you that sometimes we children of God act like we
don't have a Father? Oh, it's easy to do what's expected, especially as we worship in church—when we're aware that Father is watching. We diligently follow the order of service, participating in prayers and taking care not to talk
when it's the preacher's turn. If the music is a tune we especially like, we sing
enthusiastically; if it's not one of our favorites, we sing anyway. But when the
service ends, it's easy to completely forget Father.

Worship is more than habitual church attendance. We worship when we
practice what we hear preached—when we add relationships to ritual. That's
what Jesus did. He preached His sermons and led large Bible classes, and He
expected people to listen and learn. He also cared about His "congregation"
and expected these people to care for one another (as well as for Him). Jesus
proved this point repeatedly as He demonstrated His tenderness and compassion as well as His knowledge of Scripture. Remember the time He single-
handedly catered the potluck when everyone else left their pots at home?

Jesus and His Father (who is our Father too) have observed many people
who've confused ritual with relationship—who leave worship nestled in pews
rather than strolling the sidewalks. That's why God gave us the message we
read in Isaiah. When we catch ourselves turning a good habit into a bad one,
He'll help us break it. And the Holy Spirit will help us keep our good habits
truly good. He has a habit of doing that. Thank God.

Life Insurance

"Therefore do not be anxious, saying, 'What shall we eat?' or 'What shall we drink?' or 'What shall we wear?'" Matthew 6:31

At one time, many Christians considered purchasing life insurance a grave (really bad pun!) sin. Others refused to obtain policies because they wanted everyone to be sad when they died! But back to the sinfulness issue. If we take today's Bible passage seriously, are things we do to enhance or protect our future contrary to God's Word?

Like anything else we allow to control our lives, planning for the future can be sinful. But God has also given us resources to use wisely for ourselves and our families when we can no longer work. Death being one of those times when we can no longer work, life insurance can also be classified as wise planning not outside of God's will. And there is another kind of planning that we can do as an investment against the future. In fact, you're doing it now.

Wise planning for the future involves Bible study, meditation, prayer, and worship. It's a lot cheaper than conventional insurance, but it's also more valuable. As an added benefit, we can enjoy it even before it's paid in full. As our relationship with Jesus deepens through these investments, we begin to comprehend what Jesus meant by His words about the future. But like any insurance policy, we need to read the whole thing to completely understand it. So here is what follows Jesus' words in Matthew 6:31: "But seek first the kingdom of God and His righteousness, and all these things will be added to you" (6:33).

Jesus placed everything in perspective. As we "seek first His kingdom," we take care of our spiritual needs first. With that in place, we continue to live confidently, knowing God will always care for us.

Our future is well protected thanks to Jesus' investment on our behalf. And His coverage is a vast improvement on life insurance, which is misnamed anyway. Thanks to Jesus, we have life assurance!

July 24

Perfect Score

Blessed be the Lord who has given rest to His people Israel, according to
all that He promised. Not one word has failed of all His good promise,
which He spoke by Moses His servant. 1 Kings 8:56

Some people spend half their time making promises. Then they spend the other half making excuses. Not so with God. He has the 300 of bowling, the 0.00 earned run average, perfect 10s of skating, and 100 percent free-throw average all rolled into one. God's perfect record in keeping promises has never been and never will be equaled.

Unfortunately, people have been testing God's promises since Adam and Eve. But even after their unfaithfulness, God offered another promise—a Savior to take away their sins.

Throughout the Old Testament, God's promises continued to roll right along with His wrath over people's unfaithfulness and immorality. Each time His righteous anger flared, so did His compassion. He promised various things to His Old Testament people, but His foremost promise remained that of a Savior. And when He finally delivered on His promise, hardly anyone believed it.

Jesus made promises too. He promised to return to life after He died. Even His disciples didn't believe *that!* He kept His promise anyway. Then came the time for Jesus to return to His rightful place in heaven. As He left, He promised to return.

We live in a promising age. It's the same era in which Paul, Peter, and John preached about Jesus' promise to return. We've waited 2,000 years for Jesus to fulfill this most important vow. In the meantime, we're blessed with Jesus' other promises, like the ones to be with us and answer our prayers. Like the ones to keep His forgiveness equal to our sins.

Yes, the time approaches when God will give rest to all His people. We can count on it happening any day now. Or any decade now. Or any century now.

Eat, Drink, and Be Merry

There is nothing better for a person than that he should eat and drink
and find enjoyment in his toil. This also, I saw, is from the hand of God,
for apart from Him who can eat or who can have enjoyment? For to the
one who pleases Him God has given wisdom and knowledge and joy, but
to the sinner He has given the business of gathering and collecting, only
to give to one who pleases God. This also is vanity and a striving after
wind. Ecclesiastes 2:24–26

Solomon's words from Ecclesiastes would be widely accepted today—especially if taken out of context. Skeptics may smirk over these verses. They view them in the "Eat, drink, and be merry for tomorrow we die" category. While the opening verse sounds similar initially, the words that follow add spiritual depth unsurpassed in Epicurean epitaphs.

God used Solomon to tell us to eat and enjoy life. Surprised? Hey, isn't that what Thanksgiving is all about? Of course, the only way we truly enjoy life is by knowing God. Who can eat, drink, and be merry fearing the good life will end someday? Eating, drinking, and otherwise having fun is so much better when we're satisfied with the present and looking forward to the day when life gets even better!

The banquet of blessings doesn't end with physical merriment. Did you notice what God provides for those who please Him? God gives us wisdom, knowledge, and joy too. But, if we're really honest, we must ask, Who can please God? Isaiah said we're like filthy rags to Him (Isaiah 64:6). Even the local mechanic doesn't like filthy rags!

Eat, drink, and be merry anyway. Jesus put those rags through a three-cycle cleaning with His perfect life, sacrificial death, and victorious resurrection. We can please God because Jesus made it possible. We are wise and happy because we know Jesus. And while unbelievers sadly chase the most temporary of pleasures, our joy never ends. So eat, drink, and be merry. For tomorrow we live!

Getting High on Love

*For as high as the heavens are above the earth, so great is His steadfast
love toward those who fear Him; as far as the east is from the west, so far
does He remove our transgressions from us. As a father shows compassion
to His children, so the Lord shows compassion to those who fear Him.*
Psalm 103:11–13

The astronomer's job is always looking up. (At least she won't find any
puns in outer space!) If you've never gazed through a telescope at the
night sky, take the time to do it sometime. Besides all those stars and planets
up there, it's amazing how fast the earth spins. Look away from the telescope
just for a moment after focusing on a star, and when you look back, it's out
of focus.

The most powerful telescopes, even those located high on mountaintops,
can't scan all of space. Even the Hubble telescope discovered that the sky's the
limit. It's seemingly endless—the closest object lesson we have to explain eternity. We also can use it to describe God's love. Psalm 103:11 says: "For as high
as the heavens are above the earth, so great is His steadfast love toward those
who fear Him."

We know God loves us a lot. We know that His love stretches farther than
the entire universe. Because it is so expansive, it spurns human description.
Everything we know, except the sky, has limits. For example, there's marital
love. It begins sometime before the vows are spoken and the honeymoon
begins but, out of necessity, much later than birth. Some people love their
cars, but that love usually ends when rust spots appear and tires go bald.
(Sometimes that happens with people too.) No matter what we humans love,
it has either a beginning or an end or both. Not so with God's love.

He loved you before your birth. He knew you while He was still creating
oaks, dolphins, ladybugs, ferns, and the Mississippi River. He loved you then,
and He continues to love you though you're often unfaithful—sometimes
only remembering Him when you need help or on His birthday.

Think, for a moment, of one way in which you sinned today. (Don't think
too long—even if you're a big sinner.) That sin was an act of unfaithfulness,
brief as it might have been. But God doesn't focus on sins. In fact, He doesn't
even remember them because Jesus took them away. God loves you like He
loved His Son. God's love is unconditional and limitless because Jesus fulfilled all the conditions and took away any limits when He died for you. So
grab a telescope and look for that pie in the sky!

It's History

*"But blessed are your eyes, for they see, and your ears, for they hear. Truly,
I say to you, many prophets and righteous people longed to see what you
see, and did not see it, and to hear what you hear, and did not hear it."*
Matthew 13:16–17

Old Testament prophets, even those who preached doom and destruction, lived on hope. You know how hope works. Hope is what we have on the first day of our new diet. And like those ancient prophets, we may die long before our hope is fulfilled.

We probably have little reason to envy those Old Testament men of God, even though they had direct, two-way communication with their Lord. Jesus Himself commented on how much better off we are than they. The prophets had visions of the future, but they didn't get to see what they foresaw! How blessed we are actually to see prophecy accomplished in the life of Jesus Christ!

Sometimes, however, sin blinds us to the Savior. We may find sinning so enjoyable that we wonder how anything so great can be so bad. Usually, we create plausible excuses like "It's just a little harmless fun. I'm not hurting anybody." Or we might write sin off as invalid iniquities. "Oh, that *used* to be a sin, but not any more. Everybody does it."

Thank God that sin doesn't blind the Savior to sinners. While the prophets could only hope for the day when the Savior would revitalize the relationship of God's people with Him, we know it's history. We live in an age the prophets only dreamed about. We have the cross before us. And it's empty! So is the tomb. Jesus lives and we know all about it. In a sense, we no longer need to hope. Why would anyone hope for something they already have?

Hope does play a role in daily life, however. It's the certain hope that we'll see the Savior sometime in the future. In a way, we also hope like the prophets did—that Jesus will come. It's comforting to know that He's been here once, and He knows the way back. Then we'll live with Him forever.

Leftovers

For thus says the Lord the God of Israel, "The jar of flour shall not be spent, and the jug of oil shall not be empty, until the day that the Lord sends rain upon the earth." And she went and did as Elijah said. And she and he and her household ate for many days. 1 Kings 17:14–15

Nothing lasts longer than that jar of pickles shoved to the back of the refrigerator. (Well, maybe that box of bulgur bran cereal lasts longer.) The world record leftover, however, belongs to a widow's jar of flour in the town of Zarephath. Her tiny urn of flour fed her, her son, and Elijah for many days while the rest of the country suffered though a severe famine.

No, this meditation doesn't encourage you to stock your cabinets like Mother Hubbard's in hopes that God will keep your jars (pickle or otherwise) filled. But the story does help us focus on trusting God. And even beyond the trust issue, it serves to remind us of God's power, patience, and forgiveness.

We live in famine-stricken times. Our lives are parched and starved by sin. But God comes to our rescue. He furnishes a perpetual supply of nourishment. As Elijah became a house guest at the widow's place, Jesus came to live in us. For His sake, God gives us all we need to survive. *Survive?* That word isn't good enough. *Thrive* is more like it!

Like the food that supported the widow's household, God's love through Jesus nourishes us daily. As we sin each day, we draw on the forgiveness God gives through Jesus. We dip into the jar repeatedly, yet an ample reserve always remains. God's forgiveness for Jesus' sake is the only source of spiritual sustenance that we can trust.

Next time you clean out the refrigerator, move that jar of pickles to the front. Let it remind you that God's forgiveness is always there.

Make Like a Moth

Again Jesus spoke to them, saying, "I am the light of the world. Whoever
follows Me will not walk in darkness, but will have the light of life."
John 8:12

Moths really like to wing it. (Ugh!) Their favorite domiciles are deep in the cool grass where birds can't catch them, in closets where they can snack 'round the clock, in my wallet where they rarely get a change of scenery, and around bright light bulbs at night.

We can learn from moths. (Wait! Don't eat your socks.) Consider how this Bible passage implies what moths can teach us: "Again Jesus spoke to them, saying, 'I am the light of the world. Whoever follows Me will not walk in darkness, but will have the light of life'" (John 8:12).

For some reason, moths have a persistent urge to flutter near bright lights. Maybe they possess a genetic yearning for show biz. Once attracted to a light, they demonstrate tireless effort to stay within the brilliant, warm rays flowing from the bulb. (Of course, some venture too close and disappear in a sizzle.)

Christians exhibit an earnest craving to be close to their Light. Unlike the moth's scenario, however, it's not dangerous to rub against our Light. Our Light made personal contact safe, but there was a time when brushing against God meant immediate death. Moses wanted to see God, but God wisely denied his request. Instead, He allowed Moses to glimpse Him, which was enough to put a luminous glow on Moses' face for quite some time.

The problem with sinners seeing God face to face is that He is so holy that their spiritual immune system would utterly fail because of its imperfection. But people wanted to see God anyway, and they did when God became man and came to earth in the person of Jesus Christ. Now people could see the Light. They could touch Him. They could feel His warm and gentle hands soothe and heal the hurts of their bodies. Wouldn't it be wonderful to feel His holy touch today?

We can. He touches us daily in the means of His grace—His Word and the sacraments. He skillfully splints fractured relationships, shrinks the satanic tumors that corrode our soul, and cleanses our eyes with faith so we can see His Light and stay close to it. And when physical illness or injury closes our eyes in death, He brings us back to life where we'll live in the eternal Light. And we'll never flutter in darkness again.

The Garden

"But he said, 'No, lest in gathering the weeds you root up the wheat along with them. Let both grow together until the harvest, and at harvest time I will tell the reapers, Gather the weeds first and bind them in bundles to be burned, but gather the wheat into my barn.'" Matthew 13:29–30

Every year my yard is covered with thousands of pretty yellow flowers. Actually, I would pull them out given some time and ambition. But then my front yard might look like a strip mine! One gardener, whose lawn has nary a speck of yellow, told me the best way to eradicate weedy pests is to choke them out with good plants.

Weeds caused problems in Jesus' day too, as you can see from the passage above. Any veteran weed-puller knows that when weeds entangle their evil tentacles with the roots of the innocent, pulling them is risky. Jesus' solution to the problem was simple and eventually drastic. But Jesus wasn't giving advice to mere green thumbs.

We should always allow a few dandelions on our lawns to remind ourselves about life as Christians. Most of us prefer the company of other Christians, even if they aren't perfect. But if we are to make the most of life, we repentant sinners must live with sinners of the other variety too. And as my gardening friend suggested, we need to choke out their evil with our good—a job we can't do alone.

Our goodness comes from Jesus Christ, whose death and resurrection provided fertile fields in which to grow. As we bud with good deeds and display the beautiful blooms of the Gospel, we show our "beholders" the beauty of Jesus. He works through us to choke out evil with kindness and replace thorns with forgiveness. So don't be afraid to nestle next to some weedy characters. Maybe some of your beauty will rub off on them—or at least choke the sin from their spindly stalks.

Think Again

But turning and seeing His disciples, He rebuked Peter and said, "Get behind Me, Satan! For you are not setting your mind on the things of God, but on the things of man." Mark 8:33

Intelligence is highly overrated. If you like to fish or know someone who does, you'll probably agree. We pit human intelligence against the modest brains of our quarry and often loose the battle of wits!

Often, opinions are more overrated than intelligence. God's Word provides some excellent examples. Jesus spoke today's verse when Peter didn't like what Jesus said about His divine future. No doubt Peter wanted Jesus to look on the bright side rather than predicting His own death. And then to say that He would return to life . . . Well, that's just more than intelligent disciples can tolerate. But Peter was mistaken. He tried to pit human intelligence against divine will and wisdom.

Jesus' reprimand may seem harsh, but He needed to set the record straight. After all, if Peter's way of thinking prevailed, Jesus wouldn't die. Jesus knew the Father's plan for Him, and He knew why He needed to die. He also knew that temporary death was better than temporary joy—not that anyone would disagree. But Jesus knew He would defeat the power of death in a way that human brain power would never evaluate, assess, or statistically prove. Clearly—and thankfully—Peter's opinion didn't count.

We do well to listen too. When God says He created the world; almost obliterated it with a flood; brought plagues on Egypt; and sent Jesus to suffer, die, and rise to save us from our sins; we don't need to form an opinion. We have His Word, and it presents the facts. To rely on our own intellect is like believing that somewhere, someplace we'll figure out how to snag that world record bass.

Me, Myself, and I

Blessed be the Lord, my rock, who trains my hands for war, and my fingers for battle; He is my steadfast love and my fortress, my stronghold and my deliverer, my shield and He in whom I take refuge, who subdues peoples under me. Psalm 144:1–2

My mother had a pet expression for those who incessantly talked about themselves. "Me, myself, and I," she would say. "That's all they can talk about." The unholy trinity of self-centeredness!

But look at the excerpt from Psalm 144 above. Ten very personal pronouns weave their way into David's words of praise. Very clearly, David wants us to know that God cared about him. And there is no reason not to adopt these words as our own.

Me, myself, and I. That's who God cares about, and that's who God strengthens and protects. Isn't it thrilling to know how much God loves *me?* It's one thing to be included in a crowd, like the time presidential-hopeful Eisenhower waved to a bunch of us outside the NBC studios in Chicago. Just think how we would have felt had he approached and actually shook our hands—or called us by name! But God—our awesome, holy, omni-everything God—knows me, myself, and I personally. He knew my name long before my parents picked it. He knew about that episode of puppy love that left me whimpering and whining—and He comforted me. He knew about that time in English class when I cheated—and He accepted my repentance for Jesus' sake. He knew my unspoken needs for wife and family—and He supplied just the right one for me. He saw the drunk driver snaking through traffic behind me and led me safely away—even though I never knew it happened. Yes, He cares for me, and it's VERY PERSONAL.

Enough about me, myself, and I. What about you, yourself, and you? You know, that's one of the best things about being God's chosen child. Me, myself, and I is something everyone can say.

Don't Horse Around

Woe to those who go down to Egypt for help and rely on horses,
who trust in chariots because they are many and in horsemen because
they are very strong, but do not look to the Holy One of Israel or consult
the LORD! . . . The Egyptians are man, and not God, and their horses are
flesh, and not spirit. When the LORD stretches out His hand, the helper
will stumble, and he who is helped will fall, and they will all perish
together. Isaiah 31:1–3

Horses are not man's best friend. At least not this one's. Oh, I'll admit that Paul Revere probably rode a noble steed, and many a bow-legged sheriff of the old West patrolled the dusty trails, spilling coffee and donut crumbs all over the mane of his trustworthy horse. But the last horse I rode nearly killed me, though I must admit, I wouldn't appreciate getting backed into a barbed-wire fence either. But forward and reverse should be marked more clearly on those reins!

God became angry when His people trusted horses. All this must be placed in context of ultimate trust, of course. Isaiah talked about it. "Woe to those who go down to Egypt for help and rely on horses, who trust in chariots because they are many and in horsemen because they are very strong, but do not look to the Holy One of Israel or consult the Lord!" (Isaiah 31:1).

The soldiers of Israel rarely enjoyed the latest technology in warfare. Horses greatly impressed them, as you might imagine if you've ever stood next to a stallion. They mistakenly thought that horses could win wars much as we might rely on the newest tanks or radar-evading aircraft. But God had promised to be their strength, and He told them what He thought of their weapons inventory. Horses were only flesh and bones and hair with a tail added to chase away flies. Staunch steeds were no match for God.

God intended this message for us too. We sometimes trust horses more than Him. Our horses might live under a hood and sport a horn as well as a very large price tag. Then again, a whole stable of horses is okay if we don't treat them like gods. Our horses might spend most of their time grazing in a financial portfolio. This is acceptable, too, as long as we avoid turning them into objects that supplant God. Sometimes our horses take the form of self-made transportation to heaven. That happens when we figure we're good enough (or not bad enough) in God's sight just the way we are. After all, worship and prayer and stewardship are for all those sinners out there. God says "Whoa" (or was it "Woe") to that! Don't horse around. Live by that famous motto printed on what has become a horse for many: "In God we trust."

Open 24 Hours

"All that the Father gives me will come to me, and whoever comes to me I will never cast out." John 6:37

Twenty-four-hour service seems to be a trend. All-night truck stops are indispensable, and hospitals need to offer round-the-clock service, but do we really need ATMs when we're short of cash at 3 a.m.? (Only if our car is laid up at a garage for repairs at 2 a.m.!) Convenience and service have come a long way. One thing hasn't changed, however.

God was always open for business 24 hours a day. What service! No matter how early or late we get up, God patiently waits for us to begin our day in conversation with Him. And we don't need to worry that He got up on the wrong side of the bed! The same is true when we retire, fatigued with the day's labor. God is wide awake and all ears. Even if we fall asleep while talking to Him, He isn't insulted or hurt. In His magnificent mercy, He addresses even our unspoken needs.

We aren't limited to talking with God by appointment only. The regular times are important, but He's ready for emergency interruptions too: Junior hasn't returned from his date yet. It's snowing, the streets are slippery, and he's only had his license for eight months. Or the baby wakes up every fifteen minutes all night. The fever just won't break. She begins to convulse. That's when God's spiritual 911 swings into action. Before you even call, He's with you, meeting your needs, and giving you strength to cope.

God invites us to pray anytime. He promises never to be too busy. In His grace, God even listens to those who have never talked to Him before, and to those who only do it when they are in trouble.

Be sure you talk to God today. Any time. Even if it's just to say, "I love You."

Counting Your Blessings

As He said these things, a woman in the crowd raised her voice and said to Him, "Blessed is the womb that bore You, and the breasts at which You nursed!" But He said, "Blessed rather are those who hear the word of God and keep it!" Luke 11:27–28

The lyrics of an old song claim that if worry deprives you of sleep, you should count blessings rather than sheep. It's probably good advice. All that bleating will rob you of rest. And when you think about it, you are richly blessed, aren't you?

1. The Holy Spirit gave you faith. As a believer you recognize your blessings, and you also can see them where others see only travail or trouble. You personally know the Giver of those blessings.

2. Your senses are working. You see the pages of this book, and if noise distracts you, thank God you can hear. You feel the differing textures of your surroundings, and you smell. No, not you. I mean . . . well, you know what I mean. Put the book down and have a snack. Unless it's one of those taste-free varieties, you probably enjoy the flavor. (If one or more of your senses doesn't function, you're blessed with increased intensity in other senses to compensate.)

3. God gave you this day your daily bread. (You asked for it, didn't you?) Not only bread, but everything else you need for survival, maybe even prosperity. If you're a little hurt that God hasn't given you as much as the proverbial Joneses, remember that the more one has, the more one is tempted to feel self-sufficient and, thereby, the more one is tempted to discard faith.

4. Somebody loves you. That person might live with or near you or perhaps he or she sends thinking-of-you cards. Maybe you see this person every day and the love is so routine that you take it for granted. Maybe he or she lives elsewhere or only in memories. Even if you're terribly lonely, God loves you so much that He sent Jesus who loves you so much that He died for your sins. Now the Holy Spirit loves you so much that He keeps you faithful, even when you're tempted to roam.

5. And then there's this: "As He said these things, a woman in the crowd raised her voice and said to Him, 'Blessed is the womb that bore You, and the breasts at which You nursed!' But He said, 'Blessed rather are those who hear the word of God and keep it!'" (Luke 11:27–28).

Jesus enabled you to hear God's Word, which mercifully assures you that even when you don't obey Him, Jesus obeyed for you. You're saved! You have God's Word on it.

Keep the Change

Thus says the Lord of hosts, the God of Israel: Amend your ways and your deeds, and I will let you dwell in this place. Jeremiah 7:3

Most people welcome change—especially at the grocery store. But this really isn't the subject of today's meditation. The kind of change we shall consider is the change synonymous with reform.

Babies provide a good example for change in our own lives. Babies always know when they need changing, even though their parents sometimes practice the art of distraction and delay. (This clever ploy sometimes gets the *other* spouse to notice the predicament, and act.) With the removal of the soiled (isn't that a polite word?) diaper, the child becomes more comfortable and happy. Until the next time.

Our own sins have us wallowing in a mess too. Those around us may react in ways similar to dirty diaper episodes. For example, there's the "maybe if I ignore it, it will go away" syndrome. Conversely, there's also the "Aggggh! That baby needs changing" reaction that brazenly points out what is already obvious. We sometimes react to our sinfulness in ways that excuse it, indicate that it's nobody's business but our own, or accuse others of being equally sinful or worse. Jeremiah tells us that we better acknowledge our sinfulness and then do something about it.

Reform isn't easy. In fact, it's impossible without the Holy Spirit, and then it still takes spiritual perseverance. The initial ingredient of reform is a repentant heart. That too, comes from the Holy Spirit's urging. We respond with both sorrow and sincere aspiration to abandon our sinfulness. Then the Holy Spirit gives us the essential element of reform, namely His power to fight sin.

Empowered by the Spirit, change may not be easy, but it is possible. Like that baby in a fresh diaper, we find comfort in the cleansing Jesus brought into our lives. It brings change worth keeping.

Banner Year

He brought me to the banqueting house, and His banner
over me was love. Song of Songs 2:4

Everybody enjoys a good love story. Television cameras pan a stadium filled with cheering sports fans as a skywriter inscribes the sky with "Allison, I love you. Will you marry me?" Here's a concrete representation of our verse for today. The banner over Allison was love!

Think for a moment. Over whom would you fly your banner of love? Why would you do it? Now think again. Who would sail their banner over you? Spouse or special friend? Co-workers? The boss? Your next door neighbor? It probably hasn't happened, but that doesn't mean you're not loved.

Love is a funny thing. Young lovers often think it's a feeling. Old lovers know it's actually commitment, forgiveness, self-sacrifice, tolerance, contentment, and service. The banner may become tattered and discolored, but it soars high just the same. Such is the banner that Jesus hoists over us.

It's not unusual for Christians to yearn for spiritual feelings. You might hear, "I'm a believer, but I just don't feel close to Jesus." Or someone will ask, "Can't you just feel God's love here among us?" And your honest answer, if you dared, would be, "No. I wish I did." Love, be it human or divine, may or may not be accompanied by strong emotions. And Christ's love, not unlike the love of a couple married many years, is present whether it's consciously felt or not.

Christ's banner over us is love. He showers us with it when we're mourning and when we're whooping it up. It's there when we're sleeping or trying to stay awake during the sermon. It's at the assembly line, computer terminal, classroom desk, steering wheel, and behind the vacuum cleaner. His banner flies when we do His will, and it dips to half mast when we're sinful—but it continues to fly. Sometimes His love is pretty routine, and other times it's downright sensational. His love promises us a banner year. Every year. For all time.

Golden Rules

You shall not take vengeance or bear a grudge against the sons of your
own people, but you shall love your neighbor as yourself: I am the Lord.
Leviticus 19:18

Neighbors are those people who sometimes motivate us to keep up, thereby causing huge losses of savings, hair, and common sense. Neighbors are those who really listen to you—especially when you're arguing with your spouse or offspring. Neighbors are those whom the preacher talks about at church. In short, it's often easier to love some lost jungle tribe on another continent than it is to love the family in the next apartment or house. Despite all that, we are able to love our neighbor as ourself—and that's direct from God Himself.

Maybe we should ask if we really love ourselves. We confess in church that we're "sinful and unclean." So what's to love? The answer, of course, lies in God, who loves us despite our sinfulness. In fact, we're probably safe in saying that He loves us as He loves Himself—maybe more. God loves us enough to sacrifice His Son to save us from our sins. If God loved us that much, then we can certainly love ourselves. And if we can love ourselves, we can love our neighbors too.

In the previous devotion, you read that love isn't always accompanied by intense feelings. But love is always accompanied by concern and service, compassion and prayer, mercy and kindness. We can love our neighbors a variety of ways. It takes some work, though. We need to keep an eye on our neighbors—not to catch them doing something, but to see what they need. They need waves, smiles, and a call to see if everything is okay after the storm. It may even mean cutting the grass an extra few feet on your neighbor's side of the property line or keeping the TV volume a little lower for people on the other side of the wall. And you can't expect neighborly love to be returned. Not everybody plays by the same rules.

What Are You Worth?

Jesus, looking at him with sadness, said, "How difficult it is for those who have wealth to enter the kingdom of God! For it is easier for a camel to go through the eye of a needle than for a rich person to enter the kingdom of God." Luke 18:24–25

Back in the '70s, salespeople offered me an opportunity to invest in Wisconsin wilderness land that would someday become a popular ski area. They said I could realize my financial fantasies. I had been to Wisconsin, and aside from a few places with cliffs, I hadn't seen any hills worthy of skiing. Being no fool, I refused to invest. (You still have a hard time seeing the hills in that area these days. Too many skiers.)

The passage above is another of those we like to apply to other people. Few folks are as wealthy as they desire. On the other hand, if you don't consider yourself prosperous, you can ignore such words from the Bible, and use them to threaten others. Wealth, however, is relative, and Jesus *is* speaking to us.

Note please, that Jesus didn't say it was impossible for rich people to enter heaven. He said it was hard. Far from being a curse, wealth of any degree is actually a blessing. God gifted certain individuals with money so they could use it to His glory—just as He gave some people good voices, the ability to teach, or skill at making things. Jesus understood how easy it is for the devil and our own evil natures to distract us from what really counts. The trouble comes only when the gifts become more important than the giver. That's what Jesus was talking about.

What are you worth? Whether you need a calculator to figure it out or can do it with a pencil and scrap of paper, you're worth more than you can imagine. Jesus died to take your sins away. Believe that and you really have a good investment.

Silence Is What?

And many of the Corinthians hearing Paul believed and were baptized.
And the Lord said to Paul one night in a vision, "Do not be afraid, but go
on speaking and do not be silent, for I am with you, and no one will
attack you to harm you, for I have many in this city who are My people."
And he stayed a year and six months, teaching the word of God
among them. Acts 18:1–11

There are times when silence is golden. Note three advantages of silence:

1. *You're an unlikely candidate for leading a neighborhood or congregational committee.*

2. *More people will agree with you.*

3. *Silence is a wicked weapon during an argument.*

The Bible treats silence several ways. The first appears in Zephaniah 1:7, which says, "Be silent before the Lord God! For the day of the Lord is near." As much as God invites us to address Him in prayer, sometimes it's best to be silent. In our silence, we listen to God. We're likely to hear His voice speaking passages from the Bible or whispering comfort in the nonverbal language of faith that our souls hear.

At other times, silence isn't so golden. Acts 18:9–10 says: "And the Lord said to Paul one night in a vision, 'Do not be afraid, but go on speaking and do not be silent, for I am with you, and no one will attack you to harm you, for I have many in this city who are My people.'"

Jesus is with us too. God willing, as you read this book, you're not facing the potential persecution that Paul encountered. Persecutors in civilized society are generally more wily and sly than life-threatening, which is scary. Can you sit next to someone on the plane and tell him what you know about Jesus? Does Jesus' love creep into normal conversation—or just creep away? How hard it is for some Christians to witness! It might help to remember you're not in it alone.

A third concept of silence is in 1 Peter 2:15: "For this is the will of God, that by doing good you should put to silence the ignorance of foolish people." Peter suggests that behavior expresses more than words. Good Christians are also good neighbors, good citizens, good church members. They live good lives. Oh, foolish people will point out the many ways Christians aren't always good at being good. You know where you fall short, so it's clear that you can't rely on your own goodness. But you don't have to. God is a good forgiver, and that suggests one more way to silence foolish people.

Take a Number

"But many who are first will be last, and the last first." Mark 10:31

Does it ever fail? You're at the grocery checkout, approximately in the middle of 19 customers. The store manager orders another cash register to open. The line peels off, and now you no longer occupy the middle. You're at the end. Proof that the last shall be first and middle shall be last! The first? They're still first.

Jesus didn't shop at grocery stores, but He was right anyway. His remarks came in response to Peter who asked what the disciples could gain by following Him. A couple of them wanted to be first in line for the blessings of heaven! And while Jesus had already hinted that His closest followers could expect harsh treatment, He also reassured the disciples they would have a special place in heaven.

That answer wouldn't please anyone interested in immediate gratification. At the time, Peter had no idea how he would suffer because of his faith. Rather than rising to either political or popular heights, he would eventually be raised on a cross. Peter would be considered the lowest of low before God transformed him into a victor.

We Christians are tempted to arrogance. Those who demonstrate higher and greater Christian characteristics might also begin thinking highly of themselves. "I serve on three church boards, teach Sunday school, and send money to missions. How great I art."

That's when Jesus' words need to slap at us. Jesus' idea of being first involved being the first to serve others, the first to forgive, the first to care. The worldly equivalent happens when Grandma serves Christmas dinner. Who does all the cooking and is the last to sit? First to serve; last to fill her plate.

The "me first" practitioners are in for a few surprises come Judgment Day. They may succeed in pulling low numbers from the machine. But Jesus will call them backwards!

Unfair Labor Practices

They grumbled at the master of the house, saying, "These last worked only one hour, and you have made them equal to us who have borne the burden of the day and the scorching heat..." Matthew 20:11–12

Rule number 1 for arguing with the boss: Make sure you're right. Then stifle the urge. Rule number 2: Look at both sides—the boss' side and the outside.

Today's passage reports a labor grievance. The problem was that a vineyard owner paid everyone the same wage regardless of hours worked. Although it sounds unfair, the owner's reply was logical to any self-directed business owner. (But it does make you wonder how many showed up on time for work the next day!)

Jesus is definitely unfair according to human standards. A person can be a Christian her whole life, living in accordance with God's will, suppressing worldly desires, boldly striving towards obedience. Another person can live a wild, undisciplined, rebellious life and repent minutes before she dies. Both go to heaven. Or consider the Christian who has a weak faith. He vacillates between reading the Bible and studying the daily horoscope. He often doubts that Jesus would bother with him, and he is afraid of dying. He goes to church only once a month. Next to him on the same pew that Sunday is another Christian who occupies this space every week. He tithes, meditates, and reads devotional books daily. He's eager to meet the Lord in person. Should he be surprised to see the other man in heaven? Certainly not.

All this isn't to encourage practicing faith as little as possible because you can get away with it. The point is that faith in any quantity saves. Before we mutter about fairness, we should remind ourselves that if God were fair, none of us would get to heaven. So let's join the angels who shout "Hip, hip, hooray" every time someone is saved. And let's ask Jesus to continue His record of unfairness.

Frequent Failures

The book of the genealogy of Jesus Christ. . . . So all the generations from Abraham to David were fourteen generations, and from David to the deportation to Babylon fourteen generations, and from the deportation to Babylon to the Christ fourteen generations. Matthew 1:1–17

If the devil awarded bonuses to those who fail the way airlines award bonuses to frequent flyers, we would win a trip around the world but never get to the airport. In fact, failure is so rampant that one author wrote a book about it. It was so successful that it sold three copies.

What does failure have to do with the Bible reading listed above? Did you fail to make a connection? (Sorry about that.) The list of Jesus' ancestors seems well-rooted as far as family trees go. If we were to conduct a background check of those people, however, we would discover that even the rich and famous on this list were haunted by serious failures. Abraham passed off his wife as his sister to save his life. Isaac was careless with his will. Jacob walked funny. Ram had a penchant for fleecing people. Nashon had trouble spelling. David surrendered to lust. Solomon grew cynical in old age. So the list goes. (I probably failed to uncover the whole truth about some of the characters above.)

If Jesus' ancestors had trouble with failure, you know what His brothers and sisters of this age face. Not to depress you or anything, but nearly everything we do is a failure in some sense. Listen to the words of the prophet Haggai: "Now, therefore, thus says the Lord of hosts: Consider your ways. You have sown much, and harvested little. You eat, but you never have enough; you drink, but you never have your fill. You clothe yourselves, but no one is warm. And he who earns wages does so to put them into a bag with holes" (Haggai 1:5–6).

True, isn't it? No matter what we have or what we do, we never experience ultimate and final satisfaction. If we did, we would have heaven on earth, and we know that's not its true location.

There is something that defies failure, however. It's the power of God through Jesus Christ. The salvation Jesus earned on the cross of Calvary makes Satan a failure. Try as he might, Satan may cause us to stumble, but supported by God, we'll never fall. Empowered by the empty cross of Jesus Christ, we need not fear failure. He will not let us fail to join Him in heaven.

Private Eyes

So they watched Him and sent spies, who pretended to be sincere, that
they might catch Him in something He said, so as to deliver Him up to
the authority and jurisdiction of the governor. Luke 20:20

People hire private investigators when the police can't or won't investigate some suspicion for them. It happened to Jesus, as Luke reports.

Luke didn't mince words—or titles. He called the investigators dishonest spies. They came to Jesus asking what seemed like legitimate questions, but they hoped for answers that would doom Him. Jesus' answer was so starkly honest that they abandoned their spy mission.

Common people like us probably breathe a sigh of relief knowing we're not important enough to warrant a spy's interest. But that's dangerous. The devil spies on us constantly. His eyes see everything we do in private, and he takes notes. He's saving the evidence to present on Judgment Day when we stand before God. The devil probably won't need to lie much about our activities. We're quite sinful enough without his embellishment or exaggeration. He wants us to plead guilty without any defense.

As guilty as we are, our only defense is to throw ourselves on the mercy of the Judge. We should freely confess all we've done wrong because His own investigation revealed the same evidence as the devil's. Yet God is certain to agree when we ask Him to save us for Christ's sake. We will testify that Jesus died to save us and that we know He accomplished that mission. The verdict will be swift and very partial. We'll join the throng of other saved sinners at God's right hand.

Until that time of judgment, we need to be on the lookout. Not for spies, but for our own sinful behavior. Let's not wait for Judgment Day to throw ourselves on God's mercy.

Dark Days

For unto you is born this day in the city of David a Savior, who is Christ the Lord. Luke 2:11

M erry Christmas! Even if it's not. Christmas, that is. If you have any "child" left in you, Christmas is delightful to think about any time of year. Besides, Christmas really does last all year—especially if you have credit cards!

Have you noticed God's history of taking really drastic action when days seem the darkest? For example, just when it seemed that wickedness was so overwhelming that it would wipe out heaven's future population, God washed away the evil with a flood, devastating to all but a handful of believers and animals.

Another example: Just when it seemed that more than four centuries of slavery would blend Israelite faith with Egyptian myth, God miraculously emancipated His children so they could serve Him without distraction and receive His blessings without interference.

We don't know the exact date of Christmas, but it is certainly celebrated at an appropriate time in the northern hemisphere. December 25 is close to the shortest day of the year—the first day of winter. So much darkness! The Romans were so acutely disturbed by this phenomenon that they celebrated the "return of the sun"—*Io Saturnalia*—as soon as the days began getting longer, if only by minutes. What a great time to celebrate Christmas!

Jesus is the return of light to sinners living in darkness. We no longer live in the dark days of sin because Jesus took our sins away on the darkest of Fridays. We live, instead, in times of light and hope as we look forward to the day when Jesus returns. We'll never be in the dark again.

Super Sermons

The brothers immediately sent Paul and Silas away by night to Berea, and
when they arrived they went into the Jewish synagogue. Now these Jews
were more noble than those in Thessalonica; they received the word with
all eagerness, examining the Scriptures daily to see if these things were so.
Many of them therefore believed, with not a few Greek women of high
standing as well as men. Acts 17:10–12

Pity the poor individuals who don't have to leave the house to hear a sermon! Many of us go to church for that experience, and many preachers long to preach an immortal sermon. (Too bad some confuse immortal with eternal.) In fact, some poor preachers feel they're getting through to the congregation when they see a lot of heads nodding. But before we become too critical of preachers, we can recall that good listening usually makes good preaching.

Luke describes good listening in Acts 17:11. He noted, "Now these Jews were more noble than those in Thessalonica; they received the word with all eagerness, examining the Scriptures daily to see if these things were so."

You might think that the Bereans listened so well because they had a talented, fluent, dynamic preacher like Paul. But Paul claimed that he wasn't much of an orator. In fact, he probably didn't even make his college debate team. But those Bereans knew how to listen. Then they checked out the facts of the sermon!

We would do well to emulate the Bereans. Where do you start? Next time you listen to a sermon, make some mental notes of the chief points. (Well, maybe you better write them on paper.) Record the sermon text, and reread it in a Bible that has cross-references. Read those texts too. Or buy a study Bible that explains passages. (Your local Christian bookstore or your pastor is a source of advice on what translation to read.) As you study more about what you hear, you'll probably turn into a preacher yourself.

Too late for the seminary? Maybe. But most great sermons are preached from faces, hands, and feet rather than tongues and lips. Compassionate eyes reflect Christian concern, and smiles illustrate the joy of salvation. Helping hands are reminiscent of the service Jesus performed. Then there are those sermons that come from the sole. (Yes, it's spelled right.) Our feet carry us many places in a day, which provides opportunities to preach sermons with the rest of our body—lips, tongues, and larynx included.

Maybe now you're convinced that you're a preacher. But have pity on the nodders in your "congregation." They may be in danger of getting whiplash.

Exercise Equipment

If you put these things before the brothers, you will be a good servant of
Christ Jesus, being trained in the words of the faith and of the good doc-
trine that you have followed. Have nothing to do with irreverent, silly
myths. Rather train yourself for godliness; for while bodily training is of
some value, godliness is of value in every way, as it holds promise for the
present life and also for the life to come. 1 Timothy 4:6–8

A ren't modern inventions wonderful? Exercise equipment is a good example. People can build their bodies in the privacy of their own homes with machines that manipulate every conceivable muscle (and a few that aren't so conceivable). You can purchase walking machines, skiing machines, weight-lifting devices, and other contraptions that might have been outlawed in the Dark Ages as instruments of torture. My own experience with exercise devices is limited to teeter-totters, swings, and jungle gyms.

The craze surrounding physical fitness undoubtedly has many origins. Some people like to keep that which God called His temple trim, fit, and effi-cient. Others feel it's the avenue to attractiveness; some hope remaining phys-ically fit will help them live longer. All are good reasons when kept in per-spective, and they suggest some parallels in the realm of faith as well.

Consider Paul's words to young Timothy: "Have nothing to do with irrev-erent, silly myths. Rather train yourself for godliness; for while bodily train-ing is of some value, godliness is of value in every way, as it holds promise for the present life and also for the life to come" (1 Timothy 4:7–8).

Paul wasn't suggesting that exercise is worthless, but he knew what hap-pens to taut tummies, bulging arms, and broad chests. Gravity is vicious as the years pass, and fitness training is no guarantee of extended life. Paul also might advise, "Exercise your faith as well as your body because when your body goes, God will keep your faith strong."

No one wants a flabby faith any more than they want a frumpy physique. Therefore, someone should commend you for exercising right now. The Holy Spirit uses exercise "machines" such as devotional books, group Bible studies, chat sessions with Jesus, worship services, and the sacraments to flex and pull and twist and pump weak faith into fit faith. When faith is strong enough, God even allows adversity to push it to its limits, thereby making it firmer and even more brawny.

Maybe you've heard phrases such as "buns of steel" or "abs of steel." What can you claim? With the coaching of the Holy Spirit as you diligently exercise in God's Word, you have a soul of steel.

Star Studded

Do all things without grumbling or questioning, that you may be blameless and innocent, children of God without blemish in the midst of a crooked and twisted generation, among whom you shine as lights in the world. Philippians 2:14–15

I heard on the radio that, I could buy a star and name it for a loved one. Its name would be registered and sealed in a vault. As an additional benefit, I would receive a chart showing me just where in heaven my loved one twinkled.

Maybe having a star named after you isn't as ridicu . . . er, unusual as it sounds. Did you see what Paul told the Philippians? He said that we Christians shine like stars in an otherwise dark and depraved universe. And because our names are on those stars, we might also be inclined to heed the first part of today's note to the Philippians. "Do everything without complaining or arguing."

Perhaps Paul meant that we should avoid church meetings. No. Disregard that last lapse into sarcasm. (But if your congregation holds regular meetings to discuss its "business," you know what I mean.) So many jobs await eager Christians. They also await those who aren't so eager. But doing God's work means pitching in together even when we're tired and don't feel like pitching. Doing God's work requires unity rather than disparity, hidden agendas, private prejudices, and self-centeredness.

God helps us do His work. Perhaps we should think of ourselves like that star God sent over the stable in Bethlehem—the one registered to Jesus Christ. It showed the Wise Men where they could find their Savior. God put us on earth for the same reason. He makes us glisten with the Gospel and glitter with grace. And our names won't be secured in some musty vault. They will live forever in God's International Registry of Saved Sinners.

August 18

Cutting the Apron Strings

Therefore, thus says the Lord: You have not obeyed Me by proclaiming liberty, every one to his brother and to his neighbor; behold, I proclaim to you liberty to the sword, to pestilence, and to famine, declares the Lord. I will make you a horror to all the kingdoms of the earth. Jeremiah 34:17

God bless America. It's a nation characterized by religious freedom. Every American is guaranteed the right to attend the church of his or her choice. Or to go golfing. Or seek to restrain worship of the true God. Of course, only a radical would insist on worship of the one true God because any god can be true. Right? That's the nature of freedom.

Our religious freedom was granted by God. It was He who led our country's shapers to insist on freedom to worship as one chooses—a good idea, but one which we humans easily pervert or dilute. But that's God's way too. Had He wanted puppets, He would have given us strings instead of liberty. God indeed gives us religious freedom.

Jeremiah's "congregation" apparently took its liberty seriously. The people chose freedom from God rather than the freedom to serve and obey Him. Sound familiar? The most serious deficiency of religious tolerance is freedom to worship gods other than the true one. And while our country may promote such freedom, and while God allows such choice, we court disaster when we cut our apron strings to God. Under these circumstance, "Give me liberty or give me death" takes on new meaning.

Examined through the eyes of faith, religious freedom involves no choice at all. We clearly see the goodness of God. He gives unlimited benefits to citizens of His kingdom. Take health care, for example. In a day when medical insurance is a major concern, it's comforting to know that God sends healing to all who want it. Oh, there is a string attached. We must go to the doctor of *His* choice.

When You Don't Know What to Say

Know this, my beloved brothers: let every person be quick to hear, slow to speak, slow to anger. James 1:19

God bless America—a land that guarantees freedom of speech. Too bad it doesn't guarantee listeners! The ability to listen is almost sure to win friends and serve them in godly ways. In fact, if you listen carefully as you read today's meditation, you'll receive a bonus tip at the end. (No fair skipping to the end to see if it's worth it. Listen to me!)

Most of us are familiar with this scene: Despite the serenity they're designed to provide, the soft, pink lighting and bouquets of flowers make us uneasy. Even the stately wooden casket can't lend genuine dignity to the young, lifeless body at rest on its cushions. The damp and reddened eyes of the family search deeply, almost desperately, into your own eyes. What can you say at times like these?

The best thing to say when we don't know what to say is to say so. The best thing to do if we're slow to speak is to be slow to speak. Chances are good that people in need don't want a speech anyway. What emotionally needy people need is for someone to be there and to listen. A hug and a simple "I'm sorry" say volumes to the brokenhearted, and it invites others to open their stricken hearts to us.

But what will we hear? We'll hear memories—maybe the same ones we've heard many times before. One secret of good listeners is listening without comment to things we already know. Isn't that just what Jesus did? He knew the deepest dreads prowling the hearts and souls of all who asked His help. His words were simple, but His actions were powerful. He listened and loved.

You listened well! So here's the tip. If you want kids to listen to you, pretend you're talking to someone else. And if you don't want them to listen, pretend you're talking to them!

The Arsenal

*The night is far gone; the day is at hand. So then let us cast off the works
of darkness and put on the armor of light. Romans 13:12*

God bless America. (Again.) Where else do people have the right to
wear tank tops and sun dresses anytime they want? Whoops—wrong
arms. Wrong "bear" too.

The right to bear arms was born of fear that armed despots would easily
overcome unarmed citizens. Unfortunately, this important freedom remains
seriously abused by the very people it intended to serve. That's the nature of
freedom, though, isn't it? We have freedom to be wise or foolish.

God gave us the right to bear arms, but He took it a step further. He actually armed us. We hear Paul telling the Romans and us how we're to use this
freedom and power. No "deeds of darkness" allowed. We Christians wear the
armor of light for the many righteous battles we fight. But aside from talk,
what exactly does God give us for battle?

God's arsenal is more potent than nuclear warheads. He gave us
righteousness, His Word and Sacraments, and salvation. Soldiers with bad
attitudes are poorly equipped even if they have a tank strapped to their back.
They must believe in that for which they fight. When God made us righteous
through Jesus Christ, He gave us the right attitude. He made us one with the
Commander. Then He gave us the weapons of Word and Sacrament.
Deceptive weapons, they are. They appear so flimsy. But these mighty
weapons equip us to fight the devil. The Word tells us to resist and overcome
the enemy, and the Commander Himself touches us personally through
Baptism and His Supper. Then there's salvation. We can fight the fiercest battles of faith unafraid of dying because Jesus gives us salvation. God did indeed
give us the right to bear arms. And for that we're eternally grateful.

Hot Pursuit

*For even if I made you grieve with my letter, I do not regret it—though I
did regret it, for I see that that letter grieved you, though only for a while.
As it is, I rejoice, not because you were grieved, but because you were
grieved into repenting. For you felt a godly grief, so that you suffered no
loss through us. 2 Corinthians 7:8–9*

God bless America. (Kate Smith would be proud!) Our government
gives us the right to pursue happiness. Most Americans are in hot
pursuit. Unfortunately, a lot of money is burned trying to catch it.

Nonchristians' pursuit of happiness often differs from the Christian's.
Our quest takes us through some unusual—even unhappy—places. Let's see
where the pursuit begins.

The best place to start may be with Christ's disciple Peter outside the
building where His dear friend was on trial for His life. Unfortunately, Peter
failed miserably in returning that friendship. Before we shake a shaming finger at Peter, we need to examine ourselves, standing there next to him. How
often, by word or action, do we also deny knowing the best friend we ever
had? But enough of that for now. Happiness is well beyond us, and only the
hottest of pursuit will help us catch up.

Breathlessly, we stop at the next station of happiness—the cross. This is
happiness? The cross seems an obstacle toward happiness, and Jesus certainly didn't enjoy it there.

Our happiness, like that of the Corinthians whom Paul counseled, must
begin with sadness. Not that either God or Paul enjoyed making us feel bad.
Having spent the chilly evening with Peter and crouching beneath the cross,
how could we feel otherwise? But that sorrow is useful, for it leads us to
repentance. And repentance leads to forgiveness. And forgiveness leads to
eternal life with Jesus. So sit down and rest. The chase is over. Happiness is
yours. And it didn't cost you a cent.

Ignorance Is Not Bliss

Now the law came in to increase the trespass, but where sin increased,
grace abounded all the more. Romans 5:20

Ignorance isn't bliss. If it were, more people would be jumping for joy. Ignorance of God's Law can either be blissful or terrifying, depending on how you look at it. One thousand years passed between the first time man (and woman) broke God's Law and the time when God gave His followers 10 rules for life. When Moses lugged the two stone tables of Law down the mountain, an era of awareness began—awareness of God's will for His people.

Now His people knew what they were doing wrong. They may have sinned anyway, but at least they knew what they were doing. With that in mind, we read Paul's words to the Romans. Does this really mean that God set out to increase our sins by revealing His Law? Hardly.

Among God's many gifts is the Law, which plainly increases awareness of our own sins. This is essential information. It's like that pain on our right side that warns us to see a doctor—before our appendix explodes. The Law tells us something life-threatening is wrong. Our relationship with God is infected with sin, and we need immediate treatment. If we didn't know about it, then . . . ignorance would be deadly!

Knowing our sinfulness prompts us to run to Jesus for help. His diagnosis confirms our suspicions. We are indeed sin-full. But He is forgiveness-full. The more sins we expose, the more forgiveness we receive. (Not that we should have some kind of contest to see how much forgiveness we can get!) That's Paul's message to the Romans, and it's God's assurance to us. We don't need to be ignorant of our sins, but we can be sure that God forgets them for Jesus' sake. Now that's real bliss.

Ring around the Soul

"Woe to you, scribes and Pharisees, hypocrites! For you clean the outside of the cup and the plate, but inside they are full of greed and self-indulgence. You blind Pharisee! First clean the inside of the cup and the plate, that the outside also may be clean." Matthew 23:25–26

Aren't modern inventions wonderful? Of course, they aren't always consistent with their reputation. Take dishwashers, for example. Maybe it's because I owned an early model (two hands, a washcloth, and a towel) that I wasn't satisfied with the electrical kind. I was especially dissatisfied with its effectiveness on paper plates. It didn't do well with bones or gravy that had been dried-on for more than 11 days either. If you left coffee in a mug more than three weeks, well, the dishwasher didn't make a dent in that either!

My dishwasher must have been the Pharisee model. Listen: "Woe to you, scribes and Pharisees, hypocrites! For you clean the outside of the cup and the plate, but inside they are full of greed and self-indulgence. You blind Pharisee! First clean the inside of the cup and the plate, that the outside also may be clean" (Matthew 23:25–26). Wow! Those were some of the harshest words our Savior ever spoke.

Squeaky clean on the outside, but ring around the soul on the inside. That describes the condition of anyone who tries to masquerade as wholly holy on his or her own. Those who flaunt their facade of goodness anger us, just as they did Jesus, but sometimes the situation is more pathetic.

Think of a well-known person who, by all appearances, is someone everyone would consider good. Got a name in mind? What evidence does this person demonstrate to support this reputation? Perhaps it's large donations to worthy causes or hours of personal labor to help those living in ramshackle squalor. Maybe it's someone who participates in every fund-raiser at the local school or who chauffeurs the neighborhood kids to soccer practice. As a Christian, however, you know what the ultimate measure of goodness is, don't you?

Does this person believe that Jesus is his or her Savior from sin, death, and the devil? If not, all the philanthropy and volunteer hours in the world won't make this person good in God's judgment. How easy it is for outward goodness to deceive both the do-gooder as well as those who observe the goodness! As good as this person might be, he or she needs your witness, empowered by the Holy Spirit, to be truly good. Maybe you can start by offering to help with the dishes.

The Love of Our Life

Set me as a seal upon your heart, as a seal upon your arm, for love is strong as death, jealousy is fierce as the grave. Its flashes are flashes of fire, the very flame of the Lord. Many waters cannot quench love, neither can floods drown it. If a man offered for love all the wealth of his house, he would be utterly despised. Song of Songs 8:6–7

Solomon had plenty to say about love. Of course, He seemed to have lots of experience on the subject.

Scholars think a woman spoke the passage above for a man she deeply loved. The "seal over your heart" and the "seal on your arm" may be ancient precursors of modern wedding rings. Some women wore pierced rocks or arm bands identifying them as property of their beloved husbands. But before you start muttering about the idea of "belonging" to someone else, let's view this passage as an expression of God's love for us.

We Christians crave God's love. If ever we wanted to "belong" to someone other than ourselves or perhaps our cherished spouse, we want to be identified with Him. We want to take His name so all the world will know how much He loves us and vice versa. And so God weds us to Himself with the mark that we belong—faith in Him.

God's love for us is "strong as death" and as "fierce as the grave." We can think of God's love being strong as death—the death of Jesus on the cross. This was no deep coma or symbolic sleep as some claim. It was our real God who died a real death. The unyielding grave insisted on its way, but in the end, even the grave yielded, and Jesus rose to victory. Now His love continues not just to burn, but to blaze—a virtual inferno of love that defies extinguishing.

God's love can't be bought. His love is priceless. It's unmerited. And it's free. God loves us because—well, because He loves us. What other reason could there be?

A Sandwich to Remember

*And day by day, attending the temple together and breaking bread in
their homes, they received their food with glad and generous hearts, praising God and having favor with all the people. And the Lord added to their
number day by day those who were being saved. Acts 2:46–47*

Aren't modern inventions wonderful? Another fascinating one is the
bread maker. Older bread bakers remember the loving punches
inflicted on dough, though no loaves were pummeled in anger. It was just
something bakers kneaded to do. Next came the dough hook, which butted
dough with nary a drop of sweat required of the baker. Now we have this
machine that does everything but eat the bread.

Bread has long assumed religious significance. There was the unleavened
bread baked by the children of Israel as they packed for their escape from
Egypt. There was manna in the desert when they were far from bakeries.
Finally, there was my mother's bread, which once reminded the family of the
bricks baked by the Israelites while still captive in Egypt.

Jesus compared Himself to life-giving and life-sustaining bread. When He
instituted the Lord's Supper, He didn't break a fish or a leg of lamb. He broke
bread and told His followers to remember Him when they ate it. Together
with the wine, we celebrate today His presence and receive the forgiveness He
won for us on the cross.

Beyond Holy Communion, we can continue another tradition that helps
us remember Jesus' sacrifice. Acts 2:42 suggests something we can copy: "And
they devoted themselves to the apostles' teaching and fellowship, to the
breaking of bread and the prayers."

We "break bread" every time we eat, and we eat several times each day
(except for those who partake in one continuous meal). This presents the perfect opportunity to pray. Although we're hungry and don't want the food to
cool, we can have a few brief words with God about more than just our meals.
(After all, it's not like He's a waiter who doesn't want to hear how your day
went.) There's also the fellowship aspect. If you eat alone, it's probably the
time when you're most lonely. But you can find a cure for that loneliness if
you pull out a chair and invite God to sit with you. Then you can pray and eat
simultaneously. If you're so blessed to have companions at the table, enjoy
their fellowship and be a source of joy for them as well.

Whatever your meal, remember the time Jesus ate and prayed and led
fond conversations with His friends. Even that routine summer sausage sand-
wich can be something to remember.

That Explains It

For no prophecy was ever produced by the will of man, but men spoke from God as they were carried along by the Holy Spirit. 2 Peter 1:21

Recently, some cynical scholars have announced the "truth" about Sodom, Gomorrah, and Lot's wife (Genesis 19). (You know what cynics are, don't you? They're people who know everything and believe nothing.) You may remember the fearful story of how God demolished the sin cities with fire and brimstone. You may also remember that God spared Lot and his family, and how Lot's wife took one last, forbidden look at the hometown, becoming the first recorded victim of excessive sodium.

Now all this is hard to explain. Modern, technologically enhanced, highly educated cynics now claim that research suggests the cities were located atop a highly flammable bituminous area. As for Lot and Mrs. Lot, that was a case of mistaken identity. Their escape took them down the Dead Sea Scenic Highway where chunks of salt were known to float like icebergs, occasionally washing ashore on high waves. These scholars seem to suggest that Mrs. Lot stooped over to tie her sandal or something when Lot noticed the hunk of flotsam and ran off in horror.

God leaves no room for cynicism about His Word. Peter says that our familiar Bible stories come courtesy of the Holy Spirit, who makes the unbelievable believable. We don't need explanations about how God does things. Otherwise, how could we believe that the same God who devastated two corrupt cities would also love sinners so much that He spared their eternal lives? Our escape is through none less than God's Son, Jesus. And when God returns to turn the whole universe into a highly flammable bituminous area, He'll lead us to safety too. Just don't look back.

413 Reasons to Thank Jesus

Jesus said to her, "Everyone who drinks of this water will be thirsty again,
but whoever drinks of the water that I will give him will never be thirsty
forever. The water that I will give him will become in him a spring of
water welling up to eternal life." John 4:13–14

When we need a little prodding to thank our God and Savior, a good place to look for suggestions is in the fourth chapter, thirteenth verse of several books. John is a good place to start. He quotes Jesus, who implies that nothing in the world completely and finally satisfies us.

Isn't it peculiar that we can be so satisfied with ourselves and so dissatisfied with others? Of course, that phenomena is easily explained. Ignorance and forgetfulness! And haven't you also noticed it's hard to be satisfied when we get what we deserve?

Jesus chose water to remind us of the temporary nature of things that satisfy us. A drink of water satisfies only until we're thirsty again. Sleep fulfills our needs only until the alarm clock rings. Even the most gratifying, long-term, human relationships end in the back of a moving van or hearse.

The only real satisfaction comes from things that last forever. Take "extended warranties," for example. We buy them in hopes of having our appliances last longer. But how satisfied can we be when we're paying in advance for inevitable breakdowns? If only we could find something that satisfies forever.

As you know, only Jesus offers eternal satisfaction. Our Savior's love and care is totally satisfying. Regardless of the multitude or magnitude of our sins, Jesus always has enough love to cover them. And while we persistently seek His forgiveness for our consistent failures, His one act on the cross was all it took to slake God's anger over our rebelliousness and unfaithfulness. And so we face each day and our eternal future knowing that whatever dissatisfies us is nothing compared to God's love through Jesus Christ. Satisfaction guaranteed.

Truly Transformed

Now when they saw the boldness of Peter and John, and perceived that they were uneducated, common men, they were astonished. And they recognized that they had been with Jesus. Acts 4:13

History has recorded many changes over the years, and some people have opposed all of them. Others welcome change, but only if it favors them.

Some changes truly transform the way we live. Take electric transformers that adjust the power supply to your home. We're certainly thankful to whomever invented those devices. And that brings us to the subject of another Transformer—with a capital *T*.

Jesus has transformed our lives. And He's been doing it for quite a while. Go back to the days of Peter and John as recorded in Acts. People were surprised at the transformation of these two. Once they were blue-collar laborers, but now these men of God courageously told others about their Savior. Once they hoped to enjoy a few comforts, but now they withstood physical assault. Though they had little background in "book learning," now they matched the minds of educated critics. Had they joined the Toastmasters Club or earned some correspondence course diploma? Of course not. As the Bible passage says, they had "been with Jesus."

All of Jesus' transformations were truly electric! He changed the punishment that God's wrath demanded into salvation. Like the transformers you see hanging from electric poles, Jesus hung from the cross and changed the punishment we deserved into useful energy to serve Him in thanksgiving. Energy to praise Him. Energy to emulate Him. Then Jesus sent the Holy Spirit to transform us sinners into saints—even before we die. Now we can channel the love of Christ to others as we serve, forgive, and tell others how Jesus changes life. It's just another of the 413 reasons to thank God!

Inspired Performance

And He gave the apostles, the prophets, the evangelists, the pastors and teachers, to equip the saints for the work of ministry, for building up the body of Christ, until we all attain to the unity of the faith and of the knowledge of the Son of God, to mature manhood, to the measure of the stature of the fullness of Christ. Ephesians 4:11–13

When was the last time you were inspired? Perhaps you took on some creative plumbing project at home. (It probably wasn't "creative" until you started it.) Early morning showers sometime inspire musical creativity. Maybe you were inspired when you took on the career that you're in now or when you tackle certain tasks on the job.

Paul told the Ephesian Christians about inspiration—another reason to thank God. He listed apostles, prophets, evangelists, pastors, and teachers as inspired careers. Before we conclude that most of us aren't inspired in those ways, we need to realize that a little of those callings exist in whatever we do. Therefore, whatever our role in life, God inspired us to be His child and to serve in unique ways.

God inspires us to heal broken relationships, aimless wandering, lame excuses, and dead ambitions with bold forgiveness and the Holy Spirit's power. Though we may see ourselves as non-prophet in nature, Jesus inspires us to accurately predict the glorious future that awaits us and all believers. As for the evangelist, how can we keep secrets about what God has done? Pastors and teachers, as we know them today, are specially trained for their missions, but God also inspires each of us to act like a shepherd, seeking and finding the lost sheep of the world and then teaching them the formula for salvation.

You are inspired. Now get out there and give a performance that others will never forget.

The "I Can" Spirit

I can do all things through Him who strengthens me. Philippians 4:13

The best of our world's history is built on an "I can" spirit. "I can save some seeds to plant and move those rocks to grow food for my family," thought the first farmers. "I can translate God's Word into a language that ordinary people understand," said Martin Luther. "I can find a way for man to walk on the moon," figured some rocket scientist.

"I can do everything through Him who gives me strength," claims the Christian. And it's true too. It's essential to have power for love as opposed to having a love for power.

Sometimes we Christians lust for power—benevolent power, of course. We want to do great things for the Lord. Today's passage makes it sound as if we could do spectacular things to serve Him. There's just one little flaw in that perspective. It's the word *we*.

As we aspire to great service, we must also remember that the Mother Teresa in us may be intended to show compassion to a sick neighbor rather than to pitiful throngs in some pagan nation. And a desire to preach powerful sermons may need tempering down to proclaiming the Savior's love to our own children. Feeding 5,000 by God's miraculous power may seem a worthy goal too. But God may want us to work in that downtown kitchen that serves the grimy and hopeless once a week.

God's power doesn't always work in the way we normally understand power to work. The power of love that drives Christians to all kinds of service works by the Holy Spirit. And it's never a little thing to spark or strengthen faith in the hearts of others. It's a powerful thing accomplished only by the Holy Spirit working in us. We have the power to accomplish whatever God expects of us. We most certainly have an "I can" Spirit.

Consolation Prize

*But we do not want you to be uninformed, brothers, about those who are
asleep, that you may not grieve as others do who have no hope. For since
we believe that Jesus died and rose again, even so, through Jesus, God will
bring with Him those who have fallen asleep. 1 Thessalonians 4:13–14*

Surely you've heard the story of the wife who accepted defeat like a
man. She blamed her husband!

Consolation prizes rarely please people as much as the "first prize." "At
least it's better than nothing," is the way we might comfort ourselves. Yet the
only important prize—the very best prize—is the prize for losers. It's not as
bad as it sounds.

Nobody can deny that we're losers. Oh, we can deny our actual status to
others, but we can't repudiate it with God. He knows the truth about sinners,
and we are losers. Ever since Adam and Eve disqualified themselves from the
first prize of an all-expense-paid lifetime in paradise, only one person has
even come close to winning.

Jesus won it all. He was a winner (even when He seemed a loser). The
devil thought he had a contest when he tempted Jesus during moments when
any man would be weak, but Jesus overcame every challenge. Satan couldn't
nudge Jesus off the cross while He was dying, either. Instead, Jesus did as God
intended. He humbly paid for our sins with His life.

Jesus won first prize. And because Jesus was a winner, all us losers got the
consolation prize. What consolation it is! Though death will almost certainly
claim most of us, thank God that we'll come alive again to share eternity with
Him and everyone else who died in Christ.

Keep Your Antenna Up

"Stay dressed for action and keep your lamps burning, and be like men who are waiting for their master to come home from the wedding feast, so that they may open the door to him at once when he comes and knocks. Blessed are those servants whom the master finds awake when he comes. . . . You also must be ready, for the Son of Man is coming at an hour you do not expect." Luke 12:35–40

Aren't modern inventions wonderful? I cite cellular telephones as yet another example. In days of yore, you couldn't go to a baseball game and be bothered—I mean, remain in touch—with important business clients (or the cleaners or the fish market or the travel agent). You would have to enjoy the game completely independent of infringements on your time. Now you're never more than 11 beeps away—even when you don't want to be.

In fairness to wireless providers and all others who might take offense at the first paragraph, let me say that cellular telephones are one of God's technological blessings. They give us added measures of safety and peace of mind. They also offer good subject matter for thinking about our relationship with Jesus.

The Bible says, "Stay dressed for action and keep your lamps burning" (Luke 12:35). Were Jesus talking today, He might say, "Remain available and keep your antenna up." Unlike a demanding supervisor who insists that you're always available by phone, pager, fax, or smoke signal, Jesus sets a perfect example for us.

We're aware of Jesus' hours—simultaneously available to everyone 24 hours a day. He responds to our needs, small or large, and He's faster than a microwave signal in relieving our guilt with forgiveness. His willingness to serve us demonstrates how we can respond to Him and to those who need us.

If you're out in the public at all, you interact with or at least observe many needy people (and I'm not talking about the homeless). Among their numbers may be a family member, your boss, the kid across the street, the widower in the next apartment, the driver stopped on the shoulder of the highway, the salesperson at the store, or the man standing next to you on the elevator.

With a smile on your lips, a Scripture verse in your heart, and a friendly word on your tongue, you might be God's answer to that person's prayer. Let Jesus know that you're always available. And keep your antenna up!

Out of Sight and Out of Mind

As far as the east is from the west, so far does He remove our
transgressions from us. Psalm 103:12

If you want to be perfectly happy, you need a lousy memory and absolutely no imagination. And have you noticed that people with the worst memories seem to remember everything they've ever done for you—and even a few things they didn't?

Out of sight easily translates into out of mind. What do you lose most often because you placed it out of sight? Car keys? Your glasses? How about your purse or wallet? Or that thing of such great value that you put it where nobody, including you, will ever find it?

Psalm 103 provides excellent comfort for those who have put something down and promptly forgot where it was. The psalmist is talking about our sins here. While I don't remember how far the east is from the west—we must have learned that in geography—I do know it's a long way. If car keys disappear when only twelve feet away, just think how easy it is to lose something at opposite ends of the compass! And if there's anything worth losing, and losing for good, it's our sins.

Perhaps it's nothing to worry about, but it seems that God, being all-knowing and all-everything, doesn't have problems with His memory. Not by accident anyway. But He does subscribe to a policy of forgiving and forgetting. The one who died to take away our sins forgives us. And God the Father forgets every forgiven sin for His Son's sake. He packs our sins away, losing them forever behind mountains of His love. We should have such a memory!

Watching the Time

At that time Joshua spoke to the LORD in the day when the LORD gave the Amorites over to the sons of Israel, and he said in the sight of Israel, "Sun, stand still at Gibeon, and moon, in the Valley of Aijalon." And the sun stood still, and the moon stopped, until the nation took vengeance on their enemies. Is this not written in the Book of Jashar? The sun stopped in the midst of heaven and did not hurry to set for about a whole day. Joshua 10:12–13

We look at it often each day. Perhaps that's why we call timepieces "watches." We constantly watch our watches—watching for the precise time to begin or end something. Or simply watching time pass oh-so-quickly or ever-so-slowly—the difference between waiting for your turn in the dentist's chair or the interminable time remaining before you escape from it. Sometimes time is on our side. Sometimes not. At times we may envy God, whose existence is timeless. No clocks to punch, no deadlines, no dead times. But can this God of ours really understand what it's like to live in the dimension of time?

From Old Testament days on to our present day, our timeless Lord has lowered Himself to time on our terms. Once, He literally made time stand still to deliver His people from their enemies. Consider the passage above from Joshua.

"The Day the Sun Stood Still" sounds like a science fiction movie (of course, it was called "The Day the Earth Stood Still"!). But who needs fiction when we have the real thing from God's own Word? Time and again, God used time to shower His love and blessings on us.

God sent His Son at just the right time to live for a time among people. And His Son spent a tormented three hours—less than a half-day's work (unless you're hanging on a cross)—pouring out His life to save us from our sins. Then it was over. But it began again. New life. Endless life. A life we'll share free of those little regulators hugging our wrists, clinging to our walls, or glowing softly on our nightstands.

May God speed that day when time really flies—flies away for good. Time will stand still again as we enjoy the victory Christ won on that fatal and fabulous weekend so long ago. Until that time, may God keep your faith strong and eternal.

Take It from Smokey

Now Moses was keeping the flock of his father-in-law, Jethro. . . . And the angel of the LORD appeared to him in a flame of fire out of the midst of a bush. He looked, and behold, the bush was burning, yet it was not consumed. And Moses said, "I will turn aside to see this great sight, why the bush is not burned." When the LORD saw that he turned aside to see, God called to him out of the bush, "Moses, Moses!" And he said, "Here I am."
Exodus 3:1–4

Remember the slogan broadcast by the spokesbear for the National Forest Service? Not only was he right, he also had something in common with Moses, spokesperson for God. "Only you can prevent forest fires," said Smokey.

Moses might have laughed because what he saw defied all logic. As he inched closer, the burning bush started talking to him. The flaming shrub was really God in disguise. God had a hot message for Moses. He wanted Moses to serve Him with fervent, fiery passion. You may know the rest of the story—how Moses led God's people out of slavery to the land God had promised. But that's another story. Let's not forget Smokey.

While we can't consider Smokey some furry theologian, the truth of his slogan applies to spiritual matters as well as to forest fires. We can indeed snuff out the Spirit's fire. And the devil is willing to help extinguish the blaze. We can keep our Bibles closed, skip church, neglect prayer, live self-centered lives, refuse to forgive others, develop self-reliant intellect, and forfeit hope in difficult times.

Frightening as that prospect is, God has promised that neither "height nor depth, nor anything else in all creation, will be able to separate us from the love of God in Christ Jesus our Lord" (Romans 8:39). God has sent the Holy Spirit to set Christians on fire with the Word of God and the love of Jesus. Nobody can extinguish our spiritual fire without our consent.

We need not fear that God will stop loving us. Nor should we worry that Jesus will somehow take back the salvation that He won on the cross. No matter how we anger or disappoint God, He always stands ready to forgive and keep the fire burning in our soul. The Holy Spirit fans the flames of faith with God's Word as we hear and read it.

So keep on burning. Let your smoke get in other people's eyes so they see your fire too.

Bleep Bleep

Now we know that whatever the law says it speaks to those who are under the law, so that every mouth may be stopped, and the whole world may be held accountable to God. For by works of the law no human being will be justified in His sight, since through the law comes knowledge of sin.
Romans 3:19–20

When you think about it, car horns often are the equivalents of mechanical expletives, aren't they? They should go "Bleep! Bleep!" instead of "Beep! Beep!" Too bad we can't delete them like they sometimes do profanity on public broadcasts.

Car horns often react to our steering-wheel evil. They let us know when we've done something wrong—or at least when someone accuses us of derelict driving. Next time you hear a horn bleeping at you, think about Romans 3:20, which says, "For by works of the law no human being will be justified in His sight, since through the law comes knowledge of sin."

God's Law is like a car horn. It accuses us, and its accusations are always accurate. The Law points out every way we err. Sometimes it makes us feel guilty; at other times it fuels our anger. If we're in the right mood (or should we say the wrong mood?), the Law makes us want to give up—give up trying to meet God's uncompromising demands for perfect obedience.

The only way to avoid the bleeping horns that expose our sins is never to be born. Too late for that now. But that's okay because there is a better option. Jesus silenced the horns. He quieted them when every sin for every time blared in His ears as He hung on the cross and died. No doubt it was a very silent Sunday when He left the tomb to visit His faulty friends, whom He had every right to honk at. We're among those friends, too, but we need not fear retribution. Jesus brings only His cheer and love.

You say you still hear horns blaring? That's the devil honking. He's like those impatient drivers who bellow at you even when you're obeying the law. Satan wants to keep you feeling guilty. He wants you to be more like him. When he honks, do what you do to impatient drivers. (Well, maybe not.) Get out of his way. Let the devil race by you. Your leader is Jesus Christ, Satan slayer and silencer of the Law's bleeping horns. Jesus loves you and will take you where you're going. And you'll get there exactly when He expects you.

Ladders

*"Behold, I am with you and will keep you wherever you go, and will bring
you back to this land. For I will not leave you until I have done what I
have promised you." Genesis 28:15*

Some say it's bad luck to walk under a ladder. To me, it seems more
risky to climb one. There was that crisp, fall day when I climbed to the
roof bent on relieving the gutters of their collection of crisp color. I got up just
fine, but the ladder wouldn't let me down. It stood there and defied me, teas-
ing me to enjoy fall on its terms. It wasn't until my family returned from shopping and encouraged me (with raucous laughter) that I had the shame, er . . .
courage, to descend.

As much as ladders cause me nightmares, Jacob had sweet dreams about
his. Perhaps he hoped to dream of a fluffy pillow and a downy bed as he
arranged the rock beneath his head. You probably know the story. Jacob saw
angels walking up and down the ladder, and the Lord Himself was at the top.

God gave Jacob something better than a pleasant dream. He gave Jacob a
vision for the future. Jacob could be certain that his days on the run would
end. God said, "Behold, I am with you and will keep you wherever you go,
and will bring you back to this land. For I will not leave you until I have done
what I have promised you" (Genesis 28:15). Jacob, a scheming, cheating sinner, received God's personal attention. Undoubtedly, Jacob repented of his
sins. While he might fear his relationships with brother Esau, Jacob's dream
assured him of God's forgiveness.

How often do we climb ladders in fear? We fall into deep pits of sin
(many of which we dug personally) and struggle vainly to escape to higher living. Jacob's story suggests something different: Rest in the middle of your
clash with sin. Rest on Jesus. He's at the top of our ladder with comfort and
promise.

Jesus knows our sinfulness, and He accepts our repentance. What a life He
has planned for us! His blessings began even before we were born when He
knew who we were and what we needed. He has watched us fall to sin, and
He's repeatedly picked us up with His love and forgiveness. We continue
through life confident that we belong to Him, right now, here on earth. And
we look forward to that day when He will take us up that ladder to heaven.
And we'll never come down either.

Leave Your Message at the Tone

And I said, "O Lord God of heaven, the great and awesome God who keeps covenant and steadfast love with those who love Him and keep His commandments, let Your ear be attentive and Your eyes open, to hear the prayer of Your servant that I now pray before You day and night for the people of Israel Your servants, confessing the sins of the people of Israel, which we have sinned against You." Nehemiah 1:5–6

Alexander Graham Bell invented the telephone. Some evidence suggests that his teenage son was an inventor too. Tradition hints that he was responsible for the first busy signal! As you have experienced, telephones have been busy ever since.

Recent years have seen a proliferation of area codes as the amount of numbers increases beyond the imagination. Today you can call almost anyplace. Just the other day I must have misdialed and reached a number on the ocean floor. There was a crab on the other end of the line. Which brings us to the subject of answering machines.

Think for a moment about what it would be like if God used an answering machine. We would face the same uncertainty and anxiety we experience when we trust an important message to a tiny audiotape. Will God check for messages? Did I speak clearly enough? Will He check caller ID to see if He should pay attention to me?

Psalm 4:3 says, "But know that the Lord has set apart the godly for Himself; the Lord hears when I call to Him."

Perhaps your calls to the Lord are frequent, or maybe you call Him only when you need something special. Regardless of how often you talk to God, He always recognizes your voice. Believers always get God's personal attention, even if the conversation seems one-sided. God invites, welcomes, and commands our calls, though we can be cranky, distracted, demanding, unreasonable, distrustful, and whiny.

One benefit of daily, routine calls on God is that we get to say things we might not think of during a crisis. Opportunity abounds to express our gratitude for His love and forgiveness. We can tell Him how much we appreciate all those blessings that He continues to send, though sometimes we take them for granted. We can chat about the problems others have and ask Him to give them a call.

Call God often. Listen for His calls too. The Operator is waiting.

September 8 ⌐

See Food

When He was at table with them, He took the bread and blessed and broke it and gave it to them. And their eyes were opened, and they recognized Him. And He vanished from their sight. Luke 24:30–31

I embrace a definite preference for a see-food diet. I eat nearly every food I see. If only we could treat food like we treat people and avoid those that disagree with us! It seems the only wise move is to adopt a diet. At the very least, it'll make us gain weight more slowly.

The Bible contains many references to food. We might say food really is the way to a person's heart as we note how Jesus served thousands a satisfying meal while they listened to Him preach. Food was a daily reminder of God's menu of love when He daily fed morsels of manna to the children of Israel. And instead of feeding the birds, Elijah was fed by them as God took care of his physical needs. Of course, who can forget the bread and wine—the body and blood—at Jesus' last meal with the disciples?

Two men, citizens of Emmaus, enjoyed one particular see-food platter as they ate with a stranger. Luke says, "When He was at table with them, He took the bread and blessed and broke it and gave it to them. And their eyes were opened, and they recognized Him. And He vanished from their sight" (Luke 24:30–31). The mysterious "He" was Jesus. What made this experience so remarkable was not the eerie disappearance of Jesus after the meal, but the eye-popping revelation when He prayed and served the bread. The two men saw Jesus. Now that's our kind of see food!

Obviously, the Lord's Supper provides a regular feast that keeps our eyes focused on the Savior. Jesus supplies us with another kind of food too. Words. His words in the Bible. They're not the kind of words we're forced to eat. (We do enough of that!) Instead, we experience their sweet-sour character as we consume them to nurture our souls. God's sour words sear our souls like acid when they reveal how willingly we gorge ourselves on sin. Then, like delicacies from an opulent French menu, God heaps our plate with fresh words of forgiveness and refreshing renewal.

We may describe God's menu using mouth-watering terms, but Jesus kept it simple. He compared Himself to bread, widely known as the "staff of life." And what delicious bread He is! He gives sight to the soul, revealing to eyes once blind that He is our living God. Finally—a diet worth keeping!

How Old Are We?

Then God said, "Let Us make man in Our image, after Our likeness. . . ."
So God created man in His own image, in the image of God He created
him; male and female He created them. And God blessed them. And God
said to them, "Be fruitful and multiply and fill the earth and subdue it
and have dominion over the fish of the sea and over the birds of the heav-
ens and over every living thing that moves on the earth." . . . And God
saw everything that He had made, and behold, it was very good. And there
was evening and there was morning, the sixth day. Genesis 1:26–31

The older we get, the more things ache. Especially new ideas. Here is one of them: In 1997, scientists discovered a skull and leg bone in Kenya that not only startled them, but caused them to rethink some treasured ideas about the age and evolution of humans. Mounting evidence suggests that humans started looking and acting like humans sooner than was thought humanly possible.

The discovery in Kenya may tug at our spiritual nerves and grate on our scriptural intellect, but perhaps we should find some ironic comfort in the situation. Modern science is grudgingly discovering what we believers have known for centuries. Modern human beings began as modern human beings. The Bible tells all: "Then God said, 'Let Us make man in Our image, after our likeness. . . .' So God created man in His own image, in the image of God He created him; male and female He created them" (Genesis 1:26–27).

Rather than revile scientists who postulate unbiblical ideas, we can pray for them. How sad to earn advanced degrees and sacrifice so much for the sake of understanding humankind. It's especially disheartening when all that's needed is what many of us already have—faith and Scripture.

Science would counter that faith and Scripture are mere beliefs, figments of human hope for comfort and immortality. Better we trust in some bones and mathematical projections! Tragically, scientists convince others that religion is impotent and foolish. Yet God gave us such power! Did you read how He created us in His own image? We have to admit, though, that human history clearly refutes this. Sin has so poisoned humanity that we bear little resemblance to God. But thanks to Jesus, our blemishes are only skin deep, and we remain God's creation.

September 10 ⌐

Guide to Trees

"For behold, I create new heavens and a new earth, and the former things shall not be remembered or come into mind. But be glad and rejoice forever in that which I create; for behold, I create Jerusalem to be a joy, and her people to be a gladness. . . They shall not build and another inhabit; they shall not plant and another eat; for like the days of a tree shall the days of My people be, and My chosen shall long enjoy the work of their hands. . ." says the Lord. Isaiah 65:17–25

The Bible leaves us with the distinct impression that trees were one of God's favorite creations. Not only are trees mentioned often in a variety of contexts, no fewer than 26 specific varieties made the pages of Scripture. Wood you believe it? (Okay—no more puns.)

We often marvel at the magnificence of trees, whether it's the age and height of colossal redwoods, the girth of stout oaks, or the colors of massive maples. Trees, whether brawny or scrawny, contribute to feelings of well-being too. Consider these encouraging words from Isaiah 65:22: "They shall not build and another inhabit; they shall not plant and another eat; for like the days of a tree shall the days of My people be, and My chosen shall long enjoy the work of their hands."

Long live the tree! Long live we! And it's all because of God's love. Though God certainly loved trees, He loves us more. He gave us trees for food, shade, construction, beauty, and forgiveness of sins. No, trees aren't some new sacrament. But one of God's superb creations figured prominently in the death of His Son. We behold the tree not only as a symbol of lengthy life, but also as a symbol of death. We can praise God that life and death are as intimately entwined as ivy on tree bark.

The prophet Isaiah addressed God's people during a terrible time in their history. Isaiah voiced mostly fearful and tragic words, but God also gave him words of comfort for the faithful few. Today's reading tells believers of all eras that their lives will be as the days of the tree—long and fruitful, though not devoid of weathering.

God made us strong enough to stand firm despite infestations of sin, as well as outright attacks by the vicious, voracious devil. God takes us through the seasons of life, pruning away those parts that threaten our existence. He nourishes us with Word and Sacrament and draws us upward to Himself. We have a long way to grow, but we have forever to get there. And that leaves Satan time to count our rings!

Apple Trees

I am a rose of Sharon, a lily of the valleys. As a lily among brambles,
so is my love among the young women. As an apple tree among the trees
of the forest, so is my beloved among the young men. With great delight I
sat in his shadow, and his fruit was sweet to my taste, He brought me to
the banqueting house, and his banner over me was love. Sustain me with
raisins; refresh me with apples, for I am sick with love.
Song of Songs 2:1–5

People who don't get into nature may picture apple trees differently than you and I do. Perhaps they've seen apples growing neatly in piles and rows about 18 inches wide by 36 inches high. This is perfect for picking, especially because the lighting is good, the fruit glossy, and the temperature carefully controlled.

You may recall an old song entitled "Don't Sit under the Apple Tree with Anyone Else but Me." The lyrics stem from wartime sentiment that craved romantic loyalties while lovers were separated. The Bible's Song of Solomon speaks of apple trees and faithful love too: "As an apple tree among the trees of the forest, so is my beloved among the young men. With great delight I sat in his shadow, and his fruit was sweet to my taste" (Song of Solomon 2:3).

Song of Solomon compares the love between God and His people to the romantically poetic love between a man and a woman. Later, in the New Testament, the church is called the bride and Christ the bridegroom. How appropriate that we consider our relationship to Jesus in these terms!

We sit shaded by the One who loves us beyond any earthly love we can experience. As good as that shade is, we often wander away, seeking the shade of lesser gods who promise wealth, power, freedom, or other forms of self-fulfillment. When our hopes wither and die, Jesus remains, beckoning us to return to the shelter of His love and promise. When we return to His welcome shade, we wonder how we could have left Him in the first place. Until another temptation seduces us.

"Don't Sit under the Apple Tree with Anyone Else but Me" might be a good song for Christians. Jesus wants us to stay with Him, and the love He offers surpasses any offered elsewhere. But He also wants us to remain faithful to Him. He gives us power to resist sitting with anyone else. He feeds us with His sweet love, compassion, and care. Jesus listens to our most personal thoughts and innermost desires. Indeed, He knows them even if we don't speak them. His faithfulness to us through good times and bad assures us that we always can trust Him. So sit under an apple tree, and take a Friend.

Evergreen

Blessed is the man who walks not in the counsel of the wicked, nor stands in the way of sinners, nor sits in the seat of scoffers; but his delight is in the law of the Lord, and on His law he meditates day and night. He is like a tree planted by streams of water that yields its fruit in its season, and its leaf does not wither. In all that he does, he prospers. Psalm 1:1–3

Offering more proof of my expertise in treeology, I can tell you that evergreen is the scientific name for a group of trees that are ever green. Even more important, rarely is science so clear on the meaning of a scientific name.

Of course, evergreen really isn't the name of a specific tree. Most evergreens are members of the pine family, and the most famous member of the pine family is the Christmas tree. Nothing beats the aroma—to say nothing of the aura—of a Christmas tree. While research in this area is somewhat suspect, many people like to think that Martin Luther was the first to drag a tree through the snowy fields of Germany and into his home. He had a good idea. What better tree to "plant" in your home than one that points toward heaven?

Evergreens are great symbols of faith. Their ability to remain green during cold winters and hot summers reminds us of the characteristics of enduring faith. Let's probe this idea further. A good place to begin research is with the Bible—Psalm 1:3 in particular: "He is like a tree planted by streams of water that yields its fruit in its season, and its leaf does not wither. In all that he does, he prospers."

Psalm 1 comments on blessings that accompany those who delight in the law of the Lord. Such people are compared to a healthy, happy, fruitful evergreen tree planted in the best possible location. The water flowing nearby provides the food and moisture necessary for a productive life. The meaning of the psalm is that when Jesus is in our lives, when the Holy Spirit is at work in us, we are fed with sufficient love and wisdom to support a productive faith.

Christians aren't, however, "ever green." The devil and our sinful desires make us brittle and dry, ready to snap or burn or drop our faith, leaving us naked to destruction. That's a good time to remember that Jesus is "ever green"—without exception. He remains faithful to us, and the proof is that He sacrificed Himself for us while we were still sinners.

What consolation we have because we know Christ's love and sacrifice! We can use it to needle the devil every time He tries to chop us down.

Climbing Trees

And there was a man named Zacchaeus. . . . And he was seeking to see
who Jesus was, but on account of the crowd he could not, because he was
small of stature. So he ran on ahead and climbed up into a sycamore tree
to see Him, for He was about to pass that way. And when Jesus came to
the place, He looked up and said to him, "Zacchaeus, hurry and come
down, for I must stay at your house today." Luke 19:2–5

The huge sycamore in front of the house needed trimming, and the
wedding reception at the home across the street needed cheap entertainment. The situation was custom-made for a warm, sunny Saturday.

Propping up the largest stepladder I had, I climbed to the top step, saw in
hand. I attacked a large limb, and my labored grunting arrested the wedding
guests' attention. Only when the limb surrendered and fell did I realize my
balance depended on a left hand clinging to the now-departed limb. The saw
was in my right hand. I dropped the saw and raised both hands to the limb
above the stricken one, kicking away the ladder in the process. The audience
clapped and laughed as I dangled from the branch trying to plan my drop. But
enough about sycamores and me.

Sycamores make good trees for climbing, despite their lack of coopera-
tion for trimming. The Bible lends credence to that in Luke's reports involving a short man: "So he ran on ahead and climbed up into a sycamore tree to
see Him, for He was about to pass that way" (Luke 19:4).

Zacchaeus wanted to see Jesus. Nothing would stand in his way, including the crowds along the street, craning their necks for a closer look at the
miracle worker. Short on stature, but long on problem solving, Zacchaeus
ascended the now famous sycamore. He accomplished his goal. He even
made eye contact with Jesus, who, to the amazement of the crowd, stopped
and addressed the man infamous for his tax transgressions. The encounter
was friendly. Jesus invited Himself to Zacchaeus' place.

Witnesses didn't like what they saw. No supposedly righteous, holy person would ever personally visit brazen sinners. But these witnesses didn't
know what we know and what Zacchaeus hoped. Jesus came for sinners. He
came into their homes, into their leper colonies, into their "red-light dis-
tricts," not to join them in sin, but to save them from it.

Get a closer look at Jesus. He came for us, and He wants to stay at our
homes. Better yet, He came into our hearts and made us believers just like
Zacchaeus so we'll never have to take our lives out on a limb again.

Fresh Fish

Jesus said to them, "Children, do you have any fish?" They answered Him, "No." He said to them, "Cast the net on the right side of the boat, and you will find some." So they cast it, and now they were not able to haul it in, because of the quantity of fish. John 21:5–6

According to the *New England Journal of Medicine*, a 30-year study of nearly 2,000 people indicated that regularly eating fish cuts the risk of heart attack by 42 percent. Before you stuff yourself to the gills with sardines, note that similar studies showed no proof that eating lots of fish actually prevented heart attacks. So on a scale of 1 to 10, how do you rate fish?

Lacking research, people in Jesus' time appreciated the nutritional value of fish. So significant were fish that early Christians drew them in the sand to identify themselves as believers. That's not so strange when we remember how Jesus called His disciples "fishers of men" and showed them how much they could catch—with Him as their guide. The scene is described in John 21:5–6: "Jesus said to them, 'Children, do you have any fish?' They answered Him, 'No.' He said to them, 'Cast the net on the right side of the boat, and you will find some.' So they cast it, and now they were not able to haul it in, because of the quantity of fish."

Over the years, God has guided a whole fleet of "fishermen" in finding bigger and better catches. I'm not sure how the fish population compares with the human population, but we're talking a cavernous creel! Praise God that you're part of the catch.

Imagine that! God knew where you were, and He wanted you. Of course, God is good at that because He made you and cares for you, but it's mind-boggling nonetheless. God loved you so much that He chose you to be a prize catch—one that He could point to and say, "That one is Mine!" You're one that didn't get away only to face the snapping teeth of Satan. God caught you and you're a keeper.

Now you're a fisher too. You know that saying "There's a lot of fish in the sea"? It's true. They might be hiding out in the home next door or huddled tightly in a school. You might find them lurking in shadows or openly sunning themselves. One thing is true: You have the right bait. Dangle the Gospel in front of them. Put some action into your faith. Lure them with love. Then draw a fish in the sand together. Or even in the dust on your desk!

No Thanks

Continue steadfastly in prayer, being watchful in it with thanksgiving.
Colossians 4:2

Gratitude is rare. This was proven recently by two medical emergencies witnessed on public transportation. The bus was crammed with people swaying chaotically in the aisle as the vehicle lurched to start or stop. A skinny, sick-looking man boarded the bus and slithered his way down the aisle. Suddenly, a middle-aged woman stood up and offered the man her seat. He fainted. When he regained consciousness, he said, "Thank you." Then she fainted!

Godly people know they have much for which to be thankful. But sometimes we forget. Some of us forget often. Like ill-mannered children, we offer no thanks—and perhaps feel no thankfulness—for the many blessings of God. When that happens, we confess our ungratefulness and receive God's forgiveness. (Then, at the very least, we can be thankful that only God knows everything about us!)

Whoever wrote to the New Testament Hebrew people had this to say about thanksgiving: "Through Him then let us continually offer up a sacrifice of praise to God, that is, the fruit of lips that acknowledge His name" (Hebrews 13:15). Note the word *continue*. While prayers of gratitude and praise always need to be in our hearts and on our tongues, another way to thank God is through our actions. Colossians tells us to be wise and keep our conversations "full of grace." The Holy Spirit gives us power—energized by Jesus' life and death and life again—to live our praise to God for His goodness.

Do you need a few solid reasons for gratitude? Dig out last year's tax return. Did you make enough money to pay taxes? There's a good reason right there. (Even if you owe lots of people lots of money, you can be thankful you're not them!) Now step right up to a mirror. Put your nose close to the glass and watch. See any condensation? Yep, there's another reason for gratitude.

As you search your daily life for reasons to be thankful, remember what Jesus did for you. Then it will be easier to do something for Him—to speak those graceful words to someone who doesn't deserve your grace or to skip the wisdom of this world in favor of wisdom that's out of this world.

Lost . . .

What then? Are we Jews any better off? No, not at all. For we have
already charged that all, both Jews and Greeks, are under sin, as it is
written: "None is righteous, no, not one; no one understands; no one
seeks for God. All have turned aside; together they have become worthless;
no one does good, not even one." Romans 3:9–12

You've heard the term "necessary evil." It's how we describe an iniquity we like so well that we don't want to abandon it. When it comes to
choosing between two necessary evils, it's easy to expand the choices.
Christians, however, need not worry about such things, or do we?

How do you feel about yourself—as a Christian, that is? If someone were
to ask how you support your claim to fame as a Christian, what evidence
would you offer? Perhaps it's that you attend worship each week, or maybe
you're a regular customer at the Christian bookstore. (Sounds good to me!)
Maybe you could point to your Baptism or to the fact that you rarely swear.

Additional evidence could be the fish symbol stuck to your front door,
family devotions around the dinner table, or your faithfulness in sending the
pastor a Christmas card each year. If you can submit any of the above evidence, you must be . . . like the New Testament Jews who refused to believe
in Jesus their Savior.

Ouch! You were having a decent devotion until that came along. See what
Paul said in Romans 3:10–12: "None is righteous, no, not one; no one understands; no one seeks for God. All have turned aside; together they have
become worthless; no one does good, not even one."

Paul described the condition of all people. He might have said they were
lost. The naked truth is that we're more like dead—spiritually dead. Paul's
point was that we can't claim evidence of knowing Christ based solely on
things we do. That is nothing more than a recitation of the Law, and if we
can't keep all parts of it—if we have necessary evils in our lives—we're guilty
of disobeying the whole Law. According to Paul, we can't avoid lawlessness
even through the technicality of saying we don't believe in God. When people set up their own system of laws and morality, they can't meet those
demands either.

Talk about a bad hair day, now we're into a bad heir day! Our record of
faithfulness is filled with all kinds of evil. Even as believers, we're powerless
to "earn our keep" as Christians. Don't despair, though. Our "lost and found"
hung on the cross. Be sure to read the next meditation tomorrow—if you can
wait that long.

. . . And Found

*But whatever gain I had, I counted as loss for the sake of Christ. Indeed,
I count everything as loss because of the surpassing worth of knowing
Christ Jesus my Lord. For His sake I have suffered the loss of all things
and count them as rubbish, in order that I may gain Christ and be found
in Him, not having a righteousness of my own that comes from the law,
but that which comes through faith in Christ, the righteousness from God
that depends on faith—that I may know Him and the power of His resurrection, and may share His sufferings, becoming like Him in His death,
that by any means possible I may attain the resurrection from the dead.*
Philippians 3:7–11

Among items commonly found in a school's lost and found are some
surprises. It's hard to imagine how students can lose one shoe, a
leather coat, shoelaces, or eyeglasses. It's even harder to imagine not search-
ing for the lost article. Then again, how many people look beyond themselves
and their immediate surroundings to find what they don't have? That was yes-
terday's spiritual subject too.

After that last episode, let's get something clear right away. As masterfully
as Paul exposed our sinful nature, he also proclaimed not merely good news,
but the best news in the passage above.

Found in Christ! How does that happen? We are found in Christ when we
are found by Christ. That's true evidence of our identity as a Christian. God
found the lost, beginning with Adam and Eve and continuing through the
ages. He not only found them lost, but also wanting—wanting someone to
save them from their misery. The history of God's people clearly shows that
human attempts at self-rescue didn't work—not that God didn't provide
opportunities. Especially significant was the incident at Mt. Sinai when God
told His people how they could be saved. "Obey the Law," He said. They said,
"Okay. We'll try." We've been saying the same thing ever since!

God found every sin from the multitude of sinners and laid them on
Jesus. Christ suffered and died for our sins and left them to decay as so much
litter beneath the cross. The Holy Spirit found every sinner and offered the gift
of salvation. Some of us, by His power in a most mysterious way, accepted the
gift. The lost were found.

Recall times when you were lost—on a lonely road, at the airport, or in a
windowless office building. Then think of your relief upon finding your way.
(Unless you're still lost.) We have that sense of relief and more as we remember the difference between being spiritually lost—and found. May we always
be among the found!

The Bosssssss

Be subject for the Lord's sake to every human institution, whether it be to the emperor as supreme, or to governors as sent by him to punish those who do evil and to praise those who do good. For this is the will of God, that by doing good you should put to silence the ignorance of foolish people. 1 Peter 2:13–15

D on't you just love the boss? (Easy to say if you are the boss.) The term "boss" seems particularly appropriate—especially the way it hisses at the end. A neighbor moaned that his boss was so mean that she expected a receipt when she paid a compliment! No matter how you feel about bosses—and that probably includes you in some situations—it's good to treat them respectfully. For example, it's better to tell the boss he has an open mind rather than mumbling something about a hole in his head!

God is an expert on authority because He is King of kings, Lord of lords, and Boss of bosses. Unlike some of the earthly variety, God has real authority, and He uses it only for good. Wouldn't it make life more comfortable if all bosses looked for your mistakes so they could forget them? Wouldn't it be amazing if bosses placed responsibility for all your mistakes on one of their own family members? God did exactly that when He punished Jesus for the sins of the world. And this has implications for those of us who work under the, ahem, "guidance" of a boss.

God addresses the situation in 1 Peter and in Hebrews where He says, "Obey your leaders and submit to them, for they are keeping watch over your souls, as those who will have to give an account. Let them do this with joy and not with groaning, for that would be of no advantage to you" (Hebrews 13:17).

Aside from the practical disadvantages of becoming a boss' burden, we have more lofty reasons for avoiding this outcome. God invented leaders to prevent chaos. Back in the days of Moses and Aaron, God established lines of authority for His glory and the good of people—again, two characteristics of outstanding, godly leadership. The test, however, of being good employees, citizens, or family members is not the quality of the boss, but the quality of the follower.

The Hebrews heard of their responsibility to be good workers who brought joy to the boss. We hear it too. The love God has for us through His Son, and the love we feel toward Jesus, can be expressed through our daily family and career relationships. Showing this love probably will invite some derision and even hostility, just as it did in Bible days. But it also will provide a quiet witness to our relationship with the Big Boss.

Travel Guide

Then the Lord *God said, "Behold, the man has become like one of us in*
knowing good and evil. Now, lest he reach out his hand and take also of
the tree of life and eat, and live forever—" therefore the Lord *God sent*
him out from the garden of Eden to work the ground from which he was
taken. He drove out the man, and at the east of the garden of Eden He
placed the cherubim and a flaming sword that turned every way to
guard the way to the tree of life. Genesis 3:22–24

Like it or not, detours are designed for our good. Shake your road map
at those signs once, and you'll find out why they're necessary. Those
signs keep us from falling into rivers, plopping into wet cement, or running
over sleeping highway department workers. (Okay—they're only on break.)

Among God's many activities during the early days of our universe was
the development and design of the first detour sign. His sign was more
impressive than our simple barricade topped by a battery-operated flashing
light. Read about it: "He drove out the man, and at the east of the garden of
Eden He placed the cherubim and a flaming sword that turned every way to
guard the way to the tree of life" (Genesis 3:24).

That's the passage that usually came to my mind when a Sunday school
teacher talked about "fearing" the Lord. But like most disturbing verses (and
distressing detours), God intends His words and deeds as blessings.

The angelic detour at the east gate of Eden saved Adam and Eve from a
life of misery. Had they returned to the land from which they were evicted,
they might have eaten from the tree that offered immortality—a guaranteed
eternity of anguish on sinful earth. Instead, God sent Adam and Eve on a long
detour that led them to an eternity like the one they had first enjoyed.

Has God placed some detours in your life? Thank Him. The devil slings
obstacles and hazards onto the road to eternity. He wants us to lose faith in
God's guidance to our final destination. But God is faithful to us. His Word
leads us around desperate situations and past hopelessness and helplessness.
So be sure to keep your travel guide handy. God will lead you to the finest mil-
lion-star resort imaginable, even if it takes a few detours to get there.

Traveling Together

When Pharaoh let the people go, . . .God led the people around by the
way of the wilderness toward the Red Sea. . . And the Lord went before
them by day in a pillar of cloud to lead them along the way, and by night
in a pillar of fire to give them light, that they might travel by day and by
night. The pillar of cloud by day and the pillar of fire by night did not
depart from before the people. Exodus 13:17–22

"I know how to get there, but I can't explain it. Just follow me." Many adventures begin with those words. Traveling together is a common practice designed to drive otherwise close individuals or families apart while giving the deceptive impression of actually being close. Characteristics of such travel include bumper butting; playing the mechanical version of red light-green light; and sending coded messages via flashing turn signals.

Techniques of traveling together probably degenerated soon after the practice originated. The best method was introduced to the children of Israel by God. Exodus 13:21–22 reports: "And the Lord went before them by day in a pillar of cloud to lead them along the way, and by night in a pillar of fire to give them light, that they might travel by day and by night. The pillar of cloud by day and the pillar of fire by night did not depart from before the people."

The children of Israel didn't know where they were going. Having just escaped 400 years of slavery, they simply were anxious to get away. Like young children, though, they became restless and asked the Hebrew form of the question, "Are we there yet?" Incidentally, they often complained about their food and lodging too. But God was a good leader. He knew they would never arrive at their destination unless He led them. So He did—in a most miraculous way!

We may speak philosophically about life's journey on the road to heaven, but that trip is far more than a heady topic of conversation. It's reality. And the stark reality is that we can't possibly reach our heavenly destination without divine leadership.

Today, pillars of cloud or fire are as uncommon as free road maps at gas stations. Yet God continues to lead us. He does it through His written Word in the Bible and through personal guidance by the Holy Spirit. The Bible tells us to follow Jesus. He slows down when we lag behind, and He even waits for us when we get separated or stopped by sin. The Holy Spirit travels with us, helping us focus on our Leader, filling us with vigilance for hazards, and keeping us in the right lane. If that sounds like a backseat driver, stop now. This one belongs in the driver's seat.

Asking Directions

[Jesus said,] "You know the way to where I am going." Thomas said to Him, "Lord, we do not know where You are going. How can we know the way?" Jesus said to him, "I am the Way, and the Truth, and the Life. No one comes to the Father except through Me. If you had known Me, you would have known My Father also. From now on you do know Him and have seen Him." John 14:4–7

Few words turn travel to its dark side as easily as "Why don't you stop and ask directions?"

Travelers may laugh retrospectively about episodes of being lost, but the condition also can be dangerous. Perhaps you've seen drivers, obviously confused and shaken, veer across several lanes of traffic to exit an expressway. Then there's the driver who drifts to the curb while hunting dim addresses. Worst of all, there's finding yourself lost in a hostile neighborhood.

Although Jesus' disciples shared a face-to-face relationship with their Savior, they sometimes felt lost. Thomas is a perfect example. "Thomas said to Him, 'Lord, we do not know where You are going. How can we know the way?' Jesus said to him, 'I am the Way, and the Truth, and the Life. No one comes to the Father except through Me'" (John 14:5–6).

Thomas' statement is one that many people echo today. "We don't know how to get to heaven, so how can we ever hope to live there?" The answer remains the same as it was in Thomas' time. Jesus is the only way.

That doesn't stop some people from dispensing faulty directions. You know the kind. "Let's see, stay on this road for five or six miles—maybe more, maybe less—until you get to the public library. But you can't turn right there, so you have to go a couple blocks beyond that and make three right turns so when you go past the library, it's on your right. Then keep going until . . ." Helpful, right? To think—and tremble—that some would lead us to heaven with the same kind of "help"!

In spiritual language, such misdirection usually sounds like this: "Try hard not to sin. God will count that in your favor." Or "Volunteer lots of time at the hospital and be sure to attend worship every Sunday. God will see how good you are."

It's true that God sees how good we are, and it's not a scenic view. The only route to heaven begins beneath the cross as we confess our wretchedness and accept God's forgiveness in Christ. Then He leads us to the place we most want to be. Now those are some directions worth stopping to hear.

No Turns

And if you do not turn aside from any of the words that I command you today, to the right hand or to the left, to go after other gods to serve them.
Deuteronomy 28:14

Rush hour in a big city. Have you been there? If so, you have to wonder how anyone could call it a rush. Typical traffic jams have even changed the definition of "Sunday driver." Now it's one left over from Friday's "rush"!

One lament of rush-hour drivers is that no matter what lane you switch to, it will stop while the other lanes move. And just try to leave your lane! Too bad it's not that hard to stray from spiritual paths. God tells us to avoid lane changing—to make no turns on the road to salvation. Deuteronomy 28:14 says: "And if you do not turn aside from any of the words that I command you today, to the right hand or to the left, to go after other gods to serve them."

Next time you're in a traffic jam (and have plenty of time to think), try to enjoy it. That's right: Enjoy it. Envision yourself on the highway to eternal salvation. No wonder it's so crowded! Everyone is genuinely intent on getting home, and if others are a bit impatient, consider what awaits when they arrive safely. Oh, exit ramps slip off to the side here and there, beckoning weary travelers to greener pastures (or should we say blacker asphalt?). But those side trips, seductive as they are, only lead to delays, distractions, or dead ends. Stay on the highway. Make no turns.

That's how it is as we follow our Savior. In Deuteronomy days, the way to salvation was to obey God's commands. That was as difficult then as it is for today's drivers to obey speed limits. How can you go 60 m.p.h. when cars are bumper to bumper? How can you go only 65 m.p.h. when everyone is passing you? When it came to sins, God's people either went too slow or too fast. God knew the impossibility of obeying His Law so He sent Jesus to obey it for us.

God's new command is attainable because He sent the Holy Spirit to chauffeur us. He helps us believe in Jesus as our Savior. He helps us follow Jesus despite heavy traffic and tempting detours. He helps us accept God's forgiveness and His promise of eternal life despite temptations to follow the ways of human achievement, good works, and doctrines that fit popular lifestyles or attractive intellect. So make no turns.

Fruit Market

But the fruit of the Spirit is love, joy, peace, patience, kindness, goodness,
faithfulness, gentleness, self-control; against such things there is no law.
Galatians 5:22–23

For the next several days, we'll sample zesty goodies from the fruit market. You may be familiar with the passage from Galatians listed above. It's the one about fruit of the Spirit, and we're about to taste each. The first is love.

Love is a popular fruit. We use the word in many ways. You may love your spouse, children, a certain TV show, your parents, job, car, and sleeping late. As the song says, "Love makes the world go 'round." You've also heard of love at first sight. (Don't knock it. Some of us might not make it past a second look!)

Jesus believed in love. We might go so far as to say that He believed in love at first slight. Luke 6:32 and 35a say: "If you love those who love you, what benefit is that to you? For even sinners love those who love them. . . . But love your enemies, and do good, and lend, expecting nothing in return." Jesus didn't mince any valentines; instead, He cut straight to the heart.

Love is easy if the object of one's affection is lovable. Think for a moment of those you love most. What is it about them that makes them lovable? They probably aren't perfect, but love has a blind side—a forgiving side that might be called the "commitment component" of love.

Now think of someone you don't love. In fact, think of someone you positively dislike—perhaps someone who recently "slighted" you. However, you don't need to know someone not to love them. What dastardly criminals are in the news? Which world leaders plunder their own people? Have you heard stories of Christian persecution? There's more today than there was in Jesus' time! These questions should help you list real people. Unlovables. Now put this book down. Pray for the people on your list.

For what did you pray? Perhaps the most important thing you can ask is that these people would come to faith; however, some already may claim to be Christians. Yes, "bad" people might believe in Jesus, but they also may bear bruised fruit. Pray that they recognize their sinfulness and repent. Your enemies may never realize that you're really their lover. You may find yourself singing a song of unrequited love. "What a Friend We Have in Jesus" is a good song.

Fuzzy Fruit

You have put more joy in my heart than they have when their grain and wine abound. Psalm 4:7

Some people shiver at the fuzz, but they do enjoy what's beneath it. Peaches are my selection for the fruit closest to the spiritual fruit of joy. Ah, what juicy joy awaits those who slurp their way through a ripe peach! As my mother used to say at least once each summer, "How did you get peach juice on your undershirt?"

Life can be fuzzy on the outside, but a Christian's joy lies ripe beneath the surface of all worldly experiences. David the psalmist said, "You have put more joy in my heart than they have when their grain and wine abound" (Psalm 4:7). God not only made David happy, He also implanted a wealth of indelible joy in the psalmist's heart and soul. God gave us the same gift.

Joy is a permanent condition. Laughter and mirth usually are temporary. They depend on a set of conditions that exist at any given time. Often they're random, enjoyable events. When the "event" is over, we stop laughing, and we don't feel particularly happy. For example, a family gathering at Christmas may bring delight and laughter. Then the family returns to its normal routines, and the happiness remains as only a warm memory.

Joy is different. Joy is like that contentment deep inside that says the family that gathers at Christmas is still a family though many miles (or other obstacles) separate it. Joy is happiness well beyond any smile or sense of humor. It doesn't come or go, nor does it depend on any specific circumstances.

How often Christians forget their gift of joy! Sometimes we're like the peach eater whose errant bite squirts peach juice up his nose (or down his undershirt!). He finishes the peach but won't admit to liking it! The Spirit's gift of joy wants us to splash around in its juices and share its succulence.

At times it's formidable to find the joy the Spirit placed within us. If you have trouble digging it up, just think about who you are. You are a sinner. (Not much joy there.) You are forgiven. (Whew!) It won't be long and you'll live with Jesus in perfect joy—a joy we can't begin to imagine now. (Hooray!) That's the gift of joy that lives inside us. Isn't that peachy?

Olive Alive

*"Whoever desires to love life and see good days, let him keep his tongue
from evil and his lips from speaking deceit; let him turn away from evil
and do good; let him seek peace and pursue it. For the eyes of the Lord
are on the righteous, and his ears are open to their prayer. But the face of
the Lord is against those who do evil."*
1 Peter 3:10–12

Another fruit of the Spirit is peace, but it's unlike the human variety. When nations negotiate peace, they convene military officers, diplomats, and other experts. (It's ironic that we fight to preserve peace.) The reason their treaties don't last, however, is that they usually don't invite the Savior to the peace table. While they might argue that He lives too far beyond their boundaries, consultation by prayer remains a practical and speedy alternative.

Jesus had extensive experience in the peace process. People declared war on God. They rebelled often, and they still do, never having learned their lesson. Jesus did everything necessary to negotiate a lasting peace. He stepped between humans and God and sacrificed His life for the sake of sinners. God accepted that sacrifice and declared eternal peace between Himself and the redeemed saints.

Peace takes work, as Jesus proved. And the peace He sends our way through the Holy Spirit isn't the kind where we can sit back and relax. In 1 Peter 3:11, we read, "Let him turn away from evil and do good; let him seek peace and pursue it." The pursuit of spiritual peace requires us to make peace with God every day. We do that when we identify our personal declarations of war on God and confess our sin. God then forges the peace process with forgiveness, and He arms us to fight all that seeks to destroy our relationship with Him. We do it all again the next time.

We strive for peace with others because the Spirit makes peace an integral part of spiritual life. That takes work, too, as you know if you've ever tried to keep peace with family, neighbors, or members of your church.

An effective way to offer the olive branch of peace is to be like Jesus. It might take some personal sacrifice, and it certainly will take effort that is guided by the Spirit. Unlimited forgiveness is essential, and you won't get much rest. So always be ready to pass the olive branch. Anything else is the pits.

Watermelons

*We ourselves, who have the firstfruits of the Spirit, groan inwardly as we
wait eagerly for adoption as sons, the redemption of our bodies. For in this
hope we were saved. Now hope that is seen is not hope. For who hopes
for what he sees? But if we hope for what we do not see, we wait for
it with patience. Romans 8:23–25*

Watermelons are the fruit of patience. You have to have lots of it as
you separate the seeds from the good stuff.

I'm quite a patient person, but only when it involves doing jobs around
the house. I can wait patiently all day to accomplish those tasks. If you want
to test your patience, you might be surprised how much you have, especially
while listening to the boss argue with you. The truest test of patience, however, comes when you must listen to someone telling you what you already
know. Patience is a virtue. So hurry up and get some!

Patience is also a fruit of the Spirit mentioned by Paul. He comments on
it in Romans 8:24–25: "For in this hope we were saved. Now hope that is seen
is not hope. For who hopes for what he sees? But if we hope for what we do
not see, we wait for it with patience."

To paraphrase Paul, if you hope for a watermelon and you already have
one, it's really not a hope. However, if you hope for a seedless watermelon,
you may have to practice some patience. Okay, that's not exactly what he had
in mind, but you get the idea.

Patience usually involves waiting. Because God's plan for us is something
only He understands and because He carries it out according to His divine
time line, the Holy Spirit gives us patience. We wait confidently for God to do
His will.

We practice patience when we pray. God promises to answer prayer, and
He always does. Conflict arises when we want God to answer prayers in ways
that seem logical and timely according to human standards. Patience involves
trusting God to answer prayer in ways best for us, even if it doesn't meet our
specifications.

We practice patience as we wait for Jesus to return. Thousands of years
passed between the time God first promised a Savior to Adam and Eve and
the time the angels sang the birth announcement to scruffy shepherds. When
Christ's work on earth ended, He promised to return and take us to heaven.
How many days do you become impatient with that promise? Of course,
when He shows up unexpectedly, someone probably will ask if He couldn't
wait a little longer!

The Kind Kind

*And do not grieve the Holy Spirit of God, by whom you were sealed for
the day of redemption. Let all bitterness and wrath and anger and clamor
and slander be put away from you, along with all malice. Be kind to
one another, tenderhearted, forgiving one another, as God in Christ
forgave you. Ephesians 4:30–32*

The milk of human kindness is always a bit curdled. Someone always
tries to skim a little cream off the top. But milk serves as an object lesson if we pour it over some sugared strawberries. Consider this as an example
of the fruit of kindness—a smooth dessert, tame on the taste buds.

Kindness is a fruit of the Holy Spirit. The apostle Paul says, "Be kind to
one another, tenderhearted, forgiving one another, as God in Christ forgave
you" (Ephesians 4:32).

A wise person once defined kindness as loving someone who doesn't
deserve it. Wow! That fits you perfectly! Don't get defensive. That statement
fits every one of us. Because it does, we begin to comprehend how much God
loves us. His kindness exceeds absolutely anything we ever could expect. But
there is a catch. Paul tells us to be as kind toward others just as God is kind
toward us.

You'll discover your personal share of kindness as you go about daily routines with heightened awareness. Some examples? If you drive, you'll have
numerous opportunities for kindness—and remember our definition. There's
that guy who waited until the last minute to merge away from the lane closure and that woman strolling leisurely down the lane—in the parking lot!
What kindness can you express toward that store clerk who drops your change
or to the person stocking shelves who doesn't know where to find the bread?
Then there's that crabby, next-door neighbor who complains that your heart
beats too loudly and keeps him awake at night. Finally, there's that person
who keeps doing the same aggravating things over and over. He usually
expresses contrition, then he's back to his old tricks. (If you look in a mirror,
he might look like you!)

God gave Jesus a special measure of kindness, and the Holy Spirit has
heaped some on us too. Thank God for His unwavering kindness. Ask Him to
kindly give you some extra, especially for sharing with people just like you.
Tell Him you want to be the kind kind.

September 28

Good as Apple Pie

His divine power has granted to us all things that pertain to life and god-
liness, through the knowledge of Him who called us to His own glory and
excellence, by which He has granted to us His precious and very great
promises, so that through them you may become partakers of the divine
nature, having escaped from the corruption that is in the world because of
sinful desire. For this very reason, make every effort to supplement your
faith with virtue, and virtue with knowledge, and knowledge with self-
control, and self-control with steadfastness, and steadfastness with godli-
ness, and godliness with brotherly affection, and brotherly affection with
love. For if these qualities are yours and are increasing, they keep you
from being ineffective or unfruitful in the knowledge of our
Lord Jesus Christ. 2 Peter 1:3–8

You really need ice cream to top it off. Apple pie is good, but with ice cream, it's great. Speaking of goodness, it's mentioned by Paul as a fruit of the Spirit.

It's said that there is a little goodness in everyone. We must admit, however, that it's hard to find in some people. And for others, it's so far inside that it never gets out!

Not so with Christians who have this good gift from the Holy Spirit! Goodness is an essential ingredient in the Christian lifestyle. God's goodness—through Jesus Christ—made possible our goodness. Just being good, however, isn't good enough. We must be good for something. Passive goodness is like the air bag in your car. It's good, but it does nothing unless you're in serious trouble. God's goodness is more active. It consciously attaches itself to everything we do and remains vigilant in pursuing the course of godly behavior.

Translated into action, human goodness tries to copy God's goodness. God always makes the correct choices, which, you'll have to admit, is a bit beyond our grasp. We probably best approach God's type of goodness by hating evil and loving good. This means we avoid certain things in our vocabulary—phrases such as "Goody Two-shoes" used to describe people who obviously try to make good choices or avoid immoral behavior.

On the positive side, our intentional goodness helps us evade corruption. That's good for something. It helps us bypass situations that might weaken our faith or our relationship with Jesus.

Goodness speaks volumes to those around us. Onlookers may even wonder why we're so good, which provides an opportunity to witness about the One who bought our goodness on the cross. Jesus Christ is like the ice cream on a warm slice of apple pie!

Too Much of a Good Thing

And the king of Israel said, "Seize Micaiah and take him back to Amon the governor of the city and to Joash the king's son, and say, 'Thus says the king, Put this fellow in prison and feed him with meager rations of bread and water until I return in peace.'" 2 Chronicles 18:25–26

Pick any fruit, eat lots of it, and the results are predictable. The same might be said of our next fruit of the Spirit—faithfulness.

Understand that abundant faithfulness is excellent; it also can get you into trouble, just as it did for a not-so-memorable man in the Bible named Micaiah. He was one of God's prophets. He thought it more important to offer truthful prophecies than to say what people wanted to hear. That got him in trouble. "And the king of Israel said, 'Seize Micaiah and take him back to Amon the governor of the city and to Joash the king's son, and say, "Thus says the king, Put this fellow in prison and feed him with meager rations of bread and water until I return in peace"'" (2 Chronicles 18:25–26).

Micaiah warned Israel's king to avoid war despite the fact that the king's bevy of yes-prophets assured him of victory. The king believed the yes-men. He never returned alive.

We might point to others whose faithfulness got them into trouble—Joseph, John the Baptist, Stephen, and Paul among them. We can't let this "fact of faith" discourage us. All who have suffered for their faithfulness found the condition temporary, and some went to their "reward" sooner than others.

Faithfulness is a gift of the Spirit. Just as Christians possess different degrees of the Spirit's blessings, they also have various degrees of faith. The Holy Spirit started us with the right amount of faith. Through the years, we may have lost some of that faith as we wandered away from Bible study, the Sacrament, worship, and prayer. Or perhaps we've been blessed with a stronger faith. Strong faith becomes even more potent as we weather crises, trusting that God always brings good from bad. Stronger faith results from Bible study, our presence at the Lord's Table, and through worship where we hear God's Word of promise.

When called on to express our faith, trouble may accompany the experience. We would do well to expect it because then we won't be shattered by criticism or other persecution. Faithfulness is a benchmark of believers through the ages. The bench may be nicked, burned, and sat on regularly; nevertheless, it persists and even prospers. Better yet, faithfulness keeps us in touch with our loving, forgiving Savior. When it comes to faithfulness, there's never too much of a good thing.

Gentle Fruit

For we never came with words of flattery, as you know, nor with a pretext
for greed—God is witness. . . . But we were gentle among you, like a
nursing mother taking care of her own children. So, being affectionately
desirous of you, we were ready to share with you not only the gospel of
God but also our own selves, because you had become very dear to us.
1 Thessalonians 2:5–8

Consider the apricot a nominee for the title of gentle fruit. It's neither too juicy nor too dry; not excessively sweet yet pleasingly mellow; tasty without sending taste buds into shock. That's how gentleness is—wonderful but not spectacular.

Among the many attributes of our Savior, gentleness would rate a strong second to love. In fact, gentleness may be generally defined as love in action. All Christians have a measure of this quality as a gift from the Holy Spirit. Paul mentions gentleness in 1 Thessalonians 2:7, which says: "But we were gentle among you, like a nursing mother taking care of her own children." Gentleness characterizes the way God wants us to treat others.

God has been generously gentle with us. We deserve His wrath, but He softly sprinkles blessings on us. The world should end because of its wickedness, but God maintains it, giving more time for others to be saved. When we confess our sins, God would be justified in slapping us down and making us grovel; instead, He extends His merciful hand to forgive us and to bless and strengthen us. God is an excellent role model for gentleness.

Consider what it means to be gentle. Being considerate may be another way of stating it. Jesus always was considerate; He did what He knew people needed. He didn't set up conditions, for example, when He healed others. He simply did it, healing their physical afflictions along with their spiritual maladies. He met the needs of hurting people, often neglecting His own human needs.

Another manifestation of gentleness is a willingness to listen. Do we listen beyond words to hear the heart speak? People may offer a variety of explanations to describe what they think and feel, but beneath their words, they reveal unmet needs or aches. A good listener might determine that "what goes around, comes around" or that suffering is sometimes a direct consequence of behavior. It might be easier to bluntly tell others why they feel the way they do. It's better to listen sympathetically, perhaps offering to pray with someone for healing of mind, body, and spirit.

As with all gifts of the Spirit, if we want to learn more, we can study God's Word. We can hear it straight from the mouth of the world's foremost gentleMan.

Enough

When morning came, all the chief priests and the elders of the people took
counsel against Jesus to put Him to death. And they bound Him and led
Him away and delivered Him over to Pilate the governor. . . . Now Jesus
stood before the governor, and the governor asked Him, "Are you the King
of the Jews?" Jesus said, "You have said so." But when He was accused by
the chief priests and elders, He gave no answer. Then Pilate said to Him,
"Do you not hear how many things they testify against You?" But He
gave him no answer, not even to a single charge, so that the governor
was greatly amazed. Matthew 27:1–14

Ray was the wise man of the produce department. With only the mere trace of a benign snicker, he helped young, ignorant customers tell the difference between lettuce and cabbage. When a dozen bunches of grapes seemed good judgment because the grocery list stated "grapes," Ray would spot the bulging bag and urge a little self-control. Ray probably saved a lot of young lives!

Self-control is the last of the fruit of the Spirit. Perhaps it's fitting that the last installment is self-control.

An old proverb suggests that the emptier the pot, the quicker it is to boil. Translated loosely, it means watch your temper. Exercise self-control. Again, Jesus provided an excellent example. His trial was a sham, and both He and His enemies knew it. At the very least, we might expect Jesus to let fly a tongue-lashing befitting the situation. Instead, the Bible reports His response in the verses above.

We all admit the necessity of self-control under stress, especially if the stress happens to outweigh or outrank us. Good advice, not of biblical origin, suggests that we count to 10 when we're angry. When we're livid, it's best to count at least 10 times further—then shut up anyway. Self-control can be a challenge in good times as well.

You've probably noticed that those who have much want more. This may be evident especially at the Thanksgiving table where the turkey isn't the only thing that gets stuffed. Or how about the generous credit limit that gets stretched beyond its already bountiful boundaries?

Self-control is a gift of the Spirit because it encourages us to be content with what we have. It keeps our life in perspective. It's God's way of confining us to that which makes us truly happy and satisfied.

October 2 ⟋

Cheap Gifts

For by grace you have been saved through faith. And this is not your
own doing; it is the gift of God, not a result of works, so that no
one may boast. Ephesians 2:8–9

Most children are haunted by pet fears. For some it's thunderstorms; others dread darkness. Mine was sparrows. They were a special menace during November and December. They perched on my neighbor's gutter—a scant three feet from our kitchen window—and watched me during breakfast. They watched me during lunch and supper too. They had only one motive. My mother said they were watching me eat. If I didn't clean my plate, they would report the matter to Santa Claus. With every tweet, the gift list grew smaller!

How good to hear the news that probably appears in every worthwhile devotional book ever written: "For by grace you have been saved through faith. And this is not your own doing; it is the gift of God" (Ephesians 2:8).

God's gift is a true present. We do nothing to earn it. It's not that He doesn't know about us just like that imaginary guy at the North Pole. God has plenty of informers who roost on the gutter of life and report our sins. No, these informers aren't God's angels. They wouldn't think of doing such things because they know about His grace. The informers are employed by jolly old Satan whose happiest moments occur when he exploits our faults or divulges them to higher authorities.

God's gift of salvation doesn't depend on us. God sent Jesus because He already knew how rotten we were. He knew our destiny as sinners even before we were born! He gave us a gift that lasts forever. Despite the dossiers laid before Him, God looks past our sins to the life, death, and resurrection of Jesus.

While gifts are always welcome, they're more desirable when you don't have to qualify for them. What genuine gratitude we have when we receive something completely undeserved! What an opportunity to show our thankfulness! Like a box of candy passed around the room, we can share the gift of salvation. We share when we forgive as freely as God forgives us. We share when we're generous with our blessings, trusting that no matter how much we share, we'll never run out of what we need. We share when we pray for others and when we comfort them with the confidence we have in Jesus Christ.

Enjoy the best gift you've ever received. Open the shade so the sparrows can see.

Hang On

"Thus says the LORD of hosts: Peoples shall yet come, even the inhabitants of many cities. The inhabitants of one city shall go to another, saying, 'Let us go at once to entreat the favor of the LORD and to seek the LORD of hosts; I myself am going.' Many peoples and strong nations shall come to seek the LORD of hosts in Jerusalem and to entreat the favor of the LORD. Thus says the LORD of hosts: In those days ten men from the nations of every tongue shall take hold of the robe of a Jew, saying, 'Let us go with you, for we have heard that God is with you.'" Zechariah 8:20–23

If you want to go far, you have to stay close. Sorry if that sounds like some inscrutable, ancient, Asian philosophy. It's true. Look at this terrific Old Testament verse: "Thus says the Lord of hosts: In those days ten men from the nations of every tongue shall take hold of the robe of a Jew, saying, 'Let us go with you, for we have heard that God is with you'" (Zechariah 8:23).

We have the advantage of reading these words in a different context from that in which they were first spoken. In Zechariah's day, the world felt contempt for the Hebrew nation. So often it claimed to be God's chosen! So often it defied God or even forgot Him! The prophecy of Zechariah predicted that all this would change. And was he right!

Today, we can name the "Jew" whose hem people clung to. Jesus was the ultimate Jew, both in ancestry and history. He was so holy that merely touching His robe brought healing, as with the woman who had bleeding problems (Matthew 9:20–22). But Jesus brought healing not only from physical affliction, but also from spiritual illness.

Going back in time, imagine yourself grasping Jesus' robe as He gently nudges His way through the crowds. Do you hear His impassioned voice encouraging individuals away from their sin and into His realm of forgiveness? Do you see Him smiling, touching, hugging, and making eye contact with the disheveled, disabled, brokenhearted rabble? The people knew they had a good thing going, and they didn't let go.

Let's not dwell only on history, as awesome as it is. We have a part in this story that transcends imagination. In a way, we are the Jew mentioned by Zechariah too. We know God. Do others know we know God? If they don't, we've got some witnessing to do. If they do, get ready for them to hang on to your hem. As you share your love in actions and words, they'll want to be with you because you're something special. Let them hang on. You have more strength and power than you realize. After all, you're hanging on, too, and God will pull you through anything.

Guide to Hair Care

So Philip ran to him and heard him reading Isaiah the prophet and
asked, "Do you understand what you are reading?" And he said,
"How can I, unless someone guides me?" And he invited Philip
to come up and sit with him. Acts 8:30–31

The next several devotions will present a unique guide to hair care, in addition to the usual meditation. Be assured that I'm an expert in this field, My credentials include adolescent years spent drenching my scalp with several gallons of Vitalis.

The first piece of advice is this: Don't let your hair go to your head. If you do, you'll be devastated when it forsakes you. No amount of combing, brushing, stroking, or encouraging will help if your hair follicles are determined to drop out. This attitude toward hair might be extended to every other item of vanity—or, for that matter, anything at all.

Vanity is costly in many ways. Generally, others don't enjoy the company of haughty people, and pride also can have spiritual consequences. Taken to extremes, vanity results in self-righteousness, and self-righteousness leads to hell. Pride convinces us that either we don't need a Savior because we're not really all that bad or that we can earn our own salvation.

Today's reading from Acts, upon closer examination, offers a prime example of the opposite of pride and vanity. Acts 8:30–31 says: "So Philip ran to him and heard him reading Isaiah the prophet and asked, 'Do you understand what you are reading?' And he said, 'How can I, unless someone guides me?' And he invited Philip to come up and sit with him.'"

Each man mentioned could have allowed pride to prevent him from doing God's will. First, Philip could have reasoned, "Run to catch up with a speeding chariot? Why? If he wants to know about God, let him come to me." Second, the Ethiopian was an official of considerable status in his country. He could have tossed the book aside in frustration, writing it off as trite hogwash. Instead, he asked for help. The results? God's will was done. Philip served God, and the Ethiopian was saved.

Guard against pride, both spiritual and otherwise. It obstructs God's will and can cost lives. As you go about your business, ask the Holy Spirit to open your mind and heart to those in need of hearing some Good News. Also ask that the Spirit make you willing to learn from others more about God's love. After all, we don't want our faith to go where our hair should be.

Splitting Hairs

*All wrongdoing is sin, but there is sin that does not lead to death. We
know that everyone who has been born of God does not keep on sinning,
but he who was born of God protects him, and the evil one does not touch
him. We know that we are from God, and the whole world lies in the
power of the evil one. And we know that the Son of God has come and
has given us understanding, so that we may know Him who is true; and
we are in Him who is true, in His Son Jesus Christ. 1 John 5:17–20*

I thought split ends were positions on the football field until television
commercials enlightened me. Split ends seem to be a major plague,
especially for models, who react to this condition in the privacy of a TV commercial. For others, this isn't a problem. For example, my hair doesn't have
split ends; it just split. Hair today; gone tomorrow.

Splitting hairs isn't confined to a physical condition. It's also a pastime of
people who like to draw the finest of lines between questionable elements of
behavior. They categorize faulty behavior into big sins and little sins. It's all
splitting hairs to God. Note 1 John 5:17: "All wrongdoing is sin, but there is
sin that does not lead to death."

No excuses for splitting hairs—I mean sins—here. It's all wrong. Every sin
has consequences. Some consequences are more serious, both in how they
affect the sinner as well as the victim of the sin. For example, it's easy to
rationalize that lustful thoughts aren't nearly as serious as outright adultery.
And hating that person who broke into your house isn't as bad as murdering
her. In the same way, those caught stealing cars receive much harsher sentences than those nabbed for shoplifting groceries.

Place all our sins on a heap, both the ones we consider minuscule and the
ones that amass to several tons, and the pile reaches mountain-size nonetheless. As sinners go, we've all gone a long way. Sins normally kill people, as
today's Bible passage implies. The death is eternal. The passage also indicates
that sin isn't always a terminal situation.

The only deadly sin occurs when we abandon our faith completely. You
might say that's when people split from God for good, or rather, bad. All other
sins are forgiven forever. This time we might say that the sins split, which is
only because Jesus took them away. He brushed aside the devil and combed
our souls clean and neat.

As you confess your sins to Jesus this day, repent of all of them—even
those you might have forgotten because they seemed so small. Don't be afraid
to confess the ones that loom large either. When it comes to forgiveness, Jesus
doesn't split hairs.

October 6 ⌐

Hair Raising

*Now to Him who is able to keep you from stumbling and to present you
blameless before the presence of His glory with great joy, to the only God,
our Savior, through Jesus Christ our Lord, be glory, majesty, dominion,
and authority, before all time and now and forever. Amen. Jude 1:24–25*

A friend tried that hair-growing formula called Rogaine®. One night he
left the bottle in the shower stall. The next morning, his wife mistook
it for body gel. Too bad the stuff works as advertised.

The specter of such a hair-raising experience might leave us smiling and
shuddering. I wish the prospect of all frightening experiences would offer
such a humorous image! The truth, as you know it, isn't funny at all. Sin has
so spoiled the world that dangers lurk within seemingly benign situations. For
example, a Christian school may assemble a playground, which must be surrounded with a fence to protect the equipment from vandals and lopsided
lawsuits.

Every day is fraught with threats. Occasionally, we read of "freak" accidents—when something with paltry predictability of ever happening happens. Drive-by shootings or death by drunk driver provide other examples of
random threats. And there are those with high-risk jobs, such as firefighters,
police officers, military personnel, and dentists. (How many people do you
know who actually love their dentist?)

Life would be gloomy, apprehensive, and unbearably anxious—a truly
hair-raising experience—were it not for God's loving protection. It probably
hasn't escaped your attention, however, that believers and unbelievers seem
equally susceptible to danger. Sometimes it's hard to believe that God promises to protect us when we see what happens to faithful people around the
globe. We need to understand what God's protection is all about.

Don't be discouraged from praying for daily protection or for safety during special situations. God watches over us during those incidents. He always
cares for us despite outward circumstances. God won't let sin take us to hell.
Even if we lose our earthly life, God won't let us remain dead. Like Jesus Christ
before us, we will rise to live with our heavenly Father, never to die again. It's
like Jude says:

> Now to Him who is able to keep you from stumbling and
> to present you blameless before the presence of His glory
> with great joy, to the only God, our Savior, through Jesus
> Christ our Lord, be glory, majesty, dominion, and authority,
> before all time and now and forever. Amen. Jude 1:24–25

Hair Trigger

A soft answer turns away wrath, but a harsh word stirs up anger. . . . A
gentle tongue is a tree of life, but perverseness in it breaks the spirit.
Proverbs 15:1–4

As you read this, maybe you're upset that here's another takeoff on hair. If you've liked the hair series, perhaps you'll be angry to know this is the last installment. If you read the devotions out of sequence, you're unhappy because none of this makes sense. If you're annoyed at all, this meditation is for you. The topic is hair-trigger tempers.

Just about the time I get my temper under control, I go fishing again. My rod, reel, and bait fail to produce the desired results, and that sets me off. Can you cite some of your own eruptions caused by a hair-trigger temper?

The book of Proverbs is a good place to look for scriptural commentary on temper. Proverbs 15:1 says: "A soft answer turns away wrath, but a harsh word stirs up anger." Diplomats subscribe to this proverb as do successful salespeople, counselors, and anyone else who deals regularly with the public. Like most proverbs, the greater its truth, the harder it is to follow consistently. We need a good role model—someone with lots of experience—someone like Jesus Himself.

The gospels record many gentle words from our gracious Savior. They also report a few instances of holy and righteous frustration when kind words fell only on deaf ears. There was the "den of thieves" incident in the temple and the "brood of vipers" label pasted on those determined to destroy the Messiah. But note that Jesus' justifiable anger was aimed not at those who loved Him, but at those who attempted to arrest the Gospel's progress.

Jesus also would be excused if He did some sanctified screaming at us. Every sin we have ever committed and will ever commit caused Jesus to wince in pain as His executioners slammed the nails through His hands. We brought Him nothing but misery, and we certainly deserve His anger. What do we get instead? The most gentle words ever uttered: I forgive you.

Forgiveness is the gentle glue that cements relationships. Hair-trigger tempers are easy to set off, but repairing damage they cause may be impossible. Angry words hurled at those we love—or at those we don't love—usually fracture relationships. Pray for the kind of "temper management" our Savior practiced even in His most painful moments. Is it okay to lose your temper? Sure. Permanently.

Collector's Edition

*But as for you, continue in what you have learned and have firmly
believed, knowing from whom you learned it and how from childhood you
have been acquainted with the sacred writings, which are able to make
you wise for salvation through faith in Christ Jesus. All Scripture is
breathed out by God and profitable for teaching, for reproof, for
correction, and for training in righteousness, that the man of God
may be competent, equipped for every good work. 2 Timothy 3:14–17*

You see the advertisements in magazines. Yes, you, Annie Average and
Ozzie Ordinary, can own a collector's edition plate, suitable for display,
commemorating the very first bottle of dishwashing liquid. (Future editions
are planned depicting the entire history of dish detergent—so start your
collection now!) It's all yours for only four installments of $39.95 each. Or
maybe the collector's edition books attract you. For a small mortgage, you can
own gold-edged volumes by famous writers. These books come complete
with yellowed pages and musty odor.

Seriously, you probably own the best of any collector's edition. Between
its covers you'll find the immortal words of blessed heroes, including Jacob,
Ruth, Daniel, Jeremiah, Peter, Paul, and Mary. (Not to be confused with the
singers.) You'll read what writers such as Matthew, Mark, Luke, and John say
about the life and times of the God-Man, Jesus Christ. You can even read the
words of our great Hero (printed in red for your convenience).

The Bible offers instructional reading, but it's intended for more than
that. In addition to teaching about and strengthening faith, it prepares us to
demonstrate our faith. Once read, we put God's words into our actions.

Within the welcome and comforting Gospel passages, the Holy Spirit
whispers, "Get busy. Because God loved the world so much that He sent His
Son to pay for your sins, get out there and tell the world His story. Because
Jesus loves you so much that He suffered on your behalf, get out there and
share that unconditional love with others. Because you are forgiven, act like
it. I will help you abandon sinful ways and use My power to change your life."

Difficult tasks? Yes, indeed. But like old age, it's something into which we
gradually grow as we study God's Word and participate in His Sacrament. We
can see our faith in its resulting deeds. Someday, we'll be part of an amazing
collection too.

Christians, Go Home!

*And Amaziah said to Amos, "O seer, go, flee away to the land of Judah,
and eat bread there, and prophesy there, but never again prophesy at
Bethel, for it is the king's sanctuary, and it is a temple of the kingdom."*
Amos 7:12–13

It might have appeared on a sign at the city limits. Bethel: Population 378. Home of the Golden Calf Crusaders and the Shrine of Jacob's Ladder. Prophets Not Welcome.

Amos, God's draftee for prophet, entered town anyway. And did he get an earful: "And Amaziah said to Amos, 'O seer, go, flee away to the land of Judah, and eat bread there, and prophesy there, but never again prophesy at Bethel, for it is the king's sanctuary, and it is a temple of the kingdom'" (Amos 7:12–13).

Amos faced the same problem that many people face today. People of faith aren't always welcome, especially when they speak boldly for God. Most Christians—even outspoken ones—haven't been called seers, but they've probably been called worse. Life in the world sometimes seems like it's fenced and posted "Christians, Go Home!"

Perhaps you haven't suffered prejudice or inhospitality, but our society has gradually, subtly, posted the land with signs of intolerance. When Christians complain about immorality, unbelievers respond that everyone has a right to decide what to do as long as it doesn't impinge on anyone else's right. (Except God's!) Abortion is a good example—er, bad example—isn't it? Humans must have options, even if options mean death for the innocent and helpless. (Humans explain it away with pseudoscience—idolatry in big words.) Then there's the debate about sexual preferences. Christians cite the Bible, and disbelievers claim exclusive ownership of their bodies. Need we pursue the matter? Government isn't too friendly to the one true God either. Though we dare not impose a national religion, we risk alienating the one true God by granting sterile status to any and all gods. Were Amos to stumble into town and address the issues, he would think he was back in Bethel.

Christians should go home. Maybe we should mumble God's will to more receptive ears. Our own! It's easy to speak against the big, overt, defiant sins of the world. But we need to address our own sinfulness too. We can examine ourselves to see where pride, greed, selfishness, prejudice, hate, or self-righteousness hold God in contempt. Then we can do something about it. Repenting and accepting God's forgiveness are in order. One day, when our last confession is over, we'll hear the now welcome words of Jesus as He says, "Christian, come home."

October 10

Christians Revolt!

"If the world hates you, know that it has hated Me before it hated you. If you were of the world, the world would love you as its own; but because you are not of the world, but I chose you out of the world, therefore the world hates you. . . . But all these things they will do to you on account of My name, because they do not know Him who sent Me." John 15:18–21

As you read in the previous devotional, Christians aren't always welcome. That we should expect such treatment is confirmed by Jesus, who said, "If you were of the world, the world would love you as its own; but because you are not of the world, but I chose you out of the world, therefore the world hates you" (John 15:19).

Does this sound like a call to revolt? After all, we don't belong to the world and the world often reminds us of that reality. In fact, the world already thinks we're pretty revolting!

Now the question is, "What do we do about it?" The answer would be simple were it not so difficult or drastic to emigrate to a more God-friendly location. So how do Christians revolt? The answer, as we might expect, appears in these words of Scripture: "For though we walk in the flesh, we are not waging war according to the flesh. For the weapons of our warfare are not of the flesh but have divine power to destroy strongholds" (2 Corinthians 10:3–4).

Sounds like the ultimate terrorist weapon! Yessiree. Step right up and grab a God grenade. We'll wipe out those sniveling unbelievers and decimate the pagan population. One pop of God's awesome wrath and it'll be all over. Wait. Though God certainly possesses atomic capabilities, His way is different.

Revolutionary Christians rebel against the world by boldly proclaiming and living the Gospel. We dissidents don't seek revenge for wrongs done. We forgive them. How revolting—especially to those who neither want nor accept our forgiveness. We mutiny against the world by refusing to live according to its flimsy standards and adopting God's standards instead. We flout the world system of self-reliance in favor of complete dependence on God. We rebel against the world goal of mastery and freedom to win the right to become servants—even slaves—to our God. And all the while we look to our revolutionary leader, Jesus Christ, who won the right to live by dying on the cross. In disdain of everything for which the sinful world stands, He rose from the dead and leads us yet today.

Christians revolt. We'll soon be at peace.

Getting a Second Job

Finally, then, brothers, we ask and urge you in the Lord Jesus, that as you received from us how you ought to live and to please God, just as you are doing, that you do so more and more. For you know what instructions we gave you through the Lord Jesus. For this is the will of God, your sanctification. 1 Thessalonians 4:1–3

How often has someone said to you, "Don't work too hard"? The thought expresses kind intentions, but perhaps it's not the wisest advice. (The best way to avoid being fired by the boss is to be fired by energy.) The Bible contains vastly better advice in 1 Thessalonians 4:11–12: "Aspire to live quietly, and to mind your own affairs, and to work with your hands, as we instructed you, so that you may live properly before outsiders and be dependent on no one."

That's laudable counsel, especially as it applies to a second job. You know, the one you take on so you can afford some of the little pleasures—or the big necessities—of daily life. Perhaps you find your secondary employment as a banker, government official, checkout clerk at the grocery story, bus driver, homemaker, welder, secretary, or maintenance worker. Of course, you can never allow your second job to interfere with your primary occupation.

Your foremost calling is to serve God. No, we don't leave that task to preachers or other professional church workers. It's the vocation of each Christian. To understand this important position, we can examine a job description.

The job falls under the category of service profession and requires dedication and perseverance. Servants are willing to study the finer details of their duties through Bible study. Mistakes are expected, but the Employer offers a generous plan of forgiveness and retraining. Workers receive a generous benefit package through which all their daily needs are supplied, and the Employer provides a retirement plan that's out of this world! Because the work is so vital, workers cannot expect vacations and must sometimes serve in unanticipated ways at the will of their Employer.

Christians who hold two jobs usually work both at the same time. Neither employer seems to mind, for the Christian worker going about God's business is usually an excellent worker for an earthly boss as well (though God sometimes gets shortchanged in the deal).

Next time someone good-naturedly tells you not to work too hard, tell her thanks, but it's not an option. When you work two jobs, you're bound to keep busy.

October 12

Nag Nag Nag

And He told them a parable to the effect that they ought always to pray and not lose heart. He said, "In a certain city there was a judge who neither feared God nor respected man. And there was a widow in that city who kept coming to him and saying, 'Give me justice against my adversary.' For a while he refused, but afterward he said to himself, 'Though I neither fear God nor respect man, yet because this widow keeps bothering me, I will give her justice, so that she will not beat me down by her continual coming.'" And the Lord said, "Hear what the unrighteous judge says. And will not God give justice to His elect, who cry to Him day and night? Will He delay long over them? I tell you, He will give justice to them speedily." Luke 18:1–8

There is only one way to avoid nagging, and that's for the nag-ee to do what the nag-er wants.

Today's Bible reading is a parable about how to wear down an arrogantly apathetic judge. This information may actually come in handy, considering the foibles of the modern judicial system. Okay, so that's not the real purpose of the parable. Jesus wanted to contrast His willingness to hear prayers with a shoddy judge's willingness to administer real justice.

No, this wasn't a ploy by Jesus to escape the rasping and grating of nagers. He assured His listeners that God hears and answers prayers. The key to understanding Jesus' answer is to acknowledge that God does indeed care and that He provides answers with precise timing.

A little self-examination probably reveals that we tend to nag God in proportion to how much a specific problem or condition nags us. Illness, storms, and violence yield other opportunities for nagging.

We don't need to nag God. One simple prayer gets His divine attention, and He won't miss any details. Nagging God with a hail of redundant pleas may actually signal weak faith or foster an attitude that we can persuade God to take action on our terms. Of course, God knows what needs doing and He does it, sometimes even before we ask. And even weak faith is better than no faith because it recognizes—or at least concedes—God's control and care of our lives.

God invites us to pray, and His Son taught us a good one—one that covers every imaginable situation. Pray it (again) now. There is a difference between gently bringing our needs before God and nagging His eternal ears off.

Out of Court Settlement

*"And why do you not judge for yourselves what is right? As you go with
your accuser before the magistrate, make an effort to settle with him on
the way, lest he drag you to the judge, and the judge hand you over to the
officer, and the officer put you in prison. I tell you, you will never get out
until you have paid the very last penny." Luke 12:57–59*

If everyone had good judgment, we wouldn't need judges. As it is, court
cases abound. Even lawyers prefer to avoid court by settling out of it.
(That way the only charges levied appear on the bill for services rendered.)
Will social scientists of the future wonder about a society that established a
comprehensive system of justice and then found ways to circumvent it? Will
they pronounce our era one in which an alternative to admitting guilt was to
buy off the indignation of victims? Will they see us as prone to filing frivolous
lawsuits against huge corporations or famous people because it was an even
better gamble than the state lottery?

Apparently, the problem isn't new. Jesus once told a crowd that "as you
go with your accuser before the magistrate, make an effort to settle with him
on the way, lest he drag you to the judge, and the judge hand you over to the
officer, and the officer put you in prison" (Luke 12:58–59).

We may chuckle at or decry the details of out-of-court settlements.
However, we also must realize that we are part of the most sweeping and most
important out-of-court settlement ever.

The court date was set by the highest ranking Judge in the universe. The
problem is that He won't tell us when it is, though it matters little since we're
unable to mount an effective defense.

Imagine for one terror-filled moment that we appear before God on
Judgment Day. He hears our plea and decides that the evidence suggests a
mandatory life sentence with no hope of appeal or parole. It's hard to imagine that and remain poker-faced!

Good thing Jesus won an out-of-court settlement for us. Long before
we're scheduled to appear before the almighty Magistrate, Jesus settled the
matter once for all. He erased our sins through His life, work, and death. He
didn't hide our guilt in hopes that God wouldn't notice; instead, He took it
away completely. He bought our freedom, and now we need not fear judgment. Even better, His resurrection arranged for us to move in with the Judge.

See you in court.

Something in Your I

Every way of a man is right in his own eyes, but the Lord weighs the heart. To do righteousness and justice is more acceptable to the Lord than sacrifice. Haughty eyes and a proud heart, the lamp of the wicked, are sin. Proverbs 21:2–4

How much does an "I" weigh? Often, it's bloated and obese, though in those who value themselves little, it's as skinny as the letter. When it comes to "I," many people imitate the current trend in gas stations—self-service. Others simply serve up themselves, perhaps preferring self-sacrifice to getting sacrificed by others. One thing is certain: There's usually something interesting surrounding the shortest word in our language. We'll examine this idea in the next few devotions.

There's something in our I. A wise sage, inspired by God, once said, "Every way of a man is right in his own eyes, but the Lord weighs the heart" (Proverbs 21:2). The Lord weighs the heart rather than the "I" that either deprecates, exonerates, or accentuates itself. Sinners like us love that little word. It says so much about an important topic, doesn't it? It also leads to trouble.

When "I" comes first, it places everyone and everything below it. In religious people, "I" can be an insidious virus that weakens faith. The change is gradual, but you know you're in trouble when spiritual conversations emphasize what you are doing rather than what God has done. Spiritually inspired people want to do much for God, and the devil uses that motivation to scatter spores of self-righteousness. You'll find the problem in Christian literature too. Authors who encourage us to apply our faith sometimes forget to remind us why. All good things we do can only be done in response to God's great love for us—His forgiveness that enables us to apply and exercise our faith to the glory of God and for the good of others.

Another bleak side of "I" is just as bad: "I am guilty." You know you're in trouble if persistent guilt prevents you from enjoying the warmth of Jesus' love. His love is so expansive and expensive that He sacrificed His life to prevent guilt from searing your soul with the heat of hell.

There truly is something in your I. As one brought to faith by the Holy Spirit, Christ lives in you. He has removed the self-importance of "I" and replaced it with righteousness won by Christ. Next time something gets in your "I," ask Jesus to take it out. Once He does, your "I" really becomes worth something.

Irate

Do you not know that all of us who have been baptized into Christ Jesus were baptized into His death? We were buried therefore with Him by baptism into death, in order that, just as Christ was raised from the dead by the glory of the Father, we too might walk in newness of life.
Romans 6:3–4

An ancient proverb of uncertain origin (probably the first human to be bumped from a flight) offers this insight: "He who flies into a rage usually has a crash landing." It probably hasn't been too many days since you last took such a flight. Maybe it was at the grocery store when someone tried to cut into line. Maybe a family member committed the same extremely stupid blunder again. Or perhaps it was the neighbor's dog perusing your favorite tree or those kids cruising with windows open and bass boosters booming that set you off.

Sometimes we're rightfully angered by what happens around us. We witness or hear about so much injustice and senseless tragedy. Anger, provided it doesn't send our blood pressure surging, can be a positive outlet when expressed about people and events that seem to splinter and twist God's will. Those are the kinds of things that make God irate too.

If we're really honest, we will confess that we do much to incur God's wrath. For that, God has some cross words for us. Here they are: "We were buried therefore with Him by baptism into death, in order that, just as Christ was raised from the dead by the glory of the Father, we too might walk in newness of life" (Romans 6:4). We can summarize that passage by saying that God's cross word was indeed the cross on which Jesus suffered the rage and punishment rightly belonging to us. This is nothing short of astonishing. Indeed, it would be unbelievable—if we didn't have the gift of faith. That faith is more than rote knowledge of Bible stories and creeds such as the Apostles', Nicene, or Athanasian (ask your pastor about this one if you're not familiar with it).

Faith is that personal conviction that Jesus was thinking about you and me when He hung on the cross on that bleak Friday. Better yet, faith assures us that He was thinking about us when He emerged from the tomb on that fresh Sunday morning. Even now, Jesus is thinking about us, caring for us, bringing our future in line with His will.

God isn't irate anymore. His Son brought us into His family. Forgiveness and the desire to live according to His values persist in our hearts through the work of the Holy Spirit. Because of what He has done for us, we're free to boldly claim this truth: I rate.

Icon

And now, go, write it before them on a tablet and inscribe it in a book,
that it may be for the time to come as a witness forever. Isaiah 30:8

Icon is an old word made fashionable by the rapid growth of personal computers. Today, an icon is a graphic device that enables computer users to get themselves into trouble faster than they could before computers used such symbols. For example, my computer has a trash can icon on the screen. You can guess what that stands for, even if you aren't familiar with computers. (It's where much of my work is filed!)

The context of today's Bible reading really doesn't suggest icons unless you've been staring at screen savers for too long. I have, so I'll suggest that verse 8 might be applied to a more pristine context—one that involves icons as well.

"And now, go, write it before them on a tablet and inscribe it in a book, that it may be for the time to come as a witness forever" (Isaiah 30:8). God spoke through Isaiah because He didn't want anyone to consider His Word to be a trifling matter. Prophecies meant God cared enough to leave potent signs intended to guide believers according to His will. Perhaps we might use icons in the same way.

There's a little space on the outside margin of this page for you to doodle a personal icon that symbolizes God's love for you. Draw it now, but avoid the easy road—no crosses allowed!

Aha! Had to think for a moment, right? Plenty of situations listed in the Bible lend themselves to icons. Maybe your icon is a flaming bush like the one Moses saw or a ladder like Jacob's. Is it the head of Daniel's hushed lion or three fireproofed men engulfed in flames? Maybe you're more New Testament oriented and your icon is a shepherd's staff or, okay, even a cross.

Computer icons provide shortcuts to launch programs. The icon isn't the program, rather by the way it looks, this sign identifies a program. We need only point to it with the mouse (if you get it to quit wiggling), and it takes you where you want to go.

Use the icon you drew to remind you how much God has done for you and all sinners. Doodle it on that notepaper by the phone or, better yet, where others can see it. Maybe they'll keep their distance. Or maybe it will provide a shortcut for others to hear what you know about God's program. Would I con you?

The Evil Eye

*"Your eye is the lamp of your body. When your eye is healthy, your whole
body is full of light, but when it is bad, your body is full of darkness.
Therefore be careful lest the light in you be darkness. If then your whole
body is full of light, having no part dark, it will be wholly bright, as when
a lamp with its rays gives you light." Luke 11:34–36*

Today we'll consider an eye for an I. They're closely related. We could consider at length how evil "I" can be, but let's think about the physical eye instead. Look at someone's eyes right now. (Use a photograph if necessary.) What do you see? A cornea? Red streaks? Crust? A pupil? (Ask her to get back to school!) Or can you look beyond the obvious and see lies? Flirtation? Anxiety? Affection? Anger? Evil?

It was probably a poet who said that eyes are a mirror of the soul. Maybe they are. For a moment, let's think of eyes in a way that connects pathology with the spiritual. Before we begin, read this passage: "Your eye is the lamp of your body. When your eye is healthy, your whole body is full of light, but when it is bad, your body is full of darkness" (Luke 11:34).

Have you noticed how well eyes adjust to different conditions? For example, when you extinguish the lights in a hotel room, you're immediately plunged into darkness so overwhelming that you wouldn't dare attempt a trip to the washroom for fear of stubbing your toe, running into a wall, or accidentally letting yourself into the hallway partially clad. It doesn't take long, however, for your eyes to adjust. Soon you're able to find your way around obstacles and to your destination. In other words, the darkness becomes more routine.

Isn't the evil of sin like the initial darkness when you turn off the lights? Sins, especially those "new" to us, may seem terrible at first. We don't want to skip our evening prayers or our weekly trip to worship. Or we fear God's wrath when we utter our first curse or brush against that person who seems so much more attractive than our spouse. But sin, all sin, becomes easier to commit as we become accustomed to it. It's like the shroud of darkness in that hotel room. How much easier it is to navigate through our sinfulness once we spend some time adjusting!

Jesus knows how sin works. He wants to be our night-light in a sin-darkened world. Through His Holy Spirit, He enables us to see sin clearly and to shun it so we don't stub our soul. Jesus keeps an eye out for us.

Know It All

And the jailer called for lights and rushed in, and trembling with fear he fell down before Paul and Silas. Then he brought them out and said, "Sirs, what must I do to be saved?" And they said, "Believe in the Lord Jesus, and you will be saved, you and your household." Acts 16:29–31

It's time for a test. Circle the T . . . you know the routine.

1. **T   F**   *The Pentateuch is the first seven books of the Bible.*

2. **T   F**   *The story of the flood is found in the book of Noah.*

3. **T   F**   *Herman Neutics was a famous theology professor.*

4. **T   F**   *Intinction is like intonation, only softer.*

5. **T   F**   *We must be Greek scowlers to understand the Bible.*

Just what should we know so we can pass the ultimate spiritual test? Luke recorded this in Acts: "Believe in the Lord Jesus, and you will be saved, you and your household" (Acts 16:31). Paul and Silas spoke those words to their desperate jailer as he contemplated suicide to avoid the punishment mandated by the Roman government in jailbreak situations. That sentence answers the question of what we need to know—especially for the final exam.

If all we need to know for salvation is that Jesus is our Savior, then why bother with further study? Why take time to read the Bible or attend classes at church or listen to Christian broadcasting? The fact that you're reading this book indicates you already know—perhaps intuitively—the answer. We want to learn more and more about God's love for us. We want to understand how we fit into the history of salvation, which is explained so well in the Bible. God's Word to us is Good News, and we can never get enough of that.

Have you gone through times when you wondered if you knew enough to be saved? Satan sends those doubts. He hopes that you'll strive and strain to learn enough about salvation to earn it on your own. That's the dark side of knowing more about God. The devil tempts us to scrutinize God's Word, to study it so well that we think we know it all. In the process, we forget what is most important—Jesus Christ.

Continue to study God's Word. You'll know you're too smart if you can't answer this question in two words or less: Who took away your sins and saved you?

By the way, all the answers on today's midterm were false. But they weren't important. When you know Jesus, you really do know the right answer.

New and Improved

I tell you this, brothers: flesh and blood cannot inherit the kingdom of God, nor does the perishable inherit the imperishable. Behold! I tell you a mystery. We shall not all sleep, but we shall all be changed, in a moment, in the twinkling of an eye, at the last trumpet. For the trumpet will sound, and the dead will be raised imperishable, and we shall be changed.
1 Corinthians 15:50–53

L et's examine your advertising awareness. What type of product seems most prone to the "new and improved" angle of advertising? It's probably detergent—dish, clothes, tub, toilet bowl, tile, and carpets alike. How much better can detergent get?

The greatest new and improved cleaner ever developed is really quite simple. God was its inventor. Its liquid form—mixed with a powerful formula—cleans the worst stains of sin. This cleaner works on human beings. God applied this cleaner—water and His Word—to us in our Baptism. It changed spiritual life forever, though we still live in a body that will someday return to the earth from which the first model originated. That's when we can expect the next version of "new and improved."

Paul explains, "Behold! I tell you a mystery. We shall not all sleep, but we shall all be changed, in a moment, in the twinkling of an eye, at the last trumpet. For the trumpet will sound, and the dead will be raised imperishable, and we shall be changed" (1 Corinthians 15:51–52).

Some Christians worry and wonder what happens to loved ones blown apart in tragic accidents or what God thinks of cremation. When you think about it, though, would you find the remains of Peter, Paul, or John? God doesn't need remains any more than we need our present bodies after death. He'll find us and shape us into something new and improved. You'll still be you and I'll still be me, but we wouldn't want our old bodies in our new home. (It's bad enough that people laughed at us on earth without giving the angels cause to do the same thing.) Sin will no longer wrinkle our faces, drop our hair, bulge our tummies, or crack our joints. We'll be remade, this time using heaven's specs. But John tells about the best change of all:

Dear friends, now we are children of God, and what we will be has not yet been made known. But we know that when He appears, we shall be like Him, for we shall see Him as He is. 1 John 3:2

"We shall be like Him." That's the last time we'll ever hear "new and improved."

Never Seen Before

Then I saw a new heaven and a new earth, for the first heaven and the
first earth had passed away, and the sea was no more. And I saw the holy
city, new Jerusalem, coming down out of heaven from God, prepared as a
bride adorned for her husband. And I heard a loud voice from the throne
saying, "Behold, the dwelling place of God is with man. He will dwell
with them, and they will be His people, and God Himself will be with
them as their God. He will wipe away every tear from their eyes, and
death shall be no more, neither shall there be mourning nor crying nor
pain anymore, for the former things have passed away."
Revelation 21:1–4

One of the more difficult adjustments to make when thinking about heaven is to forget about life on earth.

In Revelation 21:1–4, John describes heaven in radiantly generic terms. (As far as we know, John was the only one to see what was never seen before or since.) John first emphasizes that God lives with humans. God personally—oops, divinely—makes tears, pain, and death extinct. He moves us from a corrupt, defunct earth to what John calls a new heaven and a new earth. Who can even begin to contemplate the glories and ecstasy of living directly in God's presence?

We won't need the moon because night will disappear; we won't need the sun because God's glory will brighten our lives. We'll be free forever from bad relationships, automobile crashes, pseudoscientific theories, human arrogance, long freight trains, dirty diapers, traffic jams, fattening foods, pornography, flat tires, gangs, fierce storms, ferocious animals, and . . . Wait a minute. All these are what will be gone. Except to say that we'll live in God's holy presence, we haven't concluded what that experience will be like.

Paul summarized eternal life in heaven by quoting this from Isaiah: "But, as it is written, 'What no eye has seen, nor ear heard, nor the heart of man imagined, what God has prepared for those who love Him'" (1 Corinthians 2:9).

No, we can't accurately imagine life in heaven. That's not to say that we can't dream about escaping the pitfalls, pain, plundering, and plagues of earthly life. It's not to say that we can't fantasize about mansions, sparkling streets, beautiful gardens, and thunderously whooshing sighs of contentment. Our best approach to envisioning heaven is to realize that we can't even begin to know what's good for us.

The Case of the Divine Dice

So [Jonah] paid the fare and went on board, to go with them to Tarshish,
away from the presence of the Lord. But the Lord hurled a great wind
upon the sea, and there was a mighty tempest on the sea, so that the ship
threatened to break up. . . . And they said to one another, "Come, let us
cast lots, that we may know on whose account this evil has come upon
us." So they cast lots, and the lot fell on Jonah. . . . He said to them,
"Pick me up and hurl me into the sea; then the sea will quiet down
for you, for I know it is because of me that this great tempest has
come upon you." Jonah 1:1–12

If you ever want to see a living (albeit faulty) definition of strong faith, watch a gambler at his favorite slot machine. Another instrument intended to give you nothing for your money is a pair of dice. If you ever have opportunity to throw them, do a good job—three or four hundred feet should do the trick.

If you've read the entire Bible, you've come across lots of instances when it seems as though God condoned and even blessed gambling. In particular, we find several cases of individuals making decisions by throwing an ancient version of dice called "lots." The disciples cast lots to determine who would replace Judas. Going back to the Old Testament, priests used lots to assign temple duties and to choose which goat would be sacrificed and which would be set free on the Day of Atonement. As in all gambling, there are winners and losers. The question here is "Which one was Jonah?" (Think about that later.)

If it's true that gambling is part of God's won't (the opposite of will), why did God allow and even ply His holy will using what seemed to be devices of random chance? The answer is as slippery as greased dice, but experts think casting lots was common in the cultures of Bible times. God has been known to use the stuff of ordinary life to convey His will, thus it appears that God once revealed His desires through this method. Therefore, casting lots involved neither luck nor statistical probability. Instead, it was God's graphic way to impart His decisions. He loaded the dice, so to speak. (Check this out in Proverbs 16:33.)

The good news about casting lots is that they've been cast off in this era, except where they're abused in the current gambling craze. Better yet, when it comes to the most important decision of our lives, there won't be any lot casting. Judgment Day will come, and God will not play games with our eternal lives. Jesus decided our future, and He took no chances. He died for our sins and returned to life so we might win. It's a sure thing.

Complaint Department

Give ear to my prayer, O God, and hide not Yourself from my plea for mercy! Attend to me, and answer me; I am restless in my complaint and I moan, because of the noise of the enemy, because of the oppression of the wicked. . . . Evening and morning and at noon I utter my complaint and moan, and He hears my voice. He redeems my soul in safety from the battle that I wage, for many are arrayed against me. Psalm 55:1–18

When all else fails, complain. But be careful. If something doesn't work, it might very well be you! Consider my first snow thrower. One winter morning as I was confronted with several inches of fresh snow. I announced this would be the last time I would shorten my life by shoveling the driveway. My wife calmly suggested, "Why don't you buy a snow thrower?"

I trekked to the store and made my purchase. I got the box home and began to complain about the assembly instructions. "Must be a translation from a dead language," I said. My wife, an expert in translating written instructions, threw them out, then mustered the parts into a machine.

I took my lifesaving machine outside, pulled the starter rope and . . . pulled the starter rope and . . . drove the machine to the shop. There I complained bitterly, loudly, and (I thought) convincingly about its stubbornness. The clerk smiled. She flipped the starter switch, gave a gentle yank, and it roared to life. I've been a more cautious complainer ever since.

Should I have prayed over the machine before I complained? After all, Psalm 55:22 says, "Cast your burden on the Lord, and He will sustain you; He will never permit the righteous to be moved." Prayer might have been wise in this situation—I could have stopped and asked for patience, perseverance, the ability to ask for help sooner, etc. Perhaps these verses are more helpful, though, when we find ourselves grousing about other people.

Human relationships, durable as they may be over time, are often fragile in the short term. When ties become strained, the easiest thing to do is to complain.

Complaining may provide some measure of immediate relief in a tense situation, but it rarely has lasting, positive effects. That's where Psalm 55:22 comes in. It's not the kind of psalm we use against someone. Instead, our Lord wants us to cast all our complaints on Him because He cares for us. He'll plant His suggestions in our hearts, though it would be good to search His manual—translated clearly from ancient experts that include Moses, David, Matthew, and John.

Gimme Gimme

The people of Israel said to them, "Would that we had died by the hand of the Lord in the land of Egypt, when we sat by the meat pots and ate bread to the full, for you have brought us out into this wilderness to kill this whole assembly with hunger." Exodus 16:3

So what has the Lord done for you lately? Has it been anything substantial since the drama of your birth or the miracle of your faith? Or has it been more or less routine or even ho-hum?

How easily we forget the miracles and blessings of everyday life! How easily we want more and more and MORE! But if you want a really bad example of G & G—greed and grumbling—read this: "The people of Israel said to them, 'Would that we had died by the hand of the Lord in the land of Egypt, when we sat by the meat pots and ate bread to the full, for you have brought us out into this wilderness to kill this whole assembly with hunger'" (Exodus 16:3).

These were the same Israelites whom God had rescued from slavery in Egypt. Did they remember the whippings and long hours in the hot sun? No. Now they preferred food to freedom. So God delivered food fresh to their tent flap every day for 40 years! Yet hear this: "But now our strength is dried up, and there is nothing at all but this manna to look at" (Numbers 11:6).

You would never be like that, would you? So what has God done for you lately? Sometimes daily breath and bread, family and friends, unfettered church doors and uncensored sermons, blood pressure and allergy medication, and a modestly functioning brain become so mundane that we don't count them among our blessings. Once in a while we hunger for a spiritual extravaganza of sorts. We can be pitifully like the Israelites.

God was the God of Israel. He cared for them like no one else. God is the God of all people. He cares for them like no one else. When we're hard pressed to remember what God has done for us lately, we can check the pulse of faith. Do you believe you're a sinner, doomed to eternal failure and punishment? Do you still believe that Jesus saved you? Do you believe that God forgives you for the sake of Jesus Christ?

In a world characterized by a gimme-gimme attitude, it's nice to know you can hunger for something without offending our God of many blessings. Ask Him for more and more and MORE faith. Be a glutton for forgiveness. Feel your soul stretch to capacity with the Holy Spirit's power. Go ahead. Put down this book and ask for it now.

Would You Buy This?

*Now faith is the assurance of things hoped for, the conviction of things
not seen. For by it the people of old received their commendation. . . .
And without faith it is impossible to please Him, for whoever would draw
near to God must believe that He exists and that He rewards those who
seek Him. Hebrews 11:1–6*

Marketing is the art and science of making a product attractive and
available to consumers. Consider the market research and strategy
that went into the Edsel. (For you post-Edselonians, the Edsel was a highly
touted car introduced by Ford in the late 1950s. It disappeared soon after.)
Every year, hopeful manufacturers introduce their own variety of Edsel to the
public in the hopes of demand that far exceeds supply. Not coincidentally this
will mean profits. It's probably feasible for effective marketing to create
demand for boats in Death Valley!

This leads us to the subject of marketing faith in Jesus. The best marketing consultants would consider this to be the supreme challenge. Well, perhaps not. They're often in the business of selling unbelievable claims. But
would you want something that had a reliable history, though some critics
question the validity of its claims? Would you desire something that had
incredible, indescribable potential that couldn't be accurately measured?
Would you really trust its value and integrity if you could have it for free?
Would your neighbors think any less if you parked a pink Edsel in front of
your house?

Marketing faith in Jesus probably doesn't seem too complex to believers.
Our faith is rooted in God's Word. We believe what He says, not because of
clever marketing strategies but because the Holy Spirit provided faith to
believe these inconceivable assertions. Furthermore, we take comfort in
knowing we're not the only ones involved in this faith thing. "By faith Noah,
being warned by God concerning events as yet unseen, in reverent fear con-
structed an ark for the saving of his household. By this he condemned the
world and became an heir of the righteousness that comes by faith" (Hebrews
11:7).

Does this suggest that we should look for a good used Edsel or shop for
a ski boat in the Sahara? Faith in Jesus is more than buying something worthless on earth. It's rejoicing in the gift of forgiveness and salvation, trusting that
God makes good on His astonishing promises. It's trusting that the best
things in life are indeed free.

Going Out for Business

And about the ninth hour Jesus cried out with a loud voice, saying, "Eli, Eli, lema sabachthani?" that is, "My God, My God, why have You forsaken Me?" And some of the bystanders, hearing it, said, "This man is calling Elijah." And one of them at once ran and took a sponge, filled it with sour wine, and put it on a reed and gave it to Him to drink. But the others said, "Wait, let us see whether Elijah will come to save Him." And Jesus cried out again with a loud voice and yielded up His spirit.
Matthew 27:46–50

No doubt you've seen "Going Out of Business Sale" signs in store windows. I wonder if merchants ever advertised a "Staying in Business Sale"? In a way, that was the message of a cleverly worded ad that appeared weekly in the newspaper. Being an astute and ethical business student in college, I yearned to uncover deceptive advertising. I had one particular appliance store in my sight when I discovered that my sight had failed me. "Going Out for Business" looks a lot like "Going Out of Business" to eyes accustomed to the more familiar message. What a deft twist on a stock slogan!

That catchphrase might remind us of Matthew 27:50: "And Jesus cried out again with a loud voice and yielded up His spirit." The handwritten sign tacked to the cross might well have said, "Son of God. Going out for business." Prior to this time, everyone crucified went out of business for good. Could the public expect anything different?

Maybe some in modern society have the same disillusioned perception of Christians. Religion doesn't seem as popular today as it once was. True religion, that is. Christians are often denounced for outdated morality and chided because they frequently fail to practice what they preach. It's true that sometimes you can't tell believers from unbelievers by the way they act.

Jesus is going out for business among us, and our weakness only confirms His strength. Christ is in the business of forgiveness, and He'll always have a steady clientele. You and I alone could keep Him working overtime. Remarkably, He's never too busy. He never has so much business that He becomes out of touch with us, though He has His Spirit on the road to rustle up more business.

How comforting to know that Jesus makes our business His business. Because He releases us from sin's devastating grasp, we can ask Him to make us more like Him in the way we think and live. We trust that He will continue to call on us despite our regular disloyalty to Him. Pray that He never simply minds His own business. We know that in the end, we won't do business with anyone else.

Heavy Wait

*But do not overlook this one fact, beloved, that with the Lord one day is
as a thousand years, and a thousand years as one day. The Lord is not
slow to fulfill His promise as some count slowness, but is patient
toward you, not wishing that any should perish, but that all should
reach repentance. 2 Peter 3:8–9*

The lady on the phone cheerily promised that the repairperson would
arrive at 8:30 a.m. to fix the air conditioner. Now it's 9:30 a.m., and
no repairperson. You can think of three reasons why the individual is late:

1. *He can't locate your home.*

2. *His truck overheated and he's stranded in an air-conditioned
   service shop.*

3. *The dispatcher never told him about you.*

You call the company, and you're again cheerily informed that there was
an emergency. "My air-conditioning is broken, the comfort index is 113, and
he has an emergency?"

"Yes," the voice says. "His wife forgot to include his iced tea, and he had
to have his tea. Will 2 p.m. be okay?"

Waiting is a common problem recorded throughout history. Sarah could-
n't wait to have a child. David couldn't postpone his lust. God's chosen people were impatient for the Messiah. We're waiting for Jesus to come again.
And it's been a long wait.

Here's what the Bible says about waiting: "But do not overlook this one
fact, beloved, that with the Lord one day is as a thousand years, and a thousand years as one day. The Lord is not slow to fulfill His promise as some
count slowness, but is patient toward you, not wishing that any should perish, but that all should reach repentance" (2 Peter 3:8–9).

If ever there was a good excuse for delays, this is it. Other believers waited, perhaps impatiently, for Jesus to return. But our Savior's delay resulted in
your salvation. More than half of the world's population still does not believe
in Jesus, and He patiently allows time for them to come to faith too. That's
not to say He'll wait forever. Forever is reserved for after judgment. All this
suggests that we need to keep busy while we wait.

Pray that unbelievers will respond to the Holy Spirit's call to faith—
before it's too late. Share your faith through whatever ability or resources you
have so others may know Christ through you. And don't tire of waiting or lose
confidence in His promises. The Dispatcher does indeed have your name written in His book. He will be here soon.

Flashback

And you were dead in the trespasses and sins in which you once walked,
following the course of this world. . . . But God, being rich in mercy,
because of the great love with which He loved us, even when we were
dead in our trespasses, made us alive together with Christ—by grace
you have been saved. Ephesians 2:1–5

Flashback is frequently experienced by people just released from the hospital. In the comfort of their own living room, they can share the exact moment when that strange pain ambushed them. They vividly recall the ride to the hospital when every bump jolted them with pain. Then there was the emergency room and that doctor that looked as if he had just graduated from high school. And that snippy nurse! Finally, the blood samples, x-rays, MRIs, and poking. Why, it took an extra week just to recover from all the tests!

It's often more enjoyable to look back on certain events than it is to experience them. As we look back, we recount abnormal life situations without the real-time pain, fear, and uncertainty. We might even embellish the event a bit—for dramatic effect.

One flashback that doesn't need elaboration is our condition prior to salvation. Ephesians 2:1 says, "And you were dead in the trespasses and sins."

Let's use flashback right now. From the safety of wherever you are, relive that time of horror, anxiety, or helplessness when you faced the most life-threatening experience humans ever face. You were actually soul dead—another victim of epidemic sin. You might have provided just the culture where sin grows most rampant. Or maybe you were a tiny baby unable to recall your inherited sin. In either case, the cure was the same—lifesaving faith in Jesus Christ.

Like many serious diseases, sin is curable, but it recurs to chronically inflict life with pain and anxiety. That's why we remain on medication once the initial healing is accomplished. That medication is daily repentance and forgiveness. It comes in small but potent doses of Bible readings, meditation on God's Word, prayers, and hymns. Group therapy helps too. It's good to join other Christians who are recovering from sin as they meet weekly to flashback on their former condition, learn how to live in a sin-infected world, and praise their divine Physician. We also participate in another form of therapy as we meet frequently for a Holy Meal with soul-healing results.

Next time someone wants your attention as they flashback on their health, be patient and look for an opportunity to share your brush with death.

The Case of Long Lives

This is the book of the generations of Adam. . . . When Adam had lived
130 years, he fathered a son in his own likeness, after his image, and
named him Seth. The days of Adam after he fathered Seth were 800
years; and he had other sons and daughters. Thus all the days that
Adam lived were 930 years, and he died. Genesis 5:1–5

Methuselah lived so long ago, rumor has it that he had only three dig-
its on his social security card. Not only did he live long ago, but he
lived for a long period. "Thus all the days of Methuselah were 969 years, and
he died" (Genesis 5:27). (It's ironic that he almost lived long enough to die
in the flood. So much for the blessings of old age!) Many others lived to
astonishing ages, as Genesis 5:1–32 attests. And mandatory retirement was
unheard of, as Noah would be happy to tell you.

Now for the question first phrased by an ancient, unknown 3-year-old.
"Why?" Why did people live so long in those early Bible days? What accounts
for such exceptional longevity?

Wherever questions arise, so do answers—even if they're only theoretical.
Some who have studied this phenomenon believe that the world's environment was more hospitable—in effect, these individuals lived during the truly
good old days. Scholars surmise that the climate included mild temperatures
with complementary levels of humidity. Because the climate was so agreeable,
serious illness was rare, food was plentiful and nourishing, and air was pure.
Besides, these were the pre-life insurance days, so adults had to live longer to
adequately care for their families.

Yes, the last statement was absurd. And we also must admit that speculation about why people lived so long is a bit silly. In fact, it's downright dis-
tracting. While the list of ages in Genesis 5 provides information God thought
useful, we should be careful to prevent our curiosity from consuming our
faith or directing our attention away from the main theme of the Bible.

God's Word is the history of salvation. We also may think of it as the
future of salvation. God proclaims His love for sinners and reveals what He
did to establish a wonderful relationship with us. He reports in detail why He
sent Jesus, what Jesus did, and how we benefit from Jesus' life, death, and resurrection. God promises that while our years on earth are unlikely to be as
many as Methuselah's, we will live forever, which should be long enough to
satisfy anyone. When it comes to forever, what difference does it make how
many years we spend on earth?

The Other Side of the Gate

So Jesus again said to them, "Truly, truly, I say to you, I am the door of the sheep. All who came before Me are thieves and robbers, but the sheep did not listen to them. I am the door. If anyone enters by Me, he will be saved and will go in and out and find pasture. John 10:7–9

Gates are usually erected for a reason—either to keep something in or to keep something out or both. Normally they serve as a portal for limited access to an otherwise secure area. In the case of our family dog, the secure area just happens to be the rest of the world. When the dog exits its pen, look out! First, she'll sit on you, effectively trapping you under her considerable weight; then she'll either lick or bark you into submission, depending on her mood.

Think of all the gates you see. Better yet, think of your own gate—if you have one. How do you feel when your gate is closed? Do you feel the same when gates belonging to others are shut? How do you feel when you discover your gate is open? Again, would you feel the same seeing an open gate elsewhere? Depending on your point of view, gates can mean either threat or welcome, entrapment or escape, anxiety or security.

Jesus compared Himself to a gate. He said, "I am the door. If anyone enters by Me, he will be saved and will go in and out and find pasture" (John 10:9). Jesus is the gate that separates eternal life from endless doom. No one has ever entered or refused to enter any gate nearly as important.

For believers like us, every gate can make us feel good, secure, and able to escape the devil's power. Our world is filled with sin and hostility. It's a dangerous place. But the gate to safety and salvation is open, inviting us to escape to Jesus' protection and care. It's a whole different world on the other side of the gate.

John saw a gate in his glimpse of heaven, which is recorded in Revelation. This gate sparkled with jewels, a prelude to the heavenly city in which we'll someday reside. The gate is open to us and all believers. In fact, it's open to everyone right now. Someday, though, that gate will close forever. If statistics are right, only about 30 percent of civilization will be on the good side of the gate. Pray that others hear and believe the Gospel. Hold the gate open and welcome those who want to enter. And when Satan saunters by, probing your defenses, be sure to show him the gate.

Sromur

Let not your heart faint, and be not fearful at the report heard in the land,
when a report comes in one year and afterward a report in another year, and
violence is in the land, and ruler is against ruler. Jeremiah 51:46

They usually get things backward. That's why I reversed the spelling of today's subject. It seems that if you want someone to believe you, tell them it's a rumor—it's more convincing than telling the truth. Too bad baseless rumors round so many bases. They apparently caused God's Old Testament people some problems too. Jeremiah says, "Let not your heart faint, and be not fearful at the report heard in the land, when a report comes in one year and afterward a report in another year, and violence is in the land, and ruler is against ruler" (Jeremiah 51:46).

Have you noticed that rumors rarely spread good news? "Rumor has it that the company will downsize next month." "I heard that Nora and Ted are separating." "The produce department is displaying salad posters. It must be their way of saying salads will cost more lettuce." "John said that Frank heard from Jared who was talking to Al that the price of Bumble & Tumble stock will plummet."

In those hours after the first Easter dawned, rumor had it that someone had stolen the body of a freshly executed criminal. It's a rumor that some preferred to believe and perhaps still do. Even Jesus' disciples thought it was a rumor when the women returned from the cemetery and reported a mysterious encounter with an empty tomb and a glorified Friend. But there's nothing like a few facts to ransack a hot rumor!

Jesus rose from the dead just as He had promised. He crippled the devil's stranglehold on our souls as predicted by the prophets. He provided tangible proof to all doubters by a show of His hands and feet.

Perhaps we would prefer rumors to truth's pain, but the fact is that we're devout sinners. Yet our faith convinces and assures us that Jesus took away our sins and continues to forgive us despite our obstinate attitude. All these truths appear in the one book we can trust without exception—the Bible. No need for rumors of a Messiah or hearsay of salvation or gossip about some vague Gospel. We have the truth. We have it in clear language. We have God's Word on it.

Rumors are ordinary annoyances of life, stimulating speculation or anxiety as we wait for their failure or their confirmation. Good thing God left nothing to idle speculation regarding our salvation. We know for sure that everything God told us about Jesus as the Holy Spirit spoke through holy men of God is true. That should end any rumors to the contrary.

The Surgeon General Has Determined . . .

Paul talked with them, intending to depart on the next day, and he pro-
longed his speech until midnight. . . . And a young man named Eutychus,
sitting at the window, sank into a deep sleep as Paul talked still longer.
And being overcome by sleep, he fell down from the third story and was
taken up dead. But Paul went down and bent over him, and taking him
in his arms, said, "Do not be alarmed, for his life is in him." And when
Paul had gone up and had broken bread and eaten, he conversed with
them a long while, until daybreak, and so departed. And they took the
youth away alive, and were not a little comforted. Acts 20:7–12

Some people are deluded into thinking it is healthy to wake revitalized and invigorated after a good sermon. But be advised that the surgeon general has determined that sleeping during sermons may harm your health. Research from Acts 20:9 confirms this theory.

It's easier to diagnose the Eutychus Syndrome in others than it is to detect it in yourself. (A sore neck after church is one symptom. An icy handshake from the preacher is another.) There was a time, however, when all of us were much like Eutychus—only worse. We once were dead in our sins.

Before the Holy Spirit granted us faith, we gradually were falling into a deep and fatal sleep. Oh, an examination would report that our eyes were open, our hearts pumping, and our lungs rhythmically inflating, but we were slipping away as insidiously as when we close our eyes in boredom. Sin is a real killer. Like falling 30 feet to the ground, sin dealt us death.

Eutychus' story had a happy ending as Paul, by God's power, revived him. Our story ends mercifully as well. Jesus, by His power as God, resuscitated us to continue living and serving Him and others. He breathed life-giving and sustaining faith into our cold, stiff souls. He applied heavy doses of forgiveness so sin's cancer would disappear and we could live to share our faith with others.

If you find yourself snoozing next time you hear a sermon, you'll probably be unable to resist. But when the sermon-ending "Amen" sounds, stretch your arms, give a mighty yawn, and hope the pastor didn't throw an "Amen" into the middle of the sermon. Better yet, thank God that He woke you in time. Not in time to go home, but in time to wake you from sin's lethal slumber. Next time, take a nap before church.

The More the Merrier?

As one trespass led to condemnation for all men, so one act of righteous-
ness leads to justification and life for all men. For as by the one man's
disobedience the many were made sinners, so by the one man's obedience
the many will be made righteous. Now the law came in to increase the
trespass, but where sin increased, grace abounded all the more.
Romans 5:18–20

One of the more successful commercial ventures is the so-called outlet store mall. It's so called because it usually is a super-effective outlet for bulging wallets and it tends to maul credit card limits. The best outlet
malls are located at interstate highway interchanges and advertised by bill-
boards and traffic backups for several miles in any direction.

Today's Bible reading sounds much like an advertisement for a sin mall.
(Again, maul is the preferred word!) Listen: "Now the law came in to increase
the trespass, but where sin increased, grace abounded all the more" (Romans
5:20). Before you spend all your faith on a sin spree, consider the risk of
potential deception here.

The self-indulgent side of us wants to view this passage as an invitation
to "shop till you drop" at Satan's Outlet Extravaganza. After all, we may reason, the more we sin, the more grace we get. Sort of a win-win situation. Of
course, that's a misapplication of the passage. The bright side of this passage
warms the soul of sinners who realize that God doesn't observe a credit limit
for sinners. He neither condones sin nor does He hold it against those who
claim Jesus as Savior.

Sin ruins our lives. It makes us unhappy, sick, despondent, and sometimes even dangerous. Certainly, God never wanted us to be this way; therefore, He hates sin and refuses to tolerate it. On the other hand, God loves sinners. Despite our past, God accepts us as His children for the sake of His Son,
who died to eliminate our debt. The more sinful the sinners, the more thankful they are because they owe their lives to the Lord many times over.

The devil's main competitor has an outlet store too. Grace comes in many
sizes, but there isn't much variety. The only kind we can trust is God's. It's
durable and comes with a lifetime guarantee. Best of all, it's free.

Think about the kind of sinner you are. If this takes a long time, don't
worry. On the other hand, if you don't think you have many sins, perhaps you
should examine yourself more closely. Our tendency to compare sins committed and forgiveness accepted may dull us to the magnitude of gratitude we
owe our Savior. If we thanked God for forgiving each sin committed, we'd be
too busy to concern ourselves with much else. Including outlet stores.

Mission Statement

Now Jesus did many other signs in the presence of the disciples, which are not written in this book; but these are written so that you may believe that Jesus is the Christ, the Son of God, and that by believing you may have life in His name. John 20:30–31

Big business has discovered the mission statement. Mission statements usually sound noble and grand. Most translate to two simple words that everybody understands: Make money. Or it might be more precisely translated as: Make lots of money. Would you like an example? Acme Universal Widget and Wowsit aspires to legally extricate as much money as possible from 98 percent of the population of New Brunswick by supplying fur-lined, electronically heated swimwear for men and women.

Those involved in writing mission statements—whether corporate, educational, or congregational—know how difficult the task is. You want to say things "just right," so when the project is a group endeavor, it's a daunting task to get everyone to agree on wording. The most well-worded mission statements—especially the commercial species—are sufficiently confusing so nobody really knows what the mission is. (After all, there are only so many ways to say, "Make money.")

Christians have a clear mission statement. It was a snap for our loving God to pour it into John's pen. "Now Jesus did many other signs in the presence of the disciples, which are not written in this book; but these are written so that you may believe that Jesus is the Christ, the Son of God, and that by believing you may have life in His name" (John 20:30–31).

God's mission statement allows no deception or confusion. All our Lord's miracles and every inspired word recorded in the Bible have one purpose, one goal: that people of every nation and every generation may have eternal life. It doesn't even cost money. In fact, it took a severe loss to abide by God's mission statement.

Christians merge under God's mission statement not only to enjoy salvation, but also to act so others will join them now and forever. Our mission is the same as God's, though we're often inept at executing it. But the Holy Spirit is with us so we, as forgiven sinners, can tell other sinners how they, too, can join the cause. The Spirit equips us to live as missionaries through what we say and do in our homes, workplaces, recreation areas, and neighborhoods. Sometimes the mission is hard. But with the Spirit's help, it's never impossible.

Seeing Things

When the servant of the man of God rose early in the morning and went
out, behold, an army with horses and chariots was all around the city.
And the servant said, "Alas, my master! What shall we do?" He said,
"Do not be afraid, for those who are with us are more than those who are
with them." Then Elisha prayed and said, "O LORD, please open his eyes
that he may see." So the LORD opened the eyes of the young man, and he
saw, and behold, the mountain was full of horses and chariots
of fire all around Elisha. 2 Kings 6:15–17

Today if you talk about seeing things, you risk acquiring an instant reputation that puts a lot of space between you and others. If you're a Christian who sees things, you'll likely be labeled a fanatic. But people of God—people with an "in" because of Jesus Christ—have a long record of "in"-sights.

A verse from today's Bible reading underscores this point. Despite the impending onslaught by fierce foes, God's almighty army formed a protective barrier around His people. Although anyone who dared to look saw the invading army, only those who looked beyond themselves saw salvation.

The same is true for us. Perils surround us. It is ironic, but the most menacing threat is the sin of complacency. We become so accustomed to "life as usual"—generally good life as usual—that we fail to perceive its dangers. You know how it is. When things go well, we sense no need to trust God. If life goes really well, we trust ourselves more and more—until the invading army of sin appears, showing its ugly side. Then, because of self-reliance, we wonder how we'll cope with the brewing trouble.

At times like this, we need to see things—things like Elisha's friend saw. Things like an army of angels to defend us from death and the devil. But most of all we need to see Jesus. The only way we can see Him is through eyes of faith opened by the Holy Spirit.

Do you see Him? You do if He's real enough to talk to in your prayers. You do if you understand the cross as something more than jewelry. You do if you see Him offering His body and blood for you in a meal of bread and wine. You do if you can close your eyes and see Him inviting you to heaven. Seeing things now? You can be sure it's not your imagination.

Continuing Education

For the good hand of his God was on him. For Ezra had set his heart to
study the Law of the Lord, and to do it and to teach His statutes and
rules in Israel. Ezra 7:9b–10

Discoveries and theories increase by the day. Those who don't keep up are left behind. It's true for medical professionals, educators, engineers, computer programmers, construction workers, and even waste managers. Those who wait to learn from their mistakes usually receive an extensive education too—too late to be helpful. What was studied and practiced in the past must be restudied and practiced anew.

Today's reading deals with a student of God's Word, Ezra. Ezra kept up with God's Word. Although nothing had changed about God, He repeated His promises (as well as His threats) through people like Ezra. However, we must take care not to give Ezra more credit than he deserves because that would rob God of the credit.

The "gracious hand of His God" was on Ezra before he ever studied God's Word or observed His laws. God has never looked for people worthy enough to receive His blessings and love. Instead, God mercifully lavished undeserved love—grace—on Ezra and also on us. He also filled us with faith so we know what He's done. Once recognizing and claiming God as our own, we're free to fruitfully study His Word.

God's grace empowers us not only to study, but also to learn—and there's a difference. If you study every medical text available and pass the certifying exams with the highest grades, it means nothing unless you actually practice what you've learned. It would be silly to endure such stringent study and then refuse to use what you've learned for the benefit of others. It's the same with God's Word. As we continue our education in His Word through private and group study, we become better prepared to practice what Jesus preached. It would be a shame to keep all that Good News to ourselves, so practice we must.

Practice is a comforting word. Here on earth, even our Christian practice never makes perfect. But Jesus died for our imperfections. He equips us to practice our faith without fear of failure because forgiveness is always a confession away.

God bless you as you continue your education in His Word. Don't forget to practice every day.

Nothing to Cry About

But this I call to mind, and therefore I have hope: The steadfast love of the Lord never ceases; His mercies never come to an end; they are new every morning; great is Your faithfulness. "The Lord is my portion," says my soul, "therefore I will hope in Him." The Lord is good to those who wait for Him, to the soul who seeks Him. Lamentations 3:21–25

Watch the faces of people coming out of Sunday services, or worse, going in to worship. Looks like some of them consider Lamentations their favorite book of the Bible, right? However, some of the most comforting and stirring words of Gospel appear in (of all places) the Old Testament book of sorrows, Lamentations. That shouldn't surprise us.

Here is a beautiful example of grace from Lamentations 3:22–23: "The steadfast love of the Lord never ceases; His mercies never come to an end; they are new every morning; great is Your faithfulness."

The prophet Jeremiah, writer of Lamentations, had much about which to mourn. But isn't it just like God to turn around the worst situations with His love? In the middle of bad times, God's faithful people can trust His care and compassion. His supply of mercy and love never dwindles. In fact, its abundance seems to increase proportionately in times of adversity. God is a faithful Father and provider.

Faith is a funny word. We often use it to describe those who believe in God. In those terms, we know faith comes in a variety of shapes, sizes, and quantities. And consistent with the Lord's compassion as proclaimed in Lamentations, we know that even the smallest atom of faith is sufficient for salvation and immortality. The tiniest grain of faith brings the believer into the very presence of the Savior.

Then there's the faith ascribed to God. God's faithfulness is anything but tiny. It's monumental, magnetic, and mmmmm, mmmmm, mmmmm! While our allegiance strays, He remains loyal even when there's absolutely no justification for such loyalty. When we forget the One who loves us beyond description, He loves us enough to remain, waiting. Even when we abuse and misuse His name, God remains open rather than defensive, patiently waiting to hear our repentance and mercifully restoring our broken relationship.

With all this faithfulness surrounding us, we're strengthened and encouraged to face even dismal or painful futures. Every wound, disease, disappointment, discouragement, injustice, setback, or loss is like that little scratch we had on our knee when we were four and our mothers said, "It's nothing to cry about."

Nothing to Laugh About?

Then Abraham fell on his face and laughed and said to himself, "Shall a child be born to a man who is a hundred years old? Shall Sarah, who is ninety years old, bear a child?" Genesis 17:17

So Sarah laughed to herself, saying, "After I am worn out, and my lord is old, shall I have pleasure?" Genesis 18:12

Consider these answers to some common questions about laughing:

Q: Are there different kinds of laughter?

A: Yes. Ho ho. Ha ha. And hee hee—or to be more gender correct: (s)hee (s)hee. If that answer isn't what you expected, here's a different one. Yes. Laughter may be described as gleeful, scornful, polite (as when strangers laugh at your jokes), or merciful (as when friends laugh at your jokes).

Q: Does the Bible ever mention laughter?

A: Yes, several times in both Old and New Testaments. We also might imagine Jesus laughing in delight at the wedding reception and when He was surrounded by little children.

Q: Did any famous Old Testament characters ever laugh?

A: Yes, and they were married (to each other). Case in point: Abraham and Sarah (a.k.a. Sarai before she laughed).

Q: How would you characterize their laughter?

A: Abraham was rolling on the floor (desert), doubled over in delight. Sarah's laugh was cynical. By way of evidence, read the verses at the top of this page again.

Q: What is the point?

A: We sometimes dupe ourselves into thinking that worship, Bible study, and prayer—foundations on which the Spirit builds faith—include nothing to laugh about. Yet laughter is most certainly appropriate when we consider what God has done for us. We're entitled to laugh with scorn at the devil, whom Jesus defeated by dying a sinner's death and returning to life in a victory only God could accomplish. We can flash a cynical smirk when the devil or any of his supporters accuse us before God because God already has declared us innocent for Jesus' sake. Then we're able to laugh in joy here on earth because what lies ahead dilutes any present sorrows or afflictions. Someday we'll roll around the heavens, laughing forever as Jesus tickles our souls with His everlasting love. Just be careful you don't fall off a cloud!

Old Friends

"This is My commandment, that you love one another as I have loved you. Greater love has no one than this, that someone lays down his life for his friends. You are My friends if you do what I command you. No longer do I call you servants, or the servant does not know what his master is doing; but I have called you friends, for all that I have heard from My Father I have made known to you." John 15:12–15

Someone defined friends as two or more people who are angry at the same person. Someone else compared friends to appliances—the less they are used the longer they will last. Friends can also be relatives, but more often they're people with whom you can choose to relate.

Look back in your personal history, and think of one of your best friends. Close your eyes (don't try this while reading), and remember one of the good times you had together—perhaps a time when you laughed together or simply luxuriated quietly in each other's company. When you open your eyes, quickly find a mirror. Are you smiling?

Where are your old friends now? When did you see them last? Probably at a reunion or a wake. How did the conversation go? Many old friends find conversation faltering after a few minutes. How can things change so much after 10 or 20 or 30 years? How did we slip away, both becoming someone different?

Time tends to thin even the thickest friendships. To help time along, there's always distance, especially in a mobile society such as ours. All this makes one yearn for friendships like the ones you used to have. Speaking of former friendships, what can happen to a 2,000-year-old friendship?

Among Jesus' many heartwarming words are these: "No longer do I call you servants, for the servant does not know what his master is doing; but I have called you friends, for all that I have heard from My Father I have made known to you" (John 15:15).

Sharing intimate secrets and desires are common characteristics of friendship. Jesus shared His dreams and His knowledge with us. His most fervent dream was that everyone would live with Him someday. He even died to make that dream reality.

We can't allow ties with our oldest Friend to slip away. We can remind ourselves of great times together like Baptism and Holy Communion. We can think about the times our Friend came to help, and how we owe Him our very life. Yes, we can do something we probably haven't done with other old friends—talk to Him regularly. You'll probably find that, in this case, you won't run out of things to say. Why not give Him a call right now?

Good Judgment

Therefore you have no excuse, O man, every one of you who judges. For in passing judgment on another you condemn yourself, because you, the judge, practice the very same things. Romans 2:1

One wonders if good judgment exists. It isn't always evident in our judicial system where criminals sometimes go free on "technicalities" and innocent people serve harsh sentences for crimes they didn't commit. If it isn't bad enough that we question the judgment of those we employ in our judicial system, we also question the judgment of those we love most— our spouses. (Hint for the day: Never, under any circumstances, question your spouse's judgment. He/she married you!)

Romans 2:1 offers the definitive judgment on judgment. "Therefore you have no excuse, O man, every one of you who judges. For in passing judgment on another you condemn yourself, because you, the judge, practice the very same things." In other words, it appears that good judgment is no judgment.

Should we believe that whatever anyone wants to do is acceptable because the Bible tells us not to judge? Should we consider ourselves blessed equally with those who believe in other gods or who choose to believe only in themselves? Should we smile approvingly at our acquaintances for their promiscuous pleasures and lewd language because "Who are we to judge?"

Like a multiple choice quiz, the answer is "none of the above." Paul's point to the Romans addressed self-righteousness—a concept that remains an issue with us. You know from experience that judging others isn't nearly as complex as judging in courtrooms. Lawyers don't get in the way of private judgments. There aren't two sides, only one—and it's yours. It's so easy to see the faults of others that we wonder why they can't see them. But they question the same thing about us!

The other point Paul implies is that God knows everything necessary to make the right judgment. The wicked will get what's coming to them. As for us . . .

If we all got what the Judge says we deserve, heaven would contain Father, Son, Holy Spirit, and legions of angels, but no humans. We're too guilty to live freely in such company. Yet God will judge us, but His judgment will reflect what Jesus did on our behalf. You know the story. It never changes. Jesus lived, died, and rose to take away our sins. God sent His Son to earth with that mission in mind. When you meet God in heaven someday, be sure to compliment Him on His good judgment!

Lousy Logic

Now the law came in to increase the trespass, but where sin increased, grace abounded all the more, so that, as sin reigned in death, grace also might reign through righteousness leading to eternal life through Jesus Christ our Lord. What shall we say then? Are we to continue in sin that grace may abound? By no means! How can we who died to sin still live in it? Romans 5:20–6:2

Logic is an exercise of human intellect (which already begins to explain its limitations). For example, simple but authentic logic suggests that the horsepower in automobiles should not exceed the driver's I.Q. Conversely, the driver's I.Q. must exceed the posted speed limit. Logic suggests that this would greatly reduce traffic so you and I could get home faster.

Often it seems that logic is a college course rather than an extension of common sense. To prove this point, let's examine the logical implications of Romans 6:1–2, which reasons, "What shall we say then? Are we to continue in sin that grace may abound? By no means! How can we who died to sin still live in it?"

Paul confronted Roman logic. He might have said, "Look here. If you hit your thumb with a hammer, it hurts. When the throbbing subsides, you feel better. However, do you hit each finger in turn with a hammer so you continue to feel better?" Paul might have said it that way, but it was probably more logical to say it the way he did. Anyway, it was especially logical because God told Paul to say it that way.

Only those looking for loopholes in God's will would suggest that we should sin more so we can receive more forgiveness. That's never been the intent of forgiveness, though mercifully it operates that way, which is not logical at all. Why would God continue to forgive sinners as they stupidly or sullenly or stubbornly plod through the same sins while adding new ones to their repertoire? The illogical answer is that God loves us. It really doesn't make sense, does it? That's precisely what makes His love so wonderful. We don't deserve it and can't earn it. He gives it freely, and He gives it often.

Getting back to Paul's point, God's grace and mercy is no reason to keep on sinning. Along with forgiveness, God has given us the power to hate sin and fight it. Motivated by God's perpetual forgiveness and His Holy Spirit, we seek to use forgiveness less and less as we struggle to live as He wants. "Why sin when you don't have to?" is the logic to which we ascribe. But when logic—good logic—fails us, we're always welcome to do the illogical: We can count on God's forgiveness once again. That's common Christian sense that hits the nail on the head, not the thumb.

But . . .

For freedom Christ has set us free; stand firm therefore, and do not sub-
mit again to a yoke of slavery. . . . For through the Spirit, by faith, we
ourselves eagerly wait for the hope of righteousness. For in Christ Jesus
neither circumcision nor uncircumcision counts for anything, but only
faith working through love. Galatians 5:1–6

The English language includes several one-word expressions that are frequently spoken when stalling for time until adequate verbiage slides down neurons from brain to tongue. One such word is *but*.

For a word that has little meaning by itself, *but* peppers vocabulary with regularity. For example, "I know I'm late, but . . ." or "Yes, that's a good point, but . . ." Then there's the stuttering triple *but* when you can't get an excuse in edgewise with an aggressive accuser.

But has a role in spiritual matters too. Consider the following passage: "For freedom Christ has set us free; stand firm therefore, and do not submit again to a yoke of slavery" (Galatians 5:1). No, you didn't miss anything. *But* doesn't appear in letters, but it certainly looms in attitude. In this case, it's a really big but.

The "yoke of slavery" is dogged discipline of the Law, especially as the Jews considered it in the apostle Paul's time. They believed they needed to obey God's Law perfectly to please Him. That wasn't the bad part. Some believed they could do so and boldly claimed that they did. The temptation to assimilate that attitude remains infectious among believers today.

The conversation goes something like this: "I know Jesus died to take away my sins, but I must do something to help my salvation along." Or: "I know lots of Christians are kind of weak when it comes to obeying God's will, but I'm pretty good at it. At least I try." Sometimes it even takes this twist: "Those people will never get to heaven, but I'm working hard to get my reward."

Paul says we're free, and in many other Scripture passages, he also says our freedom is free. Throughout the history of salvation, as noted in the Bible, people have searched in vain for ways to earn a way to heaven. Despite God's constant reminders that we are incapable of such effort, and that attempts to earn salvation are unnecessary, people have persisted in their quest. Perhaps they don't realize that doing so is abject self-centeredness and idolatry. Yet we all fall to this temptation. When that happens, the Holy Spirit reminds us of the most fundamental truth of Christianity: We are saved by God's kindness and mercy—solely by grace. No buts about it.

What?

*David said to Nathan, "I have sinned against the Lord." And Nathan
said to David, "The Lord also has put away your sin; you shall not die."*
2 Samuel 12:13

By itself, *what* is an innocent word. Yet it's often uttered with an attitude, especially when it comes from someone "caught in the act" or
at least suspected of perpetrating one. If you could spell it, it might look like
this: Waaaaaa-t? Then it's followed by a righteous excuse or declaration of
innocent ignorance. For example, a puddle of orange soda soaks into the
white carpet. Mom enters the room. After she composes herself, she asks,
"What is that orange spot on the floor?" Missy, looking as though she just
woke from a long nap, responds, "Waaaaaa-t spot?" While the impending
tempest boils behind mom's eyes, Missy hurriedly continues, "Waaaaaa-t? I
was just sitting here wiggling my toes . . ."

Sinners, when confronted with their "acts," may utter something akin to
"Waaaaaa-t?" After all, it isn't pleasant to be caught in the act or reminded of
past ones. Human nature pushes our guilt button, and we can't tolerate it. The
natural response is to deny wrongdoing or plead ignorance.

Pleading ignorance might convince others, but not God. It doesn't fool
our inner self either. But when you're guilty, you don't want to be. Perhaps
you fear the consequences. Besides, there's always the other person who's
more reprehensible than you!

King David (a man with lots of public face to lose) sat in judgment of one
of those "other guys" when Nathan reported a malicious injustice. (See
today's Bible reading.) At the time, David didn't realize that Nathan was
speaking in hypothetical terms. He didn't get it that Nathan was revealing
David's own grievous sin. David pronounced harsh judgment on the other
guy. When Nathan revealed the culprit's identity, David did the right thing. He
resisted the urge to spout a defiant "Waaaaaa-t?" Here is what happened:
"David said to Nathan, 'I have sinned against the Lord.' And Nathan said to
David, 'The Lord also has put away your sin; you shall not die'" (2 Samuel
12:13).

Sin is so much easier to see in others than in ourselves. There's always a
wealth of ways to justify our actions—as most courtrooms seem to prove. But
there remains only one way to deal with sin. Confess it. Not only does God
already know about it, He is eager to forgive it because it makes His Son's life
and death worthwhile. So when you feel like saying "Waaaaaa-t?" shake the
urge and confess instead.

If . . .

Then Jesus was led up by the Spirit into the wilderness to be tempted by the devil. And after fasting forty days and forty nights, He was hungry. And the tempter came and said to Him, "If you are the Son of God, command these stones to become loaves of bread." But He answered, "It is written, 'Man shall not live by bread alone, but by every word that comes from the mouth of God.'" Matthew 4:1–7

Sometimes the word has a flavor of anticipation: "If I save $3 from every paycheck, I can purchase a new car for cash by the time I'm 101." At other times it's colored with regret: "If only I hadn't spent so much money on lottery tickets, I'd have enough to play for this $75,000,000 purse." Finally, there's the conditional *if* of challenge: "If you work hard and flatter your boss, you'll be promoted to an office with a view of the water cooler."

Religion is full of *if*. "If I try really hard, I'll be a better person, and God will save me." That may be the worst spiritual fallacy ever uttered. There's nothing conditional about our behavior. It's universally imperfect. Take a moment and think about "How I want to be" versus "How I am." Since you really know yourself, and no one else is involved, you have the opportunity for brutal honesty. Things don't look so good, huh? We need not fret about the *ifs* of earning a home in heaven. Christ bought us a beautiful place with His suffering, death, and resurrection.

Next, let's consider the *if* of religious regret. "If only I had a better job, more time, a pastor who preached exciting sermons, I'd get closer to God." Here is the *if* that blames God for weak or evaporating faith. Yet God is patient. Even slothful sinners have opportunity to repent and enjoy God's grace.

Finally, we have the spiritually challenging *if*. The devil thought he was clever in this confrontation with Jesus: "And the tempter came and said to Him, 'If you are the Son of God, command these stones to become loaves of bread'" (Matthew 4:3). We Christians hear versions of this *if* often. "If God loves you Christians so much, why does He permit you to get cancer or suffer deadly accidents or fight through bitter divorces like everybody else?"

The truth is that people universally enjoy God's blessings as well as suffer the consequences of a sin-afflicted world. The real difference is how the believer views these life experiences. Even the worst experiences turn out well for Christians.

If we must have *ifs* in life, then only one *if* can count: If we believe Jesus took away our sins, we'll live forever with Him in heaven. If only more clung to that Good News!

Uh . . .

When the spirit saw Him, immediately it convulsed the boy, and he fell
on the ground and rolled about, foaming at the mouth. And Jesus asked
his father, "How long has this been happening to him?" And he said,
"From childhood. . . . But if You can do anything, have compassion on us
and help us." And Jesus said to him, "If You can! All things are possible
for one who believes." Immediately the father of the child cried out and
said, "I believe; help my unbelief!" . . . [Jesus] rebuked the unclean spirit,
saying to it, "You mute and deaf spirit, I command you, come out of him
and never enter him again." . . . It came out, and the boy was like a
corpse, so that most of them said, "He is dead." But Jesus took him
by the hand and lifted him up, and he arose. Mark 9:14–27

Jesus' disciples seemed to utter (or was it uhtter?) a lot of *uhs* while accompanying Jesus. There was the *uh* when Jesus told them to find food for thousands of hungry people. Their response to Jesus' command? Maybe there's no Greek equivalent for it. However, my guess is they blankly looked in the Savior's eyes and said, "Uh, sure." Then they shuffled away, scratching their heads. Then they returned with, "Uh, the stores are closed, and uh, we think, uh, these people should go home."

Uhs probably were common companions of miracles. In another incident, the disciples were stuck with an *uh* when they were unable to lure a demon from a possessed boy. The spectators demanded to know why. "And He answered them, 'O faithless generation, how long am I to be with you? How long am I to bear with you? Bring him to Me'" (Mark 9:19).

Uh can be an ugly word when it stands for uncertainty and doubt. How long can Jesus tolerate us when we wonder if the Bible could be wrong? "Uh, do we really go to heaven when we die?" "Uh, how can I prove that God created everything?" "Uh, why would God love sinners?" "Uh, how can babies have faith even before they coo?"

Uh, the Good News is that doubters and other varieties of "uh-ers" often keep their God-given faith despite doubts. (Most of us know that from experience!) Doubt and faith coexist, and sometimes this relationship is even good! Doubt drives us to prayer and Bible study because faith hints that God has answers to our questions, even if we don't always understand them. Once we accept the fact that we don't need to understand the farthest reaches of God's goodness and will, we can trust Him. That trust is so strong, we wonder how we ever could have doubted.

Get Wet

*"On that day there shall be a fountain opened for the house of David and
the inhabitants of Jerusalem, to cleanse them from sin and uncleanness."*
Zechariah 13:1

Ever since some Old Testament child discovered that a stout branch
swished and splashed in a swift-flowing stream created both visual
and tactile amusement, humans have been fascinated by the aesthetic value
of water. Thus, we have fountains.

Haven't fountains flowed a long way? Two fountain displays in Chicago
prove the point. Magnificent old Buckingham Fountain charms thousands of
visitors each year. Its beauty lies in its architecture, as well as the spewing
water illuminated by colored lights. A short distance away are the fountains
of Navy Pier, which are totally devoid of visible structure. They're simply
streams of water arching over walkways and tempting small children (and
adults who wish they were children) to get wet. The water itself is the attraction in these winsome, whimsical displays.

If you've just made it through what had to be the world's longest paragraph devoid of the divinity in a devotion book, you're probably strong
enough to stomach what's next. Perhaps you've heard or sung the spiritual,
"There Is a Fountain Filled with Blood." Picture the best fountain you've ever
seen and replace the water with . . . with . . . with the reason some hymnals
now contain the reworded and less graphic title "There Stands a Fountain
Where for Sin." How strange that in a society that watches violence any given
night on TV, we have to sterilize a graphic hymn!

Every once in a while, and probably more often than we would like, it's
good to picture the price of our sinfulness. What a reviling sight! That Jesus
died a gory, inhumane death on the cross should be enough to make us sick,
especially when we know that it should be our blood filling the fountain. But
the fountain filled with blood really isn't meant to nauseate us. Instead, it
solemnly reminds us of the immense thanks and praise we owe to Jesus.

You'll probably want to leave this devotion with a different picture of
fountains, one more familiar and refreshing. So let's close with words from
Zechariah 13:1: "On that day there shall be a fountain opened for the house
of David and the inhabitants of Jerusalem, to cleanse them from sin and
uncleanness." From that fountain flows the water of Baptism, cleansing us
from the stains of sin and rejuvenating us for an unending life of joy. Jump
right in and splash around!

A Carpenter's Tears

He committed no sin, neither was deceit found in His mouth. When He was reviled, He did not revile in return; when He suffered, He did not threaten, but continued entrusting Himself to Him who judges justly. He Himself bore our sins in His body on the tree, that we might die to sin and live to righteousness. By His wounds you have been healed. 1 Peter 2:22–24

They bought the old house. What impressed them most about the structure? The woodwork. That seems to be the stock answer when anyone asks about old houses. It's ironic that people who lived in old houses before they were old houses often painted over the rich grains and luster of the woodwork because the decor was old! It's enough to make a carpenter cry.

Then there was the era when people didn't like the "modern" woodwork in their homes because it was too sterile. So they applied "antique kits" to make the wood look rich and warm. Sometimes it turned out cheap and gaudy, but at least it was antique. It's enough to make a carpenter cry.

My aunt and uncle's house had the best woodwork, but only in the kitchen. It was red. Against the contrasting yellow walls, it warmed the artistic embers of this young boy's heart. I thought it was cool. It was enough to make a carpenter cry. The truth, of course, is that woodwork is nothing unless it adorns comfortable and happy surroundings.

Jesus worked wood. He probably learned cutting and assembling and fastening at His earthly dad's workbench. How Joseph must have marveled at Jesus' potential as a master craftsman. Could it even be that Joseph was a little disappointed when Jesus took on a different career? Was it enough to make a carpenter cry?

Jesus remained in the woodworking field. In fact, He became a master craftsman. The Bible says of Jesus, "He himself bore our sins in His body on the tree, that we might die to sin and live to righteousness. By His wounds you have been healed" (1 Peter 2:24). When this Carpenter cried from the cross, the whole universe heard, even to the very depths of hell.

Jesus fashioned the rough, unfinished wood of the cross into a work of art. He transformed that crude, lethal lumber into a symbol of forgiveness and unconditional love. His work remains functional as well as beautiful even today. Jewelers forge crosses into ornaments often worn by people ignorant of what the symbol represents. Yet for millions of us who believe, it's a reminder of what Christ has won for us.

You might not buy (or excuse!) a house based on the beauty of its woodwork, but never cease to praise Jesus for His.

Naming Names

We who are strong have an obligation to bear with the failings of the weak, and not to please ourselves. Let each of us please his neighbor for his good, to build him up. For Christ did not please Himself, but as it is written, "The reproaches of those who reproached you fell on Me."
Romans 15:1–3

On a scale of 1 to 5, how would you rate your faith? If you find this exercise incomprehensible, think of it this way: Suppose you found yourself in church and when the collection basket is passed, you have only a $20 bill. (This places a test of faith on crudely practical terms, doesn't it?)

Okay, have you rated yourself? Now think of someone whose faith probably would rate lower. Aha—lots of people fit this category, right? Finally, think of someone whose faith you would rate higher than yours. How does it feel to rate lower?

After all that evaluating, shouldn't we just forget it? Besides, God tells us to leave the judging to Him. Should we not name names? God has this to say: "We who are strong have an obligation to bear with the failings of the weak, and not to please ourselves. Let each of us please his neighbor for his good, to build him up" (Romans 15:1–2).

When God orders us not to judge others, He really means that we, of all people, aren't qualified to condemn. God could have ended the world before we came to faith, but He patiently waited for us. His patience continues, and its primary purpose is to bring more people into His heavenly kingdom. Besides, we're unable to peer into our peers to see the condition of their souls. This doesn't mean we ignore those whose faith appears weak—especially those who clearly expose their weaknesses.

What can we do for the apparently weak? We can adopt God's patience, though this may be tough. How long can you comfort and assure those believers who seem ever so forgetful about taking their troubles to God? How can you deal with that friend who persists in a pet sin (such as homosexual behavior or drug or substance abuse) despite professing faith in Jesus as Savior? Then there's that person who looks back at you from the mirror every morning—the one who intimately knows your spiritual weaknesses and persistent sinfulness—and won't free you from guilt.

Jesus is God of the sinners and the weak. He saved us despite our weakness. Now He empowers us to pray for others who are weak. So go ahead, name names. Be sure to include your own.

Here Today

*For He whom God has sent utters the words of God, for He gives the
Spirit without measure. The Father loves the Son and has given all things
into His hand. Whoever believes in the Son has eternal life; whoever does
not obey the Son shall not see life, but the wrath of God remains on him.*
John 3:27–36

Have you noticed how we work so hard to make life easy? You've
probably discovered that the best things in life are free. It's all the
"second bests" that cost so much. With all the getting and losing in life, no
wonder some call it a game. Some game. By the time we learn the rules, we're
too old to play! How good to know that despite the occasional chaos of life,
we're still in it! And things will only get better.

So much of life seems devoted to improving its quality. Scientists, engineers, educators, counselors, and physicians combine the latest technology
with personal creativity to refine everything from door handles to artificial
hearts, mosquito abatement to lip gloss, anxiety-filled nights to dousing
heartburn. They even meet with some success.

However, for every new, life-enriching invention, there is at least one life-
marring discovery—one new indication that sin continues to make life on
earth less satisfying. Therefore, it's fitting to remember what the Bible says:
"Whoever believes in the Son has eternal life; whoever does not obey the Son
shall not see life, but the wrath of God remains on him" (John 3:36).

Not only is the best thing in life free, it already has been discovered and
it's surprisingly simple. Believe in Jesus and you have eternal life, and eternal
life begins the moment you believe. In other words, we're living for eternity
right here, right now! Not that we won't be moving someday, but when we
do, it's certain to signal upward mobility.

Some might view this scriptural concept of eternal life as somewhat pre-
mature. How often haven't we thought of eternal life as commencing with
death? But living here, living now, knowing we'll live forever suggests a few
things about how we live.

We live like we've got nothing to lose. Why hold grudges and bitter memories when we can forgive as Jesus forgives? Why mourn the passing years (or
months or days or minutes) when we still have all of life ahead of us? Why
focus so much attention on ourselves when we could work to serve others?
(We'll have a long, long time for rest and recreation later.)

Enjoy life. Ask God to help you cope with its challenges and down times.
Praise God for all the good times. Thank Him for putting you here. Always
remember that your future is out of this world.

Gone Tomorrow

For to me to live is Christ, and to die is gain. If I am to live in the flesh,
that means fruitful labor for me. Yet which I shall choose I cannot tell. I
am hard pressed between the two. My desire is to depart and be with
Christ, for that is far better. But to remain in the flesh is more
necessary on your account. Philippians 1:21–24

What are your plans for tomorrow? Next week? Next month? What are your hopes for next year? God willing, those plans will reach fruition. God willing, they may not. The only significant factor is God's will. Yet this is not meant to sound pessimistic or fatalistic.

Listen to the apostle Paul: "I am hard pressed between the two. My desire is to depart and be with Christ, for that is far better. But to remain in the flesh is more necessary on your account" (Philippians 1:23–24). Paul was eagerly willing to be here today and gone tomorrow, though if God kept Him alive, he recognized its purpose. That's a great, godly philosophy for life and death.

Speaking of a life and death philosophy, have you ever thought about living life backward? In some ways, it's a reality for Christians. We begin with death and progress through life. Paul, in another letter, said that faith begins with the death of sin. When the Holy Spirit implants faith in our soul, it takes us from the catacombs of sin into fresh new life.

For many of us, our date of death was the day we were baptized. Now we're living that part of life between death and entirely new life. Like Paul, we sometimes yearn to escape our present stage of life in favor of living in greater spiritual, emotional, social, and physical ease. Yet that might not be God's will. In that case, it is God's way of saying that we still have a purpose on earth.

Just what is your God-given purpose? Are you like Paul—in the company of others who need your witness and service? Probably. Even if you're seriously ill or homebound or physically challenged, others need you. They need to see how you face life's hazards and hardships. If you're prosperous, healthy, and happy, others need to see how you handle that particular challenge too.

The neat thing about starting life at death (of sin) is that all our plans for the future are certain. Whatever happens to us today, we can trust God to do what's best. It may mean that we're here today and gone tomorrow. By the way, if you're gone tomorrow, we'll know where you went.

At Your Doorstep

But how are they to call on Him in whom they have not believed? And
how are they to believe in Him of whom they have never heard? And how
are they to hear without someone preaching? And how are they to preach
unless they are sent? As it is written, "How beautiful are the feet of those
who preach the good news!" But they have not all obeyed the gospel. For
Isaiah says, "Lord, who has believed what he has heard from us?" So faith
comes from hearing, and hearing through the word of Christ.
Romans 10:14–17

Who delivers your news? My newspaper comes regularly early every morning. And I'm doubly blessed because I don't need to bend down to pick it up off the driveway. Our dog does it. By the time I get the paper into the house, the dog has even digested some of the news for me! How's that for service?

It's convenient to have the newspaper delivered each day. It's probably the only way I'd ever routinely read the comics—er, news. Newspaper delivery reminds me of the Gospel—God's Good News delivered to our very soul by the Holy Spirit.

Now it may be stretching the point to compare the Holy Spirit to a paperboy (if you'll excuse an old-fashioned term with no sexist undercurrent intended). Paperboys of yore usually accommodated their customers. It wasn't so much altruism as straightforward economics that provided the motivation. A happy customer meant a healthy tip. So if you asked the paperboy to leave the paper inside the storm door, he did. Good paperboys delivered newspapers according to their patrons' needs.

The Holy Spirit delivers the Good News according to each individual's needs too. He knows how best to leave faith folded snugly in our souls, waiting to be unfolded and read and believed. The Holy Spirit's call to duty does go beyond that of the paperboy's, however, because the Spirit helps us as we read the news—a quiet, invisible partner who encourages us to believe and respond to God's love through Jesus Christ.

By the way, I didn't tell you everything about my delivery dog. If I don't keep her on a leash while she retrieves the paper, she likes to deliver parts of the paper to various neighbors. While that would leave me with serious gaps in the news, it's a good model for people to follow when they receive the Good News. Spread it around.

Good News—Section I

And which now has been manifested through the appearing of our Savior
Christ Jesus, who abolished death and brought life and immortality to
light through the gospel. 2 Timothy 1:10

Newspapers are good for many things. They let us know what happened—mostly bad—since the last edition. They keep us informed of what's expected to happen—such as meetings, weather predictions, upcoming trials, and local government (with the last two often in the same article). Newspapers have certain "advantages" over radio and TV news too. For example, they can be employed as a portable wall to discourage breakfast conversation or curled rigidly to smack bugs. But enough about newspapers. On to Section I—the big news.

Newspapers boldly confront you on the front page. Headlines scream, shock, scare, or sadden. Sometimes, like when the home team wins a championship, the news lifts our spirits. If we had to narrow the Good News to a front-page headline, perhaps it would be 2 Timothy 1:10: "And which now has been manifested through the appearing of our Savior Christ Jesus, who abolished death and brought life and immortality to light through the gospel."

Granted, that headline would take up the entire front page, but at least it's worth reading. It's even a direct quote! It's the most important event of the day—in fact, the most important announcement in all history. It's a scoop to fulfill the most avid reporter's dreams! For us, it's even better because it reveals Good News.

Good News, like most Section I stories, is surrounded by bad news. Surrounded may be too tame a description. Inundated would be more accurate. Just analyze the first section of your newspaper. You probably can count the good news articles on one finger. Bad news is far more typical. That truly reflects real life. So much sin and its companions suffering, destruction, and violence! It makes us yearn for Good News.

God's Good News gives our souls a lift. It tells us that even in the glut of horror, fear, and sadness, Jesus is our Protector, Comforter, and Savior. He is a real life Hero, powerful enough to frustrate the devil's attempts to rape our souls and strangle us with sin.

Most headlines lead to longer stories. The same is true with the Good News. Write your own story now, even if you only pen it in your mind. Review your personal news event—the who, what, when, where, why, and how of your salvation. Just be sure to give WHO the most space.

Good News—Section II

And He died for all, that those who live might no longer live for them-
selves but for Him who for their sake died and was raised. 2 Corinthians
5:11–15

At what age did you begin to understand why people read the obituaries as if it were a nationally syndicated column? (Excuse me if you haven't reached that age yet.) I must confess that I read them now too. I'm always relieved when I don't find my name listed.

Obituaries reveal much about people, or rather, what others thought important about the deceased. The number 1 priority seems to be family—who is left behind and who went ahead. Then comes the suggested memorials that often provide clues about what killed the person or which organization the deceased favored.

Even God's Good News has an obituary page, and you can guess the most prominent name. Jesus does deserve top billing! How might His obituary read? Try this: "And He died for all, that those who live might no longer live for themselves but for Him who for their sake died and was raised" (2 Corinthians 5:15).

While some people weep when they spot the name of a relative or an old friend in the obituaries, we need not feel sad about seeing Jesus' name. There are several reasons for this. Surely we mourn the fact that our sins caused Jesus' death. But in God's grand plan to save us, Jesus did exactly what needed doing. He obeyed His Father, lived a sinless life, and shed His blood that we might be saved. Jesus did God's will, and He did it for us.

Perhaps the most important reason not to mourn is that Jesus didn't remain dead. The Son of God rose from the tomb, demonstrating to all believers what would happen to them. Death has claimed millions for far more than three days, but to those whose earthly lives have ended, time isn't important. Isn't it wonderful to think of all our loved ones who will wake and rise just as their Savior did 2,000 years ago?

Were an obituary written for Jesus today, it would list the usual particulars—born Christmas, died Good Friday, rose Easter. There's no body to lie in state or grave to visit, but memorials of praise to God would be appreciated in lieu of flowers. The list of Jesus' siblings probably would consume the entire Sunday edition of the New York Times and more. Somewhere in that long list of famous people like Esther, David, Peter, and Paul, you would find your name. So weep if you must, but make your tears droplets of joy.

Good News—Section III

And in a little while the heavens grew black with clouds and wind, and
there was a great rain. And Ahab rode and went to Jezreel. And the hand
of the Lord was on Elijah, and he gathered up his garment and ran before
Ahab to the entrance of Jezreel. 1 Kings 18:45–46

It's often the first section located by a large segment of the population. Readers eagerly scan the columns to learn how their favorite pack of millionaires fared. Were they trounced, or was victory won by a scant margin? What indiscretions did they commit, and what did they have to say about themselves? Where do they stand in the win/loss column? What are their chances for future fame? Yes, the sports section makes for exciting reading.

Are you a sports fan? If so, you've probably enjoyed about the same ratio of pleasure to aggravation that gamblers experience. Even the great athletic dynasties eventually tumble as players are traded or sold like shares of stock. But to give sports credit where due, without pastimes such as baseball, how would kids ever learn the national anthem?

Would the Good News have a sports page? You may remember Paul's talk about running the spiritual race with perseverance and striving to win for God. A lesser figure on the sports page, however, was an old man named Elijah. One of today's athletic apparel clothing companies would have offered him a generous reward for endorsing its running sandals according to this news report: "And in a little while the heavens grew black with clouds and wind, and there was a great rain. And Ahab rode and went to Jezreel. And the hand of the Lord was on Elijah, and he gathered up his garment and ran before Ahab to the entrance of Jezreel" (1 Kings 18:45–46).

Old Elijah sounds like a speedy mudder in the fourth race at Jezreel. What were the odds of Elijah beating a horse? The odds were very odd. In fact, it was no contest because "the power of the Lord" fueled Elijah's sprint. Elijah, humble prophet that he was, probably didn't think of this as a race. (Maybe he just wanted to get in out of the rain!)

Next time you read the sports section, think of Elijah. Think of yourself too. Are you a winner or a loser? Count your name in the win column, not because you can throw a touchdown, whack a goal, fling a 97 m.p.h. fastball, arch a three pointer, or KO the devil. Instead, you have God's power to fight sin and to score victories of grace and mercy in His name. You are indeed a winner, coached by the Holy Spirit, and clinging to the triumphant robe-tails of Jesus. The best news is, He'll never trade you to another team.

Good News—Section IV

The Lord your God is in your midst, a mighty one who will save; He will
rejoice over you with gladness; He will quiet you by His love; He will
exult over you with loud singing. Zephaniah 3:17

They won't keep you current on events like the front page does, nor will they promise riches like the financial section. You might sacrifice delicious recipes, forego the marvels of new home furnishings, and be less conscious of new fashions as well. But never, never skip the section of the newspaper with the comics. Why is Sarge socking Beetle today? Is Snoopy starting another book from atop his doghouse? How has Hagar's wife tamed the lovable Hun this time? Then there's Dilbert, simultaneously exposing and suffering corporate folly.

Comic strips break the tension of breaking news. Although they create plots of their own, we know they're not real. Often they reveal some of life's foolishness and invite us to laugh at ourselves. For a few moments, we have the opportunity to eavesdrop on the thoughts and behavior of people we'd either love to meet or want to avoid.

God doesn't need comic strips. He only needs to look at the pages of human history—our personal history included—to observe many of the same situations we scan in the comics. Much of what He sees isn't funny. In fact, it's enough to make a Creator cry. Our mistreatment of others, the environment, and everything else under His bright sun must make God shake His holy head in rueful acknowledgment that such things really exist in the world for which He had such high hopes.

Certainly, God must have His lighter moments too. Zephaniah 3:17 says, "The Lord your God is in your midst, a mighty one who will save; He will rejoice over you with gladness; He will quiet you by His love; He will exult over you with loud singing." Yes, maybe God smiles just a little as He watches your attempts to do His will. He's pleased that you want to obey and honor Him. He probably grins as He anticipates that time when you'll join Him in heaven, never to bumble around again. He looks into your heart and reads your thoughts, knowing your hopes and worries, your insecurities and courage, your failures and successes, your tears and laughter.

Next time you read the comics, think of God reading your life. Do something today to delight Him. Give God a good laugh. While you're at it, laugh along with Him.

Good News—Section V

For the time is coming when people will not endure sound teaching, but having itching ears they will accumulate for themselves teachers to suit their own passions. 2 Timothy 4:3

One section of every newspaper seems to have limited criteria for its writers. It seems like any knucklehead can make it into print. People with fine ideas like your own—well, they don't seem to get many opportunities. Still, an occasional writer must really be wise. She thinks so much like you! The news may depress you, and the comics may brighten your mood, but nothing has the potential to boil your blood or invigorate your intellect like the editorials.

Perhaps you've read the weepy words of someone who considers himself broad-minded. However, in your humble opinion, he's confusing a broad mind with a fat head. Have you noticed how easy it is to assert a conviction based on a few facts? Very few?

The Bible warns against misguided, impaired opinions and those who support them: "For the time is coming when people will not endure sound teaching, but having itching ears they will accumulate for themselves teachers to suit their own passions" (2 Timothy 4:3).

Both opinions and editorials make ears itch. Sometimes they make ears red too. God sets us straight with the words recorded in Timothy, and He's not just expressing His opinion. So many viewpoints run counter to God's teachings. Equally many spite His will. Then there are notions that seem benign but cover some sinful abscess. Among these inflammatory biases are the ideas that we control our own futures and that all lifestyles and behaviors are okay. Such ideas are wicked whispers in itching ears. Perhaps the most dangerous ideas, however, involve beliefs that sin doesn't exist or that somehow we can save ourselves by being good.

Who needs opinions when we have Jesus—the same Jesus that blots out our sins and sends His Holy Spirit to help us fight our evil, human inclinations? Who needs convictions to the contrary when we have forgiveness and salvation for free, having done nothing to earn it? Why deny sin's existence when we observe the glut of tragedy-making headlines or the pangs of our personal tragedies? We have a real God who loved us so much that He sent His Son to take the form of a man, one named Jesus, to suffer and die and defeat sin. For us. That's no opinion. These are facts boldly reported in the Bible. Isn't it great to agree with a real Expert?

Whatever

"All things are lawful," but not all things are helpful. "All things are lawful," but not all things build up. Let no one seek his own good, but the good of his neighbor. 1 Corinthians 10:23–33

Our competitive world of give and take is unbalanced. Too many people are on the take! Selfishness seems to go by various names. The extent of its facade of acceptability seems expressed by the deceptively casual word *whatever*. For example, it's Sunday morning and church bells are ringing. Howie stretches and yawns, thinking his alarm clock sounds awfully far away. His wife rolls over to face him and asks, "Are you golfing or going to church this morning?" He answers, "It's a little late for golf, so I guess I'll go to church." Mrs. Howie says, "Whatever." Then she buries her head in the pillow.

Paul had a "whatever" for the congregation in Corinth, though his was less blasé. In addressing the restrictions some felt necessary for Christians, he said, "'All things are lawful,' but not all things are helpful. 'All things are lawful,' but not all things build up. Let no one seek his own good, but the good of his neighbor" (1 Corinthians 10:23–24).

Christians sometimes wonder what they can and cannot do. Paul proclaims freedom for Christians, but sometimes exercising that freedom might not seem right. Suppose you're invited to play pinnocle, er . . . peenockle, er . . . poker. You've played the penny ante variety with friends for years, but a newer friend, one who is a recent convert to Christianity, wonders aloud whether this is proper. What do you do?

A) Figure out how to spell pinochle?

B) Ask your new friend to sit and watch?

C) Explain the difference between a friendly game and abject gambling?

D) Substitute pretzels, chips (poker or potato), etc. for pennies?

Getting back to card games, should we even play cards or otherwise socialize with people who don't share the intensity of our values? Can I play cards with people who also deal cursing and dirty jokes?

Within the vast liberty Christians have for living a Christian life, restrictions—motivated by love and concern—sometimes supersede that freedom. We ask, "Will weaker Christians weaken more as they ponder my behavior? Will non-Christians lose respect for Christ because of my actions? How can I balance standing firm in my Christian convictions and maintaining friendships?"

Whatever your answers may be, don't let them be "Whatever!"

Relief Pitcher

And it shall come to pass afterward, that I will pour out My Spirit on all flesh; your sons and your daughters shall prophesy, your old men shall dream dreams, and your young men shall see visions. Joel 2:28

You know what a relief pitcher is. It's someone brought in to replace a pitcher who's suffering whiplash from watching line drives whiz past him or who's been kicked out of the baseball players' union because he doesn't understand the word strike. Of course, "relief pitcher" may be familiar to nonbaseball fans too. For example, "It was so hot that Cleve drank all the lemonade, and we had to bring in a relief pitcher."

Relief pitchers in whatever form might remind us of what God said through the prophet Joel: "And it shall come to pass afterward, that I will pour out My Spirit on all flesh; your sons and your daughters shall prophesy, your old men shall dream dreams, and your young men shall see visions" (Joel 2:28).

God kept His promise on Pentecost when He poured the Holy Spirit into a small crowd of people. Peter, remembering the words of Joel, quoted them to the crowd. Indeed, it was a day of relief and refreshment!

With Jesus returned to heaven, the apostles needed relief if they were to obey God's mission command. It's not like they were baseball players. They weren't that wealthy. Besides that, they were good at what they were doing. But they needed a platoon of "relievers" to swell their ranks as they pitched the Gospel to thousands of eager ears. The Holy Spirit met their needs by empowering others not only to know God's Word, but to continue to spread that Word to others.

The Holy Spirit has worked in similar ways ever since Pentecost. How else could we read God's Word firsthand? How else could we learn at Bible class or grow through sermons? And the Spirit recruits us to pitch in relief also. Who needs to experience God's grace and mercy today? Who needs to know that Jesus cares for them?

The Spirit's pitcher of refreshment is less like baseball and more like lemonade. We sinners feel the heat of sin and the sweat of guilt. Satan parches our souls with his accusations, and we plaintively admit that he's right. But through the refreshing, rejuvenating, regenerating outpouring of the Holy Spirit, we believe that Jesus quenches our thirst for salvation. So go ahead, ask for another drink. The Relief Pitcher is ready and waiting.

Knock, Knock. Who's There?

Everyone who goes on ahead and does not abide in the teaching of Christ,
does not have God. Whoever abides in the teaching has both the Father
and the Son. If anyone comes to you and does not bring this teaching, do
not receive him into your house or give him any greeting. 2 John 1:9–10

Have you heard the one about the grouch who bought the grump's version of the welcome mat. It says, "Go away."

You probably wish you had a mat like that when those well-dressed people carrying briefcases, brochures, and books go door to door. Once in a while, young children accompany them. Normally, they present no threat to personal safety, but sometimes they're a quiet but spiritually lethal threat. What can we do about them?

A neighbor once suggested that I should welcome these door-to-door zealots into my home. Then, because I'm a church worker, I should set them straight. After all, aren't these people bound for hell unless somebody intervenes?

Have you ever refused to answer your door when you suspected the theological persuasions of those on the other side? Maybe, according to John, that's not a cowardly idea after all. John says, "Everyone who goes on ahead and does not abide in the teaching of Christ, does not have God. Whoever abides in the teaching has both the Father and the Son. If anyone comes to you and does not bring this teaching, do not receive him into your house or give him any greeting" (2 John 1:9–10).

Many door-to-door witnesses are well trained and prepared to answer challenges. They're also capable of questioning and debating your faith. Before you invite them in, find out whom they represent. It will be either Jesus or the devil, though they will never admit the latter because they have personally been deceived. Based on the words from John, our Savior wouldn't be disappointed if you refused to engage in spiritually oriented conversation with such people, especially if you fear the impact they may have on your faith life. You may be equally at risk if you're confident in your faith! These false teachers have reasonable, logical retorts to almost anything you throw at them.

Next time you hear the knock knock on your door, find out who's there. Sometimes it's no joke.

Toothless

*Then Job answered and said: "How long will you torment me? . . . And
even if it be true that I have erred, my error remains with myself. If
indeed you magnify yourselves against me and make my disgrace an argument against me, know then that God has put me in the wrong and
closed His net about me. . . . He has stripped from me my glory and
taken the crown from my head. . . . All my intimate friends abhor me,
and those whom I loved have turned against me. My bones stick to my
skin and to my flesh, and I have escaped by the skin of my teeth."*
Job 19:1–20

Did you know the Bible mentions teeth often enough to make some
of us jealous? Consider this lover's compliment from Song of
Solomon 6:6, "Your teeth are like a flock of ewes that have come up from the
washing; all of them bear twins; not one among them has lost its young." Can
you imagine what might happen if you said that to the one you love? (A sweet
nothing that tops this is the old "Your teeth are like stars. They come out at
night.")

While we're on the subject of teeth, Job coined a phrase that is still used
today. He said, "My bones stick to my skin and to my flesh, and I have escaped
by the skin of my teeth" (Job 19:20).

Have you ever opened wide in the bathroom mirror in an attempt to discover the skin of your teeth? I hope not. You have undoubtedly experienced
the close calls or near escapes that the phrase suggests though.

If you've read Job 19, you've discovered that Job definitely sported an
"attitude." He was angry with his friends and with God because of his suffering. He watched as his family and possessions were destroyed—and he had
considerable amounts of both. He knew that he himself had escaped termi-
nation only by the skin of his teeth.

The "skin of the teeth" syndrome applies to us as well. We might use it to
describe our flight from sin's eternal effect. We were lost and condemned.
God could have ended the world at any moment, but He waited for us to
become believers. He continues to wait, mercifully patient with those who
will yet believe. He remains mysteriously silent on when time will end.
Believers from the past, present, and future will indeed escape His wrath by
the skin of their teeth.

Jesus had no such delay from hellish suffering. He refused to escape
death's pains and pangs, though to do so was within His power. Instead, He
put some skin on our teeth and pushed us past the devastating destruction we
deserve.

Are You Talking to Me?

*"But in Mount Zion there shall be those who escape, and it shall be holy,
and the house of Jacob shall possess their own possessions. The house of
Jacob shall be a fire, and the house of Joseph a flame, and the house of
Esau stubble; they shall burn them and consume them, and there shall be
no survivor for the house of Esau, for the Lord has spoken."*
Obadiah 1:17–18

Sometimes the Bible is as confusing as a jigsaw puzzle. Perhaps you're one of those patient souls who keeps a "puzzle in progress" on a card table in your living room, sliding and flipping anonymous pieces until they find a home. One old man was like that. It took him three years of retirement to finish one puzzle. Later, he learned that his wife had tossed pieces under his easy chair to keep him occupied and out of her hair.

If you've endeavored to read the Bible from cover to cover without aid from a study guide, you've probably asked God, "Are You talking to me?" One passage that might motivate such a question is the one above from Obadiah.

Does it sometimes seem the Bible is not relevant to modern life? So much of God's Word is history that we're tempted to forget that we're history too. It's just that our history is happening now. But there must be some way to relate the entire Bible to our present life, otherwise why would God leave all those words for us? The answer lies in the fact that perhaps we shouldn't read the entire Bible—or at least not without guidance from trustworthy study guides to help edify us, especially as we traverse the tough, hard to understand places.

Today's selection from Obadiah is just one piece of the Bible. It has a place in God's Word just as a plain blue piece of cardboard fits somewhere in a puzzle. Without that piece the puzzle is incomplete. It's true of Scripture too: Every verse plays a role in the complete story of God's love for sinners and His hatred of sin.

As for the relevance of Obadiah 1:17–18, a reliable commentary interprets it thusly. Mount Zion was the location of Solomon's temple to God—the home of God on earth. Despite the ravages it suffered, God promised to send the inheritance—His Promised One—to live among the people and to save them. He would be right where they could see Him. And it's really no puzzle at all who that Promised One was.

Silence Is . . .

But the angel said to him, ". . .Your prayer has been heard, and your wife
Elizabeth will bear you a son." . . . And Zechariah said to the angel,
"How shall I know this? For I am an old man, and my wife is advanced
in years." And the angel answered him, ". . .You will be silent and unable
to speak until the day that these things take place, because you did not
believe my words." Luke 1:13–20

Silence truly is what you said it was when you silently inserted a word
for ". . ." in the title. Not that everyone would agree with silence's des-
ignation as a precious metal. Take Zechariah for example.

He was a priest who served part-time in the temple at Jerusalem. One
thing bothered him. He and his wife of many years were childless—a dirty
disgrace in ancient Jewish culture. Although he and his wife, Elizabeth, probably prayed often, their prayers seemed to have gone unheard. When God
finally answered the couple's prayer, it was more than Zechariah could handle and he questioned the angel. Armed with God's power, Gabriel gave a
definitive response: "You will be silent and unable to speak until the day that
these things take place, because you did not believe my words, which will be
fulfilled in their time" (Luke 1:20). Gabriel imposed harsh consequences for
what seemed like logical doubt.

Except when it comes to God and His messengers, doubts are better left
unexpressed—especially if they're coming from someone respected as a leader
in faith. So it was for Zechariah a personal blessing that he was struck dumb.
Now he couldn't question God's Word nor could he utter skepticism or even
mild misgivings. Silence, as you probably know, provides plenty of time for
listening and thinking.

It might be good if we were struck dumb on occasion. If your faith is
active, people know that you're a Christian. People know you believe. They
watch and listen too. If they hear you angrily curse your boss or computer or
brakes or aching muscles, they wonder about you. They wonder about Christ.
Then there may be times when they see how you ignore them when they're
hurting. Failure to voice forgiveness—well, that's anything but golden silence.

Pray that God would silence all our doubts and give us golden words for
golden opportunities.

No Apologies

*For even if I made you grieve with my letter, I do not regret it—though I
did regret it, for I see that that letter grieved you, though only for a while.
As it is, I rejoice, not because you were grieved, but because you were
grieved into repenting. 2 Corinthians 7:8–9*

If you ever feel lonely and ignored, the fastest way to remedy the situation is to make a major mistake. To err used to be human, but now far
too many people are blatantly human! Of course, the best thing about blun-
ders is that we can learn from them. Some of us have a fantastic education!
Then there are the others—those who invent creative ways to blame others.

The apostle Paul crammed the postal system with letters addressed to
congregations that operated in mistake mode. One such congregation was at
Corinth, and Paul minced no words. He called the mistakes of the believers
by their proper nomenclature—sins. Paul also said: "For even if I made you
grieve with my letter, I do not regret it—though I did regret it, for I see that
that letter grieved you, though only for a while" (2 Corinthians 7:8).

Now most of us might not be so bold, which probably is proven by personal experience. When is the last time (unless you're a parent of young children) that you exposed someone's mistakes? Better yet, have you recently
called anyone's mistakes a sin? Or if you're in a position to evaluate others—
on the job, in the home, behind the teacher's desk—have you found yourself
apologetically (sometimes mistakenly called tact) exposing one's errors?

I'm not implying that we need to appoint ourselves Accuser General! We
need only examine our own lives to observe thriving sin. Admittedly, we
would bristle if our neighbor or spouse or sibling or pastor confronted us
with the ugly truth, though, like Paul, they would assist us by doing so. If
we're afraid or too pompous to identify our own sinfulness, we might just
miss the best news of our lives.

Never fear hearing about your sinfulness. Don't feel offended if someone
marks your mistakes. (Even if they feel good about it!) Thank them for bringing you to the cross where you can dump your sins. Pile them high. The cross
is no longer occupied with gasping and flinching flesh. Jesus' work is done.
He took away your sins, and He continues to forgive you.

In the end, when God finally brings you to judgment, you'll need no further apologies. Jesus has completely erased your mistakes—okay, your sins!

Relics

But Mary treasured up all these things, pondering them in her heart. And the shepherds returned, glorifying and praising God for all they had heard and seen, as it had been told them. Luke 2:19–20

You know you're getting old if others refer to your sweater, your TV, your car, or even your body as a relic. It would be better to call you or your belongings an antique, at least they're valuable. But relics? Often the word and the idea behind the word are spoken with contempt.

At one time, the Christian church was infested with relics. Any church that possessed a bizarre collection of some saint's body parts gained power and influence, members and money. (Today, it probably would gain a coroner's inquiry!) Peter's petrified ear lobe or Thomas' teeth were sure to guarantee some special spiritual blessings (or at least the need to enlarge the congregation's safe). What wasn't funny, however, was that the church misled many believers to trust the "special powers" of worthless relics.

Relics remain today. How easy to venerate the crucifix without honoring the One who hung there. Or perhaps it's the architecture of our favorite church. Could worship really be worship without flying buttresses or arched beams? Maybe it's the liturgy in worship services—an orderly organization of elements sometimes elevated to the authority of Scripture itself. Or perhaps it's that crusty, fragile Bible stuck to the bookcase shelf, the one rarely touched by human hands.

We need no relics. We have Jesus Himself. While we might think of Him when we see crosses or Bibles or pulpits, our loss would be manageable if those were to disappear. We could do what the most famous mother in Nazareth did: "But Mary treasured up all these things, pondering them in her heart" (Luke 2:19).

Like Mary, most of what we ponder about Jesus is pleasant. The dramatic birth announcement, the stunned shepherds under the starry sky, a Baby's cry punctuating the moos and baas and brays. But Mary had piercing ponderings as well. We can only begin to imagine her feelings and thoughts when she heard hammers driving nails through flesh and wood. Then the flash of a sword—and sin—stabbing her Son's side.

The best pondering of all, however, is capturing the essence of Easter in our hearts. It is the greatest treasure ever pondered! We need no splinters of cross nor shreds of burial clothes to remember what was there. Nothing remained of this death because Jesus has risen and lives. For us, His resurrection makes Satan's victory a relic of the past.

Spending Spree

And God is able to make all grace abound to you, so that having all suffi-
ciency in all things at all times, you may abound in every good work. As it
is written, "He has distributed freely, he has given to the poor; his right-
eousness endures forever." He who supplies seed to the sower and bread
for food will supply and multiply your seed for sowing and increase the
harvest of your righteousness. You will be enriched in every way for all
your generosity, which through us will produce thanksgiving to God.
2 Corinthians 9:8–11

What would you do first if you suddenly became vastly richer than
you are now? Would your lifestyle change? With whom, if anyone,
would you share your fortune? Are there any obligations you have as a
Christian? (Oh, there's that question again.) Money is never a cure for
what ails us—socially, emotionally, psychologically, or economically. But real
wealth—that's another story.

Paul assesses our worth this way: "You will be enriched in every way for
all your generosity, which through us will produce thanksgiving to God"
(2 Corinthians 9:11).

Genuine God-given wealth is like easy money. It isn't earned; it's inherited. Wealth that comes from God needs no protection either. It's there for the
taking and sharing. The "catch," of course, is that God's wealth doesn't always
mean dollars—sometimes it's time or talent.

Have you assessed your wealth? Although the Bible downplays the value
of wealth, money and possessions are gifts from God. The implications of
financial prosperity are obvious. Some of that money will do lots of good for
missionaries or hungry children or homeless adults.

Perhaps your greatest treasure is time or talent. Has God blessed you with
retirement yet? Are you working at a job that doesn't make strenuous
demands on your time? If so, count your blessings and begin sharing them
with those who need your presence as opposed to, say, your presents.

Talents? You most certainly have some. Whether it's sewing, carpentry,
telling stories, cutting grass, or solving problems, God rejoices when you use
those skills to His glory and the welfare of others.

When it comes to giving, Jesus was the perfect example, though we cannot carry it to the extremes He did. He gave until it hurt. Because of that, our
giving doesn't have to hurt a bit.

December 5 ⌒

A Handful

Now I know that the Lord saves His anointed; He will answer him from His holy heaven with the saving might of His right hand. Psalm 20:6

Y ou've heard this expression generally applied to a young, rather "active" child: "She's a handful!" Given the usual situation that prompts such a phrase, handful seems to be an understatement. A few olives or a medium tomato—now that's a handful, but trouble and bad behavior? Even a seven-foot tall basketball player lacks large enough palms to hold sin, evil, wickedness, and other varieties of imperfection at bay.

Scripture often talks about hands, especially God's. Now there's a set of capable hands! Here's how the psalmist portrays them: "Now I know that the Lord saves His anointed; He will answer him from His holy heaven with the saving might of His right hand" (Psalm 20:6). God doesn't even need two hands to keep evil in its place!

Any talk of hands leads us to the cross. Among the excruciating cruelties of Roman-style execution was the piercing of Jesus' hands. The same hands that wiped leprosy from infected limbs and tousled the hair of young children, the same hands that caressed the broken-hearted and beckoned dead bodies back to life, the same hands that endlessly broke bread and served fish were impaled to the cross. The sins of the world were indeed a handful—a bloody, throbbing handful. Those sins of the world included yours and mine, and Jesus had to die to save us.

The most common idea associated with God's hands, however, probably isn't the cross. His hand is a symbol of power. Even as they were nailed to the cross, Jesus' hands were hands of power. Jesus was doing something only God could do and live to tell about it. He was strangling sin's power while His equally pierced feet delivered that kick to the head of Satan promised back in the days of Adam and Eve.

Those powerful hands continue to gently stroke His people. Jesus holds out handfuls of mercy and kindness, sprinkling it generously on us, nudging us into the world each day to share His message and His love with others. We can almost see Him raise those hands in blessing, giving comfort and confidence as we live each day for Him. That applies to good times and bad—times when problems such as conflict, pain, anxiety, or fear are too big a handful for us.

The song is right. God does have the whole world in His hands. And that would be quite a handful for anyone but God.

Stop and Smell the Roses

Then Jesus went with them to a place called Gethsemane, and He said to
His disciples, "Sit here, while I go over there and pray." And taking with
Him Peter and the two sons of Zebedee, He began to be sorrowful and
troubled. Then He said to them, "My soul is very sorrowful, even to death;
remain here, and watch with Me." And going a little farther He fell on
His face and prayed. Matthew 26:36–39

Was it Shakespeare who said, "A rose by any other name means that you don't know your flowers very well"? He probably stole the line from his gardener. Roses are only one fragrant flower in God's bouquet of garden miracles. So important are flowers, that most states adopt one as their own. Even the Department of Transportation has an official flower—the cloverleaf!

From gas stations to corporate headquarters to concrete planters in the middle of urban boulevards, flowers brighten mundane life. We rejoice that spring blooms promise the impending death of winter. Summer blossoms soothe our eyes and sweeten the air. Perhaps you've noticed, too, that shortly before the first frost, flowers mellow into their deepest and richest hues.

Gardens, especially one particular garden, meant something different to Jesus. It's something worth remembering, even as we enjoy botanic beauty. Matthew reports this incident involving Jesus in the Garden of Gethsemane: "And going a little farther He fell on His face and prayed, saying, 'My Father, if it be possible, let this cup pass from Me; nevertheless, not as I will, but as You will.' . . . Again, for the second time, He went away and prayed, 'My Father, if this cannot pass unless I drink it, Your will be done'" (Matthew 26:39, 42).

This garden visit by Jesus didn't involve smelling roses. It involved sweating blood. It was as if a shawl of thorns entwined His entire being. Jesus prayed—for Himself, for us. He listened to God's answer as His friends snored in the garden's soon-to-be-shattered serenity. Jesus searched for some other way to take away our sins, perhaps something resembling a garden party to announce victory over sin. But it wasn't in the Father's plan, and Jesus obediently suffered and died for our sins.

Next time you're in a garden, take some time to pray. Oh, you and I are incapable of sweating blood (unless we kneel on a rose bush), and we need not limit our prayers to cries of anguish. Smell the roses, feast your eyes on the petunias, and spend some quality time with the impatiens. Remember how God sent them for your enjoyment, and recall Jesus' moment in the garden. Not the one named Gethsemane, but the one just outside the tomb.

Cheat Sheet

Behold, I have engraved you on the palms of My hands; your walls are
continually before Me. Isaiah 49:16

High school stimulated four years of intellectual creativity among my friends. Most of that creativity involved obtaining a diploma with as little work as possible.

One friend had a fresh approach to preparing for tests. (Actually, it was a historically proven method, but he wasn't very good at history.) He identified several major math formulas that he then wrote on the palm of his hand. We lectured that such behavior was dishonest. When that didn't work, we warned him about getting caught. He disregarded our lectures and made it through the test with nary a suspicious glance from the teacher. He also failed the test. We had him so worried about getting caught that his palms sweated and the ink ran!

One of the last things we would suspect God of doing is cheating, though this passage might suggest otherwise: "Behold, I have engraved you on the palms of My hands; your walls are continually before Me" (Isaiah 49:16). While we know that God doesn't "cheat" to remember us, this passage does bring some graphic comfort into the lives of sinners.

The Bible mentions the Book of Life—that record of believers who will be judged righteous for Jesus' sake. In moments when we fail to appreciate the vast and comprehensive knowledge of our Lord, we may wonder how God keeps track of the millions of saints that will join Him in heaven. Will He find our names in the book? Will He remember us? Does He think about us now?

Intellectually, at least, we know that yes correctly answers each question. But can't you picture God peering into His hand, looking for your name? And finding it, of course!

Today's Bible passage comforted Isaiah's people as they gazed on the wrecked walls of Jerusalem, wondering if God had forgotten them and their holy city. God used picture language to reassure them that He doesn't forget and that they always will be on His "mind." That same consolation is ours as we gawk at the ruins of our lives, which are wracked by sin and Satan. Through Isaiah, God assures us that He remembers how Jesus repaired our broken relationship and that our names already appear on the roles of heaven. If you're afraid you might forget that Good News, draw a cross on the palm of your hand. Just don't do it in water-based ink!

Pardon Our Dust

*And I am sure of this, that He who began a good work in you will bring
it to completion at the day of Jesus Christ. Philippians 1:3–10*

The sign looked friendly. What harm could a little dust do? After all,
renovation and remodeling keep things up to date. Entering the dust
zone, however, we encountered plastic sheets draped from ceiling to floor and
heard the din of drills and saws rattling against concrete and wood. Our noses
were the first to recognize dust. Our eyes noticed it next, releasing a few tears
to float away the grit. We felt it on our hands, too, compelling us to wash
them at the nearest sink. This was only the first of 16 more projects scheduled.
You know, it's bad enough to visit the hospital, but to pardon their dust? Well
. . .

In a way, the Father, Son, and Holy Spirit Construction Company could
hang a "Pardon Our Dust" sign around the necks of all believers. Can you
imagine the puff of dust as God took clay from the ground and breathed life
into it? Just as babies cry as they are born, Adam probably sneezed. God said,
"I bless you," and He did. He's been blessing humans ever since. But Adam
and Eve led the fall into sin, thus necessitating constant renovation projects
by the original Company.

God had a plan to remodel us, and Jesus was the only one who could
implement it. He was born with a dual identity—God and Man—and He
grew up learning the carpentry trade. (How appropriate for the one who ren-
ovates our life!) He lived as sinners should have but couldn't or wouldn't, and
He died to take away our sins. But Jesus came back to life, defeating death and
the devil. In the process, He ripped the wall of sin from our lives. Then He
sent the Holy Spirit to finish the job.

The Holy Spirit began remaking us. He gave us faith, but He also realized
that His work wouldn't end until Jesus returned. The Holy Spirit continues to
work, urging us to repent so He can continue perfecting us. He braces us with
God's Word so we stand strong against the devil. He polishes us with grace so
we have a beautiful luster for the day Jesus returns.

Pardon our dust? Jesus did already. Pardon our dust? There remains much
work as the Spirit labors within us. Will the job ever end? Listen to Paul: "And
I am sure of this, that He who began a good work in you will bring it to completion at the day of Jesus Christ" (Philippians 1:6).

All Natural

A man who had died was being carried out, the only son of his mother,
and she was a widow, and a considerable crowd from the town was with
her. And when the Lord saw her, He had compassion on her and said to
her, "Do not weep." Then He came up and touched the bier, and the
bearers stood still. And He said, "Young man, I say to you, arise."
And the dead man sat up and began to speak, and Jesus
gave him to his mother. Luke 7:12–15

God long has used nature to carry out His miracles. In Old Testament days there were burning bushes, thunder and lightning, fire and water. God often used miracles against His enemies. In New Testament times, Jesus did many miracles, all for the good of His people, which sometimes included enemies. Thus, we see natural water supernaturally transformed into natural wine. We see natural diseases—even death—healed so people could once again live a natural life.

That Jesus healed death is a gracious gift, but it should be no surprise. Along with a large crowd of mourners in the town of Nain, we witness Jesus at work. He met a slow funeral plodding its way to the cemetery. Jesus shared the grief, especially of the widow whose only child was about to be buried. Nature had taken its course in its sinful, tragic way and spoiled the life of a beloved son. But Jesus reversed nature. He commanded the son to arise. Nature yielded, and the young man returned to his mother.

The natural consequences of sin are illness, injury, and death. However, the God who created life and all of nature had power to overcome death. He came to earth as the Man who healed at Nain, and He hung on Calvary's cross as the true Man and true God who suffered, died, and rose to save sinners. How unnatural! And how we might yearn to see a Nain event with our own eyes. Or at least some miracle!

We're tempted to forget that miracles still happen. But considering that God still uses some natural means to accomplish His will, maybe those miracles are now so natural that we fail to notice them? Isn't the birth of a baby still a miracle? Isn't the food we eat, grown from seed, nurtured on sunlight and soil, and able to fuel our bodies still a miracle? Isn't it a miracle that Jesus continues to forgive us despite the suffering we cause? Maybe we should label modern miracles "All Natural!" Natural for a God who loves us in a miraculous way.

Something of Which to Be Proud

But let each one test his own work, and then his reason to boast will be in himself alone and not in his neighbor. Galatians 6:4

If God had intended for us to pat ourselves on the back, He would have made our elbows bend the other way. Experts advise us to swallow our pride. It's probably healthy advice. Pride is never fattening—unless it goes to our head. We all know—and probably dislike—proud people.

Is it ever proper to be proud? Most philosophers probably would cite statements such as "Pride goeth before the fall" or the once-famous lyrics, "You're so vain, you probably think this song is about you." (If you're well beyond or well under your 50s, you probably won't remember the song, but take my word, those were the lyrics. If I had a better memory, I would remember who sang it!)

Back to the question at hand. Is it ever proper to be proud? Paul, in his letter to the Galatians, said, "But let each one test his own work, and then his reason to boast will be in himself alone and not in his neighbor" (Galatians 6:4).

Did Paul really mean you can "be proud of your own accomplishments"? According to this inspired word that came from God through Paul, we can be proud—if our pride doesn't fool us into thinking we're better than others. Paul's "pride" comes from knowing that the Holy Spirit has empowered us to follow God's will and to live a Christian lifestyle.

Most often, pride manifests itself in sinful attitudes of arrogance or exclusiveness. It happens when we forget how sinful we are and how everything truly good about us is good only because Jesus made it that way. It's an especially easy sin for Christians as we get caught up in living according to God's will and absentmindedly give ourselves credit. It happens when we compare ourselves to other sinners and end up feeling good that we're not so bad after all. Good thing this sin, too, is one Jesus readily forgives. Over and over.

Take pride in the truth that God chose to save you for no good reason long before you had any ancestors or tradition of family faith. Be proud that the Holy Spirit works in and through you, though you certainly don't deserve it. Be proud to boast that Jesus died to take away your sin. Let others know they can boast in the same thing because they are just like you.

Cookie Crumbs

"These things I have spoken to you while I am still with you. But the Helper, the Holy Spirit, whom the Father will send in My name, He will teach you all things and bring to your remembrance all that I have said to you. Peace I leave with you; My peace I give to you. Not as the world gives do I give to you. Let not your hearts be troubled, neither let them be afraid." John 14:25–31

Often we know exactly what we will leave behind when we go. Property, investments, and cash end up in the pockets of relatives and friends—with a little on the side for the government, of course. There are all the forgotten incidentals too—memorabilia residing in basements and attics that is destined for yet another basement or attic because relatives can't bear to part with it. Besides what we can count and see and lift and dust and toss, there remains even more to leave behind—experiences take up as much space as sentiment allows.

We don't have to die to leave things behind, however. Take cookie crumbs, for example. That's a legacy I leave to the cleaning rag every day after breakfast. Feelings count too. What do we leave behind as we interact with family, friends, acquaintances, and even strangers on a daily basis?

Jesus left some things behind too. John 14:27 quotes Jesus as saying, "Peace I leave with you; My peace I give to you. Not as the world gives do I give to you. Let not your hearts be troubled, neither let them be afraid." Jesus didn't leave any crumbs. He left the whole cookie! Now we enjoy what He left behind.

Don't be deceived. The peace Jesus left isn't the kind discussed at the United Nations. It's not the peace that is shattered nightly in both random and premeditated acts of violence. In fact, it has little to do with external conditions. True peace is a matter of attitude—a condition of trust and contentment that is rooted in God's love for us. This peace exists despite war, domestic bloodshed, climatic terrors, chaotic health, or family feuds. It's a peace that is incomprehensible to all who don't have it.

You and I have the peace Jesus left behind. We know where we've been, and admittedly, we've been some terrible places. We also know where we're going, and we're going there because Jesus sacrificed the peace that was at His command to die a most unpeaceful death on Calvary. It's the peace we have because we know that Jesus waits for us to arrive in a place where tranquility and ecstasy coexist.

December 12 ～

Geography Lessons

*And he said, "Thus says the LORD, 'I will make this dry streambed full of
pools.' For thus says the LORD, 'You shall not see wind or rain, but that
streambed shall be filled with water, so that you shall drink, you, your
livestock, and your animals.'" 2 Kings 3:16–17*

This begins a series of three meditations based on geography. Was it
one of your favorite subjects in school? Many students like the subject, probably because it's easy to relate to the main ideas. Most of us have
seen geographical features such as mountains, hills, valleys, rivers, lakes, and
Uncle Egbert's nose. Like any subject, of course, geography includes many
advanced concepts and a specialized vocabulary—such as "diurnal varia-
tions," which is easily confused with plumbing terminology.

Valleys are something everybody understands. We've heard of places such
as the Hudson River Valley, the Red River Valley, and Rudy Vallee. Valleys are
normally fertile places, lower and more temperate than the landforms surrounding them. Exceptions, of course, are places such as Death Valley.

The Bible mentions many valleys. Some of them are more image than
reality as in the "Valley of the Shadow of Death" mentioned in Psalm 23.
Doesn't this sound like a pleasant place? "For thus says the Lord, 'You shall
not see wind or rain, but that streambed shall be filled with water, so that you
shall drink, you, your livestock, and your animals'" (2 Kings 3:17). Here's a
valley that sounds as though it should be named "Jesus' Valley."

Jesus' Valley is located around every Christian. In actuality, it's more an
oasis than a valley. The valley's climate is refreshing, soothing, and nourishing. It stands in stark contrast to the areas outside its boundaries—places
where sin has parched all life and decay spreads rampantly.

Sin's blight exists within the valley too, but Christians seem inoculated
against its deadly effect. They get sick from it, but they always recover. That's
because Jesus' Valley is filled with healing. We know this healing by names
familiar to Christians everywhere—grace, mercy, forgiveness, peace, and love.

Life in Jesus' Valley is pleasant, but like valley dwellers everywhere, we
need to work too. As we labor for the valley's namesake, we find ourselves
spreading the same healing that has so affected us. Grant grace, mete out
mercy, frequently forgive, practice peace, and lavish lots of love on those you
meet today. Invite them to live in Jesus' Valley with you.

Head for the Hills

I lift up my eyes to the hills. From where does my help come? My help
comes from the Lord, who made heaven and earth. He will not let your
foot be moved; He who keeps you will not slumber. Psalm 121:1–3

Hills are stubby mountains. They are easy to climb, but clumsy people are inclined to roll down them as opposed to plummeting off them. Hills may be defined as anything higher than the surrounding terrain. Therefore, my city-dwelling friends and I once belly-flopped our sleds down the hill on Lloyd Avenue. The "hill" was a mound of sooty soil, elevation approximately six feet above the vacant lot it bordered.

David (the king) didn't live on Lloyd Avenue, so when he envisioned hills, he probably had something more impressive in mind. Here's one of his "hill" psalms: "I lift up my eyes to the hills. From where does my help come? My help comes from the Lord, who made heaven and earth" (Psalm 121:1–2).

David's son Solomon reports on the hills, too, as he repeats the words of a young bride in Song of Solomon 2:8: "The voice of my beloved! Behold, he comes, leaping over the mountains, bounding over the hills." David's help and the bride's lover are the same: our Savior, Jesus Christ.

Two basic human needs are love and help. We find both in human counterparts, but they never equal the help and love we receive from Jesus. Only in Him can we find both the quality and the quantity of help and love that sinners need.

Human love, powerful and warm as it is, sometimes wears thin. Our own sinful nature, as well as the sinful natures of those who love us, create defects in love. Sometimes the defect is so deep that love stops completely or it becomes so weak that we're unsure it even exists. When it comes to human help, we're equally limited. We can help in many ways, but often we establish conditions for giving help or are too proud to take it. Then there are those times when no earthly help can help.

How good to know that invincible help and limitless love are available in Jesus! When we're down, suffering in body, soul, or psyche, we can look beyond our problems—even above the hills to heaven itself.

Look for a hill today—even a diminutive one—and remember God's love and help. By the way, isn't it great to know that even if you're over the hill, He is too?

Go with the Flow

*God is our refuge and strength, a very present help in trouble. Therefore
we will not fear though the earth gives way, though the mountains be
moved into the heart of the sea, though its waters roar and foam, though
the mountains tremble at its swelling. There is a river whose streams
make glad the city of God, the holy habitation of the Most High.*
Psalm 46:1–4

Our last lesson in geography is about rivers. (Too bad the course was-
n't this short when we were in school.) Nearly every great city has
blossomed by a river. Early man—and woman too—discovered that rivers
offered advantages that improved the quality of life. Rivers made food and
transportation readily available. They offered a primitive form of plumbing.
Then there was the music—the strains of "Old Man River" wafting above the
waves as the showboat passed by—though I don't believe geography books
cover that particular aspect. However, life along a river wasn't always idyllic.
Floods often obliterated the idylls into a viscous goo of silt and mud.

History has recorded many disastrous floods. Yet cities along rivers still
make good places to live. Scripture focuses on that asset as it compares God's
care for us to a river at its best behavior. "There is a river whose streams make
glad the city of God, the holy habitation of the Most High" (Psalm 46:4).

The river flowing through the city of our God has no history of flooding.
Even without dikes, levees, or the Corps of Engineers, it won't flood in the
future either. This river is purely beneficial because joy flows along with its
currents. Can you imagine bathing in it? How cool and cleansing the water
feels as it flushes away our sin and suffering! It's no wonder that John and the
disciples took people into a river for Baptism. In this act of washing sins away,
believers were free to go with the flow—the flow of the Holy Spirit as He guided them toward God-pleasing words and deeds.

Then there's transportation on God's river of joy. God's river leads us to
His city. Not that river travel is completely safe. Yes, there are rapids where the
devil tries to sweep us away, shoals where he tries to bash us, and sandbars
where he attempts to ground us. Nonetheless, we travel the river in happiness,
trusting God to bring us to Himself in His city.

Picture yourself cruising down the river of God. You're sprawled on a
lounge chair in the warm sun. A soft breeze coddles you into incredible contentment. A good place to read, isn't it? How about a good book? How about
a really Good Book? Just open the pages, and go with the flow.

December 15 ⌐

Get Up and Go

Bartimaeus, a blind beggar, the son of Timaeus, was sitting by the road-
side. And when he heard that it was Jesus of Nazareth, he began to cry
out and say, "Jesus, Son of David, have mercy on me!" . . . And Jesus
said to him, "What do you want Me to do for you?" And the blind man
said to Him, "Rabbi, let me recover my sight." And Jesus said to him, "Go
your way; your faith has made you well." And immediately he recovered
his sight and followed Him on the way. Mark 10:46–52

Have you heard the old line uttered by a tired old man: "My get up
and go got up and went"? It's a funny line unless it's your reality!
Most people admit to this human twist on the much feared personal energy
crisis.

Consider the blind man in today's Bible reading. Bartimaeus was tired of
being blind. You might imagine how blindness saps your energy as you summon all other senses to do what sighted persons do so easily. Though
Bartimaeus was blind, he had vision enough to recognize Jesus as his healer.
Indeed, Bartimaeus had a new infusion of "get up and go," undoubtedly
praising God as he took in all the sights.

We all suffer an energy crisis. Sin saps our strength. Perhaps you remember how a guilty conscience kept you awake nights or how anger disrupted
any attempts to relax. Maybe bitterness over past events haunts you, persistently nagging you with unsettling aggravation. Then there's all that energy we
waste jumping to conclusions and raising the roof or forging chains of credi-
ble lies with which to deceive others. Even feeling sorry for ourselves or
imprisoning silent anxiety robs us of energy.

Vitamins offer no help. Health food provides only useless calories.
Exercise won't get us back in shape either. Only one way exists to revitalize the
spiritually de-energized, and that is faith.

Faith doesn't come by our own striving. The Holy Spirit infuses faith into
our weak and worn soul. Through His holy energy we see our Savior and
believe that He took away our sins. Jesus announces to us the same proclamation He delivered to Bartimaeus: "Get up and go. Your faith has made you
well."

So now what? Get up and go where? Where else but along the trail that
Jesus walked. Because He healed us from sin, we're free to enjoy the sights of
salvation, even as we sometimes stumble along His path. We'll see even better sights someday—angels, saints, Jesus Himself!

Thanks for Sharing That

"Men of Israel, hear these words: Jesus of Nazareth, a man attested to you by God with mighty works and wonders and signs that God did through Him in your midst, as you yourselves know—this Jesus, delivered up according to the definite plan and foreknowledge of God, you crucified and killed by the hands of lawless men. Acts 2:22–23

Its intent differs depending on the circumstances. "Thanks for sharing that" sounds grateful when responding to a tip from a stockbroker. It's less than gratifying, however, when you mutter it to the state trooper who says, "Do you know you were doing 85 in a 45 m.p.h. construction zone?" Christians probably identify similar duplicity when they consider the phrase.

Which tone of voice would you expect in response to Peter's passage from Acts 2:23? "This Jesus, delivered up according to the definite plan and foreknowledge of God, you crucified and killed by the hands of lawless men."

Wouldn't we much rather hear that Jesus paved our way to heaven? Yet we need to hear precisely what Peter said to the crowd—and to us. We are responsible for Jesus' suffering and death. Our sins, along with the sins of all people, caused the death of the Son of God.

Martin Luther once suggested that Jesus was the greatest sinner of all times as He hung on the cross. Before the devil enjoys that one too much, Luther was referring to the load Jesus bore as He paid for each trespass with His own holy life and blood.

Civilized people live with regret and remorse for years if they happen to be responsible for another's death. That's exactly where we stand as we ponder the cross and what it represents. Surely you're thankful I shared that!

Jesus was great at sharing. Remember how He shared a few groceries with thousands through His miraculous power? He shared His power, too, as He sent disciples out to perform miracles of healing. But when it came to our sins, He kept them all for Himself. We couldn't begin to share the guilt because it would drive us from God's presence and send us to hell. Jesus knew where sharing had to end.

Praise God for sending Jesus to forgive our sins and to restore our relationship with Him. Praising God means more than keeping the Good News to ourselves. It means that we forgive others. Praising God also implies that we tell others why we forgive. Others may not welcome the story of Jesus in your life and theirs, but by the power of the Holy Spirit working through the Good News you share, someday they'll thank you for sharing.

Smile?

Be wretched and mourn and weep. Let your laughter be turned to
mourning and your joy to gloom. James 4:9

Smiles are highly overrated if you ask me. Of course, you didn't. Ask me, that is. But I'll tell you why they're overrated, even at the cost of my innermost psyche. A now defunct airline characterized their service by painting smiley faces on the front of their aircraft. Seeing that friendly sight, I was anticipating a pleasant flight. Then a security agent shook me from my reverie. He mentioned something about fitting a hijacker's profile—a one-way ticket, no luggage, and a nervous smile (mine, not the aircraft's). Smiley faces have left me unimpressed and even a bit hostile ever since.

Scripture isn't too keen on smiles either, especially in light of this verse: "Be wretched and mourn and weep. Let your laughter be turned to mourning and your joy to gloom" (James 4:9).

Can you imagine what business would have been like for that airline had it painted frowny faces on the jets? It would have left the business sooner than it did! Is it good for Christian "business" to publish verses such as the one above?

Grief must precede joy in Christian life. In more worldly ways, it's the other way around, isn't it? Laughter usually degenerates into tears. Not so for Christians. The sadness and gloom that James encourages originate with how we feel about our sinfulness. It's like James is saying, "Hey! Don't enjoy your sins. Any pleasure you experience is short-lived." It's sort of like the laughter you hear seeping from the local bar. It's often followed by staggering steps, loud words, false bravado, sick stomachs, and throbbing heads.

Sin is like that. James says Christians need to treat sin like the serious matter it is. Repentance involves sorrow—the mourning type—plus a sincere desire to refrain from such sin again. After that believers can smile again, knowing that God forgives them for Jesus' sake.

Are you smiling now? It's okay—go ahead. When you realize how sinful you are, you also realize how forgiven you are. Your smiles can go a long way too—farther than a flight on a failed airline. Send your smiles to those around you—your family, coworkers, antagonists, security agents—all those who need a sunny, or should we say Sonny, smile to brighten their lives. But never smile back at an airplane, even if it smiles first.

Getting Discovered

He raises the poor from the dust and lifts the needy from the ash heap.
Psalm 113:7

A veterinary scientist, digging in frozen Siberian soil, found the frozen sperm of a woolly mammoth. He wants to extract the DNA and inject it into elephants in hopes of producing woolly mammoths again.

Can you imagine what his mother thinks of his pursuits? "You found what, digging where? Go to your room immediately and throw out all those filthy science books. Get rid of that shovel too!"

Stories like this prompt us to think about the future (unless you're fixated on the private lives of woolly mammoths). One hundred, one thousand, five thousand years from now, will anyone remember us even as much as some nameless furry beast? Will they discover something about us (or our pets)? What will they conclude about life in the 21st century? Will their mothers be upset about their discoveries?

It might be well that no one "discovers" us in the future. What they are likely to find is a record of sin—greed, depravity, immorality, violence, and other news headlines. They'll have an expert guide to help them identify their discoveries. The devil will still be around, pointing out our sins to everybody in the hopes that God will notice. But God won't listen, and we're assured of that in Psalm 113:7: "He raises the poor from the dust and lifts the needy from the ash heap."

We sinners are poor and needy. One thing on which both the Bible and science agree is that, barring any morbid breakthroughs in mortuary science, we'll return to the ground someday. Perhaps some traces of DNA will remain, but even if that doesn't happen, God will "discover" us. Because Jesus rose from the dead, we will too. While our souls will already be in heaven, our bodies, long turned to dust, will rise perfect in every way to join our souls. We'll live that way forever.

Unlike those woolly mammoths of ancient times, we have something to look forward to. While we may not actually rejoice in our own inevitable passing, we never need worry about extinction. So look forward to that day when Jesus returns to summon us from the grave and take us to live with Him. There's an activity that will surely make His Father happy.

Excuses . . .

The secret things belong to the Lord our God, but the things that are
revealed belong to us and to our children forever, that we may do
all the words of this law. Deuteronomy 29:29

Some things I just don't understand. Take bowling for example.
Perhaps it's a reflection of my limited mathematical skills, but I just
don't understand the scoring. Would the game have languished so much if
bowlers simply counted the number of pins knocked down in 10 frames? A
perfect game would be 100—much more sensible than the 300 score now
required. Bowlers, of course, don't understand the beauty of this simplicity. In
addition, bowlers seem to have a complete inventory of excuses for missed
chances—everything from oily lanes to smoke so thick as to limit visibility on
the approach. As for me, I know enough to cheer at strikes or moan at gutter
balls. Do I need any excuses? Okay, for me, 100 really is a perfect game!

Many people shun or abandon what they don't comprehend. God's Word
provides an example. Much of it defies understanding; therefore, dodging it
seems appealing and logical. "Why read what you can't fathom?" becomes an
excuse. How do you respond?

A good way to respond is to remember Deuteronomy 29:29, which says,
"The secret things belong to the Lord our God, but the things that are revealed
belong to us and to our children forever, that we may do all the words of this
law." In other words, God has secrets that He prefers to keep. That's His business, and we can be certain He has reasons for such secrecy—not that we
would understand those reasons anyway. But God revealed all that we need to
know. He gave us His Son, Jesus Christ, and the Holy Spirit, who helps us recognize Jesus as our Savior.

Perhaps you know people who avoid God because they don't understand
His system of keeping score. After all, "What's fair is fair. The Bible itself
points out how good Jesus was to disreputable sinners and how critical He
was of good church people."

The deceptive problem, however, was that the good church people only
thought they were good whereas sinners seemed to recognize how miserable
they made their lives and the lives of others. Sinners were sorry and wanted
to change. If that reminds us of us, that's good because the Holy Spirit has
worked faith and repentance in us. We know Jesus took away our sins and
gave us a new life to enjoy. As for keeping score? God doesn't, so why should
we?

. . . Excuses . . .

Their condemnation from long ago is not idle, and their destruction is not
asleep. For if God did not spare angels when they sinned, but cast them
into hell and committed them to chains of gloomy darkness to be kept
until the judgment; . . . then the Lord knows how to rescue the godly
from trials, and to keep the unrighteous under punishment until
the day of judgment. 2 Peter 2:2–9

Who says love is elusive? Even if you can't get someone else to love you, you probably can do it yourself! Love is an infinitely popular topic, and it's one of the most basic and pervasive human needs. The Bible says that love is the very essence of God. Scripture urges us to love our enemies and to love our neighbors. (They're probably the same people!)

What do you know about God's love? Undoubtedly, you've experienced it often—probably more often than you realize. Like human love, however, God's abundant love can be misunderstood. Some people think that if God is as abundantly good as we claim, He would never punish anyone in hell. Everyone will go to heaven regardless of whether or not they believe in Him. People who believe this are sincere and open-minded but sadly ignorant or misguided.

God's Word says, "For if God did not spare angels when they sinned, but cast them into hell and committed them to chains of gloomy darkness to be kept until the judgment. . ." (2 Peter 2:4). The message is quite clear. It seems to paint God's picture in a different light—apparently less loving than faithful believers allege and perhaps even deceptively sinister.

We need not despair though. God truly loved us so much that He sent His Son, who took human form, lived a sinless life, suffered a ghastly death, and returned to a glorious everlasting life so sinners like us—the ones who deserve to join those wicked angels of 2 Peter—might live forever in the glow of His love. God doesn't want a single drop of His Son's blood to be wasted. He wants it used on every person. So what's the difference between those angels and us—between believers and unbelievers or the defiantly depraved who stubbornly follow their own delusions?

Faith is the difference. Evil beings, whether angels or humans, lack the Holy Spirit's work within them, which convinces them not only to believe in a real, loving God, but also to take advantage of His love through repentance and forgiveness. Faith changes life. It drives us to seek God's will, worship Him, and to love Him by loving others. God's love even includes persistent reconciliation. Even better, we can be confident that God's love story won't have a happy ending because *ending* isn't in His vocabulary.

And More Excuses

What shall I render to the Lord for all His benefits to me? Psalm 116:12

Inflation is responsible for many modern woes. You know what inflation is. It's where prices balloon to the bursting point, except they never explode themselves out of existence. Although we may complain about suffering from inflation, we're usually part of the problem—like when we are stranded in the traffic jam that we're part of. Inflation is so bad that if you ask someone to "put in their two cents," it will cost seven dollars. A person could go broke just trying to stay even!

One characteristic of inflation is a proliferation of excuse-making. Commerce excuses higher prices because production and personnel costs increase. Workers excuse demands for higher wages because products cost so much. A vicious circle, isn't it? But something even more vicious exists. It's sometimes used as an excuse for denying the offer of salvation. Psalm 116:12 says it all: "What shall I render to the Lord for all His benefits to me?"

The psalmist probably had no intention of attempting a payment plan for God's goodness. It was one of those questions uttered in a mood of gratitude for the incredible and unfathomable love of God. Yet some people mistakenly reason that they must make restitution for their personal drain on God's blessings—including the blessing of eternal life. Perhaps you've even thought about it yourself. "God has given me everything. Now I must repay Him, so I'll go to church every week (maybe I should attend both Sunday services!). I'll also give a little extra to missions, and I'll take my neighbor to church (even if she doesn't want to go!)."

You probably see the error of this thinking. No matter what the sacrifice, our sins have inflated the price of salvation beyond reach. In a moment of weakness, we may want to give up—to make excuses for weak or decaying faith—by saying or feeling that we have nothing to contribute to our salvation. That's when we confess that we're bankrupt and file for protection under the Law.

Jesus gives that protection. He paid what we couldn't afford, buying us a home not only in a good neighborhood but a mansion besides. Inflation doesn't bother Jesus. He's loaded. Loaded with grace and mercy and forgiveness and love and compassion and kindness and goodness and . . . Well, let's just say that when it comes to blessings, Jesus practices inflation!

Bones of Contention

As with a deadly wound in my bones, my adversaries taunt me, while they
say to me continually, "Where is your God?" Why are you cast down, O
my soul, and why are you in turmoil within me? Hope in God; for I shall
again praise Him, my salvation and my God. Psalm 42:10–11

How do you approach life? Would you characterize yourself as courageous or cowardly? Do you bravely hope for the future or dread it?
The only hope some people have is hope of avoiding the worst! Sometimes
courage to face the future is a matter of body language—knees down and eyes
up. Mostly, however, we demonstrate a curious mix of courage and cowardice.
How easy it is to boldly stand for something noble and weakly fall for temptations in the opposite direction.

The tension between boldness and timidity are bones of contention. We
might think of this struggle the next time we observe what's left after a hungry family devours the holiday turkey. What remains is the wishbone and the
backbone.

I don't know about you, but I haven't had good experiences with wishbones. In fact, I rarely wished for anything but to crack the bone just right.
Even then I often didn't get my wish.

Wishing is futile, especially if we count on it for anything more important
than contests inspired by dead turkeys. How much time do people lose wishing they were richer or better looking? How many wish they had a better job,
were younger, were older, were smarter, or were closer to retirement? Who
doesn't wish they had avoided something in the past? Sometimes we even
wish that God was more faithful, especially if life is going badly.

The words of Psalm 42:10–11 give some flesh to the dilemma. "As with a
deadly wound in my bones, my adversaries taunt me, while they say to me
continually, "Where is your God?" Why are you cast down, O my soul, and
why are you in turmoil within me? Hope in God; for I shall again praise Him,
my salvation and my God."

We can replace the wishbone with backbone. Today's psalm explains how
that's done. Hope in God differs as much from wishing random wishes as
wishbones differ from backbones. We're always winners with God, even when
we wait to see our hopes materialize. Our future doesn't depend on haphaz-
ard circumstances such as cracking a bone just right. We look forward with
strong backbones because God Himself is that Bone, holding us up, giving us
support, and protecting us. What a good thing to remember the next time we
have a bone to pick—with the devil!

Set Up

Accordingly, though I am bold enough in Christ to command you to do
what is required, yet for love's sake I prefer to appeal to you—I, Paul, an
old man and now a prisoner also for Christ Jesus. Philemon 1:8–9

L et's pull out our Bibles and read the book of Philemon, but don't let today's reading intimidate you. The entire book is only 25 verses. Of course, nobody says you have to read the whole thing just because it's the right thing to do, if you know what I mean. If you don't know, the next paragraph will clear it up.

"Accordingly, though I am bold enough in Christ to command you to do what is required, yet for love's sake I prefer to appeal to you—I, Paul, an old man and now a prisoner also for Christ Jesus" (Philemon 1:8–9). Just what did Paul ask of Philemon? He wanted Philemon to welcome back Onesimus, Philemon's runaway slave.

Paul didn't require Philemon to accept Onesimus without consequences, but when you read the entire account, you get the idea that Philemon's options were somewhat limited. In a way, Paul "set up" Philemon for the benefit of Onesimus. In effect, he said, "Do me a favor. Not that you have to or anything, but don't you think you owe me?"

You probably have some experience with situations such as this. "Here's two box seat tickets to a game for the team that's been sold out since 1950. By the way, I'll be out of town. Could you stop by and feed my 20-foot boa constrictor on the way to the stadium? Of course, if you don't like snakes, that's another story. But if he gets hungry, well . . ."

In all fairness, some "set ups" are only right. Paul's "cashing in his chips" was one of those situations. God's call to respond to His favor is another.

We can't do a thing to accomplish our salvation. We're like the slave Onesimus—runaways from our true Master. But Jesus wants us to return, and He knows that God will accept us. Although Jesus actually set us free, He also set us up to return the favor by the way we live and interact with others. Not because we have to, but because Jesus did so much for us that we want to return that love by serving both God and others. Had Jesus not been set up on the cross for us and had He not made us acceptable in God's sight, we would be lost forever. When you think about that, that's one "set up" that's given us a really good setup.

Make-Over

If then you have been raised with Christ, seek the things that are above,
where Christ is, seated at the right hand of God. Set your minds on things
that are above, not on things that are on earth. For you have died, and
your life is hidden with Christ in God. When Christ who is your life
appears, then you also will appear with Him in glory. Colossians 3:1–4

I suspect that someday people will come with service schedules just like new cars. Instead of new tires at 40,000 miles, we'll be scheduled to have our arches raised at 40. Then at 50, we'll get our retinas and corneas tuned to eliminate blurs and floaters. Original equipment hair can be replaced as early as 55, and after that we'll be eligible for prorated charges on make-overs of bent backs, expanded stomachs, and shriveled faces. Of course, we really don't have to wait because much of this is currently available through surgical alteration of our bank accounts.

Cosmetic make-overs provide only a temporary fix. Real change comes from deeper inside. Paul says, "If then you have been raised with Christ, seek the things that are above, where Christ is, seated at the right hand of God" (Colossians 3:1). The remainder of Colossians 3 provides details of the kind of favorable changes—the spiritual and moral make-overs—that take place when we come to faith.

Before we're "made over," our hearts are set on things below. Way below. Sin dragged us down even before we were old enough to sin on our own. Sin makes us ugly, perhaps not so much in looks but surely in attitude and behavior. Talk about needing a make-over! It's the sinner's foremost need because without it, God won't give us a second look before sending us off to hell.

Thank God we don't have to pay for the alterations that make us acceptable. Jesus paid the price. Paul reminds us that the make-over really makes us different. Now our hearts are set on higher things—things that beautiful people like us can do. Now we hate sin (though not enough to avoid dabbling in it daily). We want to do what God wants; therefore, we seek to learn His will through studying His Word. The Holy Spirit works in us to help us grow in Christ and increasingly put our faith into practice until that day when our make-over reaches full maturity.

Although Jesus did a complete job, the Holy Spirit keeps us working to maintain our beauty. Avoiding sin is difficult. Growing in faith takes time, energy, and effort. While we're doing all that, we remember how we got this far. We owe it all to Jesus, the One and only Creator of the perfect faith-lift.

Antiques

So then, brothers, stand firm and hold to the traditions that you were taught by us, either by our spoken word or by our letter.
2 Thessalonians 2:13–17

Unless you're a specialist, you probably can't tell the difference between antique and just plain old. It's similar to the difference between priceless and worthless. Antiques are what you leave in the basement for the next generation to complain about and the following generation to fight over after you're gone. "Just plain old" is something you get rid of immediately before it's deemed an antique.

However you view the issue of old versus antique, we're probably at the end of an era. Will anything today last long enough to become an antique? If we have something old, we better take care of it. A well-preserved antique increases in value the older it gets. (Don't you wish the same were true of us?)

Each of us owns an antique. No, it's not our favorite tie or wallet or shoes. (If we wait long enough, they'll be back in style before they become antiques!) The Bible says: "So then, brothers, stand firm and hold to the traditions that you were taught by us, either by our spoken word or by our letter" (2 Thessalonians 2:15).

Historic letters are sometimes worth much, and treasured old sayings remain quotable for years. Then there are family stories passed by word of mouth from generation to generation. While they might not carry the price tag of Ben Franklin's notepad, their worth is nothing short of a fortune. It doesn't take the average Christian long to determine that his or her special antique—God's Word—isn't just plain old. God's Word is beyond ancient, and its value is inestimable.

Sinners that we are, we sometimes leave this precious antique wedged on a dusty shelf or—perhaps worse—still encased in its original wrapper. We think that someday it'll be worth something if only we don't wrinkle any pages. Of course, God's Word is more than a collection of sentences, paragraphs, and chapters. Its words belong in our hearts where they come alive through the power of the Holy Spirit. How good to hear and believe all that God has done for His people! How wonderful to know that He sent Jesus to take away our sins! Isn't it beyond comprehension to have these blessings just because He loves us?

Treasure your antique, but don't baby it. Don't display it only on Christmas or Easter. Keep it right there in your heart and everywhere else. As old as it is, it will never be too old.

Proverbs

For whoever finds Me finds life and obtains favor from the Lord.
Proverbs 8:1–36

Scratch around the recesses of your memory. What are some of your favorite proverbs? Here are some of mine, though I suspect my memory is incapable of perfect wording: "A penny earned makes for little bacon in the piggy bank." Or how about this: "A stitch in time hurts a lot more than a butterfly bandage." Other memorable proverbs—well, almost memorable— include: "A watched pot boils over anyway" and "An ounce of prevention probably costs more than your medical coverage provides."

Proverbs are wise sayings. They date far back in history. The ones with which we're most familiar seem to come either from early American history or a time somewhat further removed—the time of King Solomon. The biblical book of Proverbs preserves Solomon's God-given wisdom.

Solomon's proverbs are valuable because he took them from a higher source of wisdom. While we may feel humble compared with a king long remembered for good judgment, Solomon's "source" remains available to us.

Here's one of my favorites (and this time I got it right): "For whoever finds Me finds life and obtains favor from the Lord" (Proverbs 8:35). The "Me" in this Proverb is wisdom personified, a.k.a. Jesus. Earlier in Proverbs 8 we discover how easy it is to "find" Jesus. It says that He calls to us. Now if you've ever played hide-and-seek, you normally don't call out to the one trying to find you. It's different with our loving Savior. He says, "Wisdom isn't elusive if you're looking for the right kind. I'm right here, and I want you to have My wisdom. Take it. It's free!"

The best wisdom ever is not only the knowledge that Jesus died to save sinners like us, but it is the faith to believe it—to inscribe it in our souls just as Franklin's students might have carved his sayings into desktops. And we don't have to worry that we might lose some of God's proverbs. They're safe in the Bible, even if we take them out and use them in everyday life. You know what they say—"A little knowledge is better than a lot of stupidity."

Whatsisname

Our soul waits for the Lord; He is our help and our shield.
Psalm 33:20

For you, O Lord, are my hope, my trust, O Lord, from my youth.
Psalm 71:5

Again Jesus spoke to them, saying, "I am the Light of the world. Whoever follows Me will not walk in darkness, but will have the light of life."
John 8:12

Then I saw heaven opened, and behold, a white horse! The one sitting on it is called Faithful and True, and in righteousness He judges and makes war.
Revelation 19:11

My father always had trouble with names. Whenever he started a conversation that involved news about someone, he said something like, "You know, whatsisname bought a new car, and it looks a lot like the one whatsisname bought—only a different color."

Everyone gets a name. And a good name is worth more than money. (It's tax free!) A good name comes from the person who bears it.

God has many good names—as well He should. The Bible passages at the top of this page identify some of them, so when you have time, start paging. Among them is this famous and beloved passage heard most often at Christmas: "For to us a child is born, to us a son is given; and the government shall be upon His shoulder, and His name shall be called Wonderful Counselor, Mighty God, Everlasting Father, Prince of Peace" (Isaiah 9:6).

Great names, aren't they? But consider this one: "Even now, behold, My witness is in heaven, and he who testifies for Me is on high" (Job 16:19). How often have you called Jesus your "witness"? Sounds legal rather than merciful, but it is a good name nonetheless. We sinners need a witness, but not the kind who testifies against us.

God knows we sin. We need testimony in our favor, and we have it! It comes from Jesus Christ Himself, a star witness who tells God that He knows us. We're one of the faithful, made that way by the Holy Spirit. We belong in God's eternal kingdom because Jesus took away our sins and we have His grace and mercy.

Even if you get old and forgetful, you'll never forget Jesus' name. He has so many! But in case your memory really fails, you can call Him Whatsisname. Just be sure to use a capital W.

Delayed

*It is eleven days' journey from Horeb by the way of Mount Seir
to Kadesh-barnea. Deuteronomy 1:1–46*

Airlines are good with terse messages—words that "say it all" and fit in the short space flashed on the arrival/departure screens. Delayed is one of those words. Seasoned travelers usually suspect that word because it's often the precursor of another curt communiqué: Canceled. This can be especially annoying because air travel is expensive. One might even say that the cost of flying has reached new heights. Then again, flying is probably better than the alternative for long trips. At least in the air you pass bad drivers at a safe distance!

Air journeys will never get as bad as foot travel was in Moses' times. Delayed would have been a gross understatement, considering Deuteronomy 1:2: "It is eleven days' journey from Horeb by the way of Mount Seir to Kadesh-barnea."

In itself, an 11-day trip would be long by modern standards, but this 11-day trek turned into a 40-year expedition. What took so long? It wasn't bad weather, bomb scares, over-booking, or heavy traffic. The problem was the travelers themselves. They were unruly, rebellious, and untrusting. Besides that, they seemed easily sidetracked and quarrelsome. In other words, they were a lot like us.

We're on our way to a destination where no airline goes. Like the Israelites of Moses' day, we're headed to the Promised Land. While God doesn't encourage us to hurry or hasten the trip by our own means, He has provided everything necessary to make the excursion seem short. Yet we sinners usually make the trip seem exhausting and slow as we give in to all sorts of temptations that lead us to sin. Even if we live a pretty good life, it's neither pretty nor good nor does it elude our suffering from sin in general. Yet there's a way to make travel time seem to fly.

Trust God. Easy to say; sometimes difficult to do. Perfect trust in God would result in anxiety-free life. Can you imagine how enjoyable life would be if we were 100 percent worry free? Can you imagine the joy in a life where every burden would be carried by Someone else? The possibility exists, though a bit beyond the limits of our faith. But don't let that stop you. Pray for more. Faith that is. It'll seem like no time at all until time flies faster than the speed of life.

And in Conclusion . . .

"But you will receive power when the Holy Spirit has come upon you, and
you will be My witnesses in Jerusalem and in all Judea and Samaria,
and to the end of the earth." Acts 1:8

If you're like most readers, you're anxious to finish this book and start
something new. These last three meditations will recall some "departing words" from the Bible. This one recounts what Jesus said on the day He
left for heaven.

Have you ever wondered if Jesus was anxious to get on with other divine
duties when He finished His earthly work? Perhaps He wanted to return to
heaven so He could finish getting it ready for the millions of people He invited to live there. Certainly He understood how His dear friends felt about His
departure, especially after spending those joyous and victorious post Easter
days with them. But Jesus didn't leave His followers with any sentimental
farewell address. (He left that to the angels. See Acts 1:11) Instead, He told
them they could expect a different champion and companion—the Holy
Spirit. And He also told them to get to work. So many people in so many
places needed to hear the message about their Savior!

What about us? Are we to heed Jesus' words too? Definitely. It's as if Jesus
was saying to us, "And in conclusion My friends, spread the word about Me.
Tell others the Great News about their future. And tell them the future begins
right now."

The Gospel surely is Great News, but we can't just sit around reveling in
its ecstasy. The Gospel has a goal, and Christians of all eras have the Holy
Spirit's power to carry out that goal. Our job is to make more Christians. Our
mission fields may be hallways, work stations, parking garages, hospital
rooms, the middle seat on a long flight, or a child's crib. One thing for sure—
people need to hear and observe what we know. Don't worry if you're doing
a good job or not. Let people draw their own conclusions.

Growth Hormones

But grow in the grace and knowledge of our Lord and Savior Jesus Christ.
To Him be the glory both now and to the day of eternity. Amen.
2 Peter 3:18

If only our hearts would grow as steadily as our waistlines! Some people grow up and spread Gospel cheer. Others just spread. But of course, that's not the type of growth Peter spoke of in his departing words.

All Christians aspire to grow in grace. In fact, the more a believer grows in grace, the greater the ambition to grow more. Mature Christians are never content where they are; they always want more. The way to grow in grace starts—well, gracefully. We simply ask the Holy Spirit to make us more grace-full. That's just what He wants to hear, but He will also tweak our willingness to grow by more common means.

We might find ourselves praying more often—sometimes even skipping the "Dear Jesus," salutation and launching into conversation as if we're talking to a good friend. (Isn't *that* true!) We'll also have a consistent urge to worship and receive the Lord's Supper with regularity. In turn, those experiences make us more grace-full to others—believers and unbelievers, friends and foes alike. Grace grows as we experience and share it.

We need to continue growing in knowledge too. Reading through the Bible once is a fruitful practice. But fruit needs to blossom and ripen every year if the tree or vine is of any value. Once is never enough, and always is never too much. It's good to get into some Bible study with other people too. Other Christians often have new or different insights about the same passages that mean only one thing to us. And others need to hear what we've learned too. Knowledge also grows as we read books that help us understand the Bible better. (Most pastors will eagerly help you choose some.)

Peter said his farewell perhaps the best way any Christian friend can. He praised God in his time as well as for ours. Way to grow, Peter. Way to grow.

Thank You, and Come Again

He who testifies to these things says, "Surely I am coming soon." Amen.
Come, Lord Jesus! The grace of the Lord Jesus be with all. Amen.
Revelation 22:20–21

Nearly everyone wants to go to heaven, but some people hope they live long enough to see changes in the entrance requirements.

John knew the way to heaven, and his final words in Revelation tell us about it. John knew that Jesus would return as the glorious King someday, and he hoped it would be soon. So strong was his desire to be with Jesus that he implored Him to return. Is that what we mean when we pray, "Come, Lord, Jesus?" Probably not. We're likely to be satisfied with blessed food. As far as urging Him to end the world as we know it, well that may be another thing altogether.

Many people fear the end of the world. The idea even leaves many Christians shaky. It's not that we're afraid of going to hell. Jesus took care of that problem long ago on Calvary's cross. But many of us tremble at actually seeing Jesus face-to-radiant-face. And how loudly will those trumpets blast? We can probably expect to see Satan face-to-fiery-face too—and will he be mad!

What about all the saints who ever lived? Will there be room for all of us to gather in front of the King's throne? Will He remember us by name? Lots of questions, but very few answers. John got a good glimpse of Judgment Day and heaven. We can read about it in Revelation, but that often leaves us with even more questions! (Read it anyway.)

Many Christians enjoy their earthly life, which is another gift from God. But we can't begin to compare earthly life with life in heaven. We can be confident that we're ready for Jesus' return. We can be certain that it will be as sudden and as joy-filled as the first time He came. With grateful, faith-filled hearts and souls, let's join together and say, "Thank You, Lord Jesus. Come again."

Amen.

SCRIPTURE INDEX